BIBLICA ET ORIENTALIA

(SACRA SCRIPTURA ANTIQUITATIBUS ORIENTALIBUS ILLUSTRATA)

41

FRANCIS I. ANDERSEN - A. DEAN FORBES

Spelling in the Hebrew Bible

Dahood Memorial Lecture

Preface by
DAVID NOEL FREEDMAN

ROME
BIBLICAL INSTITUTE PRESS
1986

ISBN 88-7653-342-7

© Iura editionis et versionis reservantur

PRINTED IN ITALY

GREGORIAN UNIVERSITY PRESS
BIBLICAL INSTITUTE PRESS
Piazza della Pilotta, 35 - 00187 Rome, Italy

Editor's Preface

Mitchell Dahood's eminent career and richly filled life have been rehearsed elsewhere, as well as his lamented premature death. Suffice it to say here that while he was not considered an outstanding student, and certainly not a rare universal genius like his teacher, the extraordinary W. F. Albright, Mitchell Dahood, through an endless series of brief sallies, punctuated by an occasional extended article or monograph, culminating in major volumes including the three master works on the Psalms, managed to provoke at least as much controversy as most others in our field and to alter the terms of the debate and shape the nature of the approach to a discussion of Hebrew poetry for our generation.

It is sometimes forgotten that Mitchell Dahood was Professor of Ugaritic, perhaps the first such in the world, at the Pontifical Biblical Institute, and was primarily responsible for instruction in the Northwest Semitic languages at that venerable institution. Not long before his untimely death; he informed me that Eblaite, the latest recruit in the ranks of Northwest Semitic dialects, had been added to the curriculum, and he expressed the hope that before long a new chair of Eblaite would be established at the PBI. In view of his enthusiasm for the new finds at Ebla, matched only by his unceasing efforts to untangle the by now well-studied tablets from Ugarit, there is little doubt that had he lived and had the authorities seen fit to follow his advice, he would have been named to the new chair without relinquishing the old.

The point I wish to make is that Mitchell Dahood approached the Bible from the outside, from the cultural and linguistic environment in which its literature was nourished. While he dealt very seriously with the Bible as a scholar, and even more so as an ordained clergyman (a faithful and loyal member of the Society of Jesus from youth until his life's end), nevertheless his primary concern was to show how the texts from Ugarit and other sites in the Syro-Palestinian area could illuminate the Hebrew Scriptures (and to a lesser extent the Greek Bible as well). Inevitably this interest focused his attention on biblical poetry, at the center of which were the books traditionally identified in that manner: Psalms, Job and Proverbs. His concerns did not end there, but the great bulk of his published (and unpublished) work was aimed at the elucidation of those books and the rest of the poetry of the Bible. It was inevitable too that his approach from the outside and his emphasis on external texts, such as the Ugaritic tablets, would produce distorted effects, and no doubt his preoccupation with Northwest Semitic resulted in strange renderings and stranger interpretations.

At the same time, if there was palpable excess here and there, nevertheless the net effect was to make certain that the scholarly world would not soon forget the Ugaritic connection. What the earlier champions of Ugaritic studies discerned as a necessary prerequisite for dealing effectively with the poetry of the Hebrew Bible, especially the Psalter, namely people such as Cassuto, Ginsberg, Albright, Gordon, and others, Dahood drove home with persistence, imagination, innovation, and certainly excess. It is not clear yet how much of his enterprise will stand and survive, but certainly he gave the field of biblical poetry a twist and a shake from which it will never fully recover or revert to the old internal pre-Ugaritic days.

Considering how he shook up traditional biblical scholarship, and how he approached it from the standpoint of the tablets and inscriptions of Greater Canaan, it seems very odd in retrospect that he should have been called, and that disparagingly, a masoretic fundamentalist. The fact that the label was untrue and unfair from the beginning is not nearly as important as the complete misunderstanding of Dahood's perception and evaluation of the received text, which in turn were based upon his approach to and analysis of non-biblical inscriptions and texts.

In a somewhat guileless and equally naive fashion he considered the biblical text, in particular the poetry, to be a faithful transcription of the original written version of the poem or piece. In the process of transmission there was no intent to alter or edit, only to copy. But in the course of time spelling practices changed, i.e., vowel letters were added, and vocalization (i.e., the pronunciation of words) changed even more. So Mitchell Dahood regarded the consonantal skeleton of the text to be both original and accurate, reproduced endlessly and unerringly. This skeleton formed the basic structure which constituted the underwriting of the biblical palimpsest, the most original and reliable of all the data preserved in medieval manuscripts and modern printed versions. The vowel letters were added by well-intentioned but not necessarily intelligent and certainly not inspired scribes and editors. Finally the masoretes added the vocalization, which was essentially an effort to harmonize the variety of earlier and different spelling systems and practices and to bring the great mass of biblical text into uniformity. From Mitchell Dahood's perspective the specific and special contribution of the masoretes was the least important and viable and the most dispensable element in the transmission of the text. Masoretic fundamentalist indeed!

In fact, Mitchell Dahood was rather cavalier in his treatment of the text and emended freely and extensively, in a great variety of ways. He dispensed with or disposed of both vocalization and vowel letters pretty much as he pleased, regarding all of these as secondary or tertiary additions to a pristine text. On only one point was he immovable. He would not change or permit the change of a consonant. It is easy enough now to see this conviction and determination as an oddity, but the main reason for it was, I believe, the recognition that something had to be preserved, some genuine link with the original, or it could all be blown away. When so much freedom with vowel letters and vocalization is insisted upon, much less freedom can be granted in what is left, or else the essential contact with the original text could be lost altogether.

This rather startling appraisal of the biblical text arose directly out of his study of the inscriptions, on which we touched earlier. What stands out in Canaanite inscriptions, especially Ugaritic and Phoenician, is the presence of consonants and the absence of vowel letters. Reading, rendering, and interpreting all of these texts depends finally upon the consonants, most of which are assumed to be correct, since for the most part we are dealing with autographs or very early copies. There are possible exceptions—certainly there are errors in the Ugaritic tablets, and possibly a rare vowel letter, but by and large one must read the texts from the consonantal skeleton. That is the way Mitchell Dahood read the Bible. At the least it produced interesting results, but finally was there any real basis in fact or history for such a choice?

We should say that Dahood clearly followed his teacher and master in this respect. Professor Albright, in dealing with the poetry of the Bible and more especially with early poems, regularly stripped the text of its vowel letters and vocalization to get at the naked original—the tenth century (or earlier) text as it was written by the scribe who set it down. I ought to know, since my esteemed colleague Frank Cross and I wrote out these texts in just that form in one of our joint doctoral dissertations on early Hebrew poetry under the direction of Dr. Albright.

I think that these factors may explain in large part Mitchell Dahood's predilection for a basic consonantal text. He believed moreover that Phoenician (i.e.. consonantal) spelling could be traced in much later poems of the Bible, so he did not hesitate to discard final vowel letters. He had even fewer compunctions about medial ones, which in his view arrived even later on the scene and could be removed with impunity.

It should be added that Albright did not make the same sharp distinction between consonants and vowels that Mitchell Dahood did, but the former was influenced in his approach primarily by historical factors. He reconstructed the poems on the basis of many factors and reproduced the orthography of the time of composition, omitting final and medial vowel letters as the occasion called for and including them when appropriate. He used all available tools, including versions and inscriptions, to recover or reconstruct the original text, and he practiced with great skill the fine art of conjectural emendation, even on some occasions the more notorious kind, namely *metri causa*. Mitchell Dahood dealt with such matters in a more mechanical and less severely disciplined fashion, but often with even more startling and provocative results.

We come back to the question of spelling and whether Mitchell Dahood's or W. F. Albright's or Cross and Freedman's approach and analysis were or are justified. The present volume is devoted to the subject of biblical as against inscriptional spelling. It is a massive and meticulous investigation based upon computer-generated and monitored study of the whole of the Masoretic Text. The authors can speak with some certainty about the real spelling of the Bible as it has come down to us, and they can make plausible judgments about the evolution or development of that spelling.

At the risk of stealing their thunder, let me indicate where I think matters stand, not as to details, but in the broad stretch and along chronological lines. For the pre-exilic period, in the beginning there were only consonants, no vowel letters anywhere in the writing. But very early on, certainly by the ninth century, perhaps earlier, a lot of vowels were written with the aid of a few consonant signs, which may be called "vowel letters." Final vowel letters were introduced in all of the derivative alphabetic systems, whether Canaanite or Aramean, pure consonantal writing surviving only in the land where it all started--Phoenicia (and its colonies). Everywhere else and certainly in Israel and Judah, final vowel letters were not only in use but universally used. It is barely possible that a few of the oldest poems in the Bible were written in purely consonantal style, but by the ninth century everything was written with final vowel letters including such poems. The survival of earlier spelling would be incidental, accidental, and coincidental. I know of no extended piece in the Bible (not so much as a whole line) that has survived as an example or reflection of purely consonantal spelling.

We now know that a whole panoply of medial or internal vowel letters was already available at about the same time, at least for Aramaic, and presumably for the other languages as well. This is the contribution of the recently published Tell Fekhereye bilingual from eastern Syria. The usage elsewhere was much more restricted, but it continued to spread and increase in the eighth and seventh centuries. Although the writing of word-final vowels by means of specially designated consonant letters was general everywhere, the marking of medial vowels remained sporadic if not haphazard. By the sixth century the use of medial vowel letters was not only increasing but being normalized in the inscriptions.

When we look at the biblical text as a whole, it is clear that it belongs to a period when final vowel letters were used throughout and systematically, while the use of medial vowel letters was very widespread although not entirely regularized. The biblical text essentially as it has been preserved in MT (with numerous variations, inevitably) reflects the spelling systems of the post-exilic period, more particularly the fifth-fourth centuries BCE. No doubt it is based on earlier texts, but the spelling could be normative for a period probably not earlier than the middle of the fifth century. This particular style of spelling, distinctly different from earlier as well as later practice, could be associated with the person and work of a man like Ezra, whose authority would lend weight to its preservation. What all this means is that the Bible is not consonants only but vowel letters too, and not only final vowel letters but medial ones also. While we can allow some distinctions as to age and weight, they are not nearly so great as Mitchell Dahood thought, or even Albright. Therefore it behooves us all to pay close attention to all the letters of the Bible. While we may wish to reserve judgment about the masoretic vocalization, we can surely say that it served a very worthy purpose, which was to preserve the traditional pronunciation along with the written text. It often provides clues to understanding the text which the consonants and vowel letters alone are not sufficiently precise to supply.

David Noel Freedman

Authors' Preface

It is nearly a hundred years since R. B. Girdlestone wrote: "It might be thought that the age and authorship of the Hebrew books could be tested to some degree by their orthography" (Girdlestone 1892: 176). Girdlestone was not able to advance very far into this question. He was generally aware that some names occurred in more than one form, but he did not distinguish them from the variant spelling of otherwise identical words. He did, at least, notice the two spellings of David, but did not follow through. He was not able to relate the phenomena to the history of Hebrew spelling as such. That was hardly possible before the recovery of inscriptions permitted that history to be charted. Writing in 1962, Freedman said that the variation in the use of *matres lectionis* followed a "discernable pattern" but that "this has not been clearly analyzed or described scientifically" (1962: 90). In his "History of Hebrew *Plene* Spelling" Weinberg (1975: 462) noted that available lists "tend to seek out extremes" and that "in the absence of quantitative studies that take into account the different strata of biblical writing there is not much merit in such exemplifications." This study aims to remedy this lack of systematic information. We have both the text of the Hebrew Bible and a coordinating dictionary in computer-manipulable form, so a statistical investigation of spelling practices in the Hebrew Bible is possible.

This book is an outgrowth of the Dahood Memorial Lectures delivered in the University of Michigan February 8-10, 1983. The preparation of the material for publication has permitted more ample treatment than the original oral presentation.

We attempt four things: first we describe the orthographic phenomena of the Hebrew Bible; secondly, we assess the evidence by means of appropriate statistical analyses; thirdly, we interpret the evidence in terms of the history of Hebrew spelling; finally we speculate on the significance of this evidence for studies in the production and transmission of the text.

The plan of the book is as follows. Chapter 1 introduces some examples, identifies the problems, and begins to develop mathematical models and theoretical concepts for handling those problems. Chapter 2 outlines the history of Hebrew spelling based primarily on inscriptions and related language evidence. Chapter 3 illustrates various biblical uses of *matres lectionis* for spelling long (and, very rarely, short) vowels; detailed stages in the development of their use are suggested. This is quite in line with traditional impressionistic methods of inquiry. Readers who are mainly interested in the new material could skim Chapters 2 and 3 (especially the lists of specimens) without loss of continuity. Chapter 4 hypothesizes how spelling choices are made and introduces the two extreme positions on the text transmission process (the one holding that no orthographic damage has occurred and the other holding that all historical orthographic detail has been washed out in transmission). It also looks at some theories of spelling propounded by Gesenius. Chapter 4 also proposes a formal theory of text transmission and reports investigations into its simplification. The theory is shown to be general enough to encompass both of the extreme positions. Fundamental limitations are next discussed, and possible compromise approaches to investigating our data are presented, one being singled out for further study.

The mathematical concepts introduced in Chapter 1 and the ideas on text transmission introduced in Chapter 4 enable statistical assessment of the biblical data. Naif research has all too frequently misused statistical arguments in a way that misleads the unaware reader or else loses credibility with those more informed. We have tried to be rigorous and at the same time intelligible. An attempt has been made to explain matters in an elementary way, so as to reveal the power of the concepts involved without inducing dread in non-mathematical readers. And an attempt has been made to qualify our explanations so as to avoid irritating our mathematically sophisticated readers.

In Chapter 5, we describe preparation of the data by removing irrelevant vowels from consideration. Chapter 6 explains our classification procedures for the remaining vowels. Chapter 7 describes the division of the text into portions suited to our analysis, and Chapter 8 considers the effects of proximity of the same lexeme, lexeme frequency, and stress on spelling behavior. These preliminaries completed, we reach the central questions. In Chapter 9 we study the spelling of the vowel types across the portions of the text, noting especially the outliers which contain an abnormally high concentration of distinct spellings. In Chapter 10 we study the spelling in each portion of the Bible for all vowels, and use cluster analysis to find out which portions resemble one another most closely (and which are very different) in their spelling. Having shown that orthographic information survives transmission, in Chapter 11 we apply these results to the history of the text of the Hebrew Bible.

For their support of the Australian component of this research, thanks are expressed to the Research Grants Scheme of the Australian Federal Government, Macquarie University, and the University of Queensland. There are many persons we would like to thank. Professor David Noel Freedman has supplied endless encouragement as well as a Preface which places our research in the context of Father Dahood's life work. We are grateful to our colleagues in St. Lucia and Palo Alto for all kinds of support. Supremely, we are thankful to Lois Andersen and Ellen Forbes for companionship, love, and enthusiasm.

Francis I. Andersen
A. Dean Forbes

Contents

Editor's Preface	v
Authors' Preface	xiii
Contents	xvii
Tables	xx
Figures	xxii
Chapter 1. Spelling in the Hebrew Bible	1
1.1 The general practice in Hebrew spelling	1
1.2 The spelling of 'David'	4
1.3 Interpreting relative frequencies	6
1.4 The spelling of 'three'	9
1.5 The spelling of long /ō/ and /ū/	10
1.6 The spelling of -ōt[-]	11
1.7 A useful analogy and an approach to analysis	15
1.8 The model of independence	17
1.9 Measuring goodness of fit	19
1.10 Assessing goodness of fit	20
1.11 Outliers and association	22
1.12 An illustration of independence: verse parity	23
1.13 Choice of text	25
1.14 Our problem	30
Chapter 2. The History of Hebrew Spelling	31
2.1 Introduction	31
2.2 Alphabetic writing	31
2.3 Writing vowels	33
2.4 Subsequent developments	55
2.5 Developments in post-exilic times	60
2.6 The study of Hebrew orthography	63

Chapter 3. Standard Hebrew Spelling and its Deviations   66
   3.1 *Matres lectionis* in the Masoretic Text   66
   3.2 Detailed stages of development   66
   3.3 The *plene* spelling of long vowels   81
   3.4 The *plene* spelling of short vowels   95
Chapter 4. Theories of Masoretic Text Orthography   101
   4.1 A spelling hypothesis   101
   4.2 Theories of textual transmission   102
   4.3 Spelling options as scribal opportunities   104
   4.4 Features of scribal opportunities   104
   4.5 Text transmission and information theory   105
   4.6 Markov processes   107
   4.7 The nature of the source-encoder   109
   4.8 Description of the channel   115
   4.9 Effects of Markov chains on encoder statistics   118
   4.10 The *error-free* theory   121
   4.11 Source-encoder and channel separability   124
Chapter 5. Vowels Having No Spelling Options   126
   5.1 Conditions specifying fixed spelling   126
   5.2 The forces at work   128
   5.3 Elimination of non-opportunities   130
   5.4 Nonuse of the *plene* option   131
   5.5 Nonuse of the *defective* option   132
   5.6 The mechanics of vowel marking   149
Chapter 6. Classification of Spelling Options   155
   6.1 Classification of vowels   155
   6.2 Stress patterns   156
   6.3 Word length   158
   6.4 The history of the vowel   158
   6.5 Vowel types   162
   6.6 The mechanics of type assignment   204
Chapter 7. Specification of Text Portions   205
   7.1 The need for careful text portioning   205
   7.2 The philosophy of portion definition   206
   7.3 The mechanics of text portioning   207

7.4 Specification of seventy-six portions   208
7.5 Reduction to smaller sets of portions   212
Chapter 8. Possible Confounding Factors   214
   8.1 Influences in spelling choice   214
   8.2 The spelling of nearby lexemes   214
   8.3 Lexeme frequency and spelling choice   221
   8.4 Stress   230
Chapter 9. The Behavior of Types Across Portions   240
   9.1 Assessing the *indifference* theory   241
   9.2 Detailed results of contingency table analyses   246
   9.3 Discussion   284
Chapter 10. The Behavior of Portions Across Types   288
   10.1 Ordering the portions   288
   10.2 Preparing the data   289
   10.3 Displaying the data   291
   10.4 Quantitating similarity   293
   10.5 Discovering affinities   294
   10.6 Checking results   308
Chapter 11. Summary and Conclusions   309
   11.1 The use of *matres lectionis*   309
   11.2 Spelling in the various portions of the Bible   312
   11.3 The history of spelling in the Hebrew Bible   318
   11.4 Conclusion   326
Epilog   329
Bibliography   332
Citation Index   354
Scholar Index   365
Subject Index   367

Tables

Table 1.1 Spelling of 'David' in the Hebrew Bible 5
Table 1.2 Spelling of 'three' in the Hebrew Bible 9
Table 1.3 Spelling of '-ōt[-]' in the Hebrew Bible 11
Table 1.4 Spelling of suffixed '-ōt[-]' 12
Table 1.5 Spelling of construct '-ōt' 13
Table 1.6 Spelling of stressed '-ōt' 13
Table 1.7 Observed counts of suffixed '-ōt[-]' 17
Table 1.8 Expected counts for "ignorance" model 17
Table 1.9 Estimated counts for model of independence 18
Table 1.10 Standardized residuals for suffixed '-ōt[-]' 19
Table 1.11 Observed verse parity counts 24
Table 1.12 Estimated verse parity counts 24
Table 1.13 Standardized residuals 25
Table 2.1 Stages of Northwest Semitic writing 32
Table 2.2 Spelling of suffixed qōl 47
Table 2.3 Spelling of suffixed qōl 48
Table 3.1 Differences within similar texts 71
Table 4.1 Double-vowel incidence counts 112
Table 4.2 Predicted double-vowel incidence 113
Table 4.3 Double-vowel standardized residuals 113
Table 4.4 Initial frequencies, Portion #1 & Portion #2 119
Table 4.5 Initial frequencies, Portion #1 & Portion #3 119
Table 4.6 Strong chain effects 120
Table 4.7 Weak chain effects 122
Table 4.8 Final frequencies, Portion #1 & Portion #3 123
Table 5.1a Lexemes declared fixed 153
Table 5.1b Lexemes declared fixed 154

Table 6.1 Spelling of /ō/ 162

Table 6.2 Spelling of preposition 'unto' 171

Table 6.3 Spelling of preposition 'upon' 172

Table 6.4 Suffixed preposition 'like' 182

Table 6.5 Free form prepositions 'in,' 'like,' 'to' 183

Table 6.6 Infinitives absolute 183

Table 6.7 Spelling of 'not' 186

Table 6.8 Spelling of 'is not?' 187

Table 6.9 ˀōt in the Pentateuchal sources 190

Table 6.10 ˀōt in the sources: estimates 190

Table 6.11 ˀōt in the sources: residuals 190

Table 7.1a The seventy-six portions 209

Table 7.1b The seventy-six portions 210

Table 7.1c The seventy-six portions 211

Table 7.2a Hierarchy of 5/10/30 divisions 212

Table 7.2b Hierarchy of 5/10/30 divisions 213

Table 8.1a Pair discordance as function of separation 215

Table 8.1b Pair discordance as function of separation 216

Table 8.2 Spelling in discordant pairs 219

Table 8.3 Spelling choice and stress sequence 220

Table 8.4 Distribution of 'fathers' 225

Table 8.5 Spelling of forms of 'fathers' 227

Table 8.6 Spelling of 'prophets' 229

Table 9.1 Outliers in type-portion-spelling cells 287

Table 10.1 Percent of rejected cell pairs 290

Table 10.2 Facial features and types 293

Table 10.3 Distances between pairs of portions 294

Table 10.4 First-stage resemblance matrix 295

Table 10.5 Second-stage resemblance matrix 295

Table 10.6 Third-stage resemblance matrix 296

Table 10.7 Gallery of dendrograms 297

Figures

Figure 8.1 Spelling discordance as function of separation   216

Figure 8.2 Percent of opportunities versus portion   232

Figure 8.3 Percent *plene* across portion for Type 47   233

Figure 8.4 Percent *plene* across portion for Type 48   234

Figure 8.5 Percent *plene* for all opportunities   235

Figure 8.6 Percent *plene* for Types 1-12   236

Figure 8.7 Percent *plene* for Types 13-24   237

Figure 8.8 Percent *plene* for Types 30-55   239

Figure 8.9 Percent *plene* for Types 56-65   239

Figure 9.1 Ranked v_s with 95% C.I. plus v_v 245

Figure 10.1 Chernoff faces for marginal Types 1-15   292

Figure 10.2 Spelling: five portions, all types   299

Figure 10.3 Spelling: ten portions (Threshold = 10)   300

Figure 10.4 Spelling: ten portions (Threshold = 20)   301

Figure 10.5 Spelling: thirty portions (Threshold = 10)   302

Figure 10.6 Spelling: thirty portions (Threshold = 20)   303

Figure 10.7 Spelling: without outliers (Threshold = 10)   304

Figure 10.8 Spelling: without outliers (Threshold = 20)   305

Figure 10.9 Verse-parity clusters (Threshold = 10)   306

Figure 10.10 Verse-parity clusters (Threshold = 20)   307

Chapter 1. Spelling in the Hebrew Bible

1.1 The general practice in Hebrew spelling

In Western languages words are written in linear fashion, one sign after the other, usually from left to right. Their alphabets provide some signs for writing consonant sounds, some for writing vowel sounds. Hebrew is written from right to left with an alphabet of twenty-two signs. These letters represent consonantal phonemes. There is also a distinct system for writing the vowels. Vowel signs consist of smaller dots and dashes written above, in, or beneath the consonantal letters. The two systems are autonomous, and the vowel signs may be omitted from a written or printed text. A reader who knows the language can supply the vowels to such an "unvocalized" text.

At one point the two spelling systems overlap, since sometimes certain consonant letters may be used to write certain vowel sounds. Thus the sound of the long vowel /ō/ can be represented by the consonant letter ו in an unvocalized text (ו usually represents the sound of the consonant w). There are accordingly two ways of spelling the word $qōl$, 'voice,' with or without ו -- קול or קל. When the vowel sign ("point") for /ō/ is used as well, these spelling options are קוֹל and קֹל.

The letter *waw*, ו, when used to represent a vowel sound, is called a *mater lectionis*. When it is used, the spelling is called 'full' (*plene* or מָלֵא, שָׁלֵם in Babylonian nomenclature); when it is not used, the spelling is *defective* (חָסֵר).

This complex writing system raises the question of the "correct" spelling of any word containing one or more long vowels. Introductory grammars usually supply simple spelling rules. Example: "...while the usage of vowel letters to indicate final vowels was standardized early, there is no consistency in the use of internal vowel letters in the Bible" (Greenberg 1965: 18). This suggests that there is a rule for spelling a vowel at the end of a word (Spell it *plene*!), but there is no rule for spelling a vowel within a word. Würthwein (1979: 28) says about the phenomenon of variant spelling: "...the writing of a form *plene* or *defective* is completely fortuitous, involving neither consistency of usage nor significance for the meaning of the text."

Not all scholars believe that the use or nonuse of *matres lectionis* is fortuitous. Kahle (Bauer and Leander 1922: 91-2) suggested that a *mater lectionis* could be used to prevent confusion of words which would be identical if written with consonants only. This was already Ibn Ezra's view. Murtonen (1953: 47) suggested that scribes might have omitted *matres lectionis* in order to save space.

The Jewish sages did not think that any detail in the sacred text, however slight, could be without significance. They were fully aware that many words in the Bible were spelled in more than one way. If the word occurred frequently, with a dominant or preferred spelling, they noted the less frequent deviations. Many lists of such exceptional spellings occur in the massorah (traditional marginal annotations to the Hebrew text). Esoteric significance was often discovered in such peculiar spellings, especially when the numerical value of a word was considered to be part of its meaning. (Letters were assigned numerical values.) In spite of statements that the use of *matres lectionis* is fortuitous, readers of the Hebrew Bible have noticed that there seem to be more full spellings in the later books than in the earlier ones. This has often been stated, but details have never been assembled systematically. If that were done, it might be possible to sort out early spellings from later ones, and so to gather evidence for the relative dating of the books.

If the variant spellings of what is apparently the same word reflect historical changes, these could be of two kinds. If the word itself did not change, then the alternatives represent dif-

ferent spelling conventions for the same word, in vogue at different times or in different circles. If 'voice' was always $q\bar{o}l$,
then its two spellings follow two purely graphic possibilities:
defective spelling ignores the vowel, *plene* spelling writes it. The
historical question is then whether these represent an early
and a late practice. Or were the options always available, and
was the choice a matter of taste?

It is also possible that the word was not always pronounced
in the same way, and that the two spellings represent phonetic
differences: קֹול represents the familiar $q\bar{o}l$, the theoretically
possible $q\bar{u}l$ and $qawl$ not occurring in the masoretic text
(although the latter could have been the intention of such a
spelling for a dialect or stage of the language in which the diphthong is still intact, as in Arabic); but קֹל could reflect some
other vocable, such as qal. If this were the case, at least with
some words, then the spellings could provide information about
the phonetic history of such words. If both spellings were used
side by side, they could attest the currency of two pronunciations at the same time, with the difference due to speech patterns (e.g., whether the word was stressed or not), or possibly
due to dialect (North versus South, etc.). If the spellings are
differentiable as early and late, they could document stages in
the evolution of pronunciation.

To sum up. In the Hebrew Bible the spelling of many words
is not uniform. Many suggestions have been made about the
significance of this fact. Opinions divide into four groups: 1) The
spelling is fortuitous (Würthwein's remark above) and therefore
meaningless. 2) The letters have a mystical meaning. 3) The
spelling is due to scribal whim, either to make a word less
ambiguous (Kahle) or to save space (Murtonen). Spelling
preferences could then attest the policies of different scribes,
schools of scribes, or channels of textual transmission. 4) The
spelling patterns record differences in pronunciation (diachron-
ic [historical] or dialectal [regional or social]) or systematic
changes in spelling praxis as such.

So there are two kinds of questions: 1) Are the variations in Hebrew spelling fortuitous or are there patterns? If patterns, what are they? 2) What do the patterns mean? Can they be used to recover information about the origins of the texts -- their dates (early versus late) or locations (if they reflect dialects); or about the history of the texts -- their literary production and scribal transmission?

1.2 The spelling of 'David'

What spelling patterns does the Hebrew Bible disclose? We begin with a simple example, the spelling of the word 'David.' In consonantal spelling a name such as 'David' (*dāwīd*), with long /ī/, would be written דוד (*dwd*). The vowel /ī/ was not shown -- *defective* (*ḥāsēr*) spelling. In the later standard spelling the consonant *yod* ׳ (*y*) was used to represent the long vowel /ī/ to yield דויד (*dwyd*) -- *plene* (*mālē*ᵓ) or 'full' spelling. Both spellings are found in the Bible. Their relative frequencies are shown in Table 1.1, with entries ordered from least *plene* to most. (Counts are identical whether we prefer the *ketib* or the *qere* text, since 'David' is never the object of such notes. The meaning of the rightmost column is explained in § 1.3.) The existence of both possible spellings in large numbers shows that there was no one rule for the whole Bible.

The *massora marginalis* at 1 Kings 3:14; 11:4, 36; Ezekiel 34:23; and Song of Songs 4:4 reads ה מל indicating that 'David' occurs *plene* five times. Since there are 285 *plene* spellings, the massorah evidently refers to books in which both spellings occur, reflecting a manuscript tradition in which the spelling in Psalms is uniformly *defective* and that in the Minor Prophets is uniformly *plene*. For details see Ginsburg (1897-1905: IV § 126).

Ginsburg found 1,077 occurrences of David, 791 *defective* and 286 *plene*. He has two extra occurrences in Samuel and one in Job. His count for Ezra-Nehemiah-Chronicles is 272. BDB has 1,066, 790, 276, respectively. If these differences correctly report variations in manuscripts, and not just errors in counting, they are still so slight as to make little difference to the overall picture. The most intriguing variant is found at Hosea 3:5, the only *defective* spelling in the Minor Prophets in L, where A and C both have *plene*.

Table 1.1 Spelling of 'David' in the Hebrew Bible

Text	Defective	Plene	Total	Plene %	95% C. I.
Genesis-Judges	0	0	0	-	-
Samuel	575	0	575	0.0	0.0-0.5
Isaiah	10	0	10	0.0	0.0-25.9
Jeremiah	15	0	15	0.0	0.0-18.1
Ruth	2	0	2	0.0	0.0-77.6
Proverbs	1	0	1	0.0	0.0-95.0
Qohelet	1	0	1	0.0	0.0-95.0
Psalms	87	1	88	1.1	0.0-6.2
Kings	93	3	96	3.1	0.7-8.9
Ezekiel	3	1	4	25.0	0.6-80.6
Minor Prophets	1	8	9	88.9	51.7-99.7
Song of Songs	0	1	1	100.0	5.0-100.0
Ezra-Neh-Chron	0	271	271	100.0	98.9-100.0

Only the purely consonantal (*defective*) spelling is used in Samuel. Only the full (*plene*) spelling is used in Ezra, Nehemiah, and Chronicles. Kings, Isaiah, Jeremiah, and Psalms prefer the old spelling. The three loci of *plene* spelling of 'David' in 1 Kings (3:14; 11:4, 36) are editorial, reflecting later (priestly?) interests. Broadly speaking, this contrast reflects pre- and post-exilic practice. The old spelling survives in Samuel; the new spelling begins to appear in 1 Kings and Ezekiel. The use of *plene* spelling in the Minor Prophets represents the trend to later usage, which comes to full expression in the work of the Chronicler. The spelling in 1QIs[a] is always *plene*, the prevailing Qumran practice (Kutscher 1959: 75; Freedman 1983b: 91, n. 5), as in 4Q161, 4Q174, 4Q177.

Writing to Bonk in 1891, Stade said of this phenomenon: "דוד, דויד scheint mir nur eine Schrulle des Chronisten oder *eines seiner Abschreiber* zu belegen" (Bonk 1891: 128). We have to determine whether the facts as set out in Table 1.1 are a peculiarity of this word, an idiosyncrasy of some writer, or whether they are representative of spelling patterns throughout the Hebrew Bible. See Freedman (1983b).

1.3 Interpreting relative frequencies

Consider the following assertions based on Table 1.1: 1) The relative frequency of spelling 'David' *plene* in Ezekiel (25%: 1 out of 4) is about eight times that found in Kings (3.1%: 3 out of 96). 2) The writer of Ezekiel was eight times more likely to use a *plene* spelling of 'David' than the writer of Kings.

The first assertion is a correct (if uninteresting) description of the relation between the relative frequencies (*Plene %* values shown in Table 1.1) observed for the books of Ezekiel and Kings. Assertions of the second kind are often made as if they were no more than a restatement of the first assertion, or a valid inference from it. But such assertions leap beyond simple description. The second assertion suggests that had we additional texts from the writers of Ezekiel and Kings, the observed eightfold greater preference of Ezekiel over Kings for *plene* spellings of 'David' would be maintained. Now, it is far from evident that how 'David' is spelled is writer specific. The observed spelling might be conditioned by context, by provenance, by some as-yet unfathomed spelling rule; its non-uniformity might have resulted from copyists' errors and so have nothing whatsoever to do with authorship.

But even if, for the sake of argument, we allow that the spelling of 'David' might be a marker of authorship, the second assertion is misleading. The relative frequency for Ezekiel is based on but four instances, that of Kings on ninety-six. For the reasons given above, we cannot assume that the observed frequencies reflect unvarying practice; we need to estimate the likely relative frequencies for additional material written by the authors of Ezekiel or Kings, if we had such. Such an estimation process should take account of the differing sample sizes. (That Samuel never spells 'David' *plene* in 575 instances is convincing evidence that a hypothetical, enormous text homogeneous with Samuel would most likely not spell it *plene*. That the single occurrence in Proverbs is *defective* tells us next to nothing about the behavior we might expect in a large text homogeneous with Proverbs.)

Lacking any specific mechanism explaining the variability in the spelling of 'David,' we posit a simple statistical generation process. This is done to allow us to judge the strength of evidence represented by the data given in Table 1.1. It leads to the "confidence intervals" (95% C.I.) specified in the rightmost column of the table. The model does not purport to mimic the decision processes underlying the observed data, but only to lead to a rough, useful way of comparing the observations.

Suppose the spelling used in a given instance is governed by the flip of a *biased* coin, a coin whose probability of coming up heads is not necessarily one-half. If heads comes up, the writer uses *plene* spelling; if tails, he uses *defective* spelling. If the coin is so biased as always to come up heads, the spelling will be invariably *plene*. If it comes up heads, on average, one-fourth of the time, then over a *very long* text, twenty-five percent of the instances will be spelled *plene* and so on. Now suppose the probability of coming up heads (of spelling *plene*) is given by p. (Remember that a probability, p, equal to zero indicates impossibility, while a probability equal to one indicates certainty.) It is this generation probability that we wish to estimate based on our data.

Even though the probability of heads (*plene*) may not be one, it is quite possible to observe data sets consisting only of *plene* spellings. Since the outcomes of flipping a coin are independent events, the probability of a sequence of outcomes

is simply the product of the probabilities of the individual outcomes. Thus, the probability of observing a sequence of n
plenes is simply p^n, p times itself n times. If, for example, the
single event probability is nine-tenths ($p = .9$), then the probability of observing ten *plenes* in ten instances is $p^{10} = .35$. If
$p = .1$, then the probability of ten *plenes* in ten instances is
$p^{10} = .0000000001$, profoundly unlikely. Given the value of the
probability of *plene* spelling, it is trivial to compute the probability of getting some set of observations (subject to the suita-
bility of our simple statistical model).

   We wish to go the other way: Given some limited sample of
data, we wish to infer what value the generation probability for
plene spelling should be assigned for a much larger, hypothetical, homogeneous data set. (Note that we do not address *why*
the data are homogeneous.) But a set of data may result from
any of a range of underlying generation probabilities. As we
just saw, a set of ten *plenes* in ten instances might result when
the generation probability is $p = .9$ (with overall probability
.35) or when it is $p = .1$ (with overall probability .0000000001),
or when it takes on any value except zero. To have a well-posed
problem, we do not ask what probability can account for the
observations. We ask what upper and lower probability limits
can be determined such that we can assert that the actual generation probability lies between those limits with some specified confidence of being correct. The upper and lower probabilities so specified bound a "confidence interval." If the confidence that the actual probability lies within the interval is .95,
the interval is termed a 95 percent confidence interval (95%
C.I.). (Taken over *very many* determinations of 95 percent confidence intervals, the particular generation probabilities will lie
within the associated intervals 95 percent of the time.)

   We have omitted certain subtleties from the foregoing discussion (two-sided versus one-sided intervals, specification of
unique intervals, etc.). The interested reader should consult
Sachs (1982: 333f.) or a statistical reference work under

"confidence intervals for the binomial distribution." Had we assumed some other generation model, the details of the confidence intervals would differ but the basic ideas would be the same.

The reader is now in a position to examine the 95 percent confidence intervals associated with the relative frequencies found for Ezekiel and Kings and see why assertion 2) is not statistically sound. We see that, with 95 percent confidence (one chance in twenty of erring on average), our data and model imply that the relative frequency for spelling 'David' *plene* in Kings lies between 0.7 percent and 8.9 percent. For Ezekiel, the 95 percent confidence interval lies between 0.6 percent and 80.6 percent! Because of the paucity of data, the confidence interval for Ezekiel completely covers that of Kings. The generation probability for Ezekiel might well be two orders of magnitude larger than that of Kings or it might be fifteen times smaller. Our data are too limited to allow us to decide.

1.4 The spelling of 'three'

The word 'David' occurs in a limited number of books; it can tell only a part of the story. The spelling of many words in the Hebrew Bible may have a contribution to make to the total picture. In the word 'three' ($\check{s}\bar{a}l\bar{o}\check{s}$) and its derivatives the stem may be spelled שׁלשׁ or שׁלושׁ. The distribution of these spellings in the *ketib* text of L is shown in Table 1.2.

Table 1.2 Spelling of 'three' in the Hebrew Bible

Section	Defective	Plene	Total	Plene %	95% C. I.
Pentateuch	176	3	179	1.7	0.4-5.2
Former Prophets	179	2	181	1.1	0.1-4.3
Latter Prophets	48	5	53	9.4	3.3-21.8
Writings	135	50	185	27.0	20.8-34.0

The picture for 'three' is similar to that for 'David.' The pattern does not suggest that the spelling choice was haphazard. Those portions of the Hebrew Bible that deal with or come from earlier times tend to prefer *defective* spellings, while those from later times have relatively more *plene* spellings. From the confidence intervals we see that the rate of using *plene* spelling is higher in the Writings than in the Primary History (Pentateuch plus Former Prophets). The same cannot be said of the Latter Prophets, because its confidence interval overlaps the others. This is partly because it contains less than a third as many data as each of the other samples.

1.5 The spelling of long /ō/ and /ū/

Exodus 31:18 is a specimen of conservative spelling; long /ō/ and /ū/ are always *defective* except when word-terminal. Note כְּכַלֹּתוֹ, לֻחֹת (× 2), הָעֵדֻת, כְּתֻבִים. The Midrash (*Exodus R.* 41:6) argues that לֻחֹת could be taken as singular, to show that the tablets were one (size). The point is contrived, since the singular is לוּחַ, always *plene*. But the discussion is testimony to the peculiarity of the text. The doubly *defective* spelling of *lūḥōt* occurs twenty-six times (sixteen in Exodus, its only usage; nine in Deuteronomy; and 1 Kings 7:36). לוּחֹת occurs five times, all in Deuteronomy. At each place there is a massorah that the word is spelled *defective* five times. This cannot refer to either vowel alone; it describes *this* spelling with /ū/ *plene* and /ō/ *defective*. In spite of the massorah, L has לחֹת at Deuteronomy 9:15, a scribal error. לֻחוֹת occurs five times (Deuteronomy 4:13; 9:11; 1 Kings 8:9; Habakkuk 2:2; 2 Chronicles 5:10), the more "modern" style. The doubly *plene* spelling is not found in MT. Once more the Pentateuch prefers *defective* spellings.

1.6 The spelling of -ōt[-]

A more ample picture is provided by the spelling of the morpheme -ōt[-], which marks most feminine plural nouns (including adjectives, numerals, and participles) and some masculine plural nouns. The use of *defective* and *plene* spellings of the long vowel in this morpheme for the *ketib* text is shown in Table 1.3. The confidence intervals in Table 1.3 are much shorter than those in previous tables due to larger sample sizes. They do not overlap.

Table 1.3 Spelling of '-ōt[-]' in the Hebrew Bible

Section	Defective	Plene	Total	Plene %	95% C. I.
Pentateuch	1188	544	1732	31.4	29.2-33.7
Former Prophets	276	784	1060	74.0	71.2-76.6
Latter Prophets	299	1646	1945	84.6	83.0-86.2
Writings	424	1717	2141	80.2	78.4-81.9
Total	2187	4691	6878	68.2	67.1-69.3

Once again the spelling practice is not uniform. The percentage of *plene* spellings ranges from 31.4 in the Pentateuch to 84.6 in the Latter Prophets. When the individual books are looked at separately, the range is even wider. Lowest is Exodus, with 20.4 percent; highest is Esther, with 93.5 percent. (Exodus contains 460 instances of -ōt[-]; Esther has but 46.) Study of the spelling of this vowel in the individual books supports the hypothesis that early writings prefer *defective* spelling only in a general way. The highest percentage in the Pentateuch is 51.5 (Genesis), with the other books very much lower. The lowest in the rest of the Bible is Ruth (38.9 percent) with runner-up Joshua (66.8 percent). (Genesis has 357 instances of -ōt[-], Ruth has 18, and Joshua has 193.) The differences among the individual books suggest that each has its own peculiarities.

But there are other possibilities. In § 1.1 we raised the issue of pronunciation, influenced perhaps by stress. The plural suffix -ōt[-] is found in three kinds of grammatical situations, each of which could involve a different stress pattern. The word in which it occurs could be suffixed, construct (or joined to the following word with a *maqqeph*), or neither. If suffixed, vowels in the stem are not stressed. If construct, the word is assumed to be proclitic, with little or no stress. In other situations it is stressed. When we look at suffixed nouns containing -ōt[-], the results are as shown in Table 1.4.

Table 1.4 Spelling of suffixed '-ōt[-]'

Section	Defective	Plene	Total	Plene %	95% C. I.
Pentateuch	576	28	604	4.6	3.1-6.4
Former Prophets	194	98	292	33.5	28.2-39.3
Latter Prophets	238	350	588	59.5	55.4-63.5
Writings	355	282	637	44.3	40.4-48.2
Total	1363	758	2121	35.7	33.7-37.8

The percentage of *plene* spellings of this unstressed vowel for the whole Bible (35.7%) is about half that (68.2%) for all kinds of stress. Again the sections of the Bible differ, the Pentateuch having only 4.6 percent *plene*, while the Latter Prophets have 59.5 percent. The range for the individual books is wider, the lowest being Daniel (with no *plene* spellings of its few suffixed forms), next Numbers (2.5%), the highest Judges (79.4%).

From the point of view of syntax, a construct noun is "bound" like a suffixed one, as is a noun followed by *maqqeph*. Both are governed by the following word, just as the stem is governed by the following suffix. They are less stressed than free forms. The distribution of the spelling preferences in such nouns containing -ōt is shown in Table 1.5.

Table 1.5 Spelling of construct '-ōt'

Section	Defective	Plene	Total	Plene %	95% C. I.
Pentateuch	228	132	360	36.7	31.7-41.9
Former Prophets	37	192	229	83.8	78.4-88.4
Latter Prophets	20	278	298	93.3	89.8-95.4
Writings	14	267	281	95.0	91.8-97.2
Total	299	869	1168	74.4	71.8-76.9

Again the sections of the Bible differ in overall behavior, but this time the Writings have the highest preference for *plene* spellings. In the Pentateuch, however, the *plene* spellings of constructs are not much above the average for all (31.4 -- See Table 1.3).

The choice of *defective* or *plene* spelling of the stressed -ōt in such words is shown in Table 1.6.

Compared with Table 1.3, Table 1.6 suggests there is a preference for *plene* spelling of stressed -ōt, 85.4 percent compared with 68.2 overall. The range across the books is wide: Exodus is again the lowest (24.8 percent), while Judges, Jonah, Ruth, Song of Songs, and Daniel have 100 percent.

Table 1.6 Spelling of stressed '-ōt'

Section	Defective	Plene	Total	Plene %	95% C. I.
Pentateuch	384	384	768	50.0	46.4-53.6
Former Prophets	45	494	539	91.7	89.0-93.8
Latter Prophets	41	1018	1059	96.1	94.8-97.2
Writings	55	1168	1223	95.5	94.2-96.6
Total	525	3064	3589	85.4	84.2-86.5

Compared with Table 1.4, Table 1.6 points up the preference for *defective* spelling in suffixed forms, since only 35.7 percent are spelled *plene*, compared with 68.2 percent for the whole and 85.4 percent for stressed forms. It is tempting to interpret the differences between Table 1.4 and Table 1.6 in terms of pronunciation, if the stressed vowel was longer in duration than the unstressed vowel, so that the *plene* spelling registers length as such (or stress itself, since the two would coincide). But that would only be a tendency, not a rule, and one that operated with different force in different parts of the Bible. Compared with Tables 1.4 and 1.6, Table 1.5 suggests that construct forms behave more like free forms than like suffixed forms; that is, they prefer *plene* spellings. This surprising fact suggests either that construct forms still retain some modicum of stress (if that is the deciding factor) or else that the spelling decision is guided by graphic considerations, so that suffixed forms do not become overly long.

Preliminary observations along these lines have already been made by Murtonen (1953, 1975). He used Mandelkern and studied only a portion of its entries. He obtained 1,131 *defective* and 1,984 *plene*, or 63.7 percent *plene* (compare our 68.2 percent). Murtonen worked with the ratio of *defective* to *plene* spellings (calling it "the relative frequency of defective spellings in terms of plene ones" [1975: 76]). He noticed the high proportion of *defective* spellings in the Pentateuch, especially in books containing a lot of the Priestly source. But since he held that P was the "youngest" (p. 76) source, he did not recognize that the use of vowel letters in the rest of the Bible increased with time. Murtonen's work was limited further by impressionistic references to statistical plausibility. He also attributed variants to "copyists' mistakes" (p. 77) to improve the statistics.

Murtonen was particularly interested in the differences in orthography between the MT and the Samaritan Pentateuch, which shows an enormous increase in the number of *plene* spellings. This has considerable bearing on the aims of the present study, since it underscores the distinctiveness of the spelling patterns still preserved in the MT compared with what emerged in other recensions in the late pre-Christian centuries and subsequently.

1.7 A useful analogy and an approach to analysis

In the next few sections, we shall explain a whimsical, yet helpful, analogy for visualizing the structure of Tables 1.4-1.6 and shall then introduce the simplest form of a very powerful technique for analyzing that structure. Both the analogy and the analytic technique will be used repeatedly in the following chapters. The reader should exercise special care to grasp the material in §§ 1.7-1.12. A feel for the concepts here introduced is crucial if the reader is to appreciate the developments to follow. The analogy will be enriched and the analytic technique will be sophisticated by easy stages as we examine our data. First the analogy.

Picture an urban complex consisting of a group of multi-storied tenements. Each story of each tenement has a corridor running down its center, with pairs of cubicles flanking it. To the reception area arrives a visitor, Mr. Vowel. He is assigned to a tenement based on his type (what type of vowel is he?), to a story based on the stress he is under, to a position along the corridor based on the portion of the Bible from which he comes, and to one or the other of the cubicles flanking that position based on the choice of spelling he represents (is he *defective* or *plene*?). Following this assignment scheme, each arriving visitor (vowel) is given a unique place since to each type corresponds a tenement, to each level of stress a story, to each portion a hall position, and to each choice of spelling a cubicle. Thus the long /ī/ in בְּרֵאשִׁית, the first word in the Bible, is assigned to the tenement for all feminine singular nouns with that ending; it goes into the middle story for inter-mediate stress (it is in a construct); it gets first position along the corridor because it is in the first portion of the Bible (Genesis); and it is assigned the *plene* cubicle. Other arrivals that meet these specifications go into the same cubicle.

Suppose each vowel in the Bible has been assigned its appropriate cubicle. Then vowels of type -ō t will be in their own tenement. If our classification involves three levels of stress and division of the Bible into four portions (Pentateuch, Former Prophets, Latter Prophets, and Writings), then the tenement will have three stories and each story will have eight cubicles or cells (four portions times two possible choices of spelling for each portion). By examining the patterns of cell occupancy, one can determine the association (interaction) among the variables: stress, portion, and choice of spelling. (Tables 1.4, 1.5, and 1.6 provide a "census" of the cubicles in the first, second, and third stories.) Table 1.4 suggests that portion and choice of spelling are associated for low-stress vowels of that type. Is this impression statistically significant? In this introduction, we shall investigate a very simple question: Given a fixed level of stress, is the relevant vowel population distributed among the cubicles (table cells) as one would expect were portion and choice of spelling *not* associated?

For our two-variable problem (fixed stress, variable portion and variable choice of spelling), the procedure for addressing the foregoing question is as follows: 1) Estimate how the population would be distributed were there no association between the variables (model of independence). 2) Measure the goodness of fit between the observed counts and the counts estimated under the assumed model of independence. 3) Assess the goodness of fit to decide if the differences between observed and hypothetical (model-derived) data might result from statistical fluctuations. 4) If the goodness of fit is sufficient to allow the model of independence to be true, so announce. 5) If the goodness of fit is poor enough to rule out independence of position and choice of spelling, compute an index of association allowing one to gauge the extent of the association. When tables of counts are analyzed along these lines, the tables are called *contingency tables*, and one is engaged in *contingency table analysis* (Bishop, Fienberg, and Holland 1975; Fienberg 1980). Our use of this approach is justified in § 4.10.

1.8 The model of independence

The cubicle occupant distribution in the first story of the -ōt tenement is shown in Table 1.7, simplified from Table 1.4.

Table 1.7 Observed counts of suffixed '-ōt[-]'

Section	Defective	Plene	Total
Pentateuch	576	28	604
Former Prophets	194	98	292
Latter Prophets	238	350	588
Writings	355	282	637
Total	1363	758	2121

How might these vowels be distributed across the cells were portion and choice of spelling not associated? A model based on almost total ignorance would assume that any vowel was as likely to be put in one cell as another. Thus, given our table with eight cells, we would expect each cell to hold about one-eighth of the population or about 265 vowels. Table 1.8 shows the cell count estimates and row and column subtotals such a model predicts. Note that generation of this table requires only that we assume that the data spread uniformly across the table and that we know the size of the total population involved.

Table 1.8 Expected counts for "ignorance" model

Section	Defective	Plene	Total
Pentateuch	265.125	265.125	530.25
Former Prophets	265.125	265.125	530.25
Latter Prophets	265.125	265.125	530.25
Writings	265.125	265.125	530.25
Total	1060.500	1060.500	2121.00

Ignorance-model estimates may be close to some observations, but such is not the case for Table 1.7. Nor is this surprising, since the only fact used was the total sample size.

The *model of independence* uses additional facts to arrive at estimates that usually fit better than does the "ignorance" model. Let the probability of an item's going into a cell in the rth row be proportional to that row's population and the probability of an item's going into the cth column be proportional to that column's population. Equivalently, let the estimated expected count in the cell defined by some pairing of portion and choice of spelling equal the portion's total population times the *fraction* of the complete sample observed to have that spelling. Thus, the estimate for the expected count in the Pentateuch-*defective* cell is the total population in the Pentateuch (604) times the fraction of all vowels spelled *defective*, which is $\frac{1363}{2121} = 0.6426$. Carrying out the arithmetic yields an estimated expected cell count of 388.14, which is the value in the upper left-hand cell (Pentateuch-*defective*) of Table 1.9. The other cell count estimates are derived in the same way. (In generating the estimates, we are multiplying a row probability by a column probability to yield a cell probability, as should be done when row and column probabilities are independent [Fienberg 1980: 10].)

Table 1.9 Estimated counts for model of independence

Section	Defective	Plene	Total
Pentateuch	388.14	215.86	604
Former Prophets	187.65	104.35	292
Latter Prophets	377.86	210.14	588
Writings	409.35	227.65	637
Total	1363	758	2121

1.9 Measuring goodness of fit

To decide how well the model of independence fits the observations, we need to quantitate the overall difference between observed and model-based counts. For a given cell, the divergence between tables might be assessed by subtracting the estimated expected count from the observed count:

single-cell fit = observed − estimated expected count.

Since single-cell fit can be positive or negative, simply to add all single-cell fits would lead to cancellations. To insure that all fits, positive or negative, properly inflate the overall measure of goodness of fit, one might sum the *squares* of the single-cell differences. To do so would give the same weight to a numerical difference, be it in a cell holding few or many counts. But a difference of ten, say, for a cell holding twenty counts ought to count for more than the same difference in a cell holding a thousand counts. This reasoning leads us to use as our overall measure of goodness of fit the sum over all cells of

$$\frac{(observed - estimated\ expected\ count)^2}{estimated\ expected\ count}.$$

The sum is called the *Pearson chi-square statistic*, χ^2. It suggests a better measure of *single-cell* fit, the "standardized residual" (Agresti 1984: 62):

$$\frac{observed - estimated\ expected\ count}{\sqrt{estimated\ expected\ count}}.$$

Table 1.10 shows the residuals for Tables 1.7 and 1.9.

Table 1.10 Standardized residuals for suffixed '-ōt[-]'

Section	Defective	Plene
Pentateuch	+9.54	-12.79
Former Prophets	+0.46	-0.62
Latter Prophets	-7.19	+9.65
Writings	-2.69	+3.60

Note that squaring the residuals and summing them yields χ^2. The residuals will be examined after we have discussed the method for assessing goodness of fit.

1.10 Assessing goodness of fit

The Pearson chi-square statistic measures the goodness of fit between the observed counts and the estimated expected model-based counts. (In the foregoing, the model of independence for a two-dimensional table was used. We shall see in Chapter 7 that for higher-dimensional tables, many other models are possible.) Had the estimated expected cell counts for the model of independence agreed perfectly with the counts actually observed (were Tables 1.7 and 1.9 identical), then χ^2 would have been zero. In fact, we find that $\chi^2 = 420.06$. This departure of χ^2 from zero might be because the model of independence is inadequate, as there may be association between portion and choice of spelling. But it could be that the model of independence nicely characterizes the state of affairs, and the departure of χ^2 from zero results from the finite population (sample) producing counts which fluctuate from their expected values. (That on flipping a coin four times it comes up heads three times does not necessarily imply that it is biased. The sample size is too small for the outcome to make us suspicious. But thirty heads in forty tries would be another matter! For a fair coin, the probability of three heads in four tosses is .25; the probability of thirty heads in forty tries is .0008.)

What is needed is a threshold value such that if χ^2 is below the threshold, we conclude that the small χ^2 implies the model fits the observations reasonably well. If χ^2 exceeds the threshold, we conclude that the model insufficiently accounts for the observed facts. Such a threshold is supplied by the "chi-square distribution," the probability distribution which χ^2 obeys when the model adequately predicts the observations.

Determination of the χ^2 decision threshold involves three steps: 1) specification of confidence level, 2) calculation of the problem's number of degrees of freedom, and 3) determination of the threshold value from an appropriate reference work.

1) We first specify the level of confidence we wish to have in our decision. Because of the nature of statistical fluctuations, a large χ^2 could result even were the model and observations in agreement. We choose to specify our chi-square threshold such that we will mistakenly reject the hypothesis of independence on average one percent of the time. We symbolize the threshold so specified by $\chi^2_{99\%}$.

2) But before we can determine the actual value of $\chi^2_{99\%}$ we must reckon a second quantity, our problem's number of degrees of freedom, $d.f.$. The number of degrees of freedom associated with a pair of tables of observed and estimated counts is the number of cells in the observed table minus the number of *independent* pieces of information used to generate the model-based table. *Loosely*, $d.f.$ gives the number of independent quantities needed to reconstruct the table of observations from the table of model-based estimates. The smaller $d.f.$, the more independent facts about the observations have been used to build the model. (If $d.f. = 0$, the model allows perfect recovery of the observations. But such a model is uninteresting, since it achieves exactitude at the cost of a total loss of parsimony.) As the number of degrees of freedom increases, so does the chi-square threshold value.

For a two-dimensional table having r rows and c columns, the initial number of degrees of freedom is $r \times c$. Forming the model of independence requires $r + c - 1$ pieces of independent information. (One gets subtracted because knowledge of the r row sums gives us the grand total of counts in the table. Knowing that, we need be told only $c - 1$ of the column totals since the final column total is just the grand total minus the sum of the $c - 1$ known column totals.) It follows that an $r \times c$

table analyzed in terms of the model of independence has $r \times c - (r + c - 1)$ degrees of freedom, which by trivial algebra is just $d.f. = (r - 1) \times (c - 1)$. Thus, Table 1.7 along with Table 1.9 defines a problem having

$$d.f. = (r - 1) \times (c - 1) = (4 - 1) \times (2 - 1) = 3.$$

3) Having selected an acceptable confidence level (99%) and having computed the number of degrees of freedom (three for Tables 1.7 and 1.9), the chi-square threshold ($\chi^2_{99\%}$) can be found in any statistics text. We find $\chi^2_{99\%} = 11.345$.

Since $\chi^2 = 420.06$ and $\chi^2_{99\%} = 11.345$, we have strong evidence that for Table 1.7, portion and choice of spelling are not independent. To complete our analysis, we should see which cell counts of Table 1.9 depart most from those predicted by the model of independence and should characterize the degree of association between the variables.

1.11 Outliers and association

For the model of independence to hold for the data of Table 1.7, the χ^2 value should be less than $\chi^2_{99\%} = 11.345$. This means that each cell position in Tables 1.7 and 1.9 is allotted about $\dfrac{11.345}{8} = 1.42$ toward the total allowed χ^2. Recall that Table 1.10 holds the standardized residuals for our problem: the square of each cell entry in that table is that cell position's contribution to the total chi-square sum. If that contribution, on average, should not exceed 1.42, then a cell whose residual magnitude exceeds $\sqrt{1.42} = 1.2$ draws our interest as an *outlier* cell, one whose observed count deviates excessively from the model. Letting t be the number of table cells, the quantity

$$r_{99\%} = \left[\frac{\chi^2_{99\%}}{t} \right]^{\frac{1}{2}}$$

is an informal threshold with which the magnitude of residuals can be compared in searching for observations which depart suspiciously from model-engendered expectations (Bishop, Fienberg, and Holland 1975: 137).

The residuals displayed in Table 1.10 allow us to move past intuitions based on the raw counts of Table 1.7: the Pentateuch "overuses" *defectives* and "underuses" *plenes*. The Former Prophets are not out of line with the model of independence (for these observations). Both the Latter Prophets and Writings "underuse" *defectives* and "overuse" *plenes*.

Many approaches to assessing the degree of association between a pair of variables have been proposed (Liebetrau 1983). That introduced by Cramér (1946: 443) has attractive characteristics for our kind of two-dimensional table. Cramér's v is defined *for our simple tables* by

$$v = \left[\frac{\chi^2}{N}\right]^{\frac{1}{2}}$$

where N is the grand total of counts in the table. (In Tables 1.7-9, $N = 2121$.) If there is no association between the variables, v is zero; it is unity if and only if each row contains only one non-zero count (full association). Thus, v would equal unity for our problem, if and only if each portion made all its choices of spelling one way or the other. (In terms of our analogy, at each position along the hallway, only the *defective* or *plene* cubicle would house visitors.) In fact, for Tables 1.7 and 1.9, Cramér's v has a value of .45, indicating fairly strong association of portion and choice of spelling.

1.12 An illustration of independence: verse parity

We have seen the outcome of the analysis when the involved variables are associated. To provide a measure of quality control, we next consider a situation where we have strong *a priori* reason to expect the two variables to be independent. Our faith in the statistical method should be strengthened when the method confirms our prior strong conviction.

For each vowel counted in forming Table 1.7, we now tally not whether it is *defective* or *plene*, but whether it appears in an odd- or even-numbered verse. (If it appears in a verse whose number is odd, the vowel has odd parity. If it appears in a verse whose number is even, the vowel has even parity.) The resulting counts are given in Table 1.11. We ask (with linguae abutting jowls): Is portion of the Bible associated with verse parity?

Table 1.11 Observed verse parity counts

Section	Even	Odd	Total
Pentateuch	275	329	604
Former Prophets	140	152	292
Latter Prophets	294	294	588
Writings	324	313	637
Total	1033	1088	2121

The model of independence yields the estimated expected counts shown in Table 1.12.

Table 1.12 Estimated verse parity counts

Section	Even	Odd	Total
Pentateuch	294.17	309.83	604
Former Prophets	142.21	149.79	292
Latter Prophets	286.38	301.62	588
Writings	310.24	326.76	637
Total	1033.00	1088.00	2121

We compute that $\chi^2 = 4.09$. Since $\chi^2_{99\%} = 11.345$, we conclude that verse parity is independent of section. Table 1.13 shows the residuals for this problem. The residual outlier threshold $r_{99\%} = 1.2$, so *no* cells lead to suspiciously large residuals.

Table 1.13 Standardized residuals

Section	Even	Odd
Pentateuch	-1.12	+1.09
Former Prophets	-0.19	+0.18
Latter Prophets	+0.45	-0.44
Writings	+0.78	-0.76

This illustration of independence concludes our introduction to contingency table analysis. Since the data studied were ample, since we analyzed only two variables (neither involving ordered categories), and since no combinations of categories were ruled impossible *a priori*, the analysis was straightforward. Analyses of the sort just carried out will suffice until we reach Chapter 7. At that point we shall take up the problems of limited sample size, higher-dimensional tables, ordered categories, and "structural zeros" (cells that *a priori* must always hold counts of zero).

To rehabilitate our analogy briefly: In subsequent chapters, we will consider the effects (if any) of cubicles housing but few visitors. We will introduce the multiplicity of models which arise when problems involve three or more dimensions (tenement, story, position, cubicle). We will investigate whether the story variable is ordered (low, middle, high). And we will cater to the fact that some entire stories in some tenements are allowed to house *no* visitors.

1.13 Choice of text

This is a convenient place to address another issue. Is it possible to speak at all about the orthography of the MT? To be precise, there is no such thing as *the* MT. There are texts in the masoretic tradition -- manuscripts and printed editions -- and no two of them are identical. They vary in orthography, among other things. If the scribes exercised their spelling options haphazardly, the choice of one manuscript or edition rather than another could be arbitrary. Do the variations among the manuscripts and editions matter, so far as the present study is concerned?

To answer this question decisively, it would be necessary to do a complete study independently on several such texts, assembling exhaustive orthographic information about all of them. This study takes the first step, with L as its standard. Until the same thing can be done for other manuscripts and editions, it is reassuring that several tests on selected orthographic phenomena suggest that the differences among major witnesses to the MT are negligible. Collation of major manuscripts (**A, C, L, P**) and printed editions discloses astonishing unanimity, even in the use of *matres lectionis*.

The word *hăqīmōtî*, 'I raised up,' occurs 25 times in MT, three as perfect (Genesis 9:17; Exodus 6:4; 1 Samuel 15:13), twenty-two consecutive future. It is never suffixed, so the final vowel is always *plene*. With two long vowels in the stem, there are four possible spellings -- *defective-defective, defective-plene, plene-defective,* and *plene-plene*. All manuscripts and editions consulted showed each occurrence to be spelled in the same way in all of them, with the following exceptions. At Isaiah 29:3 1QIs[a], it is doubly *plene* -- not surprising. The occurrences in Ezekiel 16:60 and 62 are respectively *plene-plene* and *plene-defective* in most, and this is attested by the massorah. Only L and P show hesitating deviations (see below).

The most conservative spelling (*defective-defective*) occurs in the Pentateuch (Genesis 6:18; 9:11, 17; 17:7, 19; 26:3; Exodus 6:4), 1 Kings (6:12; 9:5), Jeremiah (6:17; 23:4, 5; 29:10; 33:14), and Ezekiel (34:23, 29) -- sixteen times. *Plene-defective* occurs six times (Leviticus 26:9; 1 Samuel 2:35; 15:13; 2 Samuel 7:12; Isaiah 29:3; Ezekiel 16:62) and *plene-plene* three times (Ezekiel 16:60; 1 Chronicles 17:11; 2 Chronicles 7:18). Quite apart from the almost complete agreement of manuscripts and editions in the locations of the three different spellings, the picture is in line with the other evidence already adduced. The lean use of *matres lectionis* dominates the Pentateuch (Leviticus 26:9 is the only exception), Kings, and Jeremiah. Chronicles uses the fullest spelling. A mixed spelling is found in Leviticus (once), Samuel (which differs from Kings in this as in many other spelling patterns), and Isaiah. Only Ezekiel is not consistent, having all three of the attested spellings, with related turbulence in some manuscripts (see below).

Levita (Ginsburg 1867b: 166) discussed *hăqîmôtî* because of the several ways it may be spelled.

1) The commonest is doubly *defective* in the stem: הקמתי. Levita claimed to quote a *massora* to the effect that there were eleven such cases. Ginsburg (1867b: 166, note 53) could find no such *massora* but listed twelve cases (he said eleven). We find sixteen!

2) Mm 2841 gives three cases of doubly *plene* הקימותי. They are Ezekiel 16:60; 1 Chronicles 17:11; 2 Chronicles 7:18. In L, Ezekiel 16:60 is והקמותי *contra* Mm. Ginsburg knew a tradition in which 2 Samuel 7:12 was doubly *plene*; but he listed this case under two categories (1897-1905: II § 140-1). In L the word is doubly *plene* at Ezekiel 16:62. It seems as if verses 60 and 62 have been confused; either the spellings have been exchanged or else the *massora* was wrongly assigned. P (first hand) has *defective-plene* (a combination otherwise not attested, and this has been corrected to *plene-plene*) and *plene-plene*. L was originally *defective-defective* and *plene-plene*, with the first corrected to *defective-plene* (as shown in BHS) by squeezing ו into a small space. C has והקימותי (Ezekiel 16:60) and והקימתי (Ezekiel 16:62), in agreement with the *massora*.

3) Mm 816 gives six cases of הקמתי as shown above. 1 Samuel 2:35 was wrongly referenced by Ginsburg (1867b: 166) as 2 Samuel ii. 35 (it is correct in Ginsburg 1897-1905 II § 141). Levita quoted 1 Samuel 15:13 as the only case of הקמותי, claiming a *massora* to that effect, but L does not agree; according to it, Ezekiel 16:60 is the only case of this spelling. But this, as we have seen, is incorrect. The data available to Frensdorff (1876: 166) on this word were not reliable. He tracked down most of these errors but did not find a case of הקמותי, quoting Ezekiel 16:62 as והקימתי and verse 60 with every

spelling except the one in **L**.

In sum, this case throws a little doubt on the quality of **L** in the main line of the MT, at least in its use of *matres lectionis*, but not enough to suggest that any other manuscript or edition should be preferred to it.

Several other individual words were collated throughout a number of manuscripts and editions, with similar results. In addition, whole books were collated across several witnesses with an eye on variations in the use of *matres lectionis*. The Rabbinic Bible usually agrees with Snaith's edition against **L** in the use of *matres lectionis*. In Genesis **L** has /ō/ *plene* five times when the others are *defective*, *defective* three times where the others are *plene*. In Exodus **L** has /ō/ *plene* six times where the others are *defective*, *defective* six times where the others are *plene*. In Leviticus **L** has /ō/ *plene* three times where the others are *defective*, *defective* once where the others are *plene*. And so on for other books and other *matres lectionis*. Considering the enormous number of vowels in the text, the deviations are negligible. **L** shows a slight drift towards more *matres lectionis*. This drift is more marked when **L** is compared with **A**. In the portion of Deuteronomy preserved in **A** there are seventeen differences between it and **L** in the use of *matres lectionis*. **L** is *plene* fifteen times where **A** is *defective*, *defective* twice where **A** is *plene*. This suggests that the differences between these two manuscripts in such details could be usefully studied. Unfortunately, the incompleteness of **A** makes it unfit for the investigation of the whole Bible which we are engaged in.

The choice of a manuscript or edition as the immediate object of study is not the only decision to be made at the beginning. Any chosen text in the masoretic tradition presents at many points pairs of alternative readings -- *ketib* or *qere*. There are essentially two complete texts, one written, the other read. The two are identical more than ninety-nine percent of the time. The relative merits of the *ketib* and *qere* alternatives have been much debated (Gordis 1937), but many features of the system are far from clear. *Defective* or *plene* options for the spelling of the same word are seldom matter for *ketib/qere* variants, unless there is also a difference in the concomitant vowel. (The old and new spelling of the suffix pronoun 'his' with nouns constitutes a special problem, and such alternatives have dubious standing in the *ketib/qere* system, as the disagreement among manuscripts on this point shows.) But many pairs of *ketib/qere* alternatives do present contrasting orthographic features, so the choice of one or the other will make a difference in the data.

For the sake of consistency, either the entire *ketib* text or the entire *qere* text should be read. But which? The decision is insecure either way. If the *ketib* text is chosen, *ketib* variants suffer from the drawback that no canonical vocalization is available. If the *qere* is preferred, we have the benefit of canonical vocalization, but there is no canonical list. One has only to compare any two manuscripts or editions, or the inventories compiled by Ginsburg and Gordis, to realize that the number of *qere* readings is indeterminate. On top of that, the use of *matres lectionis* in *qere* variants (the very thing we are most interested in) is quite arbitrary. L, for instance, often has *plene* spelling in a *qere* form where other manuscripts have *defective*.

There is no compelling solution; the consolation is that the differences amount to a very tiny fraction of the aggregate of orthographic phenomena. In the event we followed the policy of using L, including both *ketib* and *qere* in our machine-manipulable text. In order to have *ketib* variants in a vocalized form in line with the rest of the text, we were obliged to supply vowels, making the best choice from the apparatus of BHS or Gordis' lists. We were thus able to read L in two modes, the *ketib* text or the *qere* text. All pertinent data were compiled separately for these two reading modes. There were no significant differences between the final results. Our main reports are based on the *ketib* text. When the *qere* text contains interesting systematic differences of any scope, we shall discuss them.

1.14 Our problem

The components of the problem are now evident: 1) The spellings of the word 'David,' of the word and stem 'three,' and of the morpheme -ōt are neither regular nor haphazard. Presumably this is true of other words as well. 2) The patterns differ throughout the Bible from section to section and from book to book. 3) The choice of spelling seems to have an historical basis, since "early" texts (dealing with early times, if not actually written early), notably the Pentateuch, are conspicuously abstemious in the use of *matres lectionis*. (But such differences could also be due to differences in transmission history.) 4) A phonetic factor could also be involved, since -ōt might have been spelled *defective* in the early days because the vowel was still pronounced /ā/. (A phonetic and archaic factor might combine if the traditional spelling derived from a sector, possibly Aramaic, in which the vowel was not eligible for *plene* spelling.) 5) If spelling choices were influenced by phonetic considerations, then the lengthening of a vowel under stress (and corresponding shortness when less stressed) could stimulate a preference for one or other spelling. 6) Purely graphic considerations might also have entered in. It has been suggested that scribes preferred not to have too many *matres lectionis* in the same word, or simply left them out of longer words. 7) The force of convention could give individual words fixed spellings which would resist the influences listed above. 8) Notwithstanding all these factors, occasional deviations from standard spellings and violations of rules due to scribal errors are sure to have taken place.

Chapter 2. The History of Hebrew Spelling

2.1 Introduction

The impression that *matres lectionis* are used more in the later parts of the Hebrew Bible agrees with the history of spelling as traced through ancient inscriptions. Study of the inscriptions, in its turn, could provide reference points for the development of the spellings found in the Bible. "The orthography of the inscriptions may prove useful in reconstructing the history of the biblical books and the time and place of the redaction of the Masoretic Text" (Sarfatti 1982: 63).

2.2 Alphabetic writing

True alphabetic writing uses one letter for each distinctive sound (phoneme) in a language. No system is perfect, but any adequate alphabet provides for both consonants and vowels. All modern alphabets derive ultimately from the writing systems developed by the Canaanites during the second millennium BCE (Naveh 1982). The Ugaritic alphabet distinguished vowels only to a restricted degree, in association with ʾ*aleph.* Alleged use of other letters to represent vowels are conveniently assembled in O'Connor (1983: 445). By the end of the Late Bronze Age (around 1200 BCE) the Phoenicians had an alphabet of twenty-two letters. These represented the consonantal phonemes of their language. No provision was made for writing vowels. (This view was questioned by Dahood [1982: 62, n. 11].)

Early in the Iron Age the Aramaeans took over the Phoenician alphabet. So did the Israelites and other peoples of the region. This alphabet was not entirely suitable for Aramaic, since Aramaic had a different stock of consonantal phonemes

from the twenty-two for which the Phoenician alphabet had
been developed. Instead of inventing any new signs, the
Aramaeans sometimes used one symbol to represent two
phonemically distinct but phonetically similar consonant
sounds.

It was a small step from this practice to use of the same
symbol for both a consonant and a phonetically similar vowel
sound. In time three of the consonant letters -- ה, ו, and י --
were used for writing certain vowel sounds while continuing to
serve for the established consonant values. Traditional Hebrew
grammar recognizes a fourth such consonant, א. It is not appropriate to give all four consonant letters the same status in
the eventual writing system, since each has its own story. א
wasn't a *mater lectionis* in the early stages and never acquired
a function comparable to that of the other three.

It was not until the Middle Ages that a completely autonomous system for writing all the vowel sounds of Hebrew by
means of "points" was superimposed on the original consonantal writing (Kahle 1959; Morag 1962, 1974; Yeivin 1980).
Northwest Semitic writing thus evolved through the stages
shown in Table 2.1.

Table 2.1 Stages of Northwest Semitic writing

STAGE 1	*Up to tenth century BCE*	•letters for consonant sounds only
STAGE 2	*From ninth century BCE to Masoretic Era*	•letters for consonant sounds •three letters for some vowels
STAGE 3	*Middle Ages to present*	•letters for consonant sounds •three or four letters for some vowels •points for all vowels

Obviously, the biblical period involves only Stages 1 and 2. No *purely* consonantal texts (Stage 1) have survived unmodified into the Bible, *matres lectionis* being used throughout. In fact there is no proof that purely consonantal spelling was ever used in the writing of Hebrew. Stage 1 is hypothetical. Even so it is highly likely that any written Hebrew that existed before the time of David would have been purely consonantal. The Gezer Calendar is a possible specimen. And even in the time of David it is likely that consonantal spelling was in vogue, especially if the main cultural influence came from the Phoenicians rather than from the Aramaeans. To judge from the Aramaic portion of the Tell Fekhereye bilingual, the principle of using three consonant letters to write certain vowel sounds goes back to the very beginnings of Aramaic literacy (Freedman and Andersen 1985). Developments in the southern dialects seem to have been more gradual.

The consonantal texts of the Hebrew Bible all passed through Stage 2, but some traces of the orthographic conventions of Stage 1 are still preserved in the spelling of individual words (Cross and Freedman 1952: 1). The contrast between Genesis 10:8 and 1 Chronicles 1:10 supplies an illustration. In the first, Nimrod (נמרד) is a hero (גבר); in the second, נמרוד is a גבור. The two spellings of 'David' studied in Chapter 1 are another example. Such evidence is all the more impressive when the word is a proper noun, since these were given vowel letters quite early in the development.

2.3 Writing vowels

The practice of writing some of the vowels with the aid of the three *matres lectionis* did not come into full operation all at once. The system evolved gradually. The further back we go in the process, the more difficult it becomes to discover the details. Not only does the evidence become more and more sparse; we are also less certain of the pronunciation of the words which are being written. Very few inscriptions survive from the first few centuries of Hebrew writing. This evidence can be augmented by inscriptions in other Northwest Semitic languages, and they all have a lot in common. But too much uniformity should not be assumed, especially in the sound systems. Nevertheless we can say, speaking in the broadest terms, that they all used essentially the same writing system and that common cultural influences must have been at work over the entire region. When we look at the specific details, however, it is equally clear that there is considerable variation in local usage, and we do not know to what extent the scribal practice developed independently in each of the major languages or main political centers, or how much cross-influence there might have been from one area to another.

So far as Israel is concerned, exposed as it was to continuing cultural and political influence from both Phoenicians and Aramaeans from the very beginnings of the monarchy, if not before, it is a matter of some moment to gauge the relative influences from these two quarters on the development of the writing system within Israel. It is likely that the Aramaeans and the Israelites each borrowed the alphabet independently from the Phoenicians. The situation in Transjordan was probably similar, but at one further remove. Moabite practice could interface with Hebrew to the west and with Aramaic to the north. To judge from the earliest substantial evidence from Aramaic (Tell Fekhereye), the Aramaeans immediately adapted the system by invoking the letters ה, ו, and י to write *all* vowels at the end of words (all word-terminal vowels being probably long by this time) and ו and י to write *some* long vowels in the middle of words. To judge from the earliest Hebrew evidence (the Gezer Calendar), the Israelites at first used the Phoenician alphabet just as the Phoenicians did (consonant sounds only being represented) and only later followed increasingly the practices of the Aramaeans. These historical circumstances go a long way to explain why the Israelites seem to trail behind the

Aramaeans in the *scale* of the use of *matres lectionis*, even though both groups are using essentially the same rules.

In using the term "rules" we should distinguish between a practice that was universal, or well-nigh so, and a practice that was only occasional or even sporadic. In the first case it does not make much difference whether we regard the rule as our way of describing the data, inductively, or whether it was something that the scribes were taught to do in their schools. We have ho information about the latter, and there is nothing to be gained by trying to recover the mental processes of the people who wrote the inscriptions we now have. All we know is what they wrote. A social convention, such as a spelling rule, is at once arbitrary and obligatory, and it does not matter whether we call the rare departure from the dominant pattern an "exception" or a mistake. Occasional failure to observe a rule does not mean that there was no rule. But if the "rule" is more honored in the breach than in the observance, then the term "rule" becomes increasingly inappropriate. Defined in this way, there was only one generally observed rule: every final vowel was written; and, as already said, by this time all word-terminal vowels were probably long, originally short word-terminal vowels having been either dropped or lengthened; and, since either course could be followed, the results doubtless varied from dialect to dialect. Vowels were written with the aid of one or other of the three *matres lectionis* -- ' for -$\bar{\imath}$, ' for -$\bar{u}$, ה for any others. This rule prevailed in Aramaic from the beginning, and it is evidently in force in Hebrew and Moabite as soon as we begin to get inscriptions of any length. It needs to be remembered, however, that not all occurrences of these three letters at the end of a word necessarily represent the writing of a vowel. They could still stand for consonants; but ' and ' would only be consonants in this position if the word ended in a diphthong.

A rule less consistently observed, and so more appropriately described as "optional" was the writing of word-medial

long vowels with the aid of two of these *matres lectionis*. From
the beginning this practice is more in evidence in the spelling
of proper nouns than of ordinary words. In Hebrew there is a
clear difference between the universal indication of word-
terminal long vowels, the general (and increasing) writing of
word-medial long vowels in proper nouns, and the rare (and
more slowly developing) writing of word-medial long vowels in
ordinary words.

2.3.1. Gibson (1971: vii) deplores "the prevailing and disas-
trous pedagogic device of supplying students of these documents with vocalizations derived from the centuries later
Tiberian system used in the Hebrew Bibles." This regrettable
practice creates an impression that the Hebrew of the inscriptions was pronounced in the same way as the Hebrew of much
later times; it leads to wrong identification of spelling patterns,
and false estimates of the scale of use of *matres lectionis* in the
early days. Aharoni's vocalizations of the Arad ostraca were carried out in this way, implying, among other things, that the contraction of diphthongs had already reached the stage that we
know in the masoretic text. During the pre-exilic period of
Hebrew only phonetically long vowels (and not all of them) were
written with the help of *matres lectionis*. The ו and י of diphthongs were probably still consonantal.

2.3.2. The traditional treatment of this subject explained
the emergence of *matres lectionis* (consonant letters used to
write vowel sounds) within a writing system that began as
purely consonantal as due to *historical* spelling. The classic
presentation of Kahle in Bauer and Leander (1922: 91) states
that the four *matres lectionis* (all are treated alike) *das seinen
Konsonantenwert einbüsste* change into signs for vowels. He
even asserted, in order to bring the use of ה into line with the
others, that the ה of the feminine suffix -$\hat{a}$ represented a consonant sound of sorts, *in der der gehauchte Absatz geschwun-
den war* (p. 91).

2.3.3. The parade example is supplied by Harris (1939: 59).

The letter *y* came to stand for final [-î] when the 1 sg.
possessive suffix [-iya] 'my' (after gen. and acc.), written with
y, changed to [-iy] (with loss of final short vowels), then > [-î].
The use of *y* for [-î] which had thus arisen was then extended
to other cases of final [-î], which had hitherto not been indicated in the consonantal orthography.

The development traced here is purely theoretical. The
change involved -- *yadiya* → *yādî* -- had already taken place in
Ugaritic, where the suffix is zero in the orthography. Likewise in
Phoenician this suffix is never indicated. When the suffix *-î*,
'my,' is indicated by means of the consonant ꜣ (in Aramaic,
Hebrew, and Moabite), there is no reason to believe that in any
instance it represents the original ending *-iya*; that is, there is
no reason to believe that ꜣ in such an occurrence represents a
consonant so that the spelling of the derived word *yadî* in the
same way is historical. Unless the alleged fact can be established, it cannot be any more than a conjecture that the transition *yadiya* → *yādî*, both spelled ꜣ''ꜣ, was the precursor to the
use of ꜣ to spell word-terminal *-î* which had not evolved in such
a way. As soon as evidence becomes available, ꜣ is used for any
and every word-terminal *-î*, whatever its historical origin. The
spelling is phonetic in every case.

2.3.4. The argument that the use of ꜣ to write long *û* arose
similarly as the outcome of historical spelling is even more
tenuous. Weinberg (1975: 458) lists the contraction of terminal
diphthongs as /iy/ → /i:/, /uw/ → /u:/, /ay/ → /e:/, /aw/ →
/o:/. The cases involving /y/ are not in dispute; the ones
involving /w/ are not attested for /u:/, i.e., ū. There is no basis
in historical phonology for *uw* → *ū* at the end of a word (it does
arise in some word-medial positions). Garbini (1969) has under-
scored the fact that no basis for this orthography for /ū/ in
historical spelling has been demonstrated. It represents the
invention of purely phonetic spelling. Segert (1961: 118) is

reserved; the spelling והי- could reflect a consonantizing off-
glide of /ū/ to the homorganic /w/. Bange (1971) has taken
this idea of secondary diphthongization to extremes.

It was not by analogy with any known historical spelling of
long /ū/ with ו that a purely phonetic spelling of /ū/ with ו
developed. To judge from the earliest Aramaic inscriptions,
which are more generous in literary texts than early Hebrew,
this rule was applied consistently to long vowels at the end of
words, and frequently to long vowels within words, especially if
the words were proper nouns (Freedman and Andersen 1985).
The earliest examples in Hebrew are theophoric names ending
in -yāhū (-יהו) and plural verbs, such as הכו, 'they struck'
(Siloam Tunnel Inscription).

2.3.5. The writing of long vowels with the aid of ה has been
explained in various ways. The usage is simple in one respect, in
that ה is never used to write any vowel within a word. In
another respect it is complicated by the fact that ה is used (at
least by the time when the masoretic system is complete) to
write several vowels at the end of words. In masoretic texts
vocalized in accordance with the Tiberian system, the vowels
/ē/, /ɛ/, /ā/, and /ō/ have all been supplied to various words
in which a word-terminal ה has been deemed to be a *mater lectionis*. When a word-terminal ה was recognized by the
masoretes as a consonant, it was distinguished from the *mater
lectionis* by the use of *mappiq*. If the ה used in this way as a
mater lectionis in a later form of any word should correspond
to a genuine consonant sound /h/ in an earlier form of that
word, then the spelling would be considered *historical*; the consonant /h/ has ceased to be pronounced as such. How this
might have come about in any given case is another matter.

A point to be emphasized at this stage, for its significance
does not seem to have been appreciated, is the fact that most,
if not all, of the numerous and various words in Hebrew in which
the *mater lectionis* ה is used to write a word-terminal vowel do

not evolve from an earlier form in which the ה was a real consonant. The numerous forms derived from ל״י roots illustrate
this fact. Indeed there seems to be only one candidate; the consonant /h/ occurs in several allomorphs of the pronoun 'him,'
'his,' and ה is used to write the suffix -ō, 'his,' in pre-exilic
Hebrew inscriptions.

In the masoretic tradition 'his hand' is read as *yādô*,
whether it is spelled ידו (standard) or ידה (archaic). The
reconstruction of the ancient forms of 'his hand' as *yaduhū*,
yadihū, or *yadahū* is highly probable, but the third possibility,
with the accusative case ending, has been favored as the most
likely ancestor of the eventual form because the stem-terminal
/-a-/ seems to offer the best explanation of the development to
yādô. It is generally accepted that the route followed was this:
*yadahū → *yada-ū → *yadaw → *yādô*. The steps postulated are
artificial and hypothetical, and the correlation of the pronunciation at any point along the way with the spellings attested in
ancient inscriptions and eventually in the Bible is beset with
problems.

The masoretic vocalization of such a word as ידה, 'his
hand,' with *holem* is a procedure which assumes the validity of
the medieval reading, which had become uniform over every
part of the Bible, even when the spelling differed. It was plausible enough, since there were words of other types in which ה
stood for /ō/. The possibility that ידה correctly recorded a different pronunciation was not entertained. The same policy was
adopted in the reading and pointing of other pairs of words,
such as 'Jericho,' which spelled the final vowel with either ה or
ו, as well as the pointing of words such as 'Solomon' or
'Pharaoh,' whose only spelling of the terminal vowel was with ה.
There is no reason to doubt that word-terminal ה can sometimes be used as *mater lectionis* for /ō/. Illustrations from
Aramaic are comparatively scarce, but this can be associated
with the fact that few Aramaic words end in /ō/ in any case.

When it was discovered that ה was the universal spelling of the last vowels on such words in Hebrew in pre-exilic inscriptions, and also of the suffix 'his,' it was taken for granted that the masoretic pronunciation was also in vogue at that time. The masoretic normalization was projected back on to the earliest inscriptions by modern scholars, who assumed that 'his hand' was pronounced $y\bar{a}d\hat{o}$ as far back as we can trace the word. And the same for other words with the same suffix.

Several questions have to be faced before we can accept this hypothetical reconstruction of the history of a word such as 'his hand' as a true account of what actually happened. 1) In Aramaic the evolution of the suffixes for 'his' and 'her' follows a similar path, becoming $-ih$ (later $-\bar{e}h$) and $-ah$, respectively. It must be emphasized that the ה was and remained a true consonant. The loss of the original final vowels ($-u$ and $-a$, respectively) suggests that they were anceps rather than that an originally long vowel could sometimes be dropped from final position, although the force of paradigmatic analogy should always be reckoned with as a possible factor in overriding a phonological rule. Hebrew 'her hand' followed a path similar to Aramaic 'her hand' but the paths of 'his hand' diverged in the two languages. It is assumed that the corresponding vowel in 'his,' $-h\bar{u}$, was retained in Hebrew because it was long; but, by the same token, it is hard to explain how it could ever have been lost at all, if that were so. We reach the puzzling conclusion that whereas in Aramaic ידה, whether 'his hand' or 'her hand,' the ה is a consonant, in Hebrew ידה the ה is a consonant when it means 'her' but a vowel letter when it means 'his.' We seem to have reached an impasse, and the origin or even the pronunciation of the ה in ידה in pre-exilic times has not been established for Hebrew.

The fact that 'his hand' was at first spelled ידה in Hebrew leaves open the possibility that it represents a channel of development in earlier Hebrew closer to Aramaic than to the one that eventually flowed into the masoretic tradition, and that it fits in with the consonantal spelling of the period. But this does not mean that the parent form *yadahū* survived into the eighth and seventh centuries BCE; for this would have been written יִדהו just as 'his father' is written אביהו in the Bible.

2) Phonologically the syncope of intervocalic /-h-/ presents several problems. Such a change is, of course, known in the history of languages. Also in Hebrew, and already in Ugaritic; but scarcely a characteristic, certainly not a regular, change in either language. The postulated development *yadahū* → *yādô* is, in fact, the only specimen usually given (Harris 1939: 55; Bauer and Leander 1922: 225). The existence of the alternatives *ʾabîhû* and *ʾabîw*, 'his father,' confirms the possibility; but it also suggests that a conditioning factor could have been the circumstance that the vowels before and after the ה occur in extreme mouth positions. The forces at work could not have been purely phonetic, however, because a verb such as *gabahū*, 'they were tall,' is quite stable; it did not become *gabaw* or *gabô*. The consonantal root held up, and the only changes were in the vowels, which underwent but slight and quite regular changes to *gābĕhû*.

3) The spelling of theophoric names at Samaria with the ending *-yw* attests the syncope of intervocalic *-h-* at a time when the resulting diphthong was not contracted → *-yaw*.

4) Given the postulated and similar change of *yadahū* to **yadaw*, the spelling of such a word would have been יד; but such a spelling of such a word is not attested either. The spelling of רעו, 'his companion,' in the Siloam Inscription is not an exception to this, in spite of *rēʿô* in Jeremiah 6:21, which stands out against the standard biblical *rēʿēhû*. Forms derived from ל"י roots develop stems similar to those of plural nouns, in which ו does represent the suffix 'his.'

5) This fact, that is, the existence of the suffix ו, certainly consonantal, on plural stems, demonstrates the possibility and acceptability of such a development as would have been

expected for the singular as well; *yadaw*, 'his hand,' *yadāw*, 'his
hands,' for which the standard early spelling *was* יד׳. Why did
the singular and the plural develop along such different paths?

6) More serious still is the fact that the last step in the
postulated development from *ᵊyadahū* to *yādô* requires the
contraction of the word-terminal diphthong. Even if the supposed intermediate form *yadaw* was written ידה as the theory
requires, that diphthong is stable in standard biblical Hebrew.
This is attested, not only by such nouns as *ṣāw, qāw, tāw,*
ᶜānāw, but mainly by the stability of the diphthong of the third
masculine singular suffix on plural nouns, discussed in 5).
There is no reason to believe that the short vowel in *yadaw*, 'his
hand,' would make the difference. Especially in Jerusalem
Hebrew where even the contraction of the unstressed diphthong did not take place until after the Exile. Harris (1939: 56)
explained the eventual writing of 'his' with ו on singular nouns
as due to the early existence and persistence of the diphthong
-aw in such words, so that the ו was actually written in the
usual way; and then, when the diphthong did monophthongize
ידו survived as an historical spelling, displacing the spelling
ידה. This, however, does not come to terms with the fact that
all such words were spelled with ה in all pre-exilic inscriptions,
a usage which is quite inexplicable, if, at that time, such words
were *pronounced* with the ending *-aw*. We know that ידה is the
attested spelling; but it requires very complicated explanations
to sustain both the archaic ידה and the later ידו as historical
spellings.

7) All these difficulties accumulate to throw doubt on the
generally accepted assumption that epigraphical ידה already
represents the masoretic pronunciation *yādô*.

8) If we abandon the theory that ה-, 'his,' is a graphic vestige of the loss of intervocalic *-h-* from pronunciation, and if we
read ידה as we would read any other word in a pre-exilic
inscription, then we have two options. i) The ה is a true

consonant, and the vocalization is *yadih*, as in Aramaic, or
perhaps *yaduh*. But even if the latter had become *yādōh* (*ú* →
ō is a very late development), the form would have been stable
and the consonantal ה would have survived. Although there is
some evidence for syncope of intervocalic -*h*- in Hebrew, there
is little evidence for loss of post-vocalic -*h* (the evidence from
Ugaritic that the derivational "directional" -*ā(h)* originally had
a consonant provides a case for loss of post-vocalic -*h*, but only
when the preceding vowel is not stressed). This leaves the
derivation of Hebrew -*ô*, 'his,' unexplained. ii) The use of ה to
write this word-terminal vowel, assuming that it is correct to
retroject the later pronunciation -*ô* on to this spelling (leaving
the historical derivation of this suffix unexplained), could be
another example of the general use throughout the system of ה
as the *mater lectionis* for any word-terminal vowel except -*î*
and -*û*, and therefore for any word-terminal -*ô*, irrespective of
its origin. The fact that ה is also part of the primal suffix -*hū*,
'his,' is a coincidence; there is no historical connection. On the
contrary, if this -*ô* came from *-aw*, as is most probable, the use
of ה rather than ו to spell it for the first few centuries of
Hebrew writing is contrary to the theory of "historical" spelling
as the origin of the use of *matres lectionis*.

Just as in Aramaic א displaced ה as the *mater lectionis* for
word-terminal -*ā*, so in Hebrew ו displaced ה as the *mater lectionis* for word-terminal -*ō*. This later decision to change the
spelling of a suffix which meant 'his' does not prove that this ה
always represented the sound -*õ*, nor that its use is the outcome of historical spelling. There has been no similar compul-
sion to show that ה used to spell other vowels arose from historical spelling.

Perhaps we should emphasize once more the fact that the
earliest Aramaic inscriptions show that a purely phonetic use of
ה for word-terminal long /ā/ was already in vogue, alongside
the phonetic use of ו and ו. It is ה, not א, that is already in
use to write all indubitable word-terminal long /ā/'s in the Tell

Fekhereye text. It is much harder to find certain examples of
the use of ה to write any other word-terminal vowel, such as
/ē/ or /ō/ in early Aramaic, but it is possible that ה was used
for them all from the beginning, as it certainly was in due time,
that is to write any word-terminal vowel except $-\hat{\imath}$ and $-\hat{u}$. This
is another reason why we cannot be certain about the pronunci-
ation of the early Hebrew suffix 'his' when spelled with ה.

2.3.6. The monophthongization of ancient diphthongs was
another historical change that developed a specialized use of
waw and *yod* as *matres lectionis*. In the old orthography the
spelling of a word which contained the diphthong *ᵃaw* showed
the consonantal value of *waw*. Thus 'day' *ᵃyawm* = יום. When
the diphthong monophthongized (*ᵃaw* → $\hat{o}$) and the old spelling
was still used as a kind of logogram, the *waw* came to represent
the long vowel /ō/ -- *yôm* = יום.

Because of these historical circumstances, we cannot tell
from the spelling alone whether this phonetic change has taken
place in the dialect of a particular text. We cannot tell whether
the diphthong has monophthongized; we cannot be certain in
early inscriptions whether *waw* in words like יום is still a true
consonant or whether it is a *mater lectionis* (Brock 1972: 260).
We can detect that change with certainty only when a strictly
phonetic use of consonantal spelling writes *yôm* as ים.

To be completely rigorous, it should be noted that even
this evidence is not unequivocal, since the spelling of 'day' as
ים tells us nothing about what vowel was used to pronounce it.
Note the differences between Hadad כימי (lines 9, 10, 12 -- the
last proves that it is plural) and Panamuwa כיומי (lines 10, 18)
and כיומיה (line 9). The latter show that ו can be used in the
stem of the plural. Höfner (1943: 9-12) discusses the analogous
problem in Old South Arabic. The consonantal character of the
Old South Arabic script suggests that *ywm* is *yawm*; *ym* is also
used -- *yām*? The co-occurrence of each spelling five times in
the same inscription (Gl 1209) suggests *eine schwankende*

Orthographie (p. 11). The variant is rare; *ywm* prevails, but plural can be *ymt* (Jamme 1962: 577, line 2) as well as other forms (Höfner 1943: 106). The word 'day' is spelled only ⌐' in pre-exilic Hebrew inscriptions (Siloam Tunnel Inscription [lines 1,3]; Lachish Letters [2:3; 4:1; 5:3; 8:2]; Arad ostraca [frequent]). While this is usually taken to represent *yôm*, there is no reason why a byform *yām* might not have existed. The plural *yāmīm* and especially the construct *yĕmê* point to an ancient stem with the short vowel *yam*. Akkadian *ūmu* (*yūmu*) points to another possibility. The interpretation of ⌐' as a *defective* spelling of *yôm* assumes too much uniformity in the dialects of pre-exilic Hebrew. This expectation has been fostered by the overly theoretical approach of the neo-grammarians and the general practice of reading ancient inscriptions as if they are masoretic Hebrew. The real situation is likely to have been much more complicated, especially in a non-tribal city like Jerusalem. We cannot assume that every person in Jerusalem pronounced 'day' in the same way. Blau (1968) and Rainey (1972) are in order to raise cautious doubt on this score. Because of the orthography and because *byw*[*m*] occurs in Lachish 20:1, Tur Sinay interpreted *kym* as *ky-m* = *kî* + *m(a/i)* or *kiām*, a reinforcing particle (Torczyner 1938: 110). But *kym* as used in the Arad ostraca is equivalent to MT *kywm* (Isaiah 9:3; Hosea 2:17; Zechariah 14:3; Psalm 90:4, 95:8; Lamentations 2:7, 22). Even granted Tur Sinay's point, this ' need not be word-internal *mater lectionis* for /ī/. It could be *kiyami* resembling Amarna *miyami*. Without opening the door to everything, at least it is theoretically possible that *yam*, 'day,' survives as *ym* (Althann 1982); no need to vocalize *yôm*, let alone emend to *ywm*. See also Sarfatti (1982: 63-65).

Several forces were at work to produce phonetic change. Analogy can interfere with the unconditional sound shifts highlighted by neo-grammarians. We do not have to postulate an ancient metaplastic stem *yām* or *yawm* (for singular) and *yam*- (for plural). The plural *yāmīm* could have developed by imitation of its associate *šānīm* (Barth 1906: 790-791). The analogy also went the other way, producing ימות as parallel to שנות (Deuteronomy 32:7; Psalm 90:15). Incidentally, the Samaritan Pentateuch reads יומת at Deuteronomy 32:7. (See further Bravmann [1977: 98-123].)

A secondary occurrence of the sound shift *$\bar{a}$ → $\bar{o}$ complicates things further. There is a well-known problem in Job 3:8. Are the $^{\circ}\bar{o}r\check{e}r\hat{e}$-$ywm$ those who curse 'day' (as the occurrences of $y\bar{o}m$ in verses 1-4 suggest), or those who curse Sea, $Y\bar{a}m$ (as the parallel Leviathan suggests)? Emendation to ים is not usually considered drastic, but even that is not necessary; for $y\bar{a}m$ → $y\bar{o}m$ (a later imitation in some regions of Hebrew-Phoenician of the Old South Canaanite sound shift *$\bar{a}$ → $\bar{o}$ [Kutscher 1982: § 37]) gives a variant pronunciation of 'Sea' which permits the text to be retained and only the traditional meaning adjusted. The co-existence of such variants among proper nouns (Sperber 1959: 59f.) as well as common nouns (Sperber 1959: 37) is doubtless due to such causes (although Sperber simplifies the picture too much by saying that these later changes also account for what is usually recognized as the Old South Canaanite sound shift). The same development could have occurred in feminine singular nouns with secondary lengthening of -*at* → -$\bar{a}t$ followed by $\bar{a}$ → $\bar{o}$ so that feminine singular is pronounced like feminine plural (Viganò 1977).

The word 'voice' קל in the Siloam Tunnel Inscription (line 2) presents similar problems. If the Jerusalem dialect is close to standard biblical Hebrew, קל is phonetic spelling of $q\hat{o}l$ ← *$qawl$ or ← *$q\bar{a}l$, but $q\bar{a}l'$ is also possible as an isogloss of $q\hat{o}l$. Unlike words such as $š\hat{o}r$ (← *$\underline{t}awru$) and $t\hat{o}k$ (← *$tawku$), which are nearly always *plene* in the Bible, even in the oldest texts, *$q\hat{o}l$ is often *defective* in the Bible, specifically in Exodus. The standard masoretic plural is קלות or קלת.

In MT the stem of $q\bar{o}l$ is spelled both ways. The singular is mainly *plene* (443 times out of a total of 494), the plural rarely so (one out of twelve). Five different forces could be at work.

1) The stem was actually metaplastic, at least in the early days, or in some dialect areas; the plural stem קל reflects the allomorph *qal* (compare Aramaic, Ethiopic).

2) The spelling reflects the fact that the singular word often has the stress on the stem, the plural not. But suffixed forms of the singular have stress on the suffix, yet the stem is spelled mainly *plene* (113 out of 158). The construct singular is presumably unstressed (at least less stressed); yet it is spelled *plene* 255 out of 259 times. The absolute form of the singular is *plene* 74 out of 77 times. Even so, 45 out of the 51 *defective* singulars are suffixed, so stress seems to have something to do with it.

3) It could be that the *mater lectionis* is used less often in the stem of the suffixed and plural forms because the scribes did not like to use the same *mater lectionis* twice in the same word. This could partly explain why 19 out of the 41 *qōlō*, 'his voice,' are קלו. But all the suffixed forms, when taken together, have a substantial number of *defective* spellings, whether the suffix contains a *mater lectionis* or not (45 out of 158). The preference does not seem to vary much with the nature of the suffix (Table 2.2).

Table 2.2 Spelling of suffixed *qōl*

Suffix	Stem defective	Stem plene	Total
-his	19	22	41
-her	2	7	9
-thy	5	18	23
-my	11	37	48
-their	3	26	29
-your	2	2	4
-our	3	1	4
Total	45	113	158

4) Is it possible that there is a graphic or aesthetic factor, even if only one among several? The difference between the spelling of the construct singular (presumably less stressed, but spelled *plene* all the same) and the suffixed singular (often *defective*) could be due to a disinclination of scribes to write a two-letter word alone. Yet nearly all of the suffixed forms which have a prefix as well (preposition or conjunction or both) are also spelled *plene*.

5) All of the above hypotheses assume that the practice (the operation of these influences) was uniform throughout the Bible. This is not so (Table 2.3).

Table 2.3 Spelling of suffixed $q\bar{o}l$

Section	Defective	Plene	Total
Pentateuch	33	6	39
Former Prophets	7	27	34
Latter Prophets	0	43	43
Writings	5	37	42
Total	45	113	158

Defective spellings dominate the Pentateuch; they are well represented in the Former Prophets; less so in the Writings; completely absent from the Latter Prophets.

$Q\bar{o}l$ is not the only word that suggests such possible metaplasm. שׁוּר, 'wall,' has plural שָׁרוֹת (Jeremiah 5:10). In the Pentateuch 'skin' is always עוּר, but the plural is ערת. Could the latter be a relic of *$\bar{a}r\bar{o}t$?

A different pattern, but one which involves similar issues, is presented by the word 'city' -- $^c\bar{\imath}r$, $^c\bar{a}r\bar{\imath}m$. Unlike $y\bar{a}m\bar{\imath}m$, the stem vowel of the plural $^c\bar{a}r\bar{\imath}m$ remains long in construct and suffixed stem. But in this case $^c\bar{a}r$ (עָר) (Numbers 21:15, 28; Deuteronomy 2:9, 18, 29; Isaiah 15:1) is attested as a dialectal isogloss of $^c\bar{\imath}r$ (Gasov-Ginsberg 1959).

2.3.7. The phonetic spelling of a word containing the diphthong /ay/ would use *yod* to write the consonant /y/. Thus 'wine,' *$yayn$ = יַּין. When the diphthong monophthongized (*ay → $\hat{e}$) and the consonant was still written, so that the old spelling continued to be used as a kind of logogram, the letter *yod* came to stand for the long vowel /$\bar{e}$ / -- $y\hat{e}n$ = יַּין. The spelling יּ in the Samaria ostraca shows that in the Hebrew of the central tribes the diphthong had monophthongized, even in the absolute state, the spelling being consonantal and phonetic. The *plene* spelling as such does not tell us whether the diphthong has monophthongized or not. In the Arad ostraca the full spelling יין points to the pronunciation *yayn*, but it does not absolutely prove that this must have been the pronunciation. When clear phonetic evidence eventually becomes available, we know that a word like 'house' (construct) is *bêt*, always spelled בית (historical spelling) in the Bible. At some point in time the pronunciation of this word changed from *bayt* to *bêt* . Harris (1939: 29-32) was unable to suggest a date for this (later) monophthongization of unstressed diphthongs in Jerusalem Hebrew. Freedman and Mathews (1985: 52) argue that it did not happen before the fifth century BCE

2.3.8. The long vowels written by means of א arose in words which previously contained the true consonant sound of א. Thus 'head' *ra²šu → *rā(²)šu* (the vowel lengthens to compensate for the loss of the consonant) → *rō(²)š* (ראש). The cognate *ra²šān, 'first,' followed a different path. Vowel dissimilation gave *ri²šān*, and then the usual changes yielded *rī(²)šōn* (ראשן). The plural 'heads' is *rā(²)šīm* (ראשים). Another derivative is *rē(²)šīt*, 'beginning,' ראשית.

In such ways א came to be used for writing long /ī/, /ē/, /ā/, or /ō/, but only where it was previously a true consonant. This usage is strictly "historical spelling." The א is etymological, and, as the case of ראש shows, it is not used as a true *mater lectionis* to represent one kind of vowel sound as such; it is only accidentally associated with whatever vowel sound developed in the syllable that used to contain a real consonantal א. The later idea that א is an acceptable *mater lectionis*, especially for vowel /ā/, gains a foothold in biblical Hebrew marginally as a late influence from Aramaic.

2.3.9. The consistent use of the appropriate consonants for spelling the primal diphthongs from the very beginning of attested literacy shows that these diphthongs had not contracted in the dialects of those texts. Nor is there any reason to believe that these diphthongs contracted soon after the introduction of the Phoenician writing system to other languages and dialects, so as to bring in a new value for certain consonant letters, specifically ו and י, and so to bring about, almost by accident, and not by conscious analysis and adaptation, the new principle of writing certain vowels, namely only those which had just emerged as a result of such changes, by means of consonant letters. In Aramaic at least the evidence is clear. The principle of writing long vowels at the end of words by means of consonant letters used as vowel markers was already in vogue, and indeed fully developed in the earliest stages of Aramaic literacy. The usage among southern peoples (Israel, Moab, Ammon, Edom -- the evidence is quite sparse for the last two) was not far behind. This usage was first applied to long vowels at the end of words which did not arise from the contraction of diphthongs, but which were primally long. Already ה, ו, and י were used for writing word-terminal long /ā/, /ū/, /ī/, respectively, before there is any indication that ו and י (ה was never so used) were being used to write word-medial long /ō/ and /ē/, respectively, derived by contraction from primal diphthongs.

Another point is worth making. A system based on the conscious invention and imposition of a few simple rules on a previously existing spelling system -- in this case the use of ה, ו, and י for all word-terminal vowels -- rather than one in which the rules change with phonetic changes, or in which the application and development of the rules are left open (in other words, a system in which they are not strongly felt as rules), is likely to settle down into its own kind of conservatism. This is precisely what happened to the Aramaic adaptation of Phoenician spelling. It is remarkably consistent throughout centuries of subsequent use. The Hebrew usage was not quite so hidebound. On the one hand, its use of *matres lectionis* to write all word-terminal vowels is essentially the same as that in the Aramaic inscriptions. On the other hand, it moved more slowly than Aramaic did from a strictly consonantal (Phoenician) system of spelling (this point can be made with more confidence if we can claim the Gezer Calendar as a Hebrew text) in the use of *matres lectionis* for word-medial long vowels. Here there is a conspicuous time lag. By the ninth century (here the best evidence is from Moabite, so we must allow for a possible influence from Aramaic to the north) the rule that one or other of the three *matres lectionis* should be used to write all word-terminal vowels was in force generally; the use of *matres lectionis* to write internal long vowels is still sparse, and mainly in evidence in the writing of proper nouns. The slow spread of this second part of the system can be traced right up to the beginning of the sixth century BCE. The latter part of the statement has even more force when we leave out (do not recognize as bona fide *matres lectionis*) the use of ‏ו‎ or ‏י‎ for word-medial diphthongs; that is, when we do not impose masoretic pointings on the texts, as if these diphthongs were already contracted. Even after the Exile, as this study shall demonstrate in full detail, *matres lectionis* were not used universally for word-medial long vowels in biblical texts, even though the trend in that direction was now well advanced -- most for long /ī/, high for long /ū/, only moderately for long /ō/; almost completely so for long vowels derived from primal diphthongs, a heritage from the early stages of consonantal (historical) spellings. For primally long vowels the pronunciation did not change, but the spelling did; for primal diphthongs the spelling did not change, but the pronunciation did.

2.3.10. The historical development of the spelling of each kind of long vowel needs investigation along these lines. It is possible that some individual words acquired peculiar conventional spellings which did not follow the usual rules. In order to work, any spelling system needs a measure of consistency, however arbitrary or merely conventional some parts of the system might be. Absolute consistency is too much to expect, but deviations do not prove that there were no rules. Then, as now, there were some people who were not good at spelling. Allowance must also be made for transitional usage, with persistence of archaic spellings, especially in fixed expressions. This accounts for the fact that some inscriptions present the same word in two different spellings. Thus the first spelling of 'earth' in Jeremiah 10:11 (אַרְקָא) is traditional, the second (אַרְעָא) contemporary. On this phenomenon in the Tell Fekhereye inscription, see Freedman and Andersen (1985).

2.3.11. A more complete and careful study of the epigraphical evidence would require more space than is available here. It makes it very difficult to sustain the traditional view that the use of *matres lectionis* for the phonetic spelling of long vowels arose *by analogy* from the historical spellings that came through in the system by changes in pronunciation, changes which resulted in the emergence of a long vowel at a place in a word where a consonant previously occurred, the lengthening of the vowel compensating for the loss of the consonant. This would happen in a language in which the contraction of diphthongs or the quiescence of the glottal stop took place after the introduction of and consistent use of purely consonantal spelling. If this process had been followed, there would have been three stages in the development of alphabetical writing among the Northwest Semitic languages: 1) a purely consonantal phase (Phoenician and the Gezer Calendar); 2) a stage in which historical spellings were used to write some long vowels which had developed in the language *after* the introduction of consonantal spelling; 3) a stage in which long vowels (some primally long, some long by recent changes) were spelled with a *mater lectionis* in *imitation* of the historical spelling of the same vowel.

We have found no evidence that the developments corresponding to Stage 2) ever took place in Northwest Semitic. The proposal is purely theoretical, in order to have a trigger for the new idea and practice of writing vowels. There is no epigraphical evidence for a writing system that represents Stage 2) and that would have served as a bridge between the Phoenician alphabet (twenty-two letters all used only for consonant sounds) and the alphabets used by other Northwest Semitic peoples (twenty-two letters used for consonant sounds, three of them also for some vowel sounds). Moreover, there is no indication that the changes in pronunciation needed for the transition to historical spelling of certain vowels took place at the required time to provide the needed bridge. The languages and dialects of Northwest Semitic seem to have been comparatively stable in their sound systems during the period in question (the early centuries of the first millennium BCE). The changes usually adduced under the rubric of historical spelling had either taken place already in the Late Bronze Age (e.g., the contraction of diphthongs over some parts of Canaanite), or did not take place until later on in the Iron Age (contraction of surviving diphthongs in Aramaic; contraction of unstressed diphthongs in the dialect of Jerusalem, which was mainly responsible for determining the character of standard biblical Hebrew).

Some of the historical changes which bear on this problem did not take place along clean lines and in clearly marked stages, and this complicates matters. The traditional account of the origin of the *matres lectionis*, still in evidence in Harris (1939), was abandoned by Blake in 1940, at least in hypothesis. He wrote, "A complete system of such signs indicating long vowels in all positions and its consistent use may have originated at a specific time in a single alphabet, and been copied by other forms of writing that stood in some special connection with the inventing script" (1940: 397). This overstates the case. The early Aramaic system for writing long vowels with ה, ו, and י was "complete" only in principle and potentiality. The only major change in Aramaic writing over the next millennium was the replacement of ה by א as the prime *mater lectionis* for writing long /ā/, a change in detail rather than principle. The vowel letters were not used from the first with equal facility "in all positions;" they were used "consistently" for long vowels at the end of words, sporadically for long vowels inside words, and then only ו and י were used to write word-medial long vowels.

Cross and Freedman's study found little if any evidence to support the traditional theory, and inscriptions discovered since the time of their fundamental work (published 1952) have strengthened their case, in spite of considerable debate, some of it adverse (see § 2.6). Cross and Freedman indicated the need for "a new view of the origin and development of the use of final *matres lectionis*. To regard their development as the spontaneous outgrowth of historical spelling must be discarded, at least in part" (1952: 32). The final qualification represents a reluctance to abandon the traditional explanation altogether; for they go on to say, "It is simpler to assume that an occasional historical spelling (e.g., the dropping of the final *ă* of the first person pronominal suffix, *-iyă* → *î*) suggested the principle of final vowel representation" (p. 32). A similar statement, but with the same qualification, is made at the end of the study, where the authors combine "conscious invention and elaboration in the use of vowel letters," suggested by "isolated examples of historical spelling" (p. 59).

The examples of historical spelling needed to sustain this account are not attested. So we can invert the sequence of Stages 2) and 3) above, and say that the retention of historical spelling of newly developed vowels *followed* the analogy of already established phonetic spelling of long vowels. Such historical spellings considerably augmented the spelling system in its *later* stages, especially in the later epoch when the surviving diphthongs of Aramaic and Hebrew contracted.

In the early stages of phonetic spelling it was not uncommon to drop א when its pronunciation was lost in post-vocalic position (§ 3.3.1.4). And by the same token we can generally assume that when א was written it represented a consonant, since it was not one of the *matres lectionis* at first. But the retention of א in writing after its loss from pronunciation was assisted by the analogy of historical spellings involving the already established three *matres lectionis* and so enabled א to join the ranks of the *matres lectionis*, but only in a secondary way. The spelling of vowels with **א** remained historical in Hebrew for the most part. In Aramaic, however, **א** became a fully fledged *mater lectionis* by the end of the biblical period, and this usage even had a slight influence on the orthography of the Hebrew portions of late biblical texts.

2.4 Subsequent developments

In their earliest development the Hebrew *matres lectionis* represented only certain long vowels: **א** only in historical spellings; **ה** for word-terminal /ō/, /ā/, /ē/; **י** for word-terminal /ī/ and for $\hat{e}$ < *ay* once the monophthongization had occurred; **ו** for word-terminal /ū/ and for $\hat{o}$ < *aw* once the monophthongization had occurred. It is possible that the monophthongization that changed the phonetic spelling of the diphthong into a historical spelling of the derived long vowel took place quite late in the main stream of development.

The next step was simple and logical -- the writing of other long vowels with the aid of these *matres lectionis*, even without the historical factors discussed above. Once the *mater lectionis* was perceived as a purely phonetic symbol, it could be used to write long vowels as such, whatever their history. In the early stages this was done for all long vowels at the ends of words, but only for some long vowels within words. The feminine singular suffix -ā is already spelled with **ה** in the Tell Fekhereye inscription and in the eighth-century Hebrew Tell-Qasile Ostracon -- **מאה**, 'hundred' (line 4). This is a phonetic spelling; **ה** is a pure *mater lectionis* with no historical precursor. It occurs several times in the Siloam Inscription. In another region the development of this orthography in the eighth century can be traced in the differences between the Hadad and Panamuwa inscriptions of Yaʾudi (Dion 1974: 58-59). The usage is so consistent that one might say that every word-terminal long vowel was routinely represented by an appropriate *mater lectionis*. Conversely the absence of such a vowel letter in the writing of any particular word shows that it did not have a terminal long vowel.

This interpretation has not been accepted by all scholars. The differing points of view are illustrated by the problem of עת in the Arad ostraca, reviewed with bibliography by Pardee (1978: 292f.), and by the variant spellings of the second masculine singular suffix of perfect verbs and the second masculine singular pronoun suffix, reviewed by Sarfatti (1982: 67-69). Assuming the consistent use of *matres lectionis* for word-terminal long vowels, the attested spelling of the former points to the pronunciation ʿat(t). It would require the spelling עתה (as in masoretic Hebrew) to prove that the Arad pronunciation was ʿattâ. Assuming that the use of *matres lectionis* was optional, arbitrary, sporadic at this stage, it has been argued that עת could represent the *defective* spelling of ʿattā. Assuming further that עת in the Arad ostraca does represent the ʿattā of MT, the spelling of this word has been used as evidence against the hypothesis of consistent spelling practice in pre-exilic inscriptions. In view of the circular nature of the reasoning, there is no way of settling the point. Masoretic pronunciation cannot be assumed. The spellings in the inscriptions are remarkably consistent, and a few deviations are only to be expected, reflecting either transitional stages or the persistence of archaisms. This is strikingly illustrated in the Aramaic portion of the Tell Fekhereye inscription; the few inconsistencies, mainly archaisms, do not affect the uniform practice in most of the text.

The story is different with the Gezer Calendar, the one Hebrew (or is it Phoenician?) inscription that exhibits the purely consonantal spelling of the earliest period (Stage 1 in Table 2.1). There it is possible that פשת is *pištā* rather than *pišt*. The analogy of such pairs as שערים ~ שערה, חטים ~ חטה and the attestation of פשתים points to פשתה as the singular. *Pištî* in Hosea 2:7 should be corrected to *pištay* (Freedman 1955). The spelling in the Gezer Calendar is thus *defective*. The use of ה to spell word-terminal long /ā/ is almost universal in MT. It is equivocal in a few instances.

1) There are pairs of spellings which the masoretes vocalized in the same way, creating the impression that one was *defective*, when it probably represented a dialectal variant. i) ת- and תה- were both pointed -*tā*, whereas the first could be -*āt*. ii) ך- and כה-, 'thy,' were both pointed -*kā*, whereas the first could be -*āk*. iii) ן- and נה-, feminine plural verbal suffix, were both pointed -*nā*, whereas the first could be -*ān*. iv) The word 'girl,' normally נַעֲרָה, was often spelled נער and taken as a case of *defective* spelling of the word-terminal vowel. As such it evoked a *qere* annotation, but the tradition was quite fluid. The uniqueness of the form attracts suspicion and suggests that the spelling נער documents an epicene.

2) Sometimes the masoretes accepted two variant spellings as the precise writing of distinct pronunciations, as with אֵלֶּה and אֵל. The latter occurs frequently in Phoenician and has been accepted as ᵓēl, not as a *defective* spelling. We suggest that biblical עַתָּה and Arad עת are like case 2), not 1).

With all due reserve, we accept as a working hypothesis, against which the evidence of the inscriptions presents no clear-cut exception, that from the eighth century, if not already in the ninth, word-terminal ה is either the consonant or a long vowel, and that every word-terminal long vowel except ī and ū was written with ה.

The next step was the extension of the use of the two main *matres lectionis* י and ו for writing long vowels within words. In the case of regular vocabulary this practice extended from purely logographic usage. The logographic character of ancient writing explains how י came to be used for word-medial /ī/ and ו for word-medial /ū/, while ה never came to be used for word-medial /ā/. That /ī/ and /ū/ are usually primal long vowels in Hebrew, whereas /ā/ is usually tone-long or pretonic ā < *a, was also a factor in this difference of usage.

Once the spelling of a verb such as 'they cut' was settled as גזרו, 'they cut him,' previously גזרהו (with only the terminal vowel written *plene*) became גזרוהו. Both these styles are found in the Bible. Similarly 'I cut,' גזרתי; 'I cut him,' previously גזרתהו then גזרתיהו (eventually גזרתיו). In this way it was but a small step from the *plene* spelling of word-terminal -*ī* or -*ū* to the same spelling when that vowel was word-medial in a suffixed verb. And then it was only another small step to writing other word-medial long vowels *plene*. See Dion's discussion of "internal vowels which are actually final vowels" (1974: 64-67). In Ya ʾudi, *plene* spelling under these conditions was more common with /ī/ than with /ū/. Comparison of words with vowel Type 1 (§ 6.5.1) and those with Type 56 (§ 6.5.6) shows that a similar disproportion prevailed generally in the spelling of Hebrew. (See also Ginsberg 1942: 236.)

But 'she cut' גזרה is different. 'She cut him' is גזרתהו or גזרתו. The same is true for suffixed feminine singular nouns. The terminal -*ā* of the unsuffixed forms is a by-product of the primal ending -*at*, so the suffixed and unsuffixed forms do not have a common form, and the vowel is not long when internal; so ה could not make its way into the interior of a word as a *plene* spelling of /ā/. This argument is valid for Hebrew, even if it can be shown that this -*t*- is not a primal marker of feminine but a consonantal inter-vocalic glide introduced when the case system was developed (Gelb 1969: 34f.; 74f.). Nor did 'thou didst cut,' *gāzartā*, supply an opening. 'Thou didst cut them' is never *gzrthm, possibly because the unsuffixed form was usually גזרת, not גזרתה, although the latter is found (Parunak 1978; Sarfatti 1982: 68).

So far as the historical evidence is concerned, it seems that a special indication of long vowels with the aid of a purely phonetic use of *matres lectionis* was forced into the writing system by the problem of pronouncing proper nouns. In contrast to these grammatically empty words, the syntax of nouns and verbs greatly assisted their paradigmatic identification by a reader and hence their pronunciation; but more information was needed to get a proper noun right, especially when it was exotic. It has been claimed that the earliest known Hebrew use of *yod* for the purely phonetic spelling of word-medial /ī/ is in the name *šĕmīdāᶜ* שמידע in the eighth-century Samaria ostraca (Zevit 1980: 13). This is exceptional for names of that type at that time, שמדע being usual. The point depends on two sets of facts. First, the MT pointing *šĕmīdāᶜ*; secondly, the interpretation of שמדע as *defective* spelling of the former. But neither of these points is compelling.

A similar use of *y* as an apparent *mater lectionis* is already attested for a proper noun at Ugarit: *ᶜmyṯmr* = *ᶜAmmiš tamri* (*Ugaritica 3*: 81, Figure 103). But we cannot be sure that in all such cases ' is a *mater lectionis*. אלישב is *ᵓelyāšib*, not *ᵓɛlīšāb*. So אליקא, 'El vomited' (!) would be better as *ᵓelyaqaᵓ*, 'El guarded' (Zadok 1977). Similarly the word שמידע could just as well have been *šĕmyādaᶜ* or *šĕmīyādaᶜ*. It needs to be remembered that in שמידע the ' is part of the verb root. The masoretic pointing should not be accepted naively (Cross 1961). MT is equivocal in analogous cases. Compare 'Ahiqam' with 'Elyaqim.' The grammar of such names should also be kept in mind. 'Elyaqim,' or *ᵓelîyāqīm* makes better sense as 'my God will raise up (something)' and likewise '*Ahiyaqim.' 'Eli-yashib' makes better sense than 'Elishub.' Caution is in order, and proper nouns are not the best evidence. The same applies to the case of יף and ייף (Sarfatti 1982: 59-60). Unequivocal instances of the use of word-internal ' as *mater lectionis* for /ī/ in words not proper nouns appear only towards the end of the pre-exilic period -- in the stem of some hipᶜil forms in the Arad ostraca. This usage developed more slowly in Hebrew than in Aramaic. It is already present in the Tell Fekhereye text. For vocabulary other than proper nouns, Yaᵓudi already writes קירת, 'cities' (Hadad 19; Panamuwa 4, 4, 15), כפירי, 'villages' (Hadad 10; Panamuwa 10), קתילת, 'killed' (Panamuwa 8).

By the seventh century ו is used for interior /ū/ in several
Hebrew personal names. Prior to that, the usage is first
attested at Tell Fekhereye, where it is found in both common
and proper nouns, and in the Panamuwa Inscription (about 730
BCE) in its spelling of 'Assyria' אשׁור (lines 7, 11, 12, 13, 15, 16,
17 -- the reading אשׁר in line 18 is debated). The first attested
use in Hebrew of ו as *mater lectionis* for /ū/ in the interior of
an ordinary word is ארור, 'cursed,' in the Silwan Epitaph (late
eighth century).

2.5 Developments in post-exilic times

Before the Exile the use of *matres lectionis* was restricted
to the writing of vowels anciently long or long by derivation
from diphthongs or by other changes. After the Exile the usage
was extended to the spelling of long vowels, originally short,
lengthened under stress.

The norms emerging in pre-exilic orthography became the
standard for most spellings in biblical texts. The practices that
developed after the Exile never gained a complete foothold in
biblical usage. We shall discuss these two statements in more
detail in Chapter 11.

The first major activity in compiling the canonical corpus
of the Hebrew Bible probably took place in the sixth century
BCE (Freedman 1963, 1983a). Its main product consisted of the
so-called "Primary History" (Genesis-Kings). Freedman narrows
the date of likely publication of the Primary History with
remarkable precision to "between 21 March 561 and 13 August
560 BCE, a period of a year and five months" (1983a: 169). This
is more definite and daring than the thesis of Leiman (1976: 29,
131) that the Torah and Prophets had become closed collections of inspired and canonical writings by about 450 BCE.
Leiman's weak point is his assumption that all the books which
were later called Prophets were collected and canonized

together as a distinct set.

The following study shows that the Former and Latter Prophets must have had quite different transmission histories, to judge from orthography. In the light of data presented in Chapter 1 and anticipating other results, one can say that the Hebrew Bible falls into two distinct halves -- Torah plus Former Prophets (equivalent to Freedman's "Primary History"), with distinctive and consistently conservative spelling, and the rest (Latter Prophets plus Writings), consistently less conservative. The detachment of the histories from the first collection and of the prophecies from the second, and the combining of them under the rubric "Prophets," is thus a later adjustment within the canon, due to enhancement of the status of the Torah, not a result of making the Torah the first canon as such. Even if a substantial body of texts existed in written form before the Persian Period, or even before the Exile -- and there is no reason why this should not have been so -- to judge from the spelling in what now survives, all such earlier material was edited in the context of the crisis of the Exile. By then the practice of writing certain long vowels with the aid of *matres lectionis* had been laid on top of the previous largely consonantal spelling.

The most striking difference between the orthography in pre-exilic Hebrew inscriptions and the Bible is due to the switch from ה to ו to represent word-terminal -ō, usually 'his.' Examples of -ō spelled with ו before the sixth century are few and very debatable. The best candidates are קצרו (Yavneh Yam Ostracon, line 6), if it means 'his harvest,' and רעו in the Siloam Tunnel Inscription (lines 2, 3, 4), if it is the same as רֵעוֹ in Jeremiah 6:21 (Zevit 1980: 19). Cross, indeed, goes so far as to say that this use of ו for -ō did not occur in Hebrew before the fourth century (quoted by Zevit [1980: 30, note 20], but his documentation is incomplete). The distribution of the surviving cases of -ה in the Bible will be studied below in the light of Cross' claim. See Chapter 6, Type 31.

This adjustment was probably motivated by the need to resolve the ambiguity in the reading of word-terminal ה which was already established as the letter for the abundant feminine singular suffix -ā. This fact, and the fact that elsewhere ו was established as the *mater lectionis* for /ō/, would point the way to the resolution of the scribal ambiguity in the consonantal spelling of both 'his' and 'her' with the letter ה.

We cannot be sure that the updating of ה- to ו- was always correctly done. When 'his' or 'her' would serve equally well, *ketib/qere* can result (Jeremiah 2:24).

The use of ו for 'his' resolved the graphic ambiguity of this suffix with 'her,' but it introduced another ambiguity. The eventual pronunciation of the suffix 'his' on masculine plural nouns, such as 'his sons,' was /-āw/ (phonetically בָּנוֹ) which is homographic with 'his son.' This was resolved by writing 'his sons' as בָּנָיו, making בָּנָי a logogram for the plural stem. This ו is not a *mater lectionis* in the usual sense. There are many words in which it is missing. Although L frequently supplies a *plene* counterpart as *qere* (Gordis 1937: List 3), the development must have been fairly late, since good early MSS lack the feature. Orlinsky (1966: XXVI-XXIX) has castigated such tampering.

There are also a few places where the ו is superfluous: רַגְלָיו (Psalm 105:18); דְּבָרָיו (Psalm 105:28 [in L [דברוו]); עֵינָיו (Qohelet 4:8); וּבַחֲטָאתָיו (1 Kings 16:26); שְׂפָתָיו (Proverbs 16:27); דְּבָרָיו (Daniel 9:12).

The "rules" for the use of *matres lectionis* for writing long vowels were carried through to differing degrees for the various kinds of vowels, and to differing degrees in the various parts of the Bible. The fact that biblical spelling is not homogeneous will be the major object of study in what follows. From this fact inferences may be made concerning both the history of the language and the history of the text.

2.6 The study of Hebrew orthography

This broad outline represents the historical reconstruction of the evolution of Hebrew spelling of Harris, Albright, Cross and Freedman. Although subject to criticism, it still holds the field as the best account of the majority of facts. Goodwin (1969) criticized the application of historical orthography in text criticism by Albright and his students. Some of the early attempts in this direction, especially by Albright, were somewhat adventurous and vulnerable to criticism in matters of detail. Cross and Freedman (1972) gave a spirited response. Sarfatti's review (1982) indicates the need for refinement in light of later discoveries. (See O'Connor [1983].)

An important general methodological consideration is involved here. To the extent that some biblical texts originated in pre-exilic times, it is in order to ask if the marks of pre-exilic orthographic usage might still be on them, if only in traces. Goodwin's observations merely serve to curb an over-confident use of the method to recover the original forms of archaic texts, which is another matter altogether. Probing as far back into the prehistory of a text as Albright attempted to do is so uncertain that firm proofs can hardly be expected for many of the suggestions; but that does not mean that such research should not be undertaken at all. The assumption that much early Israelite literature was written with purely consonantal spelling was used extensively by Mitchell Dahood. He assumed (too lightheartedly) that rewriting a text in Phoenician orthography was not really emendation. Cross also rewrites biblical texts into pre-exilic orthography (1973: 159, 160).

More recent evaluations of the Cross and Freedman (1952) position have been given by Bange (1971) and Zevit (1980). They go in opposite directions. Zevit argues, from the evidence of Ugaritic, that consonant letters were already in use as *matres lectionis* by 1200 BCE. (See J. Blau and S. E. Loewenstamm 1970: 25-30; also Loewenstamm 1980: 57.) The evidence is very meager; most is open to alternate explanation as historical spelling; the cases are special, and there is no indication of the extension of historical spelling to purely phonetic use of *matres lectionis*. Zevit's perspective enables him to recognize *matres lectionis* more readily than Cross and Freedman in some pre-exilic words. A notable example is Zevit's recognition of ו as *mater lectionis* for word-terminal /ô/ (1980: 24, 31). Cross thinks this development is very late indeed. Cross and Freedman wrote: "There is not a single instance of *waw-ô* in any pre-exilic Hebrew inscription" (1952: 52, note 37). This is pertinent here, since this practice has almost completely prevailed in the Bible, and it is desirable to date its triumph, whether in the sixth century or not until the fourth.

Bange (1971) argues that there was no use in alphabetic Northwest Semitic texts of consonant letters as the means for writing vowel sounds as such until 600 BCE. Prior to that the spelling was strictly consonantal. A lot depends on the definition of "consonant." The problem focuses mainly on a phenomenon already discussed above. The historical spelling of a word containing a primal diphthong may be phonetically ambiguous (§§ 2.3.6, 2.3.7). Bange's observation (Chapter 2) is correct that the earliest Canaanite inscriptions from different parts of Syria-Palestine do not indicate diphthongs, but his inference is invalid. Instead of recognizing that the diphthongs were already monophthongized in the languages of those texts and that the writing is purely consonantal, he assumes that the diphthongs might have existed, but that the consonantal phonemes /w/ and /y/ were not written when they were semivowels. He disposes of the evidence of the Ugaritic *alef*s by the argument that *in*, 'there is not,' could have been pronounced ʾ*ain* (p. 24), since he thinks that consonantal /y/ and /w/ were written only when followed by a vowel. It is partly a question of how phonetic the use of the Ugaritic *alef*s was. In spite of the complexity of some of the evidence, generally the three *alef*s

reflect the mouth position of an associated vowel. Hence *in* =
ᵓ*ên*.

Bange explains all the (proto-) *matres lectionis* in pre-exilic
inscriptions as "off-glides" which developed after long vowels,
especially when stressed. This reverses the well-known history
of the monophthongization of the diphthongs. To call these supposed graphic-phonetic elements "off-glides" rather than "consonants" or *matres lectionis* is to make a distinction without a
difference. Nevertheless Bange's attempts to explain epigraphic peculiarities in terms of stress patterns (e.g., his discussion of the inconsistent spelling of 'house' in the Mesha
inscription [p. 71]) are of methodological interest.

Between the extremes of Bange and Zevit, the Cross-
Freedman schema remains the best working basis (O'Connor
1983). With the evidence so sparse, it is not surprising that the
story is incomplete. It is not to be expected that the stages in
the evolution of a writing system will be clearly divided. A new
practice is not completely established overnight. Old and new
exist side by side, sometimes even in the same text. Spelling is
always in transition, since it moves from traditional (historical)
spelling towards phonetic spelling which reflects changes in
pronunciation. And inconsistencies (errors) will always occur.
This does not mean that there were no rules. A practical writing system which is continually changing under historical forces
will present alternate spellings of the same word, especially
when historical and phonetic spellings are different, as is often
the case. Instead of inferring from the observed irregularities
that there was little or no system, it is better to proceed with
the expectation of regularity and then to accept the deviations,
even when there is no apparent explanation for them.

Chapter 3. Standard Hebrew Spelling and its Deviations

3.1 *Matres lectionis* in the Masoretic Text

In comparative-historical studies of Semitic phonology it is usual to distinguish long vowels by means of diacritic marks which signal their different paths of evolution. Even if all long /ō/ sounds are the same phonemically, they have different origins. Hence the convention: $\hat{o}$ = long /ō/ derived from primal long vowel *$\bar{a}$ or from diphthong *aw; $\bar{o}$ = long /ō/ derived under stress from primal short *u; $\tilde{o}$ = long /ō/ derived from the loss of intervocalic consonant in *$ah\bar{u}$. This study is mainly interested in spelling, specifically in the use of *matres lectionis* to spell long vowels. Hence our convention: $\bar{o}$ = long vowel spelled *defective* and $\hat{o}$ = long vowel spelled *plene*, that is with ו as *mater lectionis*. When otiose א or ה is used as the historical spelling of /ō/ this graph will be transcribed as $\bar{o}$ (ʾ), $\bar{o}$ (h). Otherwise ʾ or h without parentheses represent true consonants. Similarly for the other long vowels.

3.2 Detailed stages of development

Put succinctly, albeit crudely, in theory any long vowel in Hebrew may be spelled either *defective* or *plene*, but the options are taken up differently with each vowel. It depends in part on the kind of word or on the identity of some individual words, as we shall see below. In the main, the spelling of /ī/ has been almost completely normalized to *plene* throughout, /ū/ less completely so. The normal spelling of word-terminal /ē/, /ɛ̄/, and /ā/ admits of few exceptions. The picture for /ō/ is completely different. The history of this sound in Hebrew is very complicated, and so is the history of its spelling. The sound

/ō/ occurs 73,471 times in the Hebrew portion of the Bible. It
is spelled *defective* a total of 39,409 times; it is spelled *plene*
with the standard use of ‫ ו‬34,062 times. Because of this abun-
dance and variety, the prospect is good that its use in the text
preserves at least some traces of the stages of its evolution.

The second stage of the developmental schema suggested
in Table 2.1 can be divided into five sub-stages and the third
stage into five sub-stages. The more recent the development of
the use of consonants as vowel letters, the less completely it
has taken hold upon the biblical text.

3.2.1. The second stage (the biblical period) decomposes
thus:

Stage 2.1. All word-terminal long vowels written with an
appropriate *mater lectionis* -- /ī/ and /ē/ with ‫ ;י‬/ē/, /ɛ̄/,
/ā/, and /ō/ with ‫ ;ה‬/ū/ with ‫ו‬.

Stage 2.2. Word-medial long /ī/ and /ū/ written with ‫ י‬and
‫ ו‬respectively. Already in train, but not on a large scale, in late
pre-exilic inscriptions. (Word-medial /ā/ did not undergo a
similar development.)

Stage 2.3. Word-medial long vowels from diphthongs -- /ē/
with ‫ ;י‬/ō/ with ‫ו‬. These changes, although typologically parallel, did not necessarily proceed at the same rate. In any case
the changes took place at different times in different dialect
areas. And it is not known how far along they were in the main
stream of southern literary Hebrew in pre-exilic times. It is possible that monophthongization was not complete until the Exile
or even later.

Stage 2.4. Long /ō/ ← *ā increasingly written with ‫ו‬, particularly when stressed. There is no unequivocal evidence for
this usage prior to the sixth century (Sarfatti 1982: 62).

Stage 2.5. Long /ō/ ← *u under stress sometimes written
with ‫ ;ו‬long /ē/ ← *i under stress not often written with ‫י‬.
These are the last developments in the biblical period, and they
gain only a slight foothold in the MT.

By 600 BCE the practice, if not the rule, was to spell all primal long vowels and long vowels derived from diphthongs *plene*.
By the time of the Mishnah the rule, if not the practice, outside
the Bible at least, was to spell *all* long vowels *plene*. This
represented a complete movement from historical to phonetic
spelling. If the Bible had been fully modernized, the result
would have been a text in which all long vowels, whatever their
origin, are spelled *plene*.

The Bible never reached this point. Its orthographic
features suggest that the text, including the spelling, was relatively fixed well before rabbinic times, but just how much
before cannot now be established. Biblical spelling approaches
nearer to saturation with *matres lectionis* with some vowels,
notably those spelled with ׳, than with others, notably those
spelled with ׳. Especially when word-terminal. This is a well-
nigh universal norm in MT.

> If older texts were standardized systematically in exilic or
> early post-exilic times, and stabilized thereafter, most traces
> of their antiquity would have been obliterated beyond
> recovery. Even so one can occasionally suspect that a textual
> problem has arisen because this work was not always done
> correctly. Plural nouns in construct and many plural verbs end
> in a long vowel, and if this was not written in the exemplar (it
> would have to be very archaic, because even in pre-exilic
> times the practice became general to write all word-terminal
> long vowels with *matres lectionis*), and not recognized by the
> scribe, an apparently singular form would survive where a plu-
> ral was required. The masoretes would be unable to add the
> necessary *mater lectionis* and there was no other way of writ-
> ing a final vowel. In 2 Kings 7:10 the referential 'to them' sug-
> gests that שער העיר should have been 'gate-keepers' שערי. The
> plural subject in 2 Kings 7:11 suggests that the verb ויקרא
> should have been plural ויקראו, although such a construction is
> often considered to be a grammatical option (GKC § 145o). A
> systematic study of such textual problems in the light of the
> history of spelling could be rewarding.

The adoption of *plene* spelling for word-medial /ō/ lagged behind the other vowels. In the lead are /ē/ and /ē̆/ ← *ay, followed by word-terminal /ā/, then /ī/ and /ū/, then /ō/, and finally /ē/ ← *i well behind, that is almost never spelled *plene*.

Midway between these two orthographic styles, when *plene* historical spelling was still traditional and *plene* phonetic spelling was as yet only optional, the general trend towards more and more *plene* spellings was slightly moderated by a counter-trend. For it became optional to spell *any* long vowel *defective*, so that the *plene* spelling of primal long vowels could actually diminish (but only in word-internal positions). This explains the behavior of *hip°ils* with ' ' פ roots. (See Type 35 in Chapter 6 below.) A relatively low incidence of *plene* spellings of vowels lengthened late in the biblical period is a hallmark of an old text. But a relatively low incidence of *plene* spellings of vowels anciently long can occur both in old texts (in which *plene* prevails as *historical* spelling) and in late texts (in which *plene* prevails as *phonetic* spelling).

These constitute pseudo-archaisms or archaizing. The spelling of *pīlegeš*, 'concubine,' illustrates the point. It passes through three phases: 1) archaic *plene* spelling -- Genesis and Judges (× 16); 2) archaizing *defective* spelling -- Samuel, Kings, Ezekiel (× 9 -- 2 Samuel 3:7 is the exception); 3) phonetic *plene* spelling -- Writings (× 9 -- 1 Chronicles 2:48 is the exception).

> For most types of words, however, the trend towards more and more *plene* spellings of long vowels is steady. 'Shilo' is an example. With two long vowels, it occurs thirty-one times and can be spelled in four different ways: 1) The doubly archaic form שלה prevails (× 22 -- all in the Former Prophets, except for Jeremiah 26:6). 2) The fully modernized שילו occurs in Judges 21:21, 21 and Jeremiah 7:12 (Mm 2489). Intermediate forms are 3) שילה (Genesis 49:10) and 4) שלו (Judges 21:19; 1 Samuel 1:24; Jeremiah 7:14; 26:9; 41:5; Psalm 78:60). Three different spellings are found in Jeremiah! 'Dishon' realizes all four possible spellings, increasingly *plene* from Genesis to Chronicles: דשן -- Genesis 36:25, 30; דשון -- Genesis 36:21; דישן --

1 Chronicles 1:38; דישון -- 1 Chronicles 1:41, 42. Similarly
'Shihor:' שחר -- Isaiah 23:3; שחור -- Jeremiah 2:18; שיחור --
1 Chronicles 13:5. 'Yeshimon:' ישמ -- Deuteronomy 32:10; ישמן --
Numbers 21:20; 23:28; 1 Samuel 26:1, 3; Isaiah 43:20; ישמון --
Isaiah 43:19 (L has *massora* ל כת כן, but P has ישימון with מל);
ישימון -- 1 Samuel 23:19, 24; Psalm 68:8; 78:40; 106:14; 107:4.
'Yeshimot:' ישמת -- Numbers 33:49; ישמות -- Joshua 12:3 and
13:20; ישימת -- Ezekiel 25:9; ישימות -- Psalm 55:16. Another
example: ערסכם -- Numbers 15:20 (triply *defective*); ערסתיכם --
Numbers 15:21 (doubly *defective*); ערסותיכם — Ezekiel 44:30;
and עריסתינו -- Nehemiah 10:38 (once *defective*).

3.2.2. The masoretic era (Table 2.1, Stage 3) can be divided
into five sub-stages.

Stage 3.1 Pre-masoretic. The earliest available evidence for
the state of the Hebrew text shows that arbitrary decisions by
scribes whether or not to use a *mater lectionis* to spell a long
vowel caused considerable divergence in detail. The Septuagint
often indicates that the translators had before them Hebrew
sources that differ from our present text in this particular
(Rahlfs 1916). The Samaritan Pentateuch reflects another tradition, with more plentiful use of *matres lectionis* (Murtonen
1975). The Qumran manuscripts are especially deviant in this
respect (Martin 1958: I 207-321). This represents the first
post-biblical period of transmission in which considerable freedom in spelling was exercised. But all was not chaos. Martin
concludes that the Qumran scribes had an "official phonetic
orthography" of their own (p. 396), and the emergence in the
mainstream of texts whose orthography is relatively conservative suggests a more authoritative and traditional practice at
some central point, almost certainly Jerusalem.

Three illustrations show that care was exercised conscious-
ly over the differences between *plene* and *defective* spellings in
very early times. First, the Murabbaᶜat phylactery texts, like
MT, are found to have the same word spelled both ways in the
same passage, as can be seen from Table 3.1.

Table 3.1 Differences within similar texts

Plene	Reference	Defective	Reference
יביא	Exodus 13:5	יבא	Exodus 13:11
ולטוטפת	Exodus 13:16	לטטפת	Deuteronomy 6:8
מזוזות	Deuteronomy 11:20	מזזת	Deuteronomy 6:9
ירכה	Exodus 13:16	ירד	Exodus 13:9

Second, C. D. Ginsburg's edition shows that many manuscripts read יביא at Exodus 13:11. But the Murabbaᶜat texts agree with MT down to the last detail at the point where texts are most susceptible to harmless fluctuations.

Third, the texts of Minor Prophets found at Murabbaᶜat show only a handful of orthographic deviations from MT (DJD II 183-4).

Stage 3.2 Rabbinic. In the second period of transmission freedom was not allowed. It became explicit policy to copy sacred texts exactly. Debates arose over the definition of a true copy. The rigorists held that a copy was not acceptable unless it was letter perfect. The claim of Josephus is often quoted as evidence that this point of view was already traditional in the first century CE: "It is evident from our conduct how we esteem our own books. For during the long bygone ages no one has presumed either to add anything to them, or to subtract anything from them, or to alter them" (*Contra Apion* VIII.42). But it is not certain that he is speaking about scribal practice, let alone spelling. The context, with its emphasis on conduct, suggests that he is commenting on the scrupulous obedience of the Jew to the injunctions of Scripture. The famous remark in the *Sayings of the Fathers* to the effect that the *massora* is a fence around the Torah probably has a similar import.

But if not already then, certainly before long, faithful reproduction of the text became a sacred duty. The standard was expressed in the injunction of Rabbi Ishmael (C1 CE):

בני הוי זהיר שמלאכתך מלאכת שמים היא
שמה תחסיר אות אחת או תתיר אות אחת
נמצאת אתה מחריב את כל העולם כולו

-- "My son, be careful, because your work is God's [Heaven's] work; because if you omit a single letter or add a single letter, you will be found to have destroyed the whole world, all of it!" (*Sota* 20a). Ramban (Nachmanides), after Ibn Ezra, conceded the preservation of the exact spelling was not necessary for the literal meaning, which was not affected. It was necessary, however, for the manipulation of the letters into other words, particularly the divine names. A Torah Scroll was disqualified if one letter had been added or subtracted (*Commentary on the Torah: Genesis* [Chavel 1971: 14]). In this connection he mentioned specifically the thirty-nine cases of *plene* אוֹתָם (see Type 33 in Chapter 6 below) and claimed that biblical scholars had counted "every full and defective word in the Torah" (*ibid.*).

Over against the rigorists, a less strict view allowed some latitude, recognizing that there were slight differences, namely in the use of *matres lectionis*, that did not make any material difference to the text, since they did not affect the identity of the words. In a passage not without obscurity (*Menahot* 29b, quoted by Ginsburg 1897: 156), the Talmud indicates that to replace *defective* with *plene* was not as serious as the reverse -- replacing *plene* with *defective*:

> "Three mistakes (in one column) may be corrected, but if there are four (in one column), it must be put into the Geniza. The rule: If there is only one correct column, it saves the whole copy. Rabbi Isaac bar Shemuel bar Martha said in the name of Rab: If the greater part of the copy is correct. Abayye said to Rabbi Joseph: If the copy has three mistakes in one column, what is to be done? He answered: It must be handed over to be corrected, and then it is

satisfactory. But this (correction of errors) is applicable to *defective* spellings only (i.e., when a *plene* was written *defective*); but in the case of *plene* (i.e., when a *defective* was written *plene*) we do not need to worry about that."

This attitude would permit a gradual increase in the number of *matres lectionis*.

Whatever the goal, there was always some shortfall between practice and ideal. There is plenty of evidence that copies of the Scriptures in use were not identical. It is not certain whether the variations (admittedly very minor) between copies to which the Talmud gives explicit testimony represent the survival of variants from pre-masoretic times or the emergence of new variants within the masoretic tradition. Gordis (1937) thinks that some ancient variants as authoritative as the official text were preserved in the *ketib/qere* apparatus. Goshen-Gottstein (1967) maintains that all variations attested in rabbinic times can be explained as deviations from the official text. Barthelemy (1976: 878-84) keeps an open mind.

Whatever the causes, there are places where the text, the Talmud, and the *massora* do not agree. We have some knowledge of the existence of textual variants during a period from which no biblical manuscript evidence as such has survived because the rabbis would sometimes settle a dispute by appealing to the precise spelling of key words. Since the argument depends on this fine detail, we may be sure that the textual information is correct.

One such case was a dispute between the rival schools of Shammai and Hillel over the number of sprinklings required by Leviticus 4 (*Sanhedrin 4a*). Shammai said "six," because the word 'horns' קרנות occurs three times (Leviticus 4:25, 30, 34), and three plurals make six sprinklings. The school of Hillel pointed out that the word was not spelled consistently. It was

קרנות once and קרנת twice, obviously the same word, but with *defective* spelling, and this gave four sprinklings. This shows that such tiny details as differences in spelling the same word were noted carefully and esteemed as the key to doctrinal truths. The most surprising thing is that neither of the texts that they were using corresponds to the text we now have, which is more conservative again, since the word is spelled *defective* in all three occurrences in the Masoretic Text.

Another dispute concerned the number of compartments in a phylactery. In *Menaḥot* 34b Rabbi Ishmael argued from the three occurrences of *ṭōṭāpōt*, spelled טוטפת once and טטפת twice. Hence a phylactery had four compartments. But the Masoretic Text reads טוטפת twice (Exodus 13:16; Deuteronomy 11:18) and טטפת once (Deuteronomy 6:8). Ibn Adoniyahu felt that the argument required a reading טטפות which he could not find (Ginsburg 1867b: 62). Rashi's grandson (Rabbi 'Tam') solved the problem by arguing that in ולטוטפת the first ו can be taken and placed between פ and ת.

A similar argument asks how many doorposts are needed in an entry for the command of Deuteronomy 6 to apply. In *Menaḥot* 34b the argument hinges on various readings of *mĕzūzōt* in Deuteronomy 6:9, whether מזות (Talmud), מזוזות (Tossafot), or מזות (Rashi). The Masoretic Text agrees with none of these -- מזוזת!

Or, how many walls are needed in a booth for the feast of Sukkot? This depends on the spelling of *sukkōt*, which occurs three times in the Pentateuch -- בסכת (Leviticus 23:42, 42), בסכות (Leviticus 23:43). There were two opinions. The consensus was that there must be two complete walls, but the third may be partial. Rabbi Simeon insisted that there must be four walls, although one may be partial (*Sukka* 6b). The positions were argued as follows. The word occurs three times. The spelling of two of them, being *defective*, is ambiguous. The one with *plene* spelling must be plural. Therefore there are four. The argument may seem forced, since one סכה is a booth, not a wall. Nevertheless the count of "four" implied by the spelling is reckoned as one for the booth and three for the walls. (The argument does not provide a textual basis for the traditional concession that one of the three may be partial.) Simeon argued from the pronunciation, which is the same for each (plural), giving a count of "six." One plural word enjoins the festival. The other two require four walls (again with the halakic provision that one of them may be partial). The language of the Talmud does not permit us to decide whether Simeon was using a text in which all three were spelled *plene*, thus guaranteeing the plural. Rather we have a case of appeal to written tradition -- יש אם למקרא -- and spoken tradition -- יש אם למסורת. They were not viewed as being in disagreement, but as two distinctive but concomitant bodies of knowledge.

Other cases involving *matres lectionis*: 1) It is evident from *Nidda* 33a that the rabbis had the spelling והנשא in Leviticus 15:10. But in MT *plene* spelling הנושא is safeguarded by the *massora*. 2) It is evident from *Sabbath* 55b that the rabbis had a spelling of מעברם in 1 Samuel 2:24 (MT: מעברים). 3) Rashi has the spelling כלת in Numbers 7:1. The *massora* notes כלות as *hapax legomenon*. See Sperber (1942-43: 318-321).

It is intriguing that arguments from textual readings are not pressed beyond the registration of opposing views. There was no penetration to the ulterior question which could have settled the issue one way or the other, namely, "Which text is correct?" The rabbis were content to accept both, but alternatives of this kind were never enshrined in the text itself as *ketib/qere* pairs: אלו ואלו דברי אלהים חיים.

Such tolerance seems inconsistent with the insistence that no variation in a single letter can be allowed. There is common-sense recognition that the ideal cannot be attained, but this does not vitiate the claims of the sacred text. The ideal was never relaxed, and there is no reason to believe that the consonantal text changed very much during the almost one thousand years of transmission from the early rabbis to the late masoretes.

Stage 3.3 Masoretic vocalization. This represented a radical change in the mode of reading the text. The traditional pronunciation of each word, which up until now had been maintained in oral tradition, was secured in writing with a most remarkable exactitude. There is now no way of knowing just how accurately the knowledge of the ancient pronunciation had been preserved. In due time the authority of the vocalization system was based on legends that it derived from Ezra, or even from Moses, or even from Adam (Owen 1659). The last serious defender of this extreme conservative position was John Gill (1767). Opposite him was Bishop Lowth, who claimed that "the true Hebrew pronunciation is totally lost" (1787: I 65), so the vowel points have no authority at all. "But the true pronunciation of Hebrew is lost -- lost to a degree far beyond what can ever be the case of any European language preserved only in writing; for the Hebrew language, like most of the other Oriental languages, expressing only the consonants, and being destitute of its vowels, has lain now for two thousand years in a manner mute and incapable of utterance" (Lowth 1868: vi).

The truth lies between these extremes. The points are not infallible, but the sounds they represent were not just invented in the Middle Ages. Barr (1968) and, more strongly, Gordis (1971a) reaffirm the claims of the masoretic tradition, with all necessary reserve. The modern phase of the discussion is succinctly reviewed by Grabbe (1977: 179-197). The matter may, however, be more nuanced. The masoretic systems for writing the vowels of Hebrew were very delicate, especially in the refined Tiberian system which eventually won the day (Morag 1962; 1974). This reached its limit in the residual disagreements between the schools of ben Naphtali and ben Asher. Even so, it was not perfect, due in part to its dependence on prior systems and also due to the fact that the oral traditions were not uniform in all parts of Jewry. The Tiberian system made better provision for distinctions of mouth position (seven vowel qualities) than of vowel length. The use of the same symbol for back /ā/ and /o/ (same position) is the most conspicuous instance, but it is not essentially different from the use of the same symbol *patah* to represent middle /ā/ and /a/. For our purposes the finer points do not matter. We are mainly interested in the consonantal text. At the same time we make use of, and fully accept, the masoretic identification of the vowels represented by the *matres lectionis*, if only in the interests of objectivity. And, in the main, there is no reason to doubt that the masoretic fixation of the vowels was the preservation of an old and reliable tradition.

Masoretic studies since the establishment of the text in the ninth century CE have concentrated mainly on matters of vocalization and accentuation. It is true that numerous masoretic notes draw attention to peculiarities of spelling, *defective* or *plene*. But these do not affect the identity of the word and have been considered by many to be details of no consequence. Their possible significance for the history of the transmission of the text has not been appreciated. Ibn Ezra (quoted by Ginsburg [1897: 138]) already spoke disdainfully about "mentally deficient" persons -- *"defective* in heart" is his pun -- who asked questions concerning *defective* and *plene* --

וחכמי המסרת בראו מלבם טעמים למלאים ולחסרים והם טובים
למלא כל חסר לב כי אחרי שהם מבקשים טעם למלא ולחסר
הנה אין כח בסופר לכתוב רק מלא אם רצה לבאר שלא
תתערב המלה כמו עולם או יכתוב חסר לאחוז דרך קצרה

In more recent times Delitzsch ridiculed such research with even more uncomplimentary language:

Es könnte im Hinblick auf alle diese mannigfachen Schreibweisen nur als der Gipfel kleinlicher Pedantarie gelten, wollte man in einem Wörterbuch alle diese verschiedenen Schreibweisen registrieren.

Fragen wie "ob יְעֵץ immer defektiv geschrieben oder ob auch יוֹעֵץ berechtigt sei" [see Type 39 below], oder Bemerkungen wie: dass "sich statt וַיִּירָא sieben-mal auch וַיִּרְא geschrieben finde" [see Type 5 below], erscheinen gegenüber diesem Durcheinander, dieser Willkür in der Setzung der Vckalbuchstaben als denk-barst gleichgültig (1920: 25).

C. D. Ginsburg, in his *Introduction* (1897), a book of more than a thousand pages, devoted just one page to the history of the *matres lectionis* (p. 299).

Breuer (1976) has deplored the neglect of this subject, declaring that the choice of L as the supreme specimen of the ben Asher text was a disaster. He says, "Had they been seeking the most error-filled of all the ancient manuscripts, they could not have made a better choice" (p. XII). He calls it "error-infested" (p. XV). This is exaggerated. Later he explains: "This manuscript [i.e., Leningrad B19a = L] is one of the best of the ancient manuscripts so far as its vocalization and accentuation are concerned, but the worst in its orthography" (p. XXX). This negative estimation poses a problem for the present study, which is based on L. The limitations of L are recognized, but no compelling alternative suggests itself. See the examples supplied in § 1.13. In contrast with better, earlier MSS, and some very good ones that are actually later than L, L shows a trend to more *plene* spellings. Goshen-Gottstein pointed out that in one chapter alone (Deuteronomy 28) there are five differences in spelling between **A** and **L** (1960: 28, note 31), and in every instance L is *plene*! Deuteronomy 32 has three differences, and again **A** prefers the *defective* against the *plene* of L. L is some-times *plene* against its own *massora*.

Examples: At Isaiah 32:11 L reads וַחֲגוֹרָה בֹּ מֵל. The accentuation shows that the masoretes interpreted this as an imperative ('put on a girdle [of sackcloth]'). In the other occurrence of וַחֲגֹרָה the word is a noun, spelled *defective*. In

Isaiah 3:24, however, it is חֲגוֹרָה, the only case where the noun is *plene*. In each case P is *defective* and knows nothing of this *massora*. At Isaiah 33:4 L reads שׁוֹקֵק בׁ מֵל. The other case is Proverbs 28:15. But P and other MSS, including A and the *textus receptus*, read שׁקֵק and do not know this *massora*. So L has not only increased the number of *plene* spellings; it (or its *Vorlage*) has canonized its innovations with new *massorot*. Some of the historical reasons for this kind of confusion are discussed by Sperber (1959: 50).

L often has *plene* /ō/ where P is *defective*. With /ū/ it is the other way around. P is often *plene* where L is *defective*. Example: At Isaiah 33:7 A reads חָצָה לׁ חֹס, but P reads חוּצָה, as did L (it was corrected to match the *massora*). The differences are, admittedly, very small indeed and should not make any material difference to the overall results. There is a lot to be said for beginning with one good manuscript and getting the complete picture for it. Others can then be compared. For the time being L has a good claim, even if not yet proven to be the best to everyone's satisfaction.

Stage 3.4 Post-masoretic. With the completion of the masoretes' task, the work of the scribe was vastly transformed. Now he had to preserve the entire text -- consonants, vowels, cantillations and all. The perfection and autonomy of the vowel pointing now had a negative effect on the consonantal text. *The matres lectionis did not matter any more!* It did not make any difference whether /ō/ was spelled *defective* or *plene*. Hence we can understand the indifference to this detail expressed by Ibn Ezra. Within quite a short period the manuscripts began to diverge, and the divergences in the use of *matres lectionis* were more extensive than divergence in punctuation, even in good manuscripts. Comparison of L with A and other good manuscripts soon reveals this, although the main impression is one of identity. This new trend must have begun already in the eleventh century. Not everyone took it as lightheartedly as Ibn Ezra. The rabbi Abulafua recorded his dismay at the loss of

wisdom because in his day no one knew any more how to tell
which spelling (between *defective* and *plene*) was correct. It
was precisely in the matter of *plene/defective* that **A** enjoyed
prestige among medieval scholars. While Maimonides attests
his own reliance on it in the matter of open and closed para-
graphs, and the correct way of writing the poems, the Rabbi
Joseph Ashkenazi quotes the actual colophon of the codex (now
lost), in which the scribe explicitly claims that the manuscript's
orthography may be trusted.

 וגדלה מצאתי כי הסופר כתב בסוף הספר
וכל מי שירצה לראות מתוכו חסר או יתר
פתוח או סתום סדור או סתור

"And furthermore, I discovered that the scribe had written at
the end of the book: 'And everyone who would like to see from
inside it *defective* or *plene*, opened or closed, *seder*-ed or continued...'" (Scholem 1959: 75). Rabbi Meir Neḥmad (*Textus 1*
1960: 14) also says explicitly that the codex served as a standard of דברי יתר או חסר 'words of excess or deficiency.'

It is different with inferior manuscripts, especially those
which seem to have been made for private use. This is shown
strikingly by the British Museum manuscript G86, the so-called
"Tittle Bible." The agreement of the first hand with *textus
receptus* is uncanny. There is scarcely a difference in a single
letter. But the manuscript suffered wear and tear, and a later
user repaired it by patching over the worn places and writing
that piece of text again. Time after time, when that was done,
the secondary text adds *matres lectionis* quite freely, as they
were currently used to write Hebrew in non-biblical texts. This
shows what can easily happen. It underscores once more by
contrast the remarkable stability of most texts, in spite of the
deviations introduced unwittingly or even condoned openly in
the use of *matres lectionis*. These deviations account for the
majority of the variants collected by Kennicott and de Rossi,
and in more recent times by Ginsburg. Because they are of

little consequence, these variants have not been studied systematically; but, more seriously, they have obscured the completely different question of the broad spelling patterns in the consonantal text which are not substantially altered by these recent and minor fluctuations. The former is what we are investigating, and we do not need to incorporate the latter. See the discussion in § 1.13.

Stage 3.5 Modern. Since the Hebrew Bible has been printed, something like a *textus receptus* has been in circulation. The main editions do not vary significantly among themselves in the main object of our inquiry, the use of *matres lectionis*.

3.3 The *plene* spelling of long vowels

When biblical usage stabilized, some time during the Persian Period, the *matres lectionis* had the following functions.

3.3.1. א was used only, but consistently, in historical spellings of /ī/, /ē/, /ā/, /ō/, word-terminal or word-medial.

We include א in the following discussion for the sake of completeness and out of regard for the fact that it is called a *mater lectionis* in standard reference works. We shall show that it is not a *mater lectionis* in the way that the other three vowel letters are, and so eliminate it altogether from the ensuing investigation. There is not a single indubitable instance of the use of א as a true vowel letter in any pre-exilic Hebrew inscription. That usage is strictly post-biblical (Qumran and Talmud) and barely intrudes into the MT (see § 5.5.1). In the examples of the use of א as a *mater lectionis* in pre-exilic inscriptions that are usually put forward, the א is etymological. The only possible exception is לא, 'not.' But the history of this word is far from clear, and it is mere dogmatism to declare the א "not etymological" (Zevit 1980: 22, 29). Reserve is called for, as also with the א of the Aramaic article, whose junctural origin betokens a glottal consonant which is certainly not primal, so etymology is not the only consideration (Lambdin 1971). The uniqueness of these two cases should be set against the consistent use in both Aramaic and Hebrew from the first available evidence onwards of ה for word-terminal /ā/ in those languages.

We cannot be sure that א was not consonantal in certain other particles, such as לֻא, 'would that,' נָא, 'please,' at least in the stages in the language when post-vocalic א was still pronounced. In late texts the use of א for /ā/, especially word-terminal, when it is not etymological, is due to the influence of Aramaic, and the development in Aramaic is secondary, due to quiescence of word-terminal א. This is particularly evident in the replacement of terminal ה ָ - by א ָ - in many personal names in later books (Sperber 1959: 59). Another Aramaizing trend is the palatalization of intervocalic א in the vicinity of a front vowel. Four instances in 2 Kings 11 -- המאיות in verses 4, 9, 10 and המיאות in verse 15 -- have been corrected to המאות in *qere*. In A and other MSS the reading in verse 15 is the same as the others. A similar consequence is the alternation of א and י in intervocalic position (Gordis 1937: Lists 26, 27).

The modern listing of א as a simply phonetic *mater lectionis* survives from a time when the historical (that is, etymological) origin of most of its occurrences in this apparent role was not appreciated, and its sporadic use as an ancillary *mater lectionis* for other long vowels when it is not etymological is probably due to the analogy of its use in Hebrew historical spelling. So, strictly speaking, א never attained the full status of a *mater lectionis*. It has marginal status in the following cases.

3.3.1.1. א rather than ה may be used for word-terminal /ā/, mainly for the feminine singular suffix (Ginsburg 1897-1905: IV 11 § 21):

לֵדָא -- Numbers 11:20

גְּבְהָא -- Ezekiel 31:5

כְּלָא -- Ezekiel 36:5

שֶׁנָא -- Psalm 127:2

מָרָא -- Ruth 1:20

כַּמַּטָּרָא -- Lamentations 3:12

בְּחֵמָא -- Daniel 11:44

It may appear in locatives:

וְהָרָא -- 1 Chronicles 5:26

Verbs with ל"ה roots may use it:

יוֹרֶא -- Proverbs 11:25

כְּלָא -- Proverbs 16:30 (L has כְּלָה.)

Other words may use it:

אַרְצָא -- 1 Kings 16:9

גִּבְעָא -- 1 Chronicles 2:49

וְאַתִּיקֶיהָא -- Ezekiel 41:15 (*Qere*)

By the same confusion, ה can be used for א:

לֹה -- Deuteronomy 3:11

בֹּה -- Ezekiel 14:4

יִכְלֶה -- Genesis 23:6

3.3.1.2. When א rather than ה is used for word-medial /ā/, it is often corrected to *qere*:

בַּלָּאט -- Judges 4:21

חֶלְאָמָה -- 2 Samuel 10:17

הַמְּלָאכִים -- 2 Samuel 11:1 (But see **L**.)

רָאשׁ -- 2 Samuel 12:1, 4; Proverbs 10:4

הַשְּׁאָאוֹת -- Ezekiel 16:57

שָׁאטְךָ -- Ezekiel 25:6

הַשָּׁאטִים -- Ezekiel 28:24, 26

וְאֶמְאָסְאָךְ -- Hosea 4:6

קָאם -- Hosea 10:14

פָּארוּר -- Joel 2:6; Nahum 2:11

דָּאג -- Nehemiah 13:16

נָאוֶה -- Isaiah 33:20 in P

3.3.1.3. Redundant א may be used for a vowel other than /ā/ (Mm 907; Ginsburg 1897-1905: IV 10 § 20):

הֲהָלְכוּא -- Joshua 10:24

הַקְּלִיא -- 1 Samuel 17:17

וַיִּרְאוּ -- 2 Samuel 11:24

הַמּוֹרְאִים -- 2 Samuel 11:24

אָבוּא -- Isaiah 28:12

הִבְאִישׁ -- Isaiah 30:5 (P has qere הוֹבִישׁ.)

שָׁאסַיִךְ -- Jeremiah 30:16

רָצוֹא -- Ezekiel 1:14

נֶאְשַׁאַר -- Ezekiel 9:8

וְרָצְאָתִי -- Ezekiel 43:27

וְנִרְפָּאוּ -- Ezekiel 47:8 (Not all MSS have qere וְנִרְפּוּ.)

נָקִיא -- Joel 4:19; Jonah 1:14

נֹשְׁאִים -- Nehemiah 5:7 (L has no qere.)

לְמוֹאֵל -- Nehemiah 12:38

לוּא -- 1 Samuel 14:30; Isaiah 48:18, 63:19

> לוֹ is the norm, but לָא occurs (Qere לוֹ): 2 Samuel 18:12, 19:7. (Compare Genesis 23:11.)

רְבוֹא -- Ezra 2:64; Nehemiah 7:66, 71 (רִבּוֹ × 4)

Compare the two spellings of ʾĕlîhû in Job 32-35, and compare 1 Chronicles 26:7; 27:18.

Some of the words which the *massora* gives under quiescent word-terminal א are probably not germane, for the א could be etymological: רָפוּא -- Numbers 13:9.

Koehler (1950-51: 138-40) lists מָאזְנִים, לִקְרַאת, and צַוַּאר as words in which א is not necessary for pronunciation. He

recognizes the א in לקראת as etymological; in מאזנים, א
arises from a false etymology. It was introduced to צואר to distinguish it from צור, 'rock?' See also Gordon (1978) for the idea
that this letter could soften an offensive text.

3.3.1.4. The summary at the beginning of § 3.3.1 shows
that א never developed in Hebrew as the standard *mater lectionis* for any specific vowel. Being otiose in many cases, it was
vulnerable to omission. Quite early it was possible to leave out
an etymological א to obtain a purely consonantal spelling. The
variation in the el-Kadr javelin heads already shows this:

חץ עבדלבאת (I, III)   חץ עבדלבת (II)

Compare the two spellings of the same name חי and חיא in the
Kilamuwa inscriptions. Bange's explanation (1971: 36f.) that
the difference is due to stress is unconvincing. There is no
basis for transferring the stress patterns of Hebrew (masoretic
attestation!) to old Phoenician. Other epigraphical examples:

רשה 'its chiefs' (Mesha, line 20)

לקרת 'to meet' (Siloam Inscription, line 4)

The number of biblical examples of this omission cannot be
determined because often the etymology is uncertain, or the
identity of the word is unsure. Omission of א is standard spelling of first person singular imperfect of some verbs with פ"א
roots: אׁמַר, אֹמֵר, 'I shall say.' With other persons we have:
Root אכה

תָּבׂא -- Proverbs 1:10
Root אזן

אָזִין -- Job 32:11
Root אזר

וַתַּזְרֵנִי -- 2 Samuel 22:40 (Psalm 18:40 has תְּאַזְּרֵנִי.)
Root אחז

תֹּחֶז -- 2 Samuel 20:9

Root אכל

יוֹכְלוּ -- Ezekiel 42:5

Root אמר

תֹּמְרוּ -- 2 Samuel 19:14 (also Psalm 11:1 in some MSS)

יֹמְרוּךְ -- Psalm 139:20
A and Textus Receptus, with a note that א is missing. L
has the massora, but reads יֹאמְרֻךְ.

Root אסף

תֹּסִיפוּ -- Exodus 14:13

Root אסר

הָסוּרִים -- Qohelet 4:14

Root אפה

וַתֹּפֵהוּ -- 1 Samuel 28:24

Root אשׁף

הָשְׁפוֹת -- Nehemiah 3:13 (Compare הָאַשְׁפֹּות at 3:14.)

Roots with א in other positions:

Root בא

בָּגָד -- Genesis 30:11 (The *qere* has בָּא גָד.)

בָּנוּ -- 1 Samuel 25:8

וְהַמֵּבִי -- 2 Samuel 5:2
Gordis (1937: 95; List 7) points out that in several similar cases (1 Kings 21:21; Jeremiah 19:15; 39:16) word-
terminal א is lost when א begins the next word; contrast
Ruth 3:15.

וַיָּבֹו -- 1 Kings 12:12 (Not all MSS have *qere* ויבוא.)

אָכִי -- 1 Kings 21:29; Micah 1:15

Root גיא

בַּגַּי -- Deuteronomy 34:6 (Compare Joshua 8:11.)

Root חטא

מֵחֲטוֹ -- Genesis 20:6

חַטָּה -- Numbers 15:24

הֶחֱטִי -- 2 Kings 13:6

הַחֲטִי -- Jeremiah 32:35

Root טמא

וְנִטְמֵתֶם -- Leviticus 11:43 (Compare Job 18:3.)

Root יצא

הַיּוֹצֵת -- Deuteronomy 28:57

יָצָתִי -- Job 1:21 (L has *qere* יָצָאתִי.)

Root מאס

וַיִּמַּסוּ -- Judges 15:14 (Compare יִמָּאֵסוּ in Psalm 58:8.)

לָמֶס -- Job 6:14

Root מלא

מָלוּ -- Ezekiel 28:16 (Compare Ezekiel 41:8.)

מָלֵתִי -- Job 32:18

Root מצא

מָצָתִי -- Numbers 11:11

Root נבא

וְהִתְנַבִּיתָ -- 1 Samuel 10:6 (Compare 10:13; Jeremiah 26:9.)

Root נשא

וְתִשֶּׂנָה -- Jeremiah 9:17

וַתִּשֶּׂנָה -- Ruth 1:14

     Zechariah 5:9 in *textus receptus*; L has א.

וְנָשׁוּ -- Ezekiel 39:26

     There is a masoretic tradition (*Okla we-Okla §199*) that
נָשָׁא in Psalm 139:20 reads נָשׂוּ.

מָשֵׁתוּ -- Job 41:17

Root צואר

צַוְּרָם -- Nehemiah 3:5

Root צמא

צָמֵתִי -- Judges 4:19 (Thus, some MSS: L, C, A: צָמֵאתִי)

וְצָמֵת -- Ruth 2:9

Root קרא

וְקָרָהוּ -- Genesis 44:29 (Compare Isaiah 41:22.)

Root ראש

רֵשִׁית -- Deuteronomy 11:12

רִישׁוֹן -- Job 8:8

Root רפא

וַיֵּרָפוּ -- 2 Kings 2:22

Root שאה

לַהְשׁוֹת -- 2 Kings 19:25 (Isaiah 37:26 has לְהַשְׁאוֹת.)

Root שאל

שְׁלָתֵךְ -- 1 Samuel 1:17

Compare the name 'Shealtiel' which lacks א in Haggai
1:12, 14 and 2:2.

Root שאר

שֵׁרִית -- 1 Chronicles 12:39

Root שוא

בַּשֻּׁו -- Job 15:31 (*Qere* reads בַּשָׁיו, followed by שָׁוְא in 31b.)

Root שמאל

הַשְׂמִילִי -- Ezekiel 21:21

וּלְהַשְׂמִיל -- 2 Samuel 14:19

Root תאם

תוֹמִם -- Genesis 25:24 (In Genesis 38:27 we find תְאוֹמִים.)

See Ginsburg 1897-1905: IV § 15 for additional possibilities.

3.3.1.5. As an intermediate stage between the maintenance
of consonantal א and its development into a pseudo *mater lectionis* or else its omission altogether, there are words in which
the historical א is still written, even though it is neither pronounced nor used as a *mater lectionis* (Mm 898):

וְהָאסַפְסֻף -- Numbers 11:4

וַיֵּאָצֵל -- Numbers 11:25 (Compare וְאָצַלְתִּי in verse 17.)

מַשַּׁאת -- Deuteronomy 24:10

בָּארוּמָה -- Judges 9:41

פֶּלִאי -- Judges 13:18

וַאֲעֶנֶּה -- 1 Kings 11:39

כַּאבִיר -- Isaiah 10:13

וַיֵּאת -- Isaiah 41:25

שֹׁאסַיִךְ -- Jeremiah 30:16

וַאעְשַׁר -- Zechariah 11:5

מְאוּם -- Daniel 1:4 (מְאוּם or מוּם; in L, Job 31:7 is מְאוּם.)

כּוֹדָאם -- Nehemiah 6:8

The loss of the pronunciation of etymological א, even though still written, produces such curiosities as:

חֹטְאים -- 1 Samuel 14:33

נֹשְׁאים -- Nehemiah 5:7

קֹרְאים -- Psalm 99:6

The spellings of such foreign names as 'Tiglath-Pileser,' sometimes without א (2 Kings 16:7; 1 Chronicles 5:26), and '(B)Merodak,' sometimes with א, are marginal to Hebrew spelling. Compare אַרְבְאֵל (Hosea 10:14).

3.3.1.6. The preservation of otiose א probably fostered a bookish pronunciation of some words against the popular development. Thus בְּאֵר, 'well,' is related to בֹּאר, perhaps בְּאַר, but spelled also בּוֹר, as well as בֵּיר. The usual pointing is בְּאֵר, but the pronunciation was probably *bēr*. The retention of א prevents confusion with *bār*. But it may be lost -- בְּרוֹתָה (Ezekiel 47:16). Compare 'buffalo,' רְאֵם -- Numbers 23:22; 24:8; Deuteronomy 33:17; רֵים -- Job 39:9, 10; רְאֵים -- Psalm 92:11; רְאֵמִים -- Isaiah 34:7, but P has רֵאימִים; Psalm 29:6; רֵמִים -- Psalm 22:22. Compare שָׁאף = שׁוּף, and the *ketib/qere* מְאוּם and מוּם (Daniel 1:4). In these cases the variants show that such words had become monosyllables. The Qumran spellings of נָאם (always that in MT), נָאוּם and נֹאוּם, indicate **nūm* (Kutscher 1974: 56, 498-499). Similarly 'very' is **mōd* -- מוֹאר

or מאוד. Compare the two spellings of 'Beth-Shan.'

3.3.1.7. To guard against its elision, intervocalic א was given a *dageš* in a few cases:

וַיָּבִאוּ -- Genesis 43:26; Ezra 8:18

וַתָּבִאוּ -- Leviticus 23:17

רָאוּ -- Job 33:21

For more on this practice see Ginsburg 1897-1905: IV, p. 2.

3.3.1.8. There is little sign in the Bible of the practice of using א as a supplement to the other *matres lectionis*, a practice which proliferated in the Qumran texts (Kutscher 1959; Martin 1958: I 207ff.; Wernberg-Møller 1958). Note, however:

מְראוֹן -- Joshua 12:20

מואל -- Nehemiah 12:38

Apart from these instances, the circumstance that the spelling of /ō/ as א arises historically (see above, § 2.3.8 and Path 2 below [§ 6.4.5]) casts the otiose א in the role of a pseudo *mater lectionis*. This blocks, or at least minimizes, the use of ו in its standard role as *mater lectionis* for /ō/. It rarely supplements א. ו can be used instead of א, as when *yōmar*, 'he will say,' is spelled יומר instead of the usual יאמר. Compare הַבְּאֵר (2 Samuel 23:20) with הַבּוֹר (1 Chronicles 11:22). The use of ו in the first person singular is different:

אוֹכַל -- Psalm 50:13

אוֹמַר -- Nehemiah 2:7, 17, 20

אוֹמְרָה -- Psalm 42:10

אוֹסֵף -- Hosea 9:15

In these words, ו does not replace the א of the original root, which is not written in any case. Leaving aside the first person, יוּכְלוּ (Ezekiel 42:5) seems to be the only example; some MSS correct this to יאכלו. וַיּוֹחֶר, 'and he delayed,' at 2 Samuel 20:5 is *qere*; the text is וייחר. Some MSS have ויאחר. But a spelling such as יוֹאמֶר is never found. It is a different

story with the Qumran MSS. There 'this' is spelled זואת, זאות,
זות, as well as the regular זאת; 'head' is spelled ראוש, רואש,
רוש, as well as the regular ראש (Kutscher 1959: 124-128). When
ו replaces א, the /ō/ in such words is not recognized in this
study as an opportunity for *plene* spelling with ו. This constraint is illustrated by several common words whose spelling is
invariant. Thus zō(ʾ)t, 'this,' is always זאת (× 605) in contrast
to Qumran. Rō(ʾ)š, 'head,' is always ראש (× 462) and ṣō ʾn,
'sheep,' צאן (× 273); but צאון occurs once in Psalm 144:13, a
Psalm replete with *plene* spellings.

There are, however, some words (like this last exception) in
which a supplemental ו has been added to א; this *mater lectionis* ו is redundant. When the combination או is used, it is
pointed אֹו, not אֹ. This is the standard spelling of 'left,'
שְׂמאוֹל (× 29), and it is common for 'sins,' חַטָּאות (× 31). Also in
'full,' מְלֵאות (× 6); נֹאוד -- Judges 4:19; קְרָאות -- Judges 8:1;
רְבָאות -- Ezra 2:69. It is found once in יֹאושִׁיָהוּ -- Jeremiah 27:1;
this word is elsewhere *defective* fifty-one times.

3.3.2. ה was used as *mater lectionis* for nearly every
word-terminal /ā/ and, in certain word classes, for word-
terminal /ē/ and /ε̄/, the reflex of ל″י roots. Archaically, it
was used for word-terminal /ō/. The mnemonic שְׁנַת″ךָ 'thy
sleep,' covered the four main categories: 1) ל″ה roots; 2) feminine singular nouns and verbs; 3) verb suffixes of imperative
and cohortative (the Jewish grammarians included infinitives
here too, but this suffix is really feminine); 4) ה *locale* (they
put לַיְלָה here because it is *milᶜel*).

There are fourteen cases of word-terminal הָ -, all with
ketib/qere (*Okla we-Okla* § 113; Gordis 1937: List 18). These are
competing words, not orthographic variants. Often they
represent a survival of the old feminine plural suffix -ā as in
Numbers 34:4; Deuteronomy 21:7; Joshua 15:4; 18:12, 14, 19;
1 Kings 22:49; Jeremiah 2:15; 22:6; Psalm 73:2; Job 16:16;
Lamentations 4:17. Or they may be a grammatically possible

singular as in 2 Kings 24:10; Jeremiah 50:6; Ezekiel 35:12; 37:22. Or they may be Aramaic as in Daniel 3:29. Or they may simply be errors as in Leviticus 21:5 or Ezekiel 23:43 -- the latter very difficult. Compare Genesis 49:22; 1 Samuel 4:15; Jeremiah 48:41; 51:29, 56; Ezekiel 26:2; Psalm 18:35; 68:14; Nehemiah 13:10.

ה is never used as a word-internal *mater lectionis*. This fact renders nugatory the speculation of Bange (1971: 69, 114) that ה in the divine Name יהוה and in theophoric names of type יהו- developed from *yāwe through the introduction of ה as an "off-glide" after the long vowel. Proper nouns are not the best evidence for a phonetic change that is to be advanced as a rule. And another swallow is needed. In each case the explanation of the internal ה as etymological is still satisfactory. It is only by accident that this rule is occasionally violated. Oriental and occidental manuscripts vary in practice for writing two-word names, such as בית־אל. In the Pentateuch at least forty-six such words are single in the East, hyphenated in the West (lists in Weil 1981: 673-679). L is mixed in this detail, Kedorlaomer being spelled both ways in Genesis 14. The spelling of פרה־צור, פדה־אל, עשה־אל as one word brings the word-terminal graph into the interior of those words. This constitutes the only deviation from our previous statement.

3.3.3. ו is mandatory for word-terminal /ū/ and nearly always used for word-terminal /ō/, except where etymological א or archaic ה is used. It is frequently used for word-internal /ō/ and /ū/.

3.3.4. י is mandatory for word-terminal /ī/, is frequently used for word-internal /ī/, and nearly always used for stem-terminal as well as word-terminal /ē/ and /ɛ̄/, especially when these derive from *ay in the stem and construct forms of plural nouns. It usually is mandatory for stem-medial /ē/ ← *ay, rarely for stem-medial /ē/ ← *i.

3.3.5. Because of the numerous historical factors at work, the system was very untidy. Each long vowel could be represented by more than one *mater lectionis* and each *mater lectionis* could represent more than one vowel. This untidiness was never overcome. One can always speculate that an original long vowel, particularly word-terminal /ī/ or /ū/, whose spelling was zero in purely consonantal orthography, was not recognized by the scribes who modernized very old texts, and still masquerades as something else. In particular, verbs that should be plural, with suffix -$\bar{u}$, in consonantal orthography are unsuffixed, evidently singular. Emendation of such suspects at this late hour would hardly ever be warranted. That the extant form has satisfied the scribes for so long ensures that there is something to be said for it. Numerous cases have attracted the attention of textual scholars. Thus the singular בטח in the middle of plurals in Job 6:19-20 can easily be read as בטחו. But the singular can be explained as distributive (GKC § 145u; Dhorme, *ad loc.*). The lone apparently singular imperative in Amos 4:4-5 is usually made plural. But it is infinitive absolute, for variation.

The uncertainty of more finely balanced cases is often reflected in *ketib/qere* pairs. Of the fourteen such pairs which add ו in *qere*, the *ketib* is archaic, or already ends in one ו (Genesis 27:29; 43:28; Judges 21:20; 1 Kings 9:9). Occasionally the pronoun suffix -הו is spelled *defective* (1 Samuel 7:9; 2 Kings 22:5; Ezekiel 7:21). Otherwise the choice is between a singular or plural verb (1 Samuel 10:10; 13:19; 1 Kings 12:7; 2 Kings 20:18 [Isaiah 39:7 is plural]; Isaiah 37:19 [singular has been read as infinitive absolute]; Esther 9:27; Ezra 3:3). It is only under the rarest circumstances that we can present an argument for reading MT singular as plural; i.e. for claiming that an archaic spelling with zero for terminal -$\hat{u}$ escaped the attention of the scribes who updated such words by adding -*w*. When אִישׁ is used as distributive ('each') subject, the verb is usually plural -- ויאמרו איש אל־רעהו. But Genesis 44:13 has: ויקרעו שמלתם ויעמס איש על־חמרו וישבו העירה. Read: ויעמסו. Harder to explain are the eight pairs in which *ketib* has a redundant וּ, when the subject of the verb is evidently singular (Joshua 6:7; 9:7; 1 Samuel 15:16; 1 Kings 12:3, 21; 2 Kings 14:13; Ezekiel 46:9; Nehemiah 3:15). In 2 Kings 9:33 and 16:15 the suffix -הוּ is erroneous. Eighteen of these twenty-two pairs are in the Prophets. Thus the text of the Torah seems to have been established with more certainty, and in post-exilic books the spelling of such words would not be the decision of a copyist; they would have the standard spelling from the beginning.

3.3.6. To summarize, the long vowels are represented by *matres lectionis* in the following ways:

/ī/ by א (etymological, historical spelling; compare רִפְאתִי [2 Kings 2:21]; רִפְאֻנוּ [Jeremiah 51:9]; דְּכָאת [Psalm 89:11]), and by י (standard);

/ē/ by א (historical), by ה (word-terminal -- nouns and verbs from ל״י roots), and by י (standard);

/ɛ̄/ by א (historical), by ה (word-terminal -- nouns and verbs from ל״י roots), and by י (standard);

/ā/ by א (historical or Aramaizing), and by ה (standard, but only word-terminal);

/ō/ by א (historical), by ה (word-terminal and archaic), and by ו (standard);

/ū/ by א (etymological; rarely *mater lectionis*; compare פֻּארָה [Isaiah 10:33]), by ה (an artifact in *ketîb/qere* pairs), and by ו (standard).

Note that in all cases א remains an etymological vestige, associated with all the vowels, and so cannot be regarded as a true *mater lectionis* in a phonetic writing system.

3.4 The *plene* spelling of short vowels

The *matres lectionis* were almost never used to write short vowels in biblical texts.

3.4.1. The *plene* spelling of short /i/. The spelling of 'Ziqlag' is usually צקלג, and the two or three cases of ציקלג (in most MSS 1 Chronicles 12:1, 21; in L 1 Chronicles 4:30 as well) are sometimes cited as specimens of *plene* spelling of short /i/. But it is more likely that צקלג is *defective* spelling of long /ī/, as the use of *gaᶜya* often shows (GKC §§ 16f,i). Apart from that all we have are:

וַהֲמִיתִּיו *(wahă̆ mî tti̅ w)* -- 1 Samuel 17:35

לִיקֲהַת -- Proverbs 30:17

בִּיקְרוֹתֶיךָ -- Psalm 45:10 in some MSS (But L has בִּיקְרוֹתֶיךָ.)

לִיסוֹד -- 2 Chronicles 31:7 (But L has לִיסוֹד.)

In 1 Chronicles 11:31 אִיתַי, *ʾittay,* could have been another case, but the masoretes did not use *dāgeš*. One might add עיור (Isaiah 43:8 in Babylonian MS240 [*Textus 1*, p. 143]).

This phenomenon is attested in the *massora*. Item § 216 in the Paris recension of *Okla we-Okla* notes three cases -- Psalm 45:10; Proverbs 30:17; Isaiah 42:24. Both the textual readings and the *massora* for the third case are actually post-masoretic (Ginsburg 1867a: 34). A has מְשָׁסָה in the text, with a curious *qere*, and is confirmed by *Codex Babylonicus Petropolitanus*. L has *ketib* לִמְשׁוּסָה, *qere* משסה -- incorrectly in BHS as משׁסה to agree with the *massora*, without a note!

One may safely regard these few and dubious cases as the exceptions (due doubtless to the intrusion of rabbinic practice of spelling some short vowels with *matres lectionis*) that prove the rule.

3.4.2. The *plene* spelling of short /u/. The use of *waw* for spelling short /u/ has developed more than the use of *yod* for spelling short /i/.

The Torah has four instances:

עֲרוּמִים -- Genesis 2:25 (Mm 18)

מֵאוּמָה -- Genesis 22:12 (L!)

תְּלֻנּת -- Exodus 16:12

תְּלֻנֹּתָם – Numbers 17:25

The Former Prophets have a total of nine instances:

יוּטָּה -- Joshua 15:55 (L!)

הַיִּוּלָד -- Judges 13:8

הַכְּבוּדָה -- Judges 18:21

יוּלָד -- Judges 18:29 (*nip*ᶜ*al?*)

גְדוּלָה -- 2 Samuel 7:21, 23

מָעוּזִּי -- 2 Samuel 22:33 (L!)

דּוּמֶשֶׂק -- 2 Kings 16:10 (L: [Kutscher 1959: 5f.])

זְבוּדָה -- 2 Kings 23:36 (*ketib Zĕ bî dāh?*)

The Latter Prophets have fifteen instances:

מְשׂוּכָּתוֹ -- Isaiah 5:5

שְׂרוּקֶיהָ -- Isaiah 16:8

בְּמָעוּזִּי -- Isaiah 27:5

מוּסָּד -- Isaiah 28:16

מִסָּד precedes; MSS are confused.

יוּסָּב -- Isaiah 28:27

וּלְאוּמִּי -- Isaiah 51:4

לְאוּמִים -- Isaiah 55:4

הַמּוּלָה -- Jeremiah 11:16

כּוּלָּם -- Jeremiah 31:34

זוּנָּה -- Ezekiel 16:34

בְּחוּקֵּי -- Ezekiel 20:18

כְּבוּדָה -- Ezekiel 23:41

מָעוּנָּם -- Ezekiel 24:25

מָאוּזָל -- Ezekiel 27:19

יוּשַׁד -- Hosea 10:14

The Poetry contains thirteen instances:

מָעוּזִּי -- Psalm 31:5

מָעוּזָּם -- Psalm 37:39

מָעוּזִּי -- Psalm 43:2 (*defective* in MSS)

כְּבוּדָּה -- Psalm 45:14

יְסוּבֵּנִי -- Psalm 49:6

מָעוּזּוֹ -- Psalm 52:9

עוּזָּה -- Psalm 68:29 (preceded by עֻזְּךָ)

הוּלָּלוּ -- Psalm 78:63

עוּזֵּנוּ -- Psalm 81:2

הוּכָּה -- Psalm 102:5

וּגְדוּלָּתְךָ -- Psalm 145:6

יוּלָּד -- Job 5:7

עֲרוּמִּים -- Job 22:6 (There is no *dageš* at Job 5:12, 15:5.)

The other Writings contain fourteen instances:

הַגְּאוּלָּה -- Ruth 4:7

גּוּמָּץ -- Qohelet 10:8

גְּדוּלָּתוֹ -- Esther 1:4

וּגְדוּלָּה -- Esther 6:3

לְמָעוּזִּי -- Daniel 11:19

וְתוּמִּים -- Nehemiah 7:65

בּוּנִּי -- Nehemiah 11:15

נוּלְּדוּ -- 1 Chronicles 3:5; 20:8

הַגְּדוּלָּה -- 1 Chronicles 17:19

אַלְגוּמִּים -- 2 Chronicles 2:7; 9:10,11

וְתוּכִּיִּים -- 2 Chronicles 9:21

The Aramaic has five examples:

תְהוֹדְעוּנַּנִי -- Daniel 2:5

וְסוּפֹנְיָה -- Daniel 3:10

יְבַהֲלוּנֵּה -- Daniel 5:6

יְטַעֲמוּנֵּה -- Daniel 5:21

יְשַׁמְּשׁוּנֵּה -- Daniel 7:10

The sixty cases of the *plene* spelling of short /u/ are spread fairly evenly through the Bible. They are so anomalous that we may suspect that they are "mixed." The doubling of the consonant in words like *gĕdullā* preserves the short /u/. Otherwise it would be *gĕdūlā*. The mixed spelling permits either of these readings.

3.4.3. The *plene* spelling of short /o/. When a *mater lectionis* ʾ or ו is used to write short /i/ or /u/, the masoretic pointing treats the vowels as if they were long. Having only *ḥireq* for long and short /i/, there was no choice. But the masoretes did not use *qibbūṣ* for short /u/ when it was spelled *plene*, as they might have done, and as they were obliged to do when long /ū/ was spelled *defective*. As a result both long and short /u/ can be spelled either *defective* or *plene*. The situation is different again with short /o/. Strictly speaking, there is no such vowel in the Tiberian system. *Qameṣ* was used for long /ā/ and short /o/ because they were phonetically similar, even though historically different. Short /o/ is usually a reflex of primal short /u/ when unstressed, so it is morphophonemically related to /ō/ ← *ú. When short /o/ is spelled *plene*, it is not an alternative spelling of the same word in the usual sense. It is rather the result of a choice between two different words, different because of difference in stress. The evidence of the Qumran texts, where this kind of spelling is quite common, suggests a tradition in which these vowels were perceptibly longer than the ordinary under stress, or an orthographic tradition in which the choice of *plene* spelling registered stress as such.

This raises the question of the extent to which the same kind of spelling in the Bible is due to a similar attitude on the part of copyists. In all such instances the Tiberian system has not recognized the *mater lectionis* and has usually eliminated it in *qere*. But not always. In Jeremiah 27:20 יכוניה occurs without *qere* in C, L, A; יכניה in P. Breuer's edition has *qere*.

Because we have the facility to read either the *ketib* or the *qere* text, we are able to keep track of these alternatives. (Frensdorff 1876: 362; Ginsburg 1867b: 182).

במותי -- Deuteronomy 32:13

אכרות -- Joshua 9:7; contrast Isaiah 61:8.

לשאול -- 1 Samuel 22:15

לשפוך -- 1 Samuel 25:31 (L has לשפך.)

קסומי -- 1 Samuel 28:8 (not in Frensdorff)

אשקטה -- Isaiah 18:4

יעבור -- Isaiah 26:20

לכרות -- Isaiah 44:14 (in P)

יסגוד -- Isaiah 44:17 (not in Frensdorff)

במותי -- Isaiah 58:14 (not in Frensdorff nor Ginsburg)

אצורך -- Jeremiah 1:5 (not in Frensdorff)

לכול -- Jeremiah 33:8

כסוס -- Ezekiel 21:28

כתוב -- Ezekiel 24:2

והובנים -- Ezekiel 27:15

לאכול -- Ezekiel 44:3

אכתוב -- Hosea 8:12 (not in Frensdorff)

עבור -- Amos 7:8; 8:2

   Both are in Ginsburg (n.3); the first is in Frensdorff; neither L nor P have them.

במותי -- Micah 1:3

   This is not in Frensdorff; P has במתי without any note.

וגדול -- Nahum 1:3

לעבור -- Nahum 2:1

תדרוש -- Psalm 10:15 (L has no *qere*.)

אשמור -- Psalm 89:29

מלושני -- Psalm 101:5

וגדול -- Psalm 145:8 (Hahn)

   Ginsburg, L, A, and Snaith have גדל. See Mm 3440.

יקצור -- Proverbs 22:8

טהור -- Proverbs 22:11

יפול -- Proverbs 22:14

ואשקולה -- Ezra 8:25

אשדודיות -- Nehemiah 13:23

עמוניות -- Nehemiah 13:23

ורוהגה -- 1 Chronicles 7:34

לשאול -- 1 Chronicles 18:10

תוקהת -- 2 Chronicles 34:22

למעול -- 2 Chronicles 36:14

Five of these thirty-six cases occur in the Primary History, seventeen in the Latter Prophets, fourteen in the Writings.

3.4.4. Some of the instances of the use of י to spell short /i/ and of the use of ו to spell short /o/ or /u/ are textually dubious. The *plene* spelling of indubitably short vowels is rare. Considering that the texts were copied so many times during the ages when these later spellings were in vogue, it is astonishing that the Bible does not contain more of them. We do not consider that the few sporadic deviations from standard spelling represent a real option. While such deviations could represent a variant pronunciation in the dialect of a scribe, in which the vowels in question were longer than usual, this is outside our control. Our study is restricted to vowels which the masoretes took to be long.

Chapter 4. Theories of Masoretic Text Orthography

In this chapter we present several ideas about spelling practice. We investigate three theories of text transmission, developing one general theory. And we set the stage for Chapters 5 through 7, which describe the data preparation necessary for evaluating the general theory.

4.1 A spelling hypothesis

For simplicity, the history of a written text may be considered to run from the autograph's scribe through some indeterminate number of copyists, to the manuscript in hand.

Unless the first scribe was aware of historical spelling changes and wished to simulate antiquity, the autograph reflects the spelling practice of the scribe and of his time and place. We shall assume no attempts at archaizing have been made. Under this assumption, having the autograph would allow determination of epoch (and, perhaps, provenance).

How *might* the *autograph writer* decide on an item's spelling? Scribes were not walking dictionaries. A plausible spelling procedure might involve two approaches: 1) ready access to the memorized spelling of frequently used items (or items of great significance), 2) knowledge of orthographic shapes allowing analogical spelling of infrequent items. One might expect that the former approach would give way to the latter over some ill-defined range of frequency of occurrence *typical of a given scribe*. And one might expect frequent items to behave differently from infrequent ones.

If and when a subsequent *copyist* made a spelling decision, he first had to recognize the word. The full identity of any encountered word required knowledge of the vowels to be supplied to the written consonants. It is likely that this knowledge existed as oral tradition in the Bible-reading community, even if not absolutely fixed for every word. Indeed, it has been argued that the text existed primarily in this oral form with the (less complete) written form serving as an aid to memory (Diakonoff 1976). This puts limitations on our capacity now to recover the phonology of a language which we know only through such texts. It is therefore psychologically unreal to represent the copyist or translator as a kind of codebreaker, who worked out each time what the vocalization was or, perhaps, if he could manage without it, left out that step and worked directly from an unvocalized text (Barr 1967b).

4.2 Theories of textual transmission

We, of course, have a copy of a copy of... The copyists' care determines what we see. As far as orthography is concerned, five change mechanisms may operate during copying:

1) Intentional updating, be it thoroughgoing or haphazard, tends to replace older forms by newer forms.

2) Aesthetic improvement, based on some changeable norm of what constitutes a beautiful form, might suppress one of a pair of otherwise adjacent graphemes, and so on. (See § 4.7 below.)

3) Simple errors (misreading, miswriting, as in inadvertent modernization) work in either direction but might be expected mainly to introduce new *plenes*. (See §§ 4.8 and 4.9 below.)

4) "Correction" of previous "errors," based on collational study, self-evidence, and double-checking, has an outcome strongly dependent on the scribe's *competence* and reverence for his original.

Correction within **L** can be seen at Isaiah 33:7,
where חוּצָה has been changed to חֻצָּה by expunging
the unwanted ו, leaving an obvious gap.

5) Hypercorrection (when limited knowledge of spelling conventions of rare words or misidentification
leads to wrong application of a spelling rule) introduces further errors.

Different notions as to the extent to which these change
mechanisms have affected the text lead to differing theories of
transmission. At one extreme is the *error-free theory*, which
posits that the error mechanisms were so defeated that the
text was transmitted unscathed. At the other extreme is the
indifference (and/or incompetence) theory, which posits that
the change mechanisms operated so extensively over so many
copyings that our received texts are devoid of reliable historical orthographic information. Were the former theory correct,
we would expect texts from similar epochs to exhibit homogeneous spelling practices. Were the latter theory correct, we
would expect all texts to exhibit orthography independent of
their origins, the original spelling having long since been randomized by copyist changes. These extreme theories make no
allowance for changing scribal practice over the life of a text.
The *mixed theory* posits that the incidence of changes
decreases over time. Early in the transmission process modern-
izing may take place, either systematically or haphazardly.
Alteration of spelling may be viewed as an appropriate copyist
function, and so on. As the text inspires increasing reverence,
these activities are inhibited and greater care is exercised to
avoid introducing errors. Copyist errors are still made but not
so extensively as to blot out all traces of historical practice.
The evidence cited in Chapters 2 and 3 leads us to suspect this
theory likely best accounts for the facts. If properly formulat-
ed, its limit forms will be the two extremes presented above.
So, in evaluating the *mixed theory*, either extreme can result if
the facts warrant. What data are relevant to statistical

analyses that might allow us convincingly to choose among our three theories of transmission?

4.3 Spelling options as scribal opportunities

The text contains two kinds of vowels -- vowels which present the author or scribe with an opportunity to make a choice between *defective* and *plene* spelling and vowels which present no such opportunity.

We are interested only in vowels which could have been spelled either way. All others can be left out of consideration. It is desirable, in fact, to set aside ineligible vowels; their presence in the text dilutes the sample while contributing nothing to our knowledge of spelling alternatives. (However, they are part of the context in which candidates for scribal choice are immersed.) In Chapter 5, we describe in detail the winnowing process used to eliminate non-opportunities for scribal choice.

4.4 Features of scribal opportunities

In the study that follows, each opportunity presented in the text to write a long vowel either *defective* or *plene* is classified using four features: type, stress, portion, and orthographic choice made. We shall here briefly reiterate the meaning of each of these features and will fill in details in Chapters 6 and 7. (Our analogy in § 1.7 involved these features.)

    1) The type of vowel under investigation is given in terms of a system of classification based on historical and morphophonemic considerations. In Chapter 6, sixty-five types are defined and discussed.

    2) The relative stress placed on a vowel may also influence spelling choice (§ 1.6). In Chapter 6, the vowel-type census includes stress levels.

    3) Text portion is the part of the Bible in which the

vowel is found. In Chapter 7, seventy-six portions are specified.

4) Spelling choice indicates whether *defective* or *plene* spelling was used.

These four features are by no means exhaustive. One can conceive of spelling being affected by item frequency, by genre, by adjacent graphemes, and so on; the four features introduced above have been selected as likely the four most important independent interacting variables. The possible influence of proximity, frequency, and stress are discussed in Chapter 8.

Our central goal is to determine, for each type and stress level, the patterns of spelling found in various portions of text.

In the remainder of this chapter, we shall develop a *mixed theory* of text generation/transmission. We shall then use it as a vehicle for examining various mechanisms that have been proposed to account for spelling practice; the outcomes of these examinations will allow us to simplify the theory. Next, we shall use it to illuminate the *error-free theory*. Finally, we shall use it to assess what aspects of spelling practice can and cannot be recovered from L.

4.5 Text transmission and information theory

The fundamental matters we would prefer to study are the initial orthography of our texts and how that orthography changed in the process of transmission. What influences operated on the texts in their passage from "then" to "now"? Can the received orthography be used to cluster the portions in some helpful manner? Some concepts from information theory are admirably suited for such investigations. As Richard Hamming remarks (1980: 129), information theory is concerned "with sending information from here to there (transmission), or from now to then (storage)."

In information theory, a general communication system is analyzed in terms of five basic entities:

1) a *source* which produces the information to be communicated;

2) an *encoder* which converts the information into a signal suitable for transmission;

3) a *channel* through which the signal is sent;

4) a *decoder* which converts the received signal back into a readily intelligible form;

5) a *sink* which uses the transmitted information.

To get a feel for these concepts, consider the case of radio broadcasting: the announcer is the source; the radio station is the encoder (encoding the speech-produced air pressure fluctuations as variations in the transmitter's carrier); the path between transmitter and receiver is the channel; the receiver is the decoder; and the listener is the sink.

Our text-transmission system also has the five components of a general communication system:

1) the portion's creator is the information source;

2) the writer of the autograph is the encoder;

3) the many copyists who relayed the text through time make up the channel;

4) the masorete who fixed the pointing of the text we have received can be viewed as the decoder;

5) we are the information sink.

Standard sorts of problems addressed by information theory include:

1) removal of excess redundancy during encoding so that channel capacity is not wasted;

2) matching the channel capacity to the source's rate of information production so that parts of the message are not lost;

3) encoding redundancy into the data stream so that the decoder can recover the message in spite of any noise introduced by the channel.

Telephony provides instances of each sort of problem:

1) "Telephone speech" is readily identifiable as such, in part because some of its high-frequency components have been suppressed so the voice requires less channel capacity.

2) Multiple telephone lines are often used to link a concert hall with a radio station for live broadcast, since a single line hasn't sufficient capacity to convey music with adequate fidelity.

3) One can often understand a speaker in spite of noise, because natural language involves redundancies that allow meaning to be extracted from noise-corrupted utterances. (Subject-verb agreement is an example of such redundancy.)

Below, we shall introduce a few of the fundamentals of information theory. We shall use them to formulate and begin investigation of our *mixed theory* of text transmission.

4.6 Markov processes

Information theory is at base a statistical way of studying communications systems; one examines the statistics of *ensembles* of signals as they are encoded, transmitted, and decoded. The mathematics for approaching language from a statistical perspective are highly developed in the theory of Markov processes (Hamming 1980; Isaacson and Madsen 1976). Because of the long-range dependences that may exist between the words of any discourse, a full statistical treatment can be very complex. Since we wish to describe only the orthography of a text, we are able to use quite simple models. It is reasonable to expect spelling dependences to be of a much shorter range than overall word dependences. Also, because texts use a finite alphabet for communicating information, their elementary statistical treatment involves algebra rather than calculus.

Suppose we have seen the text up to some point and wish to guess what the next letter will be. (We wish a probabilistic model of text generation.) Suppose our alphabet consists of a total of A symbols (A stands for some number): $s_1, s_2, ..., s_i, ..., s_A$. If all we knew about the language involved was the size of its alphabet, our best guess would be that the letters were equiprobable, so that guessing any particular one would be unjustified. In symbols, we would write:

$$p(s_i) = 1/A \text{ for } i = 1, 2, ..., A, \qquad (4.1)$$

$p(s_i)$ being the probability of occurrence of letter s_i. (In words: The probability of encountering symbol s_i equals one divided by A, the size of the alphabet.) Equation 4.1 holds in the equiprobable case, since the A equal probabilities must sum to unity, it being certain that some symbol will be generated (assuming we have not reached the end of the text).

The crude uniform statistical model of text generation can be improved on if we scan a large text and estimate the actual probabilities of occurrence of the various symbols. For English texts, $p(a) \approx .080$, $p(b) \approx .015$, and so on. ($\approx$ means "is approximately equal to.") Thus, there are about eighty chances in a thousand of seeing an a in any position and fifteen chances in a thousand of seeing a b. (In the literature, these probabilities are termed one-gram or unigram probabilities, since they give the probability of seeing a particular single grapheme [Suen 1979].)

This model still is insufficient since we know, for example, that in English a q will (almost) inevitably be followed by a u. The probabilistic embodiment of this dependence is the concept of conditional probability written $p(s_i | s_{i-1})$: the probability of seeing symbol s_i is conditioned by which symbol immediately preceded it, s_{i-1}. Thus, in terms of a conditional probability, our observation about qu would read $p(u | q) \approx 1$. (In words: The probability of a u following a q is approximately unity.) This dependence of the probability of an event only on its immediate predecessor is termed the *first-order Markov property*. (The model using only simple probabilities in the preceding paragraph is zeroth-order Markov.)

If longer-range dependences need considering, one may define higher-order Markov conditional probabilities. Thus, $p(s_i | s_{i-2}, s_{i-1})$ is the probability of observing s_i, given that its immediate predecessors are s_{i-2} and s_{i-1}. Consider an example from English: the probability of d following an is $p(d | a,n) \approx .6$ (Suen 1979). In summary, if the probability of an event depends on the identity of the previous k events, we have a kth-order Markov process.

The concept of a Markov process will be used to characterize both the source-encoder and the transmission channel.

4.7 The nature of the source-encoder

Suppose the encoder has an alphabet of size A and is Markov of order k. Then to specify the full model, one uses A^{k+1} conditional probabilities, there being A^k possible predecessor strings and A possible next symbols. Thus, if Hebrew consonantal text generation required a fifth-order model over an alphabet of twenty-three symbols (א through ת plus space), one would use 148,035,889 conditional probabilities. A zeroth-order Markov source would use twenty-three simple probabilities. A low-order Markov model is devoutly to be sought. Therefore, we now turn to an examination of the minimal order needed in our model's Markov process.

In theory, the vowel orthography used at any point in a text might depend on remote and/or close-by words, word affixes, spellings in adjacent syllables, and/or adjacent consonants. If some nearby event forces a spelling choice, a spelling rule is said to be operating. Viewed probabilistically, if the presence of X requires the use of Y, the "law" is $p(Y|X) = 1$. For example, if w represents some word, then it may be that $p(s_i|w) \approx 1$; that is, symbol s_i almost always is used in word w. (Such invariant word spellings are discussed in § 5.6.3.)

Gesenius-Kautzsch-Cowley (GKC 1910: § 8k-l) make four laconic assertions regarding vowel-spelling conditioning factors which cover the possibilities well and which translate neatly into statements about the source-encoder Markov probabilities. Let V_d and V_p stand, respectively, for any *defective* and *plene* vowels, let W stand for ﬡ, let Y stand for ﬡ, and let C stand for any consonant. Then the assertions and their probabilistic approximants are: 1) Word-terminal vowels are *plene*. That is: $q(V_d|space) \approx 0$. The q-notation is used for a *backward* Markov process (Feller 1968: 414). This expression asserts that in reading the text backward, the probability of seeing a space and then a defectively written vowel is approximately zero. 2) *Defective* writing is common when using the *plene* would have resulted in the repetition of a grapheme. We take this to imply that: $p(W_d|W) \gg p(W_p|W)$ and $p(Y_d|Y) \gg p(Y_p|Y)$. ($\gg$ means "is much greater than.") 3) *Plene* in successive syllables is avoided. That is: $p(V_p|V_p,C) \ll 1$ and $q(V_p|V_p,C) \ll 1$. ($\ll$ means "is much less than.") Here we ignore the difficulties produced by *shewa quiescens*. 4) In the later books *plene* "is more usual" while *defective* "is more usual" in the earlier. (This assertion is the topic of our book.)

The first two assertions imply first-order Markov models, since they specify situations where the spelling used is conditioned by the adjacent symbol. The third assertion appears to imply a second-order model.

Although we have couched GKC's assertions in terms of encoder-model probabilities, GKC make no distinction between encoder and channel. They are describing the output resulting from the passage of the encoded source information through the (as-yet unspecified) channel. Therefore, we examine their

assertions in terms of our *ketib* transcription of the *complete* L
to see if the evidence supports them. Whether the received data
reflect the encoder characteristics will be examined below.

1) $q(V_d | space) \approx 0$. GKC lists seven instances of words
ending in a *defective* vowel. They give גּוֹ at Jeremiah 26:6,
44:8; Ezra 6:21; 2 Chronicles 32:13; we find this form at Ezra
6:21; 2 Chronicles 32:13, 17. They give גּוֹ at Zephaniah 2:9,
while L has גּוֹי as *ketib* modified by *qere* to גּוֹיִי. We agree that
Isaiah 40:31 has וְקֹוֵי. In Jeremiah 38:11, they report בְּלֹוֹי; we
find it there twice. Of 55,439 words ending in *plene*-able vowels,
only six are *defective*. Thus, since we remove these vowels from
our data on the grounds of their being rule-governed, this situation is irrelevant for our choice of the minimal Markovian order
needed to model the remaining data. (See § 5.6.4.)

2a) $p(W_d | W) \gg p(W_p | W)$. Of the 523 tokens that involve a
consonantal ו followed by vowel וֹ or וּ, only 110 are *plene*
(twenty-one percent). Thus $p(W_d | W) = .79$ and $p(W_p | W) = .21$.
The assertion is true. Such forms involving ו make up only 0.5
percent of all opportunities. Therefore, leaving these items in
our data and, for simplicity, approximating the first-order Markovian dependence by a zeroth-order Markovian dependence
will have a negligible overall effect.

2b) $p(Y_d | Y) \gg p(Y_p | Y)$. Of the 18,688 tokens that involve
a consonantal י followed by vowel יִ, יֵ, or יֶ, 725 are *plene*
(four percent). Thus we find $p(Y_d | Y) = .96$ and $p(Y_p | Y) = .04$.
The assertion, as stated, is true. However, all but a couple
thousand of these vowels are dropped in Chapter 5 as not involving opportunities for spelling choice. Of the remaining
vowels, about sixty percent are *plene*. Thus, there appears to
be no strong pressure to avoid *plene* spellings, when only true
opportunities for choice are considered.

3) $p(V_p | V_p, C) \ll 1$ and $q(V_p | V_p, C) \ll 1$. The probability
statements assert that *plene* vowels rarely occur in adjacent
syllables. (GKC reads: "*Scriptio plena* in two successive

syllables was generally avoided.") As noted earlier, our data allow us only to investigate this matter for open syllables, since we write all *shewas* identically. The complete *ketib* text of L includes 67,844 pairs of opportunity vowels in VCV contexts. Two of the examples cited by GKC do show a lack of *plene* pairing. The form קוֹלֹת* never occurs. (The underlying word appears twelve times, never doubly *plene*. See § 2.3.6.) And in 218 occurrences, יְהוֹשֻׁעַ is doubly *plene* only twice. (As was noted previously, the names of major players tend to have fixed, conservative spelling, with the notable exception of דָּוִיד.) The example of מְצָאָהוּ and מְצָאַנִי is of little force, since it only occurs nine times. However, six of these are doubly *plene*. נְבִיאִים and צַדִּיקִים also are more often doubly *plene* than not: the former is doubly *plene* in sixty-four of its one hundred occurrences, and the latter is doubly *plene* in fifty of its sixty occurrences.

Table 4.1 shows the distribution of doubly *defective*, *defective-plene*, *plene-defective*, and doubly *plene* opportunities in VCV strings in sections of the Bible.

Table 4.1 Double-vowel incidence counts

Section	DD	DP	PD	PP	Total
Torah	8953	5100	2403	1533	17989
Former Prophets	7646	4276	1613	1733	15268
Latter Prophets	5869	4496	2342	2702	15409
Poetry	2633	2976	960	1769	8338
Other Writings	4129	3352	1222	2137	10840
Total	29230	20200	8540	9874	67844

Overall, 9,874 of the 67,844 paired instances are doubly *plene* (14.6%). Thus, there are about two-thirds the number of *plenes* in successive syllables as we would expect were the choice of *defective* or *plene* equiprobable. This is hardly evidence that double *plenes* were avoided.

The data summarized in Table 4.1 provide us an occasion to perform contingency table analysis to learn something about the distribution of paired opportunities. (Contingency table analysis was introduced in § 1.7 and following.) Under the model of independence, we would expect the counts to be as shown in Table 4.2.

Table 4.2 Predicted double-vowel incidence

Section	DD	DP	PD	PP	Total
Torah	7750.4	5356.1	2264.4	2618.1	17989.0
Former Prophets	6578.1	4545.9	1921.9	2222.1	15268.0
Latter Prophets	6638.8	4587.9	1939.6	2242.6	15409.0
Poetry	3592.4	2482.6	1049.6	1213.5	8338.0
Other Writings	4670.3	3227.5	1364.5	1577.6	10840.0
Total	29230.0	20200.0	8540.0	9874.0	67844.0

We find that $\chi^2_{99\%} = 26 \ll \chi^2 = 2169.4$, suggesting there is strong evidence that our data are not spread evenly across our categories. But the association between section and kind of vowel pair is not strong. Cramér's v equals .18.

The standardized residuals are shown in Table 4.3.

Table 4.3 Double-vowel standardized residuals

Section	DD	DP	PD	PP
Torah	+13.66	-3.50	+2.91	-21.21
Former Prophets	+13.17	-4.00	-7.05	-10.38
Latter Prophets	-9.45	-1.36	+9.14	+9.70
Poetry	-16.01	+9.90	-2.76	+15.95
Other Writings	-7.92	+2.19	-3.86	+14.08

For twelve degrees of freedom, the outlier threshold $r_{99\%} = 1.14$. We see that the DD realization of paired opportunities goes from overuse to underuse as we pass from Torah to Other Writings. The PP realization goes from underuse to overuse as we pass from Torah to Other Writings. Examining the relative usage within sections, we see that the Primary History overuses DD and underuses PP, while the other sections do the reverse.

To summarize: We have seen that the first GKC assertion is correct, justifying our removal of word-terminal vowels from our data. We have also seen that their second assertion holds for ו (for a very small collection of vowels) but is not true for י when only situations involving opportunities for choice are considered. And we have seen that their third assertion is not borne out by the evidence. We have thus seen that the reduced data do not exhibit significant non-zeroth-order Markov dependences. Properly speaking, this may be because the sources are zeroth-order Markov or because the channel destroyed higher-order Markovian source dependences. (How this can occur will become clear below.) In the interest of simplicity, we model the encoder as a *zeroth-order* Markov generator.

We are not interested in studying the incidence of the various vowel types to be defined in Chapter 6. Rather, we wish to study how choices were made in spelling each type. When the information source called for a certain vowel type, how did the encoder write it, *defective* or *plene*? How did the channel transmit it? To address these questions, we study each vowel type in each portion. The spelling used by the *encoder* (the autograph's scribe, copyist zero) of portion p for vowel type t is characterized statistically by the simple Markov probabilities $p_{pt}^{(0)}(D)$ and $p_{pt}^{(0)}(P)$, which are the probabilities that the encoder of portion p "wrote" vowel type t *defective* and *plene*, respectively. (Of course, for a *defective* spelling, nothing was written in the consonantal text.) Rather than complicate all the equations with repetitious subscripts, we shall henceforth drop the subscripts pt, with the understanding that they apply to all probabilities introduced. Since either *defective* or *plene* must be used, we write:

$$p^{(0)}(D) + p^{(0)}(P) = 1 \qquad\qquad (4.2)$$

(In words: For portion p and vowel type t, the probability of encoding a *defective* plus the probability of encoding a *plene* must equal unity.) For each portion, the encoder spelling practice for each vowel type is given once we know either of the generation probabilities, since the other can be obtained from the foregoing equation. (The probabilities are often referred to collectively as the source statistics.)

4.8 Description of the channel

The actual channel our portions passed through doubtless was quite complicated. Before the Masoretic Era, the information was relayed in parallel written and oral sub-channels. Further, many copyists were at work at any time, giving rise to multiple pairs of sub-channels. Also, early on, there may have been local text types (Cross 1985), each with its own idiosyncrasies. Finally, the masoretes collated various manuscripts to produce the texts we have received. Rather than formulating a complex theory including all possible phenomena and then simplifying it to allow useful insights, we shall attempt only to characterize the copyists' activities. We distinguish *updaters* from *copyists*. The former may "improve" the aesthetics or modernize the spelling of the documents being relayed. The latter strive to reproduce exactly the texts being copied. For the former, changes may be intentional or accidental, for the latter, accidental only. We are forced to lump the updaters with the encoders, since a late updater could so transform a text as to abolish the orthographic imprint of the original encoder. In terms of the generation probabilities introduced above, this amounts to observing that the updating of the spelling of a vowel type would change the encoder's probabilities, $p^{(0)}(D)$ and $p^{(0)}(P)$, into those characteristic of the updater. Thus, suppose a late updater modernized the spelling of type t' in portion p; then the probabilities describing all the other types would remain unchanged while those of type t' would become modern. Therefore, when we studied the portions, we would be misled by statistical anomalies introduced by updaters. This is an unfortunate fact about updating activity that there is no way around.

As we shall see, the effects of the copyists can also hide all evidence of the encoders' original statistics. But their activities are less pernicious than the updaters', since the changes they introduce erode the text rather than transforming it wholesale. We have seen that the encoders' activities can be modeled by zeroth-order Markov processes. The copyists' activities can be modeled as first-order Markov processes. To do so requires only a slight reinterpretation of the conditional probabilities introduced above. Suppose the copyist did his best simply to copy the graphemes before him. (If he indulged in "cosmetic improvements," Markov models of order higher than one would be needed to describe his functioning.) Let us assume that in dealing with a type t vowel, the copyist reproduced a type t vowel with the same or changed spelling. This assumption makes the model far simpler, but it ignores the possibility that a ٱ might have been copied as a ٭ and so on. Having assumed "type preservation," the work of a given copyist is characterized by four probabilities for each type:

$p^{(c)}(D|D)$, the probability that copyist c was given a *defective* type t vowel in portion p and "wrote" it *defective*.

$p^{(c)}(P|D)$, the probability that copyist c was given a *defective* type t vowel in portion p and wrote it *plene*.

$p^{(c)}(D|P)$, the probability that copyist c was given a *plene* type t vowel in portion p and "wrote" it *defective*.

$p^{(c)}(P|P)$, the probability that copyist c was given a *plene* type t vowel in portion p and wrote it *plene*.

Each pair of probabilities must sum to unity. In copying a *defective* vowel:

$$p^{(c)}(D \mid D) + p^{(c)}(P \mid D) = 1 \qquad (4.3)$$

since a *defective* vowel must emerge either *defective* or *plene*. And in copying a *plene* vowel:

$$p^{(c)}(D \mid P) + p^{(c)}(P \mid P) = 1 \qquad (4.4)$$

since a *plene* vowel must emerge either *defective* or *plene*. Knowledge of one probability in each equation suffices to describe a copyist's activity for a given type. If the encoder (or updater) of portion p tended to "write" type t *defective* $p^{(0)}(D)$ of the time and tended to write it *plene* $p^{(0)}(P)$ of the time, then these probabilities of occurrence would describe the original seen by the first copyist. The results after the first copying would be estimated by:

$$p^{(0)}(D)p^{(1)}(D \mid D) + p^{(0)}(P)p^{(1)}(D \mid P) = p^{(1)}(D) \qquad (4.5)$$

(In words: The fraction of *defectives* produced by the encoder, times the probability that a *defective* remains *defective*, plus the fraction of *plenes* produced by the encoder, times the probability that a *plene* gets converted into a *defective*, equals the estimated fraction of *defectives* in the first copy.) Also:

$$p^{(0)}(D)p^{(1)}(P \mid D) + p^{(0)}(P)p^{(1)}(P \mid P) = p^{(1)}(P) \qquad (4.6)$$

These equations assume that the output depends only on the symbol presented as input. We shall investigate one possible departure from this assumption in § 8.2, where we study the effects of proximity on spelling practice. When such channels are connected together so the output of one becomes the input of the next, the resultant structure is termed a *Markov chain*. If the output from copyist c is the input for copyist $c + 1$, equations 4.5 and 4.6 describe the expected output with suitable changes in the superscripts:

$$p^{(c)}(D)p^{(c+1)}(D \mid D) + p^{(c)}(P)p^{(c+1)}(D \mid P) = p^{(c+1)}(D) \quad (4.7)$$

$$p^{(c)}(D)p^{(c+1)}(P \mid D) + p^{(c)}(P)p^{(c+1)}(P \mid P) = p^{(c+1)}(P) \quad (4.8)$$

Each of our portions has passed through the hands of some indeterminate number of copyists, has passed through the

Markov chain associated with that portion. Portions from differing times have passed through differing chains.

4.9 Effects of Markov chains on encoder statistics

We can see what repeated copyings do to the spelling of vowel types by considering several simple situations, ones having the same set of conditional probabilities for each copying stage. That is, we fix the error rates $p^{(c)}(P|D)$ and $p^{(c)}(D|P)$, for all c. Since the errors depend on spelling practice at the time a copyist is working, the true situation doubtless involved differing probabilities for successive copyings.

Let us first see what happens when the error rates associated with each copying are large. For concreteness, suppose we track the spelling of some hypothetical vowel type in four hypothetical text portions. Suppose each portion is copied every fifty years, the latest copy becoming the basis of the next copying. Suppose Portion #1 and Portion #2 are first set down in 900 BCE, Portion #3 and Portion #4 in 400 BCE. Portion #1 has nine hundred *defectives*, while Portion #2 has ninety. The second two portions each have equal numbers of *defective* and *plene* instances of the vowel type being studied. Portion #3 has a total of a thousand such vowels, Portion #4 a hundred.

To magnify channel effects, we use very high error rates: $p^{(c)}(P|D) = .2$ and $p^{(c)}(D|P) = .1$ for all copyists c. That is, eight times out of ten, when a copyist is given a *defective* vowel, he "writes" a *defective* form; two times in ten he mistakenly writes it *plene*. Given a *plene* form, nine times in ten he reproduces it correctly, "writing" it *defective* one time in ten. These choices, though arbitrary, recognize the general trend towards more *plene* spellings by both encoder and copyist.

A contingency table analysis of the initial statistics for Portion #1 and Portion #2 involves the two-by-two table shown as Table 4.4. Hence the analysis involves one degree of freedom.

Here and below, we display counts rather than probabilities. (The count N(D), more properly $N^{(c)}(D)$, is obtained by multiplying $p^{(c)}(D)$ by N, the number of type t vowels in portion p.)

Table 4.4 Initial frequencies, Portion #1 & Portion #2

Portion	N(D)	N(P)	Total
#1	900	100	1000
#2	90	10	100
Total	990	110	1100

Using the model of independence, we find that $\chi^2 = 0$, so Portion #1 and Portion #2 are indeed homogeneous. No surprise.

Comparison of Portion #1 and Portion #3 is more interesting. Table 4.5 shows the initial frequencies.

Table 4.5 Initial frequencies, Portion #1 & Portion #3

Portion	N(D)	N(P)	Total
#1	900	100	1000
#3	500	500	1000
Total	1400	600	2000

Using the model of independence, we find $\chi^2 = 381.0$. Since $\chi^2_{99\%} = 6.63$ (for one degree of freedom), we conclude that Portion #1 and Portion #3 are *not* homogeneous. Cramér's v equals .44.

Table 4.6 shows the hypothetical vowel type undergoing a sequence of identical copying operations. (That each portion has lost a vowel instance is a round-off artifact that need not concern us.)

Table 4.6 Strong chain effects

Date	Portion #1		Portion #2		Portion #3		Portion #4	
	N(D)	N(P)	N(D)	N(P)	N(D)	N(P)	N(D)	N(P)
900 BCE	900	100	90	10				
850 BCE	730	270	73	27				
800 BCE	611	389	61	38				
750 BCE	527	472	52	47				
700 BCE	469	530	46	53				
650 BCE	428	571	42	57				
600 BCE	400	599	40	59				
550 BCE	380	619	38	61				
500 BCE	366	633	36	63				
450 BCE	356	643	35	64				
400 BCE	349	650	34	65	500	500	50	50
350 BCE	344	655	34	65	450	550	45	55
300 BCE	341	658	34	65	415	585	41	58
250 BCE	338	661	33	66	390	609	39	60
200 BCE	337	662	33	66	373	626	37	62
150 BCE	336	663	33	66	361	638	36	63
100 BCE	335	664	33	66	352	647	35	64
50 BCE	334	665	33	66	347	652	34	65
0 CE	334	665	33	66	342	657	34	65
50 CE	333	666	33	66	340	659	34	65
100 CE	333	666	33	66	338	661	33	66
150 CE	333	666	33	66	336	663	33	66
200 CE	333	666	33	66	335	664	33	66
250 CE	333	666	33	66	334	665	33	66
300 CE	333	666	33	66	334	665	33	66
350 CE	333	666	33	66	334	665	33	66
400 CE	333	666	33	66	333	666	33	66

The proportions in the outputs by 400 CE are identical. Equilibrium has been reached: each copyist produces as many *defective*-to-*plene* errors as *plene*-to-*defective* ones. (For Portion #1 we have two-tenths of 333 equals one-tenth of 666.) It is intuitively evident and mathematically demonstrable that there is *no* way to recover source statistics once the channel has reached equilibrium. (If a portion enters the copy chain with its source statistics in equilibrium [that is, with numbers of *defectives* and *plenes* such that errors cause equal numbers to change categories during each copying], the category totals will not be altered by copying, even though *which* items are *defective* and *which* are *plene* may be quite different between input and output.) We can detect if the copy channel has reached equilibrium by examining the outputs for statistical homogeneity.

Our example illustrates that given a sufficient number of shared copyings, the statistics of two received portions can be the same even though one has been in the copy chain much longer than the other. For example, very old poetry and very late narrative might show similar spelling distributions if the shared time in the copy channel (say from just before the Common Era until the Masoretic Era) allowed equilibrium to be reached.

4.10 The *error-free theory*

The *error-free theory* posits that the copy chain introduces no errors into the portions that pass through it. In terms of the Markov-chain parameters, this implies that each copy stage has zero probability of introducing errors. In mathematical terms, this requires:

$$p^{(c)}(P|D) = p^{(c)}(D|P) = 0 \text{ for all } c \qquad (4.9)$$

In light of the variable orthography in the manuscripts, this absolute theory is not tenable. It is, however, reasonable to ask how far from zero the error probabilities were.

If the error probabilities used to generate Table 4.6 are greatly reduced, then the results of successive copyings are as shown in Table 4.7. Again we display counts rather than probabilities. In this case we have selected modest error rates: $p^{(c)}(P|D) = .02$ and $p^{(c)}(D|P) = .01$ for all copyists c. Over the long run, ninety-eight times out of a hundred, when a copyist is given a *defective* vowel, he will "write" a *defective* form; two times in a hundred he will mistakenly write it *plene*. When given a *plene* form, ninety-nine times in a hundred he will reproduce it correctly, "writing" it *defective* one time in a hundred.

Table 4.7 Weak chain effects

Date	Portion #1		Portion #2		Portion #3		Portion #4	
	N(D)	N(P)	N(D)	N(P)	N(D)	N(P)	N(D)	N(P)
900 BCE	900	100	90	10				
850 BCE	883	117	88	11				
800 BCE	866	133	86	13				
750 BCE	850	149	85	14				
700 BCE	834	165	83	16				
650 BCE	819	180	81	18				
600 BCE	805	194	80	19				
550 BCE	791	208	79	20				
500 BCE	777	222	77	22				
450 BCE	764	235	76	23				
400 BCE	751	248	75	24	500	500	50	50
350 BCE	738	261	73	26	495	505	49	50
300 BCE	726	273	72	27	490	509	49	50
250 BCE	714	285	71	28	485	514	48	51
200 BCE	703	296	70	29	480	519	48	51
150 BCE	692	307	69	30	476	523	47	52
100 BCE	681	318	68	31	472	527	47	52
50 BCE	670	329	67	32	467	532	46	53
0 CE	660	339	66	33	463	536	46	53
50 CE	651	348	65	34	460	539	46	53
100 CE	641	358	64	35	456	543	45	54
150 CE	632	367	63	36	452	547	45	54
200 CE	623	376	62	37	448	551	44	55
250 CE	614	385	61	38	445	554	44	55
300 CE	606	393	60	39	442	557	44	55
350 CE	597	402	59	40	438	561	43	56
400 CE	590	409	59	40	435	564	43	56

Because the channel effects are not as strong as previously, the texts received in 400 CE allow partitioning into affinity groups. Contingency table analysis confirms intuition, demonstrating that Portion #1 and Portion #2 *as received in 400 CE* are homogeneous, as are Portion #3 and Portion #4.

Note, however, that the proportions of *defectives* to *plenes* are quite different from those at the inputs, due to channel errors. While we can cluster the texts into groups, the observed spelling practices at the channel output do not mirror those at the channel input.

Deciding whether Portion #1 and Portion #3 are homogeneous at the output requires a contingency table analysis. Table 4.8 shows the chain output frequencies.

Table 4.8 Final frequencies, Portion #1 & Portion #3

Portion	N(D)	N(P)	Total
#1	590	409	999
#3	435	564	999
Total	1025	973	1998

Using the model of independence, we find that $\chi^2 = 48.1$, and since $\chi^2_{99\%} = 6.63$ (for one degree of freedom) we conclude that Portion #1 and Portion #3 are *not* homogeneous. Cramér's v now equals .16, whereas it equalled .44 at the input. The channel has substantially reduced the degree of association between the portion and spelling choice variables.

As was noted at the beginning of § 4.9, successive copyings likely involved differing error probabilities. Analysis of this situation involves the theory of nonstationary Markov chains (Isaacson & Madsen 1976: 136). When such chains converge with loss of memory (akin to the stationary chain example shown in Table 4.6), their outputs exhibit complete independence (Harary, Lipstein, and Styan 1970: 1169). It is then legal to test the (null) hypothesis that the resulting portions are homogeneous (by virtue of equilibrium having been reached) via contingency table analysis (Bishop, Fienberg, and Holland 1975: 62).

4.11 Source-encoder and channel separability

We have presented a simplified theory of text transmission involving zeroth-order Markov encoders and first-order Markov channels. We have seen that encoder characteristics may survive passage through the copying chain, but we will only be in a position to demonstrate that such survival has occurred for L in Chapter 9. A basic question remains: can encoder and copyist effects be separated? Algebraic arguments show that the cascade of channels is characterized by four conditional probabilities describing the complete chain (Parzen 1962: 197; Isaacson and Madsen 1976: Chapter V).

If the superscript C refers to the entire chain, then the relevant equations for the *chain* outputs are:

$$p^{(0)}(D)p^{(C)}(D\,|\,D) + p^{(0)}(P)p^{(C)}(D\,|\,P) = p^{(C)}(D) \qquad (4.10)$$

$$p^{(0)}(D)p^{(C)}(P\,|\,D) + p^{(0)}(P)p^{(C)}(P\,|\,P) = p^{(C)}(P) \qquad (4.11)$$

In words, equation 4.10 reads: The fraction of *defectives* produced by the portion's encoder, times the probability that a *defective* remained *defective* in passing through the chain occupied by portion p, plus the fraction of *plenes* produced by the encoder, times the probability that a *plene* got converted into a *defective* in passing through the chain occupied by portion p, equals the estimated fraction of *defectives* out of the chain.

The characteristics of the encoder of portion p for type t vowels are given by $p^{(0)}(D)$ and $p^{(0)}(P)$, the fractions of *defective* and *plene* type t vowels likely used by the encoder of portion p. These source statistics obey equation 4.2, as must the chain outputs with the superscript 0 replaced by C. The characteristics of the complete Markov chain transited by portion p type t vowels are given by the four conditional probabilities $p^{(C)}(D\,|\,D)$, $p^{(C)}(D\,|\,P)$, $p^{(C)}(P\,|\,D)$, and $p^{(C)}(P\,|\,P)$. Pairs of conditionals must add to unity, must obey equations 4.3 and 4.4 with c replaced by C. Equations 4.2-4.4 can be used to eliminate one input (encoder) probability, one output probability, and two of the conditionals in equations 4.10 and 4.11. When the algebraic dust has settled, we are left with *one* equation involving four quantities (an input probability, an output probability, and the two chain error probabilities):

$$p^{(0)}(D)\left[1 - p^{(C)}(P\,|\,D)\right] + \left[1 - p^{(0)}(D)\right]p^{(C)}(D\,|\,P) = p^{(C)}(D) \quad (4.12)$$

We know only $p^{(C)}(D)$. Absent further information, the equation is not solvable. Encoder effects and channel effects cannot be separated. Had we a way of knowing the chain error probabilities, we could solve for the encoder probability, provided the chain had not reached equilibrium. (Solving equation 4.12 yields an expression which evaluates to the indeterminate form $\frac{0}{0}$ when the chain has reached equilibrium.)

We must introduce additional assumptions to make the equation solvable, must put aside the equations and let the data speak to us via other routes, or must accept the combined effects of the channel and encoder in our data and make no attempt to separate channel from encoder effects.

In this book, in Chapters 9 and 10, we shall take the third way and study the channel outputs as we have received them. We shall study portions in terms of their realizations of the various types. This will allow us to cluster our portions in terms of their affinities. The rationale for clustering channel outputs is that, as our equations indicate and our hypothetical examples demonstrate, portions from similar times and places which have similar histories of transmission should emerge from the channel with similar, though modified, orthography.

We next take up three data-preparation tasks. In Chapter 5 we identify and drop from consideration vowels which present no spelling choice. In Chapter 6 we classify the remaining vowels into sixty-five types. In Chapter 7 we divide the Hebrew text into seventy-six portions.

Chapter 5. Vowels Having No Spelling Options

5.1 Conditions specifying fixed spelling

We declare vowels (usually in a specific context) to be non-opportunities for scribal choice when either of two sorts of conditions hold: 1) strong theoretical arguments can be produced that they involve no option for spelling choice, or 2) they appear very frequently and are almost always spelled one way, so that one may conclude that their spelling is fixed in practice. (We say "almost always" because transcription errors can introduce rare spurious instances.)

Certain vowels are never candidates for *plene* spelling: *shewa* and the *hatefs*; but also *patah*. *Patah* might be considered phonetically long under stress in certain word positions by analogy with other vowels which are certainly long in similar positions. The primal short vowels /i/, /a/, and /u/ have similar histories. In shut unstressed syllables they generally remain unchanged, or at least short. (/a/ can be deflected to /i/ by the Barth-Ginsberg dissimilation, or to /ɛ/ by various assimilations or dissimilations.) But under stress all three undergo a change in mouth position, becoming more central, and are presumed also to lengthen (*í* → *ē*, *a* → *ā*, and *u* → *ō*). But in verbs such as *qāṭál*, and in some segolate nouns, *patah* is retained under stress. In matching forms, such as *kābēd* and *qāṭōn*, the stressed vowel is considered long. There are three ways of handling this inconsistency: 1) Admit an inconsistency in the sound system, with otherwise identical word shapes having vowels of differing length in the same position -- /ē/, /ō/ long, /a/ short. 2) Recognize /a/ as long in such a position because /ē/ and /ō/ are long. 3) Infer that /ē/ and /ō/ in these positions must be short because /a/ is short.

The fact that /ē/ and /ō/ in such positions are rarely spelled *plene* and the fact that *plene* spelling is not used for these vowels in segolate nouns support the third way. No orthographic provision was ever made for distinguishing such a long *pataḥ* (Blau 1976: § 3.6.3.1). Similarly short /i/, /e/, /u/, and *qāmeṣ qāṭōn* in shut unstressed syllables and in analogously structured syllables virtually shut are never *plene* (but see § 3.4 above).

Even if theoretically any of the long vowels might have been spelled *defective* or *plene*, this does not mean that every occurrence of a long vowel presented a writer with a real opportunity to use one or the other kind of spelling.

That could have depended on the kind of vowel or word, or even on the individual word in which it occurred. It could have depended also (and to differing degrees) on such factors as date, locality, and scribal tradition (including conventions that preferred one style of spelling rather than another in a particular kind of literature -- monumental, cultic, secular, informal, etc.). There are some archaic spellings that have been so nearly completely superseded by the later, standard practice that the archaic style can hardly be considered a live option, especially in the generation of new texts, in the later period of formation of biblical manuscripts, and certainly in the main period of their transmission. The surviving occurrences of an archaic spelling are fossils.

An example will illustrate this phenomenon. Hebrew contains many personal names based on -אֲבִי, 'father,' and -אֲחִי, 'brother.' In the inscriptions this long /ī/, when word-medial, was not shown at first in purely consonantal spelling. It is possibly the first attested instance of the *plene* spelling of a word-medial /ī/ in Hebrew (see above, § 2.4). Yet in the Bible the spelling of this vowel is nearly always *plene*. The rare אֲבְגִיל is a fossil. אֲחִיטוּב is twelve times *plene*, three times *defective*.

For some names, the *defective* spelling has survived with different vocalization -- אָבְנֵר alongside אֲבִינֵר. A few other examples: אֶלְצָפָן אֱלִיצָפָן, אַבְשָׁלוֹם אֲבִישָׁלוֹם, אַכְשַׁי אֲבִישַׁי, יַחְצְאֵל יַחֲצִיאֵל, אַשְׂרֵאל אַשְׂרִיאֵל, עַזְרֵאל עַזְרִיאֵל. The scribes misinterpreted such *defective* spellings as if the form were short.

With some words, however, the archaic spelling was never superseded. Thus 'Solomon' is always שְׁלֹמֹה and 'Pharaoh' is always פַּרְעֹה.

If a theoretically possible spelling is never attested, the question is whether that is merely an accident of attestation or whether it represents a real prohibition within the system.

5.2 The forces at work

Several different historical and psychological forces were active, sometimes working against each other. Historically there was a general trend to more and more *plene* spellings. This trend could be arrested or advanced by convention, producing practices so invariant that the standard orthography for some words is uniform, one way or the other. That is, the long vowels in some words are always spelled *defective*, others always *plene*. The forces operated to differing degrees at five different levels of the system.

5.2.1. The first level is that of individual words. An archaic spelling of an individual word may enjoy such prestige as a logogram that it holds its own, even to modern times. The names 'Moses' (× 766), 'Aaron' (× 347), 'Solomon' (× 293), and 'Pharaoh' (× 274) all contain the vowel long /ō/ which is never spelled *plene* in these words in the Bible. The Qumran spellings are consistently מושה, אהרון; פרעוה is found in 1QIs[a]. These four names occur quite frequently, and the significance of the nonoccurrence of *plene* variants can be calculated. Other proper nouns of the same kind are spelled either way, to say nothing about nouns in general -- nouns with unstressed long /ō/ in the penultimate syllable (one does not have to go as far as the folk etymology and identify *Mōšɛh* as a participle), nouns ending in -*ōn*, nouns ending in -*ō*.

But if a word is attested only once -- to go to the other extreme -- obviously only one spelling is known, and the inference that this is an invariant standard spelling is unwarranted. Thus חִזוֹ is *hapax legomenon* (Genesis 22:22); if it occurred a hundred times, who knows how many times it might have been spelled חָזוֹה*? Similarly if a word occurs only two or three times with only one spelling.

5.2.2. The second level is that of a class of words. Looking at all of the proper nouns that end in -*ōn*, or in -*ō*, or which have -*ō* as the first vowel, as in 'Moses,' or even including similar common nouns with them, we find that both kinds of spelling are used. Defining a class of nouns by such a feature will relieve the problems of *hapax legomena* and others with low incidence. If all such nouns were put together into a single set, the words which are spelled with וֹ would be swamped by the abundant and invariant archaic spelling of 'Moses,' 'Aaron,' 'Solomon,' and 'Pharaoh.'

5.2.3. The third level is that of a class of vowels defined on grammatical grounds. On historical grounds (the history of the language) as well as by convention (the history of spelling), one might expect that all the instances of such a vowel would be spelled in the same way. On this level the /ō/'s in all *qal* active participles of type גֹּזֵר would be considered "the same." As a matter of fact, there are 5,309 such /ō/'s, 4,269 spelled *defective*, 1,040 spelled *plene*. Our classification operates mainly on this third level. The definition of such a class is not always straightforward. The word כֹּהֵן, 'priest,' and its derivatives, occurs 750 times, always spelled *defective* in the Bible (against כוהן at Qumran). Was this spelling a fixed convention because the scribes did not feel that this word was a participle for which they exercised the option of *plene* spelling? If so, should such a word be segregated from the rest at the first level as an invariant whose presence among the participles would dilute that set and give a wrong impression of the utilization of the *defective* option?

5.2.4. The fourth level is that of a class of vowels defined on historical grounds. The *plene* spelling of /ō/ ← *aw* is historical; the *defective* spelling is a secondary development. Hence it is appropriate to gather together all the long /ō/'s which share this history. The *qal* active participles mentioned above would then be treated as members of a larger class containing /ō/ ← *ā*.

5.2.5. The fifth level disregards paradigmatic and historical classification and treats all long /ō/'s as "the same" on phonetic-phonemic grounds. This level could be pertinent if it could be shown that scribes made their spelling decisions on phonetic grounds, regardless of historical or morphological factors. This cannot be assumed.

5.3 Elimination of non-opportunities

In practice each long vowel occurs in words or sets of words which fall into three main classes.

5.3.1. The vowel occurs in a commonly occurring word, or in a large well-defined set of words, in which it is almost always spelled *defective*. (The words "almost always" in this statement will be given a more rigorous definition below.) Usually there is a basis for this in the phonological history of the language, or else it represents the establishment of an invariant convention.

5.3.2. The vowel occurs in a commonly occurring word, or in a large well-defined set of words, in which it is almost always spelled *plene*. Again there are likely to be historical reasons for this, but it could be a strong convention.

5.3.3. The vowel occurs in a commonly occurring word, or in a large well-defined set of words, in which the frequency of use of both spelling possibilities points to the existence of a live option. Vowels of this third kind have statistically interesting variability in spelling. They will be the prime object of the ensuing study.

Vowels of the first two kinds, whose spelling is virtually invariant in one way or the other, can be left out of the analysis, but their elimination should not be intuitive or arbitrary. It must be justified. See § 5.6.2.

The elimination of some vowels which have virtually invariant spelling can be justified on historical grounds, since we are mainly interested in the evolution of Hebrew spelling during the most formative period of the biblical text.

5.4 Nonuse of the *plene* option

At the other end of historical development, perhaps only after the close of the biblical period and in the age of scribal transmission, new kinds of spelling began to creep in. The most obvious examples, already discussed above, are the use of *matres lectionis* to spell short vowels (§ 3.4). But there is one kind of long vowel which is so rarely spelled *plene* in the Bible that the few exceptions must be regarded as scribal errors. There are three kinds of segolate nouns in Hebrew, derived from primal forms of type **sipru*, **malku*, and **qudšu*. These yield *sēpɛr*, *mɛlɛk*, and *qōdɛš*. In the presence of a laryngeal consonant either vowel may be *pataḥ* (*zɛraᶜ*, *naᶜar*, *ᵓōraḥ*). All these words have the same prosody, but stressed /ē/ and /ō/ are considered long, while stressed /ɛ/ and /a/ are considered short. In any case the /ē/ in such words is never spelled *plene*, and the /ō/ in such words is almost never spelled *plene*. There are over two hundred different Hebrew words of type *qōdɛš*, accounting for more than 2,300 tokens in the text. קוֹדֶשׁ in

Daniel 11:30 is usually cited as the only *plene* spelling of such a
word in the entire Bible. A harbinger. שׂוֹבְךָ in 2 Samuel 18:9
could be added, but the accent is *milra*ᶜ. In contrast to other
manuscripts, in L אוֹמָר (Job 22:28) is *plene*. The evidence of the
Dead Sea Scrolls on this point is striking. In 1QIs[b], which is
proto-masoretic, segolates of type *qōdeš* are never spelled
plene; in 1QIs[a] they frequently are. It is reasonable to conclude
that the /ō/ in such words is not a real candidate for *plene*
spelling in the MT. The most common such words are קֹדֶשׁ (×
292), אֹהֶל (× 245), חֹדֶשׁ (× 231), בֹּקֶר (× 209). Similarly כֹּל, 'all'
← *kullu* occurs 853 times (*ketib* כּוֹל once or twice). כּוּל is
standard in Qumran texts. מְאֹד (× 300) is always *defective* (at
Qumran מאוד is usual).

5.5 Nonuse of the *defective* option

When the use of any *mater lectionis* is obligatory, these
cases are excluded from our study. We discuss each of the
seven vowels.

5.5.1. The preceding discussion of the use of א as *mater
lectionis* has shown that it never acquired a systematic role in
the spelling of any particular vowel beyond the level of individual
words in which it is usually etymological. Its omission is generally
the result of switching to another root (א"פ to י"פ or
א"ל to י"ל), while its addition is due to Aramaic influence or
simply bad spelling. In any case the instances are few, and the
patterns cannot be considered as part of the mainstream of
Hebrew spelling practice. So these are not included in our
study. See § 3.3.1.

5.5.2. The spelling of /ā/ has been almost completely
standardized. Word-medial /ā/ is always *defective*, except for a
handful of cases in which א has been introduced (see § 3.3.1.2).
The *plene* spelling is standard for /ā/ at the end of a word,
except for -*hā*, 'her,' which is never הָ-. Example: דְּבָרֶיהָ, 'her

words.' There could be one Aramaizing exception (הָ‑אֵ) in
Ezekiel 41:15. When written -*āh*, the *h* has *mappiq* (הַ -). The
few classes of words in which /ā/ presents a spelling option are
discussed below (Types 27-29 in Chapter 6). Apart from these,
on the word level there is נַעֲרָ, 'girl,' which is spelled *defective*
twenty-one times (Levita, following Abravanel [Ginsburg 1867a:
45], said twenty-two [Ginsburg 1867b: 109]). These are restricted to the Pentateuch. Manuscripts vary widely in the extent to
which they invoke *qere* for the *plene* spelling of this word. It is
not a fossil, which would be נערת; possibly it is epicene. The
plene spelling of terminal /ā/ is already attested in early
inscriptions, notably the Tell Fekhereye bilingual, so it is likely
that a word without the vowel letter ה did not have a terminal
vowel. The common practice of taking masoretic pronunciations back to such spellings as נער in the Bible and ען at Arad
is dubious. Because נער is unique among feminine singular
nouns and because it is circumscribed in location, we did not
include it in this study. Had we included it, the archaic character of the Pentateuch would have been enhanced.

In many cases the decision of a scribe at the stage when
old texts were being normalized into standard spelling must
have been difficult. In consonantal spelling there is sometimes
an ambiguity in certain homographic pairs of words. This is one
of the reasons why the use of *matres lectionis* was so welcome.
Many roots generate nouns in pairs, one masculine, one feminine, with similar meanings; example: צדק, צדקה, 'righteous-
ness.' A feminine form with *defective* spelling could be taken as
masculine, unless there are semantic or grammatical indications to the contrary. The difficulty of deciding between such
synonymous pairs is reflected in *ketib/qere* (Genesis 27:3;
1 Kings 7:23; Jeremiah 18:10, 31:39; Micah 3:2; Zechariah 1:16;
Proverbs 27:10; 31:18). Parallel texts within the Bible often
differ by such detail (Sperber 1943). Qumran texts often deviate from the MT in this specific (1QIs[b] as well as 1QIs[a]; 1QIs[b]
reads בצדק, not בצדקה, at Isaiah 63:1, for instance). Other

recensions, notably the Samaritan Pentateuch, often deviate from the MT in the addition or omission of הָ- (Sperber 1939).

A famous story tells about the three scrolls in the Azarah (Talmon 1962; Zeitlin 1966), which exhibited variant readings (מעונה מעון) in Deuteronomy 33:27. This need not be masculine versus feminine; it could be *defective* versus *plene* spelling of the feminine (Talmon 1962: 23).

There are only two verbs for which this happens: הָיָת (2 Kings 9:37) and נָטְעָ (Proverbs 31:16), both normalized in *qere*. Some other *ketib/qere* pairs arise because masculine and feminine forms are equally attractive, as with numerals (Ezekiel 45:3; Proverbs 30:18).

The rabbis had a rule, attributed to Rabbi Nehemiah (Jerusalem Talmud: *Yebamot* i.6; less accurately stated in Babylonian Talmud: *Yebamot* 13b), that a locative noun should have ה *locale* if it was not governed by a preposition. The Samaritans were criticized for not using this rule (Jerusalem Talmud: *ibid.*). Here grammatical doctrine could lose genuine cases in which a noun was used adverbially without either suffix or preposition (see 1 Samuel 9:26). This phenomenon evoked numerous entries in *Massorah Gedolah*.

The difference between an imperfect and a jussive often depends on terminal ה- and this also distinguishes cohortative from imperfect. But the difference is often difficult to sense, and some *ketib/qere* pairs reflect the uncertainty. Jussive/imperfect: 1 Kings 1:37; Jeremiah 40:16. Imperfect/cohortative: Haggai 1:8 (the Talmud explains that Haggai omitted the ה to signify the five things that were lacking in the Second Temple); Ruth 4:4; Lamentations 5:21.

It is hard to tell the difference between the normal imperative שׁוּב and the intensive שׁוּבה. Hence the old spelling שׁב, later שׁוּב, is ambiguous, since it could be *defective* spelling of שׁוּבה. The MT has stabilized this; *defective* spelling of the intensive form is rarely recognized and then always adjusted to

plene in *qere*, as with הָבִיטָ (Lamentations 5:1). The final adjustment of all such cases has been achieved only in modern editions. See the condemnation by Orlinsky (1940-41). *Qere* adds
ה to a verb in Joshua 24:3, Isaiah 41:23, Jeremiah 17:8, Ezekiel
23:16 and to עָשׂ in Ezekiel 23:43, Psalm 74:6.

The masculine pronoun אַתְ, 'thou,' is indistinguishable in
defective consonantal spelling from the feminine אַתְ. Spelling
the masculine *plene* resolves the ambiguity, but this was not
resorted to on the same scale with *qal* perfect verbs in -*tā* (see
Type 27 below). אַת masculine survives eight times in the
Masoretic Text, but all have been made *plene* in *qere* or else
pointed as feminine: Numbers 11:15; Deuteronomy 5:27(24);
1 Samuel 24:19; Ezekiel 28:14; Psalm 6:4; Job 1:10; Qohelet 7:22
(Frensdorff, p. 228, wrongly has verse 23); Nehemiah 9:6.
(Ginsburg [1897-1905: II 80] also cites Jeremiah 18:23.) The normalization achieves consistency, but the survival of apparently
feminine vocalization of clearly masculine forms (Numbers
11:15; Deuteronomy 5:24; Ezekiel 28:14) suggests that אַתְ was a
variant masculine form. Who knows how many times הֵם might
have been הֵמָּה, הֵן might have been הֵנָּה (Frensdorff pp. 234-
237)? But in these cases the existence of long and short forms
caused no problem.

The addition of ה could be carried too far (Joshua 7:21;
24:8; Psalm 51:4; Ruth 1:8; Daniel 9:18).

5.5.3. While theoretically any /ī/ could be considered an
opportunity to use either spelling, in practice the following are
invariably *plene*: 1) הִיא, 'she' (there is also the well-known but
still unexplained fact that the Pentateuch uses הִוא for 'she' in
most cases [× 194 in L] [Rendsburg 1982]); 2) /ī/ in word-final
position.

Any word-medial /ī/ may be spelled either way.

5.5.4. Theoretically any /ē/ could be considered an opportunity to use either spelling. The following are invariably *defective*: 1) the disjunctive *nota accusativi* אֵת; 2) ē ← i. Examples:

אֵם, 'mother,' and the like; סֵפֶר, 'book,' and similar segolates (see above); כָּבֵד, 'heavy,' and verbs such as יֵשֵׁב, 'he will sit,' and *pi'el* יְשַׁבֵּר, שִׁבֵּר, and participles like קוֹטֵל, etc. A solitary exception to the rule that /ē/ ← *i in the first syllable of an imperfect *nip'al* of a verb with *prima* laryngeal root is likewise *defective* is תֵּיעָשֶׂה (Exodus 25:31). Nor is -ē- joining a pronoun object suffix to a verb stem ever *plene* in MT. But וִיפְרִשִׂיהוּ occurs in Babylonian MS240 (*Textus 1* 1960: 137).

In contrast to the consistent *defective* spelling of ē ← *i, ē ← *ay is rarely *defective*, especially in the suffix of the construct and stem forms of masculine plural nouns and participles. See Type 14, § 6.5.2. The exceptions are mainly due to *gōyē*, גּוֹיֵ, and *qōyē*, קוֹיֵ (Isaiah 40:31); they avoid the double י of *plene* spelling. Compare the related problem of the *defective* spelling of גּוֹיִם discussed below in § 6.5.1 (Type 6). This *defective* spelling makes it difficult to distinguish singular from plural in some suffixed forms. See the similar problem with /ē/ discussed in § 5.5.5.2. Note *ketib* גיים (Genesis 25:23). The *ketib/qere* גוייך גויך occurs three times in Ezekiel 36:13-15 and illustrates this quandary. P recognizes only the third of these. In the other two a corrector has changed the original ו to י, thus securing the syllable -yay- but making /ō/ *defective*. גּוֹיֵ occurs as a stem in Genesis 10:5, 20, 31, 32; as construct in Ezra 6:21; 2 Chronicles 32:13, 17. The construct גּוֹיֵי occurs in Genesis 18:18; 22:18; 26:4; Deuteronomy 28:1; Jeremiah 26:6; 33:9; 44:8; Zechariah 12:3. A construct without י in 2 Kings 17:31 (אֵלֶה סְפָרִים) has generated *qere*. Perhaps אֶל־הַסְּפָרִים?

Other instances where the stem ends in י are:

בְּלֹוִי -- Jeremiah 38:11, 11

לְוִיֵּנוּ -- Nehemiah 10:1

חֲלָיֵנוּ -- Isaiah 53:4

Nouns derived from ל״י roots (lexical entries conventionally ל״ה) often present an ambiguity because the proclitic forms of both singular and plural are homophonous. Thus *maḥăne* can be 'the camp of' (the singular conventionally spelled as מחנה) or 'the camps of' (the plural conventionally spelled as מחני -- the deviant spelling שְׂרֵי in Ruth is not plural, usually שׂדות, but archaic). In Genesis 5:29 LXX reads απο των εργων ημων and other versions confirm 'works' as in some manuscripts; but מעשׂנו and מעשׂינו are equally ambiguous.

As genuine cases Levita (Ginsburg 1867b: 160) cites נְשִׂיאֵהֶם (Numbers 17:17) and אֲבוֹתֵכֶם (Deuteronomy 1:11). Samaritan is usually *plene*: לְמִינֵיהֶם (Genesis 1:21) and וּמֵחֶלְבֵיהֶן (Genesis 4:4). These could, however, be rare cases of the use of the suffixes -hεm or -hεn (usually -ām or -ān) with a singular noun.

Another cause of ambiguity is the fact that certain suffixes use -ē- as a joining vowel with the stem of a singular noun, so that singular and plural are homonymous. *Dĕ bārēnū* can mean 'our word' or 'our words,' conventionally written דברנו and דברינו, respectively. At Micah 5:4 L reads ארצנו, but P reads ארצינו. This cannot be plural. It shows that the joining vowel ē ← *ĭ of the singular stem could occasionally be spelled *plene*. The Babylonian scribes were more inclined to do this than the Tiberian (Ginsburg 1897-1905: IV 31 § 139). The fact that either vowel can be spelled either way compounds the problem. The analogous problem with -ε- is discussed below (§ 5.5.5.2).

Keeping these uncertainties in mind, the probable cases of *defective* spelling of stem-terminal ē ← *ay are:

לְמִינֵהֶם -- Genesis 1:21

וּמֵחֶלְבֵהֶן -- Genesis 4:4

מִקְנֵהֶם -- Genesis 34:23; 47:17 (*Plene* occurs earlier.)
Numbers 31:9; 32:26; Deuteronomy 3:19

עֲרִסֹתֵכֶם -- Numbers 15:20 (triply *defective*!)

נְשִׂיאֵכֶם -- Numbers 17:17

וְנִסְכֵּהֶם -- Numbers 29:33

אֲבוֹתֵכֶם -- Deuteronomy 1:11

וַאֲשֵׁירֵהֶם -- Deuteronomy 7:5

מִשְׁנֵהוּ -- 1 Samuel 8:2

חֵילֵהֶם -- Isaiah 30:6

מִפְּשָׁעֵנוּ -- Isaiah 53:5

נְוֵהֶם -- Jeremiah 23:3; 49:20; Ezekiel 34:14

נַפְשֹׁתֵכֶם -- Jeremiah 44:7

רָעֹתֵכֶם — Jeremiah 44:9

מֵהֶמֵה -- Ezekiel 7:11 (L thus!)

וְגַבֵּהֶם -- Ezekiel 10:12

וּפְאֵרֵכֶם -- Ezekiel 24:23

וְעֵינֵכֶם -- Ezekiel 33:25

וּמַעֲלֹתֵהוּ -- Ezekiel 43:17

אֹפֵהֶם -- Hosea 7:6

לִכְבֵהֶן -- Nahum 2:8

עֲלֻמֵנוּ -- Psalm 90:8 (The parallel shows it is plural.)

יְדֵכֶם -- Psalm 134:2

אַשְׁרֵהוּ -- Proverbs 29:18

מִגֹּאֲלֵנוּ -- Ruth 2:20

מִלְּפָנֵנוּ -- Qohelet 1:10

וְלִנְבִיאֵנוּ -- Nehemiah 9:32

Considering that the Hebrew Bible contains many thousand plural nouns ending in /ê/, these few cases (some dubious) of its *defective* spelling represent an insignificant deviation. They are not conspicuously congregated in any one place.

It is an outstanding feature of the consonantal orthography of MT that the phoneme /ē/ is distinguished so clearly as ē ← *ay and ē ← *i. The former is rarely spelled *defective*, the latter almost never *plene*. This distinction that ē ← *i is almost never *plene* suggests that the monophthongization ê ← *ay was quite late in the main (Judaean) stream, possibly post-exilic; so

in all inscriptions and in standard biblical spelling this *y* is a
consonant. Freedman (1962: 95) asserts:

"It is too much to expect that the Hebrew scribes
could have maintained a formal, i.e. orthographic, distinction for any length of time or with consistency
when the phonemic support for this distinction had
been lost."

This somewhat *a priori* argument is valid in a general way, but
it needs refining by considering further factors and by more
exact use of empirical data. N. B.: In this discussion we must
leave out the /ē/ in the stem of *hip*ᶜ*il* verbs. Here the picture
is chaotic. This /ē/ is spelled either *plene* or *defective*, and it
alternates freely with $\hat{\imath}$, also spelled either way. See Types 4
and 17 in Chapter 6. The inference that the *plene* spelling of
the vowel that the masoretes took as $\hat{e}$ shows that it was still *ay*
(because otherwise the phonemically identical $\bar{e}$ ← *ǐ* would
have been spelled in the same way, at least sometimes) -- this
inference does not absolutely follow. Another factor is at work.
The rule in masoretic Hebrew is different from that of both old
Northern Hebrew (all diphthongs monophthongized) and old
Southern Hebrew (all diphthongs retained). In its final development the stressed diphthong is retained (*báyt*), the unstressed
not (*bêt-*). The spelling בית for both forms is astonishingly consistent in the MT. If the construct had become *bêt* in biblical
times, it would have been written בת at least sometimes. Both
spellings are used in the Tell Fekhereye bilingual (Freedman
and Andersen 1985). The evidence of the Hebrew inscriptions is
unequivocal. Whenever the grammatical distinction between
absolute and construct can be determined, there is no difference in spelling. In the North, all such forms are contracted; in
the South, all are written as if they were not contracted. This
suggests that the contraction of the diphthong was universal in
the North, its survival universal in the South.

Our study of the spelling of nouns with the suffix -$\bar{o}t$[-] in
Chapter 1 showed that the spelling of both absolute and

construct tended to be *plene*, in contrast to the preference for *defective* spelling in suffixed forms. This suggests that absolute and construct were pronounced alike, possibly stressed alike, when these spelling patterns prevailed. If this was true also for words like 'house,' the diphthong did not contract, even in the construct, perhaps because it was still stressed. That change occurred quite late, after the spelling was fixed. בית remained a logograph, and the *defective* spelling never came into use in biblical texts.

The history of the pronunciation and spelling of $\bar{e}$ ← *ay has implications for the history of the spelling of $\bar{e}$ ← *í under stress. Assuming that $\bar{e}$ ← *ay and $\bar{e}$ ← *í have fallen together, and that there is no phonemic distinction between them, it is remarkable that the historical distinction between them is preserved so consistently in the spelling.

It should not be overlooked that $\bar{e}$ ← *í is stressed, $\hat{e}$ ← *ay is unstressed, and in Hebrew stressed vowels tend to be longer than unstressed. Our study shows that at least in the case of /ō/ the *mater lectionis* ו was preferred when /ō/ was stressed, as if it served to mark the length as such. The practice for /ē/ seems to be the opposite, but that is because historical spelling continued to prevail. The cogency of Freedman's first argument is borne out by Qumran practice. In 1QIs[a] both kinds of long /ē/ are spelled both ways (Kutscher 1974: 151-153). The MT is nearer to the inscriptions than post-biblical texts. Its spelling of long /ē/ is consistently conservative (excepting /ē/ in *hip[c]ils*), that is, it preserves the distinction between $\bar{e}$ ← *ay and $\bar{e}$ ← *í. The usage was frozen while diphthongs were still intact and also, for all we know, before the change $\bar{e}$ ← *í had taken place. The MT spelling of /ē/ is historical and was fixed before a phonetic spelling of the two eventually identical /ē/'s could blur the historical distinction. Unfortunately, we cannot put dates to these changes.

It is probable that $\bar{e} \leftarrow$ *$\check{\imath}$ and $\bar{o} \leftarrow$ *$\check{u}$ had a similar orthographic history. Freedman (1962: 96) observed that these
vowels "are not represented in the orthography because they
remained short vowels." But the spelling of these two vowels is
not at all the same in the MT. True, $\bar{e} \leftarrow$ *$\check{\imath}$ is practically never
plene, but $\bar{o} \leftarrow$ *$\check{u}$ is frequently so. (See § 6.5.5.) The spelling of
$\hat{o} \leftarrow$ *$\bar{a}$ and $\hat{o} \leftarrow$ *aw varies considerably in the Bible, as seen in
the two main word classes *qal* active participles ($q\hat{o}\underline{t}\bar{e}l$) (Type
39 in Chapter 6) and feminine plural nouns in -$\hat{o}\underline{t}$ (Types 47 and
48). These vowels were always long, but they are spelled *defective* in old texts. We infer that ו (masoretic $\hat{o}$) in such texts
should generally be read as /aw/, not /$\hat{o}$/, as it was before,
and perhaps even after, the Exile.

5.5.5. It is not certain whether the spelling ֵי - represents a
long /$\bar{\varepsilon}$/ (a lowered version of /$\bar{e}$/) or a diphthong /εy/ (a
raised version of /ay/). It can be written *defective* (Types 25
and 26).

5.5.5.1. It occurs in five kinds of words:

1) Feminine plural verbs, ל''י roots, which end in -$\varepsilon y n\bar{a}$:
imperfect (51 entries, 143 tokens), imperative (3 entries, 3
tokens) -- Some verbs with ל''א roots have been captured by
this class and develop a spelling with two apparent *matres lectionis*: תִּמָּצֶאינָה (Jeremiah 50:20), תִּשָּׁאֶינָה (Ezekiel 23:49).

2) Suffixed singular nouns with ל''י roots, which could retain the etymological י -- Thus, 'thy field' is שָׂדֶיךָ (1 Kings
2:26), which would be homonymous with the plural, if it followed
the masculine pattern. The ambiguity was evaded by basing
suffixed singular forms on a shorter stem, שָׂדְךָ, and this is what
many manuscripts have done with 1 Kings 2:26. The pausal
form of this שָׂדֶךָ could be *defective* plural. Cases are rare because the normal plural is שׂדות. Compare מַרְאֵיהֶם (Daniel
1:15), where the verb and complement are singular.

Deuteronomy 23:15 contains both מַחֲנֶךָ and מַחֲנֶיךָ. On
the presumption that the reference is the same, manuscripts

and versions have leveled the text both ways. Syntax supports the Masoretic Text that the first one is singular.

3) Plural (and dual) suffixed nouns -- This includes cardinal numerals and participles, either masculine, e.g., דְּבָרֶיךָ, or feminine, e.g., חֹומֹתַיִךְ.

4) Some prepositions presenting pseudo-plural stem forms in suffixation -- for example, אֵלֶיךָ.

5) Three miscellaneous words, possibly mixed readings: גֵּיא (Isaiah 40:4), שְׂנֵאָתִיךָ (Ezekiel 35:11), מַה־יָּגֵיל (Psalm 21:2). In these instances the י is historical or follows historical analogy. The *plene* spelling of /ɛ/ as such, even when stressed and so possibly lengthened, never developed in the Bible. *Segol* alone, however, in the appropriate position, can be *defective* spelling of יֶ -. This, whether regarded as long /ē/ or as a diphthong /ɛy/, is the result of dissimilation of *ay before a following vowel /ā/. By this rule it might be thought that this spelling would be found in certain suffixed verbs derived from ל''י roots, such as תַּעֲשֵׂהָ, 'thou shalt make it.' What occurs is תַּעֲשֶׂה (Genesis 6:16).

5.5.5.2. The diphthong /ɛy/ is rarely spelled *defective*.

1) There are no *defective* spellings of /ɛy/ in feminine plural imperative verbs. In imperfect verbs *defective* spellings are:

וַתִּדְלֶנָה -- Exodus 2:16

תְּהֶינָה -- Jeremiah 18:21; 1 Chronicles 7:15
   (manuscripts: Jeremiah 48:6; see L Mp)

תְּהִימֶנָה -- Micah 2:12 (hollow root)

תִּכְלֶנָה -- Job 17:5

תְּמוּשֶׁנָה -- Isaiah 54:10 (hollow root)

תְּמוּתֶנָה -- Ezekiel 13:19 (hollow root)

תִּשֶּׁנָה -- Jeremiah 9:17; Ruth 1:14 (ל''א root)

תְּעֶגֶּנָה -- Ezekiel 4:12 (hollow root); תְּעֻגֶּנָה in editions

וַתַּעֲלֶנָה -- Daniel 8:8

וְהִשְׁלַכְתֶּנָה -- Amos 4:3 (mixed form?)

Only five are genuine instances of *defective* spelling of verbs with ל"י roots. Examples come from all over the Bible.

2) Because of the uncertain morphology of nouns with ל"י roots, there are no indubitable instances of *defective* spellings. The following words are interesting:

מַחֲנֶךָ -- Deuteronomy 23:15

מִקְרֶהָ -- Ruth 2:3 (singular)

עָלֶהָ -- Isaiah 1:30 (collective)

3) Since *segol* alone in an appropriate position could be *defective* spelling of יֶ-, there are some instances of words containing ֶ which are ambiguous. Thus pausal singular suffixed nouns of type דְּבָרֶךָ, 'thy word,' could also be *defective* spelling of דְּבָרֶיךָ, 'thy words.' Unless the number of the noun stem is determined by syntax, the ambiguity may be insoluble. For this reason the list below cannot be definitive.

This ambiguity represents a point of turbulence in textual transmission. The whole drift was towards resolving the ambiguity of the *defective* spelling by inserting a י. This produced some secondary *ketib/qere* pairs, as with חֲסִידֶיךָ (Psalm 16:10 -- the best manuscripts have חֲסִידְךָ without *qere*). Psalm 119 contains many examples, because of the frequent use of such plural nouns as משפטיך, דבריך, and חקיך. The corresponding singular forms can often be construed as *defective* plurals, as many manuscript variants show.

The *massora marginalis* of Genesis 30:34 states that there are thirteen instances where דְּבָרֶךָ is *defective* plural, but there is no list in *Massorah Gedolah*. Mp at Genesis 47:30 and Numbers 14:20 (where manuscripts have plural דבריך) read יג חס כליש. The same Mp is used at Psalm 119:9, 16, 17, 25, 28, 42, 65, 101, 105, 107; and all but verse 107 have a note in BHS that manuscripts have plural (compare verse 160). Ginsburg

(1867a: 161, note 43) missed verse 17 (he rectified the omission on page 183, note 6) but added Psalm 119:169; this, however, is not an instance, being patently singular. Incidentally, verse 169 shows that the singular as well as the plural is part of the vocabulary of Psalm 119, even though other singulars do have plural variants in manuscripts (verses 74, 81). Since the vocabulary is common and the difference in meaning between 'word' and 'words' is slight, it is no surprise that seven or more *ketib/qere* pairs prefer the singular: Judges 13:17; 1 Kings 8:26; 18:36; 22:13; Jeremiah 15:16 (second occurrence); Psalm 119:147, 161; Ezra 10:12; and in some manuscripts and Targum, Psalm 119:37, *Okla we-Okla* § 131. In most instances it is 'the word(s) of God,' and the singular is preferred for theological reasons (Andersen and Freedman 1980: 149-51). Mp at Psalm 119:11, 148 says that אִמְרָתֶךָ occurs *defective* twelve times. It is hard to know how to interpret this. The spelling אמרתך occurs twenty-one times. This would be *defective* spelling only if the word were plural אִמְרוֹתֶיךָ. This variant is found in manuscripts. But feminine plural occurs only twice in the Masoretic Text (Psalm 12:7). Otherwise for plural the masculine is preferred (× 48).

Mm 605 gives three cases of דְּרָכֶךָ as plural *defective* (Exodus 33:13; Joshua 1:8; Psalm 119:37). Similarly:

חַסְדֶּךָ -- Psalm 119:41 (could be singular, see LXX);

וְאֶסְרָהָ -- Numbers 30:8 (contrast verse 6)

מִשְׁבַּתֶּהָ -- Lamentations 1:7

מִשְׁפָּטֶךָ -- Psalm 36:7

> Singular so not *defective*? Some MSS are *plene*.

עֲבָדֶךָ -- 2 Samuel 11:24; 14:31

עֵינֶךָ -- Job 14:3; Isaiah 37:17

> The first is pausal and so is possibly singular; the second is not pausal and so is plural. P and Babylonian MS240 (*Textus 1*: 137) read עיניך. עֵינֶךָ is ambiguous when pausal but *defective* plural when not in pause. The *massora* (Mm 1145) recognizes six cases. 1 Kings 8:29 is

proved plural by syntax, and the same idiom supports
belief that the noun is plural in Isaiah 37:17 and Job
14:3. But in Isaiah 37:17 'eye' is parallel to 'ear' and
Amos 9:4 and Job 42:5 show that 'eye' can be singular in
that idiom (עֵינִי could have been read as עֵינַי). Other
cases: Deuteronomy 15:18; 19:21; 25:12 (manuscripts
have plural). The versions reflect the ambiguity in most
cases.

נְעֻרֶךָ -- Proverbs 5:18
   Usually plural; manuscripts: נעוריך.

וּפְתִילֶךָ -- Genesis 38:18
   Plural, as פתילים in v. 25 shows.

מַכֹּתָה -- Jeremiah 19:8

מַכּוֹתָה -- Jeremiah 49:17

אֹהָלֶךָ -- Judges 19:9 (manuscripts have plural)

יזכר כל־מנחתך ועולתך ידשנה -- Psalm 20:4

   LXX has leveled to singular, manuscripts to plural.

בְּרִיחֶהָ -- Isaiah 15:5

מִגְרָשֶׁהָ -- forty-six times in Joshua 21
   Plene in Chronicles (see § 8.3.4).

מִצְוֹתֶךָ -- Psalm 119:98; Daniel 9:5

וְכִגְבוּרֹתֶךָ -- Deuteronomy 3:24

וּגְבוּרֹתֶךָ -- Isaiah 63:15 (L and others; MSS plural)

קְבָרֹתֶךָ -- Ezekiel 32:25

גַּרְגְּרֹתֶךָ -- Proverbs 6:21

בְּחוּרוֹתֶךָ — Qohelet 11:9 (*plene* in *textus receptus*)

מָנוֹתֶהָ -- Esther 2:9

צִדְקֹתֶךָ -- Daniel 9:16

The *defective* spelling of a suffixed plural noun can thus
masquerade as a singular. Once the *plene* spelling is established
as the norm, the possibility of reading such a *defective* spelling
as plural would no longer be possible, unless the context com-
pelled it, usually by means of concord with a plural adjective,
verb, or pronoun. Doubtless the scribes took advantage of this
long ago in most cases. We might suspect that an apparently

singular word is really plural, but it is now too late to entertain more than a suspicion. Thus the Lord said to Moses (Exodus 3:5):

שַׁל־נְעָלֶיךָ מֵעַל רַגְלֶיךָ

but to Joshua (Joshua 5:15):

שַׁל־נַעַלְךָ מֵעַל רַגְלֶךָ

It is no wonder that some manuscripts and versions read duals at Joshua 5:15. In some manuscripts Isaiah 20:2 reads:

וּנְעָלְךָ תַחֲלֹץ מֵעַל רַגְלֶךָ

C, L and P have:

וּנְעָלְךָ תַחֲלֹץ מֵעַל רַגְלֶיךָ

1QIs[a] and versions read:

וּנְעָלֶיךָ תַחֲלֹץ מֵעַל רַגְלֶיךָ

Sandals normally come in pairs, and the singular is met only in a special ceremony (Deuteronomy 25:9-10; Ruth 4:7-8). Hence the apparent singular in 1 Kings 2:5, which is inconsistent, should be plural -- 'and on his sandal [sic!] which is on his feet.' On רַגְלֶךָ see Mm 1267. Compare Jeremiah 38:22. A case of this sort sometimes evokes *plene* (plural/dual) as *qere*. The versions are unanimous that 'sandal' and 'foot' in Deuteronomy 29:4 are plural (dual). The Masoretic Text, however, has anchored the singular in the verb בָלְתָה. This, perhaps, is an illusion, for the suffix ה- could be the archaic feminine plural. (See § 3.3.2.) Deuteronomy 21:7 (יָדֵינוּ לֹא שָׁפְכָה) presents a similar case. Versions have leveled either the singular (*ketib*) or plural (*qere*). But the *ketib* verb could be feminine plural. Compare פִּתְחָה אָזְנֶךָ (Isaiah 48:8). In Jeremiah 38:22 רַגְלֶךָ is pointed singular, but the verb is plural. The noun is plural in manuscripts. In Psalm 77:13 פָּעֳלְךָ is pointed as singular, but it is probably plural, as in many manuscripts. This phenomenon is akin to the use of י to distinguish the plural from the singular. At 1 Kings 3:12 (Masoretic Text plural) manuscripts and versions have singular, but there is no *qere*. At 2 Samuel 1:16 the masoretes pointed דָּמֶיךָ as singular. At Genesis 16:5,

וּבֵינֶיךָ, the *punctum extraordinarium* shows that the second י is redundant. Samaritan reads וביניך.

4) Prepositions with pseudo-plural stems do not present any *defective* spellings of יָ.

In summary, there are eighty-eight (Types 25, 26) *defective* spellings of -יָ and they are fairly evenly distributed throughout the Bible.

5.5.5.3 The use or nonuse of י on the stem of suffixed masculine plural nouns produces similar problems, whether the stem is *děbārā(y)-w* (§ 2.5), *děbārē(y)-nū* (§ 5.5.4), or *děbārɛ(y)-kā* (§ 5.5.5). In each case the *defective* spelling of plural could be mistaken for singular, and the normal spelling of singular could be mistaken for *defective* spelling of plural. Even the *plene* spelling could be interpreted as an incorrect writing of the singular. As the discussion in §§ 2.5, 5.5.4, and 5.5.5 shows, some "corrections" were supplied in the *ketib/qere* apparatus, but this is rather haphazard. The manuscripts and versions point to many cases which did not attract *ketib/qere* annotation. For many cases the contextual syntactic control was enough to distinguish singular from plural, no matter what the spelling. When this failed, doubtless the oral tradition which always accompanied the consonantal text served as a control. But even this had its limitations. The pronunciations of 'our word' and 'our words' are identical; the only difference is orthographic. The pronunciation of 'thy word' in pause is the same as 'thy words.' 'His word' would always be different from 'his words' in reading, but the suffix וֹ- (-*āw* or -*ō̃*) was quite ambiguous, and the addition of י to the plural served as a purely logographic marker with no phonetic value. But the convention of writing all plural stems with י and the makeshift of *ketib/qere* were too late and too haphazard to preserve the genuine readings with certainty. And even then, we cannot be sure that these scribal decisions were correct. (See § 11.3.10.)

The manuscripts and versions preserve abundant evidence for this, and now there is no possible remedy. Thus the parallelism suggests that מקלל֖ך (Genesis 12:3) is plural. Because of their regard for the consonantal text, the masoretes preferred to read such a word as singular rather than as *defectively* spelled plural. We must accordingly regard the lists in §§ 2.5, 5.5.4, and 5.5.5 as minimal.

5.5.6. Theoretically any long /ō/ could be considered to be an opportunity to use either spelling. 1) Some individual words which occur frequently have invariant spelling (§ 5.2.1 and Table 5.1a,b). 2) /ō/ ← *ŭ in segolate nouns of type קֹדֶשׁ is almost always *defective* (see above § 5.4). This historical development is parallel to the change *ĭ → /ē/, but the orthographic treatment of the two resultant vowels is quite different. The latter is rarely spelled *plene*. Apart from segolate-type words containing /ō/ ← *ŭ, which are invariantly *defective* within our terms of reference, /ō/ ← *ŭ otherwise is open to the *plene* spelling option.

5.5.7. While theoretically any /ū/ could be considered an opportunity to use either spelling, in practice the following are invariantly *plene*: 1) the pronoun הוא, 'he,' 2) /ū/ in word-final position. Others in Table 5.1a,b. Any word-medial /ū/ may be spelled either way. The only frequently occurring word in which it is never *plene* is נאֻם (× 376), assuming that it is *qal* passive participle and thus a genuine archaic spelling.

5.5.8. In describing spelling options we have discussed only one part of the scribes' task. Recall the distinction between the decision of the scribe of the autograph and the later decision of a copyist (§ 4.1). The copyist, unconsciously or deliberately, could update an old spelling. The reverse is less likely. The copyist could be restrained by veneration for a canonical text, but the variations among old manuscripts (as distinct from the incredible uniformity among medieval manuscripts) suggests that such restraints were not strong. But the copyist had another problem. If he always knew the identity of each word and its pronunciation, all he had to do was to decide the spelling. For many written words, especially in the old and lean consonantal spelling, there could be more than one possible identification. If, then, the copyist supplied *matres lectionis* the original ambiguity could be lost. In our present perspective we cannot hope to recover such prehistoric (i.e., before surviving manuscripts) details with much certainty.

Some *ketib/qere* pairs seem to endorse both possibilities when it is the pronunciation, not just the spelling of the word, that is in doubt, as when the copyist had to decide whether the word contained /ī/ or /ū/. Levita (Ginsburg 1867b: 118) listed seventy-five pairs with *yod* in the text and *waw* in *qere* (Gordis 1937: List 35) and seventy pairs with *waw* in the text and *yod* in *qere* (Gordis 1937: List 34). Of course some of this could be a legacy from the Herodian era, when *waw* and *yod* were practically identical paleographically.

5.6 The mechanics of vowel marking

Applying the foregoing observations to the identification of fixed vowels was straightforward if tedious. As the analysis proceeded, any vowel judged fixed was so marked; any morpheme containing only fixed vowels was immediately removed from our data. The winnowing process involved four stages. The full *ketib/qere* text we started with had 41,687 segment types and 473,669 tokens.

5.6.1. First, the Aramaic sections (Jeremiah 10:11, Daniel 2:4-7:28, and Ezra 4:8-6:18; 7:12-26) were removed. Following this removal, the reduced text consisted of 40,216 segment types and 466,858 tokens.

5.6.2. Next, a battery of winnowing rules was applied to the vocabulary of the Hebrew text. These rules save entries which present the scribe with an opportunity to make a spelling choice and discard entries which present no such opportunity. First distinctions are made among words ending in -ā. See § 5.5.2. The majority are either feminine singular nouns or verbs, or locatives. They are invariably spelled with ה. Four other sets of entries are of orthographic interest, since they may be spelled without the ה. They arc: 1) perfect verbs ending in -tā, 'thou' (Type 27); 2) feminine plural verbs ending in -nā (Type 28); 3) the pronoun suffix -kā; and 4) the ending on insistent imperatives (Type 29). In the event, the third of these was later eliminated from the data on statistical grounds.

5.6.2.1 Very short vowels (šewa and ḥaṭefs) as well as pataḥ are never opportunities for plene spelling, and any entries containing only these vowels were eliminated.

5.6.2.2 The noun ending ה ֶ- is never plene, and such entries were eliminated when they contained no other opportunities.

5.6.2.3 The spelling א in פ״א verbs is not eligible for אי. Entries with no other opportunities were discarded.

5.6.2.4 The /ē/ in nouns or adjectives of type zāqēn is never spelled plene (the one exception in Joshua 9:11 proves the rule), and all such entries which contain no other opportunities were winnowed out.

5.6.2.5 Entries in which the first syllable is closed, not stressed, and contains i or u, which are always short, are never spelled plene. These were removed.

5.6.2.6 Entries, not verbs, which end in î or û are always spelled plene and were dropped.

5.6.2.7 Likewise for segolates and duals containing -ayi- or -āyi- with the same proviso.

> This set draws attention to the case of 'Jerusalem' with qere perpetuum for Yĕrûšālayim, a pronunciation confirmed by the spelling ירושלים at Qumran. MT ketib points to an alternative pronunciation, not just a different spelling.

5.6.2.8 Other segolates of type קֹדֶשׁ or סֵפֶר or מֶלֶךְ and so on, and other entries in which short *i*, *u* and $\bar{e}$ ← *$^*i$ are never spelled *plene* in the MT. Same proviso.

5.6.2.9 Prefixed verbs whose first vowel is $\bar{e}$ or *i* derived from weak roots, such as יֵבֵן or יֵרֵד, were dropped. The only *plene* spelling of such a vowel known to us is אֵילְכָה (Micah 1:8); the $\bar{e}$ in the first syllable of imperfect *nip^{c}als* of weak roots, such as יֵעָשֶׂה (in some editions [not L], Exodus 25:31) contains the anomalous תיעשה.

5.6.2.10 Many entries still remained which contained one or more ineligible vowels but which were needed because they also contained one or more opportunity vowels. Such ineligible vowels in entries which would have been discarded by the preceding rules, were it not for the presence of these opportunity vowels, had to be masked in various ways so that the computer would ignore them in the studies that followed.

5.6.2.11 Following this winnowing, the text consisted of 24,358 segment types and 143,854 tokens. All results were double-checked for correctness.

5.6.3. After this reduction, the inventory still contained items appearing many times in L, always spelled one way, that is, seemingly fixed. The vowel involved was declared fixed in practice if (two-sided) confidence-interval assessment allowed us to assert with 95 % confidence that the item would not be spelled in the "deviant" way more than one percent of the time in a much bigger, but statistically identical, text. (The 95 % confidence limit and one-percent threshold are arbitrary, but they fulfill the requirement of supplying an objective criterion for declaring a form fixed in practice.) If an entry occurs 367 times, and the opportunity vowel in it is always spelled in the same way, it satisfies this statistical criterion for rejection from the study as invariant. If an entry occurs 556 times and has only one deviant spelling, it is considered virtually fixed according to the criterion. With two exceptions, the dominant form

must occur 721 times to be considered fixed; with three, 874
times, and so on. Thus the pronoun suffix 'me,' -$\bar{e}n\hat{i}$, is spelled
plene once, but since the regular *defective* spelling occurs 569
times, this is considered fixed. The word $g\hat{o}y$ is spelled *defective* twice, but since the normal *plene* occurs only 439 times, it
is not "fixed" according to the criterion. The infinitive 'to say,'
לֵאמֹר, occurs *plene* three times (Ginsburg 1897-1905: IV § 827),
but since the normal *defective* occurs 942 times, it is considered fixed. We assume that entries with virtually fixed spellings did not present scribes with real spelling choices (or, even
if they did, the choice of the alternative would not be statistically significant), and so they are excluded from this study.

These policies raise some additional questions. The word
אֱלֹהִים is invariant; the same spelling occurs 1,077 times. The
construct and suffixed forms of אֱלֹהֵי, 'god(s) of,' occur 1,526
times, and only three spell $\bar{o}$ *plene*, so the form is "fixed." Other
rarer, suffixed forms are occasionally *plene*. Should they be
lumped with the others because they are the same, or kept
separate because they are different? Assuming that the stem
vowels are the same in all of them, the $\bar{o}$ can be regarded as
fixed in all of them. The rarer forms must be kept in this study,
however, because their stem-terminal vowels are genuine
opportunities for spelling choices.

By similar logic עֵין, 'eye of,' is excluded (767 *plene*, one
defective), and the stem vowel is masked out. The singular כֹּהֵן,
'priest,' occurs 440 times, never *plene*, and so the $\bar{o}$ in the plural was also considered fixed.

We did not extend this principle indiscriminately. Thus
יְהוּדָה is fixed by the criterion; but various derivatives, such as
the ethnic, which amounts to some 100 tokens in all, we retained, considering it to be different, so that the stem vowel $\bar{u}$
is an opportunity (as attested in inscriptions).

Twenty-six lexemes, accounting for 36,094 tokens, met
these criteria. Tables 5.1a,b show the *lexemes* dropped on

these statistical grounds. The 95% C.I. column shows the *percentage* range within which the true proportion of deviants most likely lies. Note that some of the lexemes involve multiple theoretical opportunities. Application of the rules and removal of the statistically invariant items reduced the inventory to 24,143 segment types representing 107,760 tokens.

Table 5.1a Lexemes declared fixed

Lexeme Head	Total	Deviants	95% C.I.
וֹ	7765	55	.53-.95
דְּ	7035	38	.54-.74
בְּנֵי	2231	0	.00-.13
אִישׁ	1657	0	.00-.18
בֵּית	1527	0	.00-.20
אֱלֹהֵי	1526	3	.04-.57
יוֹם	1505	0	.00-.20
פְּנֵי	1344	0	.00-.22
אֱלֹהִים	1077	0	.00-.28
אמר	945	3	.07-.92
כֹּל	853	1	.00-.65
יְהוּדָה	821	0	.00-.36
עֵינֵי	767	1	.00-.71
מֹשֶׁה	766	0	.00-.39
אִין	746	0	.00-.40
עִיר	680	0	.00-.44
יְרוּשָׁלַם	643	0	.00-.46

Table 5.1b Lexemes declared fixed

Lexeme Head	Total	Deviants	95% C.I.
זאת	605	0	.00-.49
כֹּה	577	0	.00-.52
נִי	570	1	.00-.97
כֹּחַ	440	0	.00-.68
אַחֲרֵי	423	0	.00-.71
בֵּין	409	0	.00-.73
שָׁאוּל	407	0	.00-.73
טוֹב	399	0	.00-.75
נְאֻם	376	0	.00-.79

5.6.4. The final phase of winnowing involved performing operations on the actual texts rather than the dictionary. The Hebrew part of L was adjusted using the dictionary produced by the previous two stages. The resulting text was examined, and any word-terminal ׳ or ׳ was marked as fixed. As a result of all these operations, the *ketib/qere* text was reduced to 20,915 segment types and 95,006 tokens, some of which contained multiple opportunities. In the *ketib/qere* text there remain 109,640 opportunities; 36,177 are *defective* and 73,463 are *plene*. In the *ketib* text there remain 108,943 opportunities; 36,040 are *defective* and 72,903 are *plene*.

Chapter 6. Classification of Spelling Options

6.1 Classification of vowels

The reduced text obtained via the methods discussed in the last chapter contains vocabulary items (words or parts of compound words -- we call all such units "segments") of two kinds: 1) segments containing one or more vowels, each presenting a scribe with an opportunity to spell it *defective* or *plene*; 2) segments containing both opportunity vowels and vowels which do not present the scribe with an opportunity. To study how the scribes used the opportunities presented by the text for choice of spelling, these segments must be examined. Vowels in the second set which do not present opportunities have been marked as fixed.

The segments in which a long vowel presents a writer with an opportunity to choose either *defective* or *plene* spelling may be classified into types on the basis of: 1) the behavior of individual words, 2) paradigmatic word classes, 3) words of particular phonetic shape, or 4) the path followed by the vowel in its historical development. Cases not fitting any of the type-defining rules are placed in a residuum.

This typology is serially exclusive, since no vowel is classified twice, even if it fits more than one type. An individual word or segment, singled out for its distinctive behavior, may also be a member of a paradigmatic class; it may belong, too, with other words of the same phonetic shape or stress pattern; and, of course, there will be other words which contain vowels with the same history.

In the system of classification now to be described, the stress pattern, which is a combination of vowel length, syllable type (open or closed), and stress position, will be considered a possible factor in its own right. The historical development of the vowel will be considered a second factor. In the former case we are forced to rely on masoretic tradition, which we accept as a given in spite of its late attestation. In the latter we do our best to recover the history of the vowel with the aid of comparative-historical grammar.

6.2 Stress patterns

It is possible that stress patterns influenced the spelling choices of scribes. Hebrew words differ in their stress patterns. We have only a rough idea of the evolution of these patterns; we do not know with any exactitude how specific words were pronounced in biblical times. Certain stress patterns stabilized by masoretic times and were fixed in masoretic pointing and accentuation. These patterns were imposed uniformly on the entire biblical text. This is quite artificial. It is highly unlikely that these patterns were in vogue without change over the millennium or so during which the Bible was being produced.

In spite of this limited knowledge, it would be a pity to ignore stress altogether. The masoretic system can be used as an approximation, and it has the advantage of givenness, whereas any historical reconstruction which we might attempt would be open to the objection that it would be speculative.

In the masoretic system there is a clear connection between stress and morphophonemics. Only the last two syllables of any word are eligible for stress, and there are constraints on the combinations of syllable type (open or closed), vowel length, and stress which may occur. The addition of a suffix can change the position of stress. The imposition of stress can lengthen a vowel; its removal can shorten a vowel. It is therefore a valid question whether the presence or absence of stress (or of concomitant lengthening or shortening) influenced a scribe in his choice of spelling. Since *matres lectionis* were used only for long vowels in any case, was the tendency to use them enhanced when the length of a vowel was made even more conspicuous by stress?

Some Hebraists distinguish as many as four grades of stress, with corresponding differences in the length of (the vowels in) a word, where such changes are phonologically possible. An unsuffixed word in context is considered normal. Words in pause (typically at the end of a verse) have the greatest stress, and some have distinct (pausal) forms of maximum length in that environment. A word with a stressed suffix has no stress on the stem, which is often shortened as much as the phonological rules of the language will permit. Between these limits, nouns in construct (and other proclitics) have less than normal stress and are often shorter than normal forms. Some, however, are considered to have secondary stress and are consistently written as separate words, never as parts of compound words, in the masoretic tradition.

Such refinements are not called for in the present study. It is enough to classify long vowels which are opportunities for scribes' spelling choices into three groups. 1) The vowel in question occurs in a word which has a stressed suffix, and therefore is less stressed than the corresponding vowel in the same word when it is not suffixed. When the vowel occurs in a word that is not suffixed, a distinction can be made between 2) construct (or other proclitic) forms, and 3) free (absolute) forms, including pausals. The latter have high stress, the former intermediate. The distinctions are relative and can be made without knowing the exact patterns of stress. The distinctions permit a contrastive classification of corresponding vowels in words which occur in all three states. By analogy the distinctions can be extended to words which occur in only one state. Thus *nota accusativi* אֵת is always suffixed, and its vowel is never stressed. Proper nouns are never suffixed; they are always stressed. It can be assumed that all unsuffixed words bear a stress, except when there are grounds for regarding them as proclitic, as with לֹא, 'not.' A word with an unstressed suffix is stressed on the last syllable of the stem.

We distinguish three stress classes: *Low*, words with a stressed suffix, the stem presumably unstressed; *Middle*, constructs and proclitics; *High*, words with an unstressed suffix (stem stressed on the last syllable) and unsuffixed words (not proclitic) stressed on the last or second-last syllable.

6.3 Word length

A suffixed word is obviously physically longer than its unsuffixed counterpart. It is therefore possible that a scribal tendency to avoid *matres lectionis* in such words arose not from phonetic considerations (because the candidate vowel is less stressed) but from purely graphic considerations (to avoid over-long words). Whatever the psychology, we are interested immediately in any differences in the use of *matres lectionis* in suffixed versus unsuffixed (or unstressed versus stressed) words. But in addition we shall sometimes distinguish segments of the same type that differ only in length.

6.4 The history of the vowel

6.4.1. The vowels /i/ and /ī/ are very stable in Hebrew, and most specimens are primal. The simple spelling *ḥireq* can represent either an historically short /i/ or a *defective* spelling of /ī/. The former has been screened out. In due time the standard spelling of /ī/ *plene* prevailed, and *defective* spellings are relatively few (a little more than ten percent in our data).

6.4.2. Most cases of the vowel /ē/ took one of two historical paths: 1) monophthongization of primal *ay*; 2) lengthening of primal *i̯ under stress. Vowels with the former history are generally spelled *plene*; vowels with the latter history are generally spelled *defective*. As discussed in § 5.5.4, it is not always possible to distinguish the two kinds of /ē/.

6.4.3. Short /ɛ/ derives by dissimilation from primal *i̯ or *a̯ and has been eliminated from this study because it never became a candidate for *plene* spelling in biblical texts. Long /ɛ̄/ derives by dissimilation (perhaps monophthongization) from primal *ay and is usually spelled *plene* (about ninety-seven percent in our data). As discussed in § 5.5.5, it is not always possible to distinguish short from long ɛ.

6.4.4. Long /ā/ presents the scribe with an apparent opportunity for a choice of spelling only at the end of a word. It was not really an option, since every such vowel had to be spelled with ה. The variants found in the MT, apparent *defective* spellings of this vowel, are probably the result of artificial normalization by the masoretes. As discussed in § 5.5.2, the nonuse of terminal ה in these special cases is probably a pseudo *defective* spelling, since the word probably did not have a terminal vowel. Such pseudo-opportunities can make only a marginal contribution to the present study.

6.4.5. The vowel /ō/ is an innovation in Hebrew. It arose in the language over a long period of time as the result of a number of quite different changes in the sound system. At least five distinct paths of change may be traced.

Path 1. Example: *yadahū → yādõ (see § 2.3.5).

Path 2. Example: ra'šu → rō(')š (see § 2.3.8). The mixed consequences of the loss of א and its use in historical spellings as a pseudo *mater lectionis* were discussed in § 3.3.1. For the reasons given there, the use of א as a pseudo *mater lectionis* is not relevant to the study that follows.

Path 3. Example: *mawtu → mõt. The writing of /ō/ with the aid of ה, א, or ו when it has developed along one of these three paths is historical when the consonant used attests the previous history of the /ō/ sound. In due time the use of ה became obsolete (Type 31 below) and א became otiose, leaving ו as the standard *mater lectionis* for the *plene* spelling of /ō/. Path 3 yields the only kind of /ō/ that is spelled *plene* in pre-exilic inscriptions (unless sporadic -ō, 'his;' see § 2.3.5), and even then we cannot be sure that ו does not still represent the consonant in the uncontracted diphthong. The development of phonetic out of historical spelling in this case meant a trend to *defective* spelling in later texts, the opposite of the trend with the other kinds of long /ō/.

Path 4. The primal Semitic long vowel *ā became /ō/ by an unconditioned sound shift in Old South Canaanite. Thus all *qal* active participles of type *šāmiru* became *šōmēr* (Type 39 below). This statement needs to be qualified a little. Some primal long /ā/ vowels evidently slipped through the net and remained long /ā/. Example: words of the type *gannāb*, 'thief.' How this happened has not yet been explained satisfactorily. There are two main theories. One is that the change did not take place if the vowel was not stressed. This is how a whole class of words, with a distinctive stress pattern, could evolve differently from others (Blau 1976). The other is that there was a dialect in which the change *ā → ō did not take place. Subsequently the two streams merged, with some sets of words, such as *šōmēr*, pronounced as in one dialect and other sets of words, such as *gannāb*, pronounced as in another dialect (Bauer and Leander 1922: 192; Kutscher 1982: § 33).

This matter needs to be kept in mind so that we do not assume too much uniformity in Hebrew in its early stages. We may be sure that שׁומר reflects *šōmēr*, but how do we know that שׁמר is *defective* spelling of *šōmēr* and not rather a representation of archaic or dialectal *šāmir*?

Path 5. In Hebrew the primal short vowel /u/ lengthens and moves forward in the mouth under stress: *ú → ō. Example: *kullu, 'all,' כל כול כֹּל.

In due time the vowel point *holem* came to be used to write every occurrence of /ō/ in the Bible, either by itself (*defective*) or as a supplement to one or the other of the *matres lectionis*, ה and ו, or as an adjunct to historical א.

Of the 73,471 long /ō/'s in the complete *Hebrew* portion of the Bible (that is, leaving out the Aramaic), 34,062 (46.4 percent) are spelled *plene*. This proportion is not found uniformly throughout the Bible. The counts of *plene* and *defective* spelling of /ō/ for the individual books are shown in Table 6.1.

The percentage of *plene* spellings in individual books ranges from about twenty-eight (Exodus) to above sixty percent. The Pentateuch, Kings, and Ruth have less than forty; Samuel and Jeremiah are between forty and fifty; Ezra (Hebrew only) plus Nehemiah and Daniel (Hebrew only) are just below fifty percent; the other prophets lie between fifty and fifty-five, along with Job, Qohelet, Lamentations, and Chronicles. Psalms and Proverbs have between fifty-five and sixty; Song of Songs and Esther are above sixty percent. Even as a rough index these percentages are of interest, and it is striking that the eight large books with the lowest scores are the Pentateuch (all less than 40 percent), 1 Samuel, 1 and 2 Kings. There is a tendency for more *plene* spellings to be used in later books. The relative high use in Joshua-Judges could indicate either later composition or more modernization of this detail than in other books of the Primary History. When the data are refined by winnowing out /ō/'s which did not present the scribes with a spelling choice, the extremes move to twenty-five percent for Exodus and sixty-five percent for 1 Chronicles. But this observation is not precise enough for our purposes. We want to trace the history of the spelling for each path taken to reach /ō/ in each type of word. We wish to investigate the emergence of a strictly phonetic use of ו for the spelling of /ō/ ← *ú or *ā out of the historical use of ו for the spelling of /ō/ ← *aw.

Table 6.1 Spelling of /ō/

Book	Defective	Plene	Total	Plene %
Genesis	3147	1982	5129	38.6
Exodus	3181	1240	4421	28.0
Leviticus	1925	1250	3175	39.4
Numbers	2541	1266	3807	33.3
Deuteronomy	2286	1280	3566	35.9
Joshua-Judges	2191	2340	4531	51.6
Samuel	3047	2564	5611	45.7
Kings	3570	2275	5845	38.9
Isaiah	2086	2315	4401	52.6
Jeremiah	2553	2297	4850	47.4
Ezekiel	2202	2392	4594	52.1
Minor Prophets	1747	1950	3697	52.7
Psalms	2220	3011	5231	57.6
Job	1054	1112	2166	51.3
Proverbs	684	1019	1703	59.8
Megillot	1055	1344	2399	56.0
Daniel	291	282	573	49.2
Ezra-Nehemiah	955	948	1903	49.8
Chronicles	2674	3195	5869	54.4

6.4.6. The Hebrew vowels /u/ and /ū/ are very stable, and most specimens are primal. The simple spelling *qibbuṣ* can represent either an historically short /u/ or a *defective* spelling of /ū/. The former has been screened out of our data. In due time the spelling of /ū/ *plene* prevailed but not on the same scale as with /ī/. *Defective* spellings of /ū/ are relatively frequent (about nineteen percent in our data).

6.5 Vowel types

The following series of sixty-five vowel types has been defined so that we can keep vowels with varying histories separate in our analyses.

6.5.1 Words containing /ī/

This vowel presents the opportunity for a scribal choice in the following twelve types of words:

•Type 1. Suffix -ī- on finite verb

Type 1	Low	Middle	High	Total
Defective	X	X	35	35
Plene	X	X	445	445
Total	X	X	480	480

> Note. An "X" in any of the "type summaries" in this chapter indicates a *structural zero*. This means that the rules defining that type exclude the possibility that the cell so marked could ever have an occupant. The vowel of Type 1, for instance, is always stressed, so the columns for low and middle stress must be vacant. When a cell is empty by chance (the type is not attested), the *sampling zero* will be shown by "0." These two sorts of zero have differing significance in contingency table analysis.

Verbs ending in /ī/ present an opportunity for *defective* spelling when they have a pronoun object suffix. Example: śamtîm, 'I put them,' שַׂמְתָּם שַׂמְתִּים. All are stressed.

In the qere text there are 444 *plene* spellings. With four curious exceptions -- יָדַעְתָּ (Psalm 140:13; Job 42:2); בָּנִית (1 Kings 8:48); וְעָשִׂית (Ezekiel 16:59) -- such verbs are not eligible for *defective* spelling unless they have a pronoun suffix. Over 3,000 unsuffixed verbs ending in /ī/ have been left out for this reason. The most common is יְהִי (× 866).

The thirty-five cases of *defective* spelling of suffixed verb-terminal /ī/ may be classified as follows:

1) Verbs derived from ל"י roots with /ī/ in the stem (× 24). The *plene* writing of the root is thus historical, but the vowel is not necessarily /ī/. (When it is, we have Type 3.)

וְזֵרִתָם -- Ezekiel 30:23

כְּלִתְנִי -- 1 Samuel 25:33

הִמְצִיתִךָ -- 2 Samuel 3:8

מְשִׁיתִהוּ -- Exodus 2:10

וְהִכִּיתִךָ -- 1 Samuel 17:46

וְהַעֲלִיתִהוּ -- Judges 11:31

וְעִנִּתִךָ -- Nahum 1:12

עָשִׂיתִם -- Genesis 6:7; Isaiah 42:16; Ezekiel 37:19

עֲשִׂיתִנִי -- Ezekiel 29:3

צִוִּיתִךָ -- Exodus 23:15; 31:6,11; 34:18; Deuteronomy 12:21;
          1 Samuel 21:3

צִוִּיתִם -- Exodus 32:8; Deuteronomy 9:12; 24:8;
          Jeremiah 29:23

הִרְאִיתִם --2 Kings 20:15

וְהִרְבִּיתִךָ -- Genesis 48:4

רְמִיתִנִי -- 1 Samuel 19:17

2) Biconsonantal roots yield three cases.

וַהֲבִאוֹתִךָ -- Ezekiel 39:2

הַעִירֹתִהוּ -- Isaiah 45:13; *plene* in P with Mm ל.

וְשַׁתָּה -- Hosea 2:5

3) Regular roots supply seven cases.

גֵּרַשְׁתִּהוּ -- Ezekiel 31:11

יְלִדְתִּנִי -- Jeremiah 15:10

וְהֵינִקָהוּ -- Exodus 2:9

לִבַּבְתִּנִי -- Song of Songs 4:9; *plene* later in verse.

הִכְרַעְתִּנִי -- Judges 11:35

הִשְׁאִלְתִּהוּ -- 1 Samuel 1:28

שִׁלְּחָנִי -- 1 Samuel 19:17

The vowel /ī/ is frequent in the stem of such verbs, and twenty-three of them already have /ī/ spelled *plene*. This phenomenon has given the impression that there is a constraint against spelling the same long vowel *plene* more than once in the same word. Recall the full discussion of this problem in Chapter 4. And notice that even here there are some words with both /ī/'s *defective*. That *defective* spelling is archaic. It occurs only once in the Writings. There are 265 opportunities for such a spelling in the Latter Prophets, but only eleven are *defective*. There are sixty-one such opportunities in the Pentateuch, and twelve of them are *defective*. Incidentally, they are evenly distributed among the sources J, E, D, P -- exactly three each!

•Type 2. Stem -*ī*- in *qal* of hollow root

Type 2	Low	Middle	High	Total
Defective	14	0	19	33
Plene	40	21	508	569
Total	54	21	527	602

Some *qal* verbs of hollow roots have long /ī/ in the stem. Example: *yāsîm*, 'he will put,' יָשִׂים יָשֵׂם.

The *qere* text has 571 *plene* spellings. Of the thirty-three *defective*, fourteen have suffixes, so the vowel in question is not stressed. Of the *defective* spellings, six are in the Pentateuch, sixteen in the Former Prophets, seven in the Latter Prophets, three in Poetry, one in the other Writings.

•Type 3. Stem -*ī*- in perfect of ל״ה root

Type 3	Low	Middle	High	Total
Defective	13	0	17	30
Plene	94	2	1144	1240
Total	107	2	1161	1270

Some perfect verbs of ל״י roots have /ī/ in the stem. Example: *bānîtî*, 'I built,' בָּנִיתִי בָּנִתִי.

Of the thirty examples of *defective* spelling, more than half (× 16) are in Samuel and Jeremiah. This represents an

intermediate stage when *defective* spelling is used because it is
traditional, as in the rest of the Primary History (seven more
defective examples), and *plene* spelling is used because
phonetic, as in the Latter Prophets and Writings (seven *defective* examples).

•Type 4. Stem -*î*- in *hipᶜil* forms

Type 4	Low	Middle	High	Total
Defective	299	1	419	719
Plene	890	39	4006	4935
Total	1189	40	4425	5654

The long /ī/ in the second syllable of some *hipᶜil* stems,
such as *hizgîr*, is an opportunity for spelling choice. The short
vowel in the shut first syllable is not an opportunity for *plene*
spelling. Example: הִזְגֵּר הִזְגִּיר.

The manuscripts are rather labile in this matter. They vary
considerably and do not always agree with the descriptions of
selected cases by the masoretes. The uneasiness of the
masoretes with the *defective* spelling is reflected in the addition of *dageš* to the following consonant in some cases.

The history of this vowel is not clear. To judge from comparative Semitic evidence, it was not primally long. This is seen
within Hebrew, too, in the fact that the reflex is often /ē/ or
/a/ (Philippi's Law). It was not written in early Hebrew inscriptions until shortly before the Exile (sixth century Arad ostraca
[Aharoni 1970: 20-21; Parunak 1978: 30; Zevit 1980: 31; Sarfatti
1982: 59]). Thus, the absence of ' does not necessarily mean
defective spelling of /ī/, although this is how it is usually taken
in the normalizing phonology of the masoretes. The /ī/ probably arose by analogy with the stem vowel of some עַ״י roots,
in which *î* ← *iy (Type 2). We have no way of knowing when that
took place. In any case, whatever the actual vowel at any stage
-- /i/, /ē/, /a/, or /ī/ -- the absence of ' in words of this type
is an archaism. So this *defective* spelling is of interest.

•Type 5. Stem -ī- in forms from י״פ roots

Type 5	Low	Middle	High	Total
Defective	46	X	X	46
Plene	316	X	X	316
Total	362	X	X	362

Some *qal* derivatives of verbs with י״פ roots have /ī/ in the first position. Example: *yīrā* ᵓ, 'he will fear,' יִירָא יִרָא.

Note וַיִּצֶר (Genesis 2:19) and וַיִּיצֶר (Genesis 2:7). These details of MT are confirmed by *Genesis R.* 9:7, which argues from the double י that God created man with two *yēṣer*'s. This optional *plene* spelling is realized only when the verb begins with /y/. Thirty-four of the *defective* spellings are in the Primary History (fairly evenly distributed), twelve elsewhere. Confusion with another root is possible: *metheg* shows that וַיִּרְא (Joshua 4:14) is *defective*. Compare Exodus 14:10. Many words in this set could be derived from a biconsonantal byform of the root in which the initial י has been lost (Andersen 1970b), so they are not really *defective*. But by the nature of the problem, it is impossible to tell if יִרָא (× 8) is a *defective* spelling of a form with root ירא or a derivative of the alloroot רא. Similarly with the fourteen or so cases of plural ירא (Deuteronomy 13:12; 17:13; 19:20; 21:21; 1 Samuel 4:7; 7:7; 17:11; 2 Samuel 12:18; 1 Kings 8:40; 2 Kings 10:4; Qohelet 3:14; Nehemiah 6:16; Micah 7:17; compare 2 Samuel 10:19). The versions show that וַיִּרְא (Exodus 20:18) was read as וייראו (compare verse 20). See also Type 15.

•Type 6. Suffix -ī (m) of plural nouns

Type 6	Low	Middle	High	Total
Defective	X	X	575	575
Plene	X	X	11890	11890
Total	X	X	12465	12465

Example: *nĕ bî ʾî m*, 'prophets,' נְבִיאִם נְבִיאִם. Always
stressed. This spelling begins to appear in Hebrew inscriptions
just before the Exile (Arad 24:19). Its scope is indeterminate.
Are all geographical names which end in /-īm/ derived from
plural common nouns? The *defective* spellings are dominated
by גּוֹיִם and לְוִיִּם, which are invariant under the influence of
the י of the stem. הַגּוֹיִים occurs in Babylonian MS240 (*Textus
1:* 143). Leaving these out, there are only 164 others (121 in the
Pentateuch). Many of these have /ī/ in the preceding syllable.

The full picture of the spelling of this morpheme cannot be
recovered from the MT. The unique עִבְרִיִּים (Exodus 3:18)
requires *ʿibriyyî m*; the more usual עִבְרִים could be *ʿibriyyīm*,
but it is always *ʿibrî m*. Similarly for other gentilics: כִּתִּים
(Genesis 10:4; Numbers 24:24; Isaiah 23:1; Daniel 11:30; 1 Chronicles 1:7); כִּתִּיִם (Ezekiel 27:6 -- qere כְּתִיִּים); כִּתִּיִּים (Isaiah 23:12
[qere כִּתִּים]; Jeremiah 2:10 [no qere]). The tradition moves
between the two, with preference for the old spelling with the
later pronunciation. The same word in the Arad ostraca is to be
read *kittiyyī m*, not *kittî m*; it cannot be used as evidence for
the general use of *plene* spelling for this morpheme.

•Type 7. Stem -*ī*- (first vowel) in other nouns

Type 7	Low	Middle	High	Total
Defective	340	X	X	340
Plene	705	X	X	705
Total	1045	X	X	1045

Some nouns which do not have a hollow root have first
vowel /ī/, never stressed. Example: *tīrōš*, 'wine,' תִּירוֹשׁ תִּרֹשׁ.
Common nouns of this type are *plene*, except for פִּילֶגֶשׁ. Proper
nouns are mixed, some preserving the archaic *defective* spelling, notably in the Former Prophets (× 29); there are none in
the Pentateuch. Thirty are due to *šīlō* (שִׁלֹה [× 22] and שִׁלוֹ [×
8]). In Genesis 49:10 *šî lōh*, if it is *the same word*, is the only
exception. But this difference tells against reading 'Shiloh' or

'what is his' (šellô) and even more against remedies requiring greater consonantal changes. The orthography tips the balance to šay lô, 'tribute will come to him' (Isaiah 18:7). Most of the proper nouns of this type which are *defective* present the *plene* as well.

•Type 8. Stem *-ī-* in nouns with hollow roots

Type 8	Low	Middle	High	Total
Defective	14	2	13	29
Plene	269	70	286	625
Total	283	72	299	654

Some nouns with hollow roots have /ī/ in the stem. Example: qīr, 'wall,' קִיר קָר. See Isaiah 22:5. Ten of the *defectives* are contributed by the archaic spelling צָן, which is never *plene*. אֵשׁ is found in the Siloam Tunnel Inscription, אִישׁ in the Lachish Letters. In the Bible ʾīš (× 1,657) is never *defective*; it has been dropped on statistical grounds (§ 5.6.3).

•Type 9. Stem *-ī-* (second vowel) in nouns

Type 9	Low	Middle	High	Total
Defective	241	38	874	1153
Plene	1470	531	3064	5065
Total	1711	569	3938	6218

Example: nāgīd, 'prince,' נָגִיד נָגִד. 'David' contributes to the large count of *defective* high-stress words (§ 1.2).

•Type 10. Stem *-ī-* in other proper nouns

Type 10	Low	Middle	High	Total
Defective	22	2	161	185
Plene	69	0	298	367
Total	91	2	459	552

Since vowel position is not specified, this residuum contains several different phonetic shapes.

•Type 11. Suffix $-\bar{\imath}\,(t)$ of feminine nouns

Type 11	Low	Middle	High	Total
Defective	4	11	23	38
Plene	58	133	393	584
Total	62	144	416	622

Example: ʾaḥărīt, 'end,' אַחֲרִת אַחֲרִית. The *plene* spelling of this morpheme appears in Lachish Letter 20:1, but Arad 20:1 still has *defective* spelling. Of the 622 feminine singular nouns with suffix $-\bar{\imath}t$, only thirty-eight (six percent) are *defective*. Twenty-nine of these are in the Pentateuch (none in Genesis), two in 2 Samuel, six in the Former Prophets, and only one -- רֵאשִׁתוֹ in Job 42:12 -- in the Writings. An archaism of the Pentateuch. Twenty-six are ordinals with /ī/ in the stem.

•Type 12. Residuum of $-\bar{\imath}$- opportunities

Type 12	Low	Middle	High	Total
Defective	12	1	13	26
Plene	42	5	48	95
Total	54	6	61	121

6.5.2 Words containing /ē/

This vowel presents the opportunity for a scribal choice with the following twelve types of vowels:

•Type 13. Stem-terminal $-\bar{e}$- in prepositions

Type 13	Low	Middle	High	Total
Defective	152	X	X	152
Plene	854	X	X	854
Total	1006	X	X	1006

Some suffixed prepositions have a *defective* pseudo-plural extension of the stem. Example: ʾălēhem, 'to them,' אֲלֵיהֶם אֲלֵהֶם.

Table 6.2 shows that in suffixation אֶל, 'unto,' behaves in three ways: 1) *defective* preferred (Pentateuch and Chronicles), 2) *defective* never used (Samuel), 3) a mixture, but *plene* preferred (the rest of the Bible, especially the Latter Prophets and Writings).

Table 6.2 Spelling of preposition 'unto'

Book	Defective	Plene	Total
Genesis	24	19	43
Exodus	28	9	37
Leviticus	14	5	19
Numbers	17	7	24
Deuteronomy	9	12	21
Torah	92	52	144
Joshua	3	20	23
Judges	6	13	19
1 Samuel	0	11	11
2 Samuel	0	8	8
1 Kings	3	9	12
2 Kings	10	19	29
F. Prophets	22	80	102
Major Prophets	6	113	119
Minor Prophets	1	11	12
L. Prophets	7	124	131
Poetry	1	10	11
Megillot	2	5	7
Ezra-Neh-Chron.	12	12	24
Writings	15	27	42
Total	136	283	419

Suffixed forms of עַל involving -ֶי- occur 523 times, ninety-six in the Pentateuch. The distribution is shown in Table 6.3.

Of the 151 cases of these two prepositions with *defective* spelling, 129 are in the Primary History, 107 in the Pentateuch (nine in Deuteronomy).

The remaining sixty-four specimens include בֵּינִי (× 31), בַּלְעֲדֵי (× 9), בַּעֲדִי (× 1), עֲדִי (× 13), and תַּחְתִּי (× 10). Apart from בֵּינְכֶם (Isaiah 59:2), all of these are *plene*.

Table 6.3 Spelling of preposition 'upon'

Book	Defective	Plene	Total
Genesis	1	14	15
Exodus	7	14	21
Leviticus	4	10	14
Numbers	3	27	30
Deuteronomy	0	16	16
Torah	15	81	96
Rest	0	427	427
Total	15	508	523

Awareness of facts such as these brings a control to decisions made in textual studies. Thus *ʾălēhem* is *defective* in three-quarters of its occurrences in Exodus. This enhances the possibility that אלהם, which is not normal spelling of anything by post-exilic standards, would press a scribe to normalize it one way or the other according to his best judgment. Thus MT at Exodus 2:25 reads אלהים where LXX αυτοις points to אליהם, each tradition having resolved the ambiguity of the purely consonantal spelling in its own way. The evidence of Table 6.2 lends support to LXX, aided by the fact that the syntax of MT is problematical. This, however, is neutralized by the fact that MT וידע is not simply a graphic variant of the reading used by LXX ויודע, unless the latter existed as a *hipᶜil*, read in *defective* form as *qal* by MT and in *plene* form as *nipᶜal* by LXX. Attention to these orthographic details then shows that the choice does not simply lie between MT and LXX as to which is the "correct" (original) reading. For וידע אלהם is purely consonantal spelling in which both words are ambiguous, a reading which has the virtue of explaining both MT and LXX as derivative, rather than trying to explain one as a (mistaken) variant of the other. Innumerable instances of this sort might be given. The example serves to alert textual scholars to the need to take such orthographic factors into account whenever the text (or texts) present curious spellings or even when a textual possibility is hidden in a quite innocent spelling.

•Type 14. Stem-terminal -$\bar{e}$- in nouns

Type 14	Low	Middle	High	Total
Defective	41	6	X	47
Plene	2236	5022	X	7258
Total	2277	5028	X	7305

Plural nouns (construct or stem) ending in /-$\bar{e}$/ may be spelled *defective*. Example: *gōyēhem*, 'their nations,' גּוֹיֵיהֶם גּוֹיֵהֶם. See the discussion under § 5.5.4.

•Type 15. Stem-initial -$\bar{e}$- in verbs

Type 15	Low	Middle	High	Total
Defective	11	X	X	11
Plene	106	X	X	106
Total	117	X	X	117

Some verbs derived from פ"י roots and from טב, which has a pseudo-פ"י alloroot as a byform in many verb derivations, may have /$\bar{e}$/ as the first stem vowel, which admits of either spelling. This belongs in the category /$\bar{e}$/ ← *ay*. Example: *mēṭīb*, 'doing good,' מֵטִיב מֵיטִיב.

The /$\bar{e}$/ in the first position of many verbs with פ"י roots, such as 'he will sit,' יֵשֵׁב, behaves as if derived from *i* and is never spelled *plene*. We cannot be sure that all these cases are correctly categorized, for the identity of the root is often uncertain. Thus the root of תֵּחַד (Genesis 49:6) is a notorious problem. Even if a פ"י root is etymological, an apparently *defective* spelling could attest a biconsonantal byform. See the discussion of Type 5. This explanation is more obvious in the case of the derivatives of טב ~ יטב.

Some manuscripts present a remarkable and possibly unique exception to this statement in the spelling תֵּיעָשֶׂה in Exodus 25:31; L reads תֵּעָשֶׂה. This unparalleled spelling of a *nipᶜal* seems to be a safeguard against reading *qal*.

•Type 16. Stem -*ē*- in verbs from ל״י roots

Type 16	Low	Middle	High	Total
Defective	1	4	61	66
Plene	3	1	127	131
Total	4	5	188	197

Some verbs derived from ל״י roots have /ē/ as the second vowel in the stem. Example: *hikkētī*, 'I struck,' הִכֵּיתִי הִכֵּתִי.

Defective spelling is conventional for the imperative, as in הַכֵּה (× 12). The spelling -ֶיה is never found. Other *defective* spellings are וְהִפְרֵתִי (Genesis 17:6); הָרְאֵתָ (Deuteronomy 4:35); שׁוֹשֵׁתִי (Isaiah 10:13); כְּסֵתִי (Ezekiel 31:15); וְהַעֲלֵתִי (Ezekiel 37:6); הֶלְאֵתִיךְ (Micah 6:3); הוֹרְתָנִי (Psalm 119:102). Deuteronomy 33:21 can hardly be included. There is only one case in the Writings.

•Type 17. Stem -*ē*- in verbs from other roots

Type 17	Low	Middle	High	Total
Defective	15	2	867	884
Plene	4	1	36	41
Total	19	3	903	925

Example: *haškēm*, 'to rise early,' הַשְׁכֵּם הַשְׁכִּים.

We cannot assume that the vocalization of the *hipᶜil* stem was stable enough to permit phonological inferences from the orthography. Comparing Type 4 above, how do we know (or rather, how did the masoretes know) which vowel to choose between /ī/ and /ē/? If *mater lectionis* י originally distinguished /ī/ from /ē/, then *plene* spelling of /ē/ under Type 17 points to /ī/ and *defective* spelling of /ī/ under Type 4 points to /ē/. The former is found only three times in the Pentateuch but is spread fairly evenly through the rest of the Bible. It seems, however, that the masoretes pointed words with *defective* spelling with /ē/ wherever possible, thus reducing the number of *defective* spellings of /ī/; and they pointed the *plene* spelling with /ī/ wherever possible, reducing the number of *plene* spellings with /ē/. Thus the same word *hkn* (*hākēn*) (Joshua 3:17) and *hkyn* (*hākîn*) (Joshua 4:3). In this way the text becomes bland, with fewer archaic spellings of /ī/ and fewer modern spellings of /ē/.

•Type 18. Stem -$\bar{e}$- in nouns from hollow roots

Type 18	Low	Middle	High	Total
Defective	18	0	0	18
Plene	520	220	40	780
Total	538	220	40	798

Some nouns derived from *media-yod* roots have $\hat{e}$ ← *ay* as the first vowel of the stem. Example: *hēl* (← *hayil*), 'force,' חֵיל חֵל. There are five *defective* spellings of *hēl* (2 Samuel 20:15; 1 Kings 21:23; Isaiah 26:1; Obadiah 20; Lamentations 2:8). Compare Frensdorff 64; Ginsburg 1897-1905: IV § 197.

It is not always possible to determine which words of shape *XēX*, where *X* is any consonant, have a biconsonantal root (*bēn*, 'son'), a hollow root (*rēq*, 'empty'), or a geminate root (*ʾēm*, 'mother'). The words meaning 'empty' are interesting (Ginsburg 1897-1905: IV § 201). Perhaps it is a case of a metaplastic stem rather than differences in spelling. The adverb is always רֵיקָם. רִיק is usually *rîq*, no suffixes. רֵק is *rēq*, and this is considered the stem of all suffixed forms (feminine and plural), even when spelled *plene*. In detail: רֵק (Genesis 37:24; Deuteronomy 32:47; Nehemiah 5:13) is rarer than רִיק (× 12), feminine רֵקָה (Ezekiel 24:11), רִיקָה (Isaiah 29:8), and רֵקוֹת (Genesis 41:27). But *rēqîm* can be רֵקִים (Judges 7:16; 2 Samuel 6:20; 2 Kings 4:3; 2 Chronicles 13:7 [Proverbs 28:19 in L]) or רֵיקִים (Judges 9:4; 11:3; Proverbs 12:11).

Other examples: הַר הַזֵּיתִים, 'Mount of Olives' (Zechariah 14:4); הַיֵּמִם (Genesis 36:24 -- doubly *defective*!); אֵלִים, 'rams' (Exodus 36:19; compare the discussion under Type 19 below of

אֵלִים in Isaiah 1:29); עָנֵי (Isaiah 3:8). The preposition *bên*, 'between,' is usually *plene* but *defective* in אִישׁ־הַבֵּנַיִם (1 Samuel 17:4, 23). With so few cases, and so much uncertainty over the actual pronunciation, little can be inferred from the spelling of nouns of this type.

•Type 19. Stem -*ē*- (first vowel) in other nouns

Type 19	Low	Middle	High	Total
Defective	418	27	102	547
Plene	51	48	62	161
Total	469	75	164	708

Nouns not based on *media-yod* roots may have /ē/ as the first vowel of the stem. Example: 'permanent,' אֵיתָן אֵתָן. (הֵיכָל is a major contributor, a loanword.) In most monosyllabic nouns of this type, such as ʔēm, 'mother,' אֵם, ē ← i and is not eligible for *plene* spelling.

The elaborate massora (Ginsburg 1897-1905: IV § 369) illustrates the confusion between 'rams,' 'oaks,' and 'gods.' In 1QIs[a] Isaiah 1:29 reads אלים (LXX reads επι τοις ειδωλοις) as if the Masoretic Text אילים is *plene* spelling of ʔēlîm, 'gods.' See Wernberg-Møller (1958: 254). But is ʔêlîm ← *ʔayil, 'terebinth'? This is interesting since things are usually the other way around -- MT *defective*, Qumran *plene*. Since LXX seems based on a text identical with 1QIs[a], the MT *plene* could be a late adjustment. If the opposite could be proved, then an early occurrence of the MT reading would point to 'oaks.' But a late development of the *plene* reading does not prove a new scribal belief that the word is 'oaks,' for the *plene* spelling of 'gods' also emerges, especially in Samaritan orthography of biblical and other texts. See Baillet 1979, but this development is probably much later. In Ezekiel 40:48 אַיִל, 'porch,' is spelled אַל, with Mp that this is a unique *defective* spelling of this word. Similarly, אֵיל פָּארָן (Genesis 14:6) is not *plene* spelling of ʔēl but construct of ʔayil, 'terebinth,' LXX τερεμινθον.

•Type 20. Stem -ē- (second vowel) in nouns

Type 20	Low	Middle	High	Total
Defective	202	40	4	246
Plene	28	126	8	162
Total	230	166	12	408

Example: *ḥăšēkā*, חֲשֵׁכָה חָשֵׁכָה. Nouns which have /ē/ as the second vowel of the stem are mostly of the type *kābēd* ('heavy') ← *kabidu*, and so are ineligible for *plene* spelling on historical as well as statistical grounds. וְקֵינִנוּ (Joshua 9:11) is the exception. Forms derived by preformative modification from ע"י roots, however, may be spelled either way.

•Type 21. Stem -ē- (first vowel) in proper nouns

Type 21	Low	Middle	High	Total
Defective	203	X	X	203
Plene	185	X	X	185
Total	388	X	X	388

Some proper nouns have /ē/ as the first vowel in the stem. Example: תֵּמָן תֵּימָן. In that position the vowel is not stressed.

This Type illustrates the complication introduced by possible differences in dialect. In the North, where the diphthong more readily monophthongized, the *defective* spelling (as in Job 6:19; 9:9; 22:1) represents archaic consonantal spelling, not late *defective* phonetic spelling. See Freedman 1969a.

•Type 22. Stem -ē- (second vowel) in proper nouns

Type 22	Low	Middle	High	Total
Defective	54	X	276	330
Plene	14	X	15	29
Total	68	X	291	359

Some proper nouns have /ē/ as the second vowel in the stem. Example: 'Yabesh,' יָבֵשׁ יָבֵישׁ.

•Type 23. Stem -$\bar{e}$- (first vowel) residuum

Type 23	Low	Middle	High	Total
Defective	15	X	X	15
Plene	102	X	X	102
Total	117	X	X	117

•Type 24. Stem -$\bar{e}$- residuum

Type 24	Low	Middle	High	Total
Defective	52	3	44	99
Plene	9	0	6	15
Total	61	3	50	114

Residuum of all words containing /$\bar{e}$/ not covered by any of the preceding rules. Example: אַרְאִיל ,אַרִיאֵל.

6.5.3 Words containing /$\bar{\varepsilon}$/

This vowel presents an opportunity for scribal choice in the following two types of words:

•Type 25. Stem-terminal /$\bar{\varepsilon}$/ in nouns

Type 25	Low	Middle	High	Total
Defective	X	X	78	78
Plene	X	X	2388	2388
Total	X	X	2466	2466

The plural ending εy in the stem of some suffixed nouns may be spelled *defective*. Example: $^c\bar{e}n\bar{\varepsilon}k\bar{a}$, 'thy eyes,' עֵינֶיךָ עֵנֶךָ. The number of *defective* spellings is indeterminate for reasons given above (§ 5.5.5.2). In any case it is very small.

•Type 26. Stem /ɛ̄/ in verbs

Type 26	Low	Middle	High	Total
Defective	X	X	10	10
Plene	X	X	136	136
Total	X	X	146	146

Feminine plural verbs of certain roots ending in -ɛ̄ynā may have -ɛ̄y- spelled *defective*. Example: *tihyɛ̄ynā*, 'they will be,' תִּהְיֶ֫נָה תִּהְיֶ֫ינָה. See above § 5.5.5.2.

6.5.4 Words containing /ā/

Apart from the four main categories of word-terminal /ā/ which are invariably *plene* (see § 3.3.2) and so have been eliminated as not presenting scribes with a choice, this vowel presents a choice in the following three types of words:

> •Note. The pronoun suffix -*kā*, 'thy,' may be spelled either way. The pseudo *plene* spelling of this suffix is so infrequent that it is disqualified from consideration as a spelling option for a scribe on statistical grounds, as explained in Chapter 5. Furthermore, as we have already pointed out, the variant spelling probably preserves some meager evidence of an alternate pronunciation. It is possible that some of the cases of *plene* spelling in the Bible are due to pressure to resolve the ambiguity with the feminine or simply to conform to the general practice of spelling terminal -*ā* with ה. It is also interesting to note that the scribes did not recognize a *defective* spelling of ʾêkâ. They did not point אֵיךְ, only אֵיךְ or אֵיכָה.

•Type 27. Suffix -*tā* of perfect verbs

Type 27	Low	Middle	High	Total
Defective	930	0	855	1785
Plene	89	0	60	149
Total	1019	0	915	1934

Second person singular perfect verbs ending in *-tā* may be spelled either way. The *defective* spelling is more frequent. In discussing this phenomenon, the point is always made that the *plene* spelling is more likely to be invoked when the root is irregular. נָתַתָּה is the parade example; it accounts for sixty-five of the examples, whereas נָתַתָּ occurs twenty-seven times. To the extent that this is so, a purely graphic consideration has been imposed on other factors. The *plene* usage is found throughout the Bible, and it can give rise to *ketib/qere*, as with שַׁתָּ (Psalm 90:8). The *plene* spelling with regular verbs is found everywhere except in the late prose writings.

As has already been mentioned in the note preceding this section, this phenomenon is better explained in phonological terms. Qumran texts prefer the *plene* spelling. It now seems that in this case the consonantal text preserves a real difference in pronunciation, which the masoretes reduced to uniformity by their vocalization. But, unlike the Qumran scribes, they did not add the *mater lectionis* (Kutscher 1974), or rather, they did not carry it through completely. (We know that in the case of ה *locale* there is a tradition that it was added to nouns used locatively but not governed by a preposition.)

•Type 28. Suffix *-nā* of feminine plural verbs

Type 28	Low	Middle	High	Total
Defective	41	X	X	41
Plene	301	X	X	301
Total	342	X	X	342

The suffix of feminine plural verbs ending in *-nā* may be spelled either way.

Twenty-seven of the forty-one *defective* spellings occur in the Pentateuch, three in Samuel, seven in Ezekiel (showing that the old spelling, or rather pronunciation, was still in use in the sixth century), one in Zechariah, and three in Ruth. So we have yet another characteristic archaism of the Pentateuch,

evidence of a variant pronunciation rather than an optional
defective spelling.

•Type 29. Suffix -$\bar{a}$ of intensive imperatives

Type 29	Low	Middle	High	Total
Defective	X	X	3	3
Plene	X	X	312	312
Total	X	X	315	315

The three apparent *defective* spellings all give rise to *qere*
variants of dubious authenticity (Orlinsky 1940-1).

6.5.5 Words containing /$\bar{o}$/

We specify twenty-six types of words involving /$\bar{o}$/ which
present the scribes with a spelling choice.

•Type 30. The preposition כְּמוֹ

Type 30	Low	Middle	High	Total
Defective	X	X	33	33
Plene	X	X	51	51
Total	X	X	84	84

The preposition 'like' has an alloform כְּמ- which occurs as
free form or suffixed. These are archaic or at least poetic.
When suffixed, it may be spelled *defective* כְּמ or *plene* כְּמוֹ. The
defective form occurs only when suffixed.

Suffixed *kāmō*- is used throughout the Bible, but half the
defective forms are found in the Pentateuch, where there are
twice as many *defective* as *plene*. Elsewhere *plene* are more
numerous than *defective*(except in Job); see Table 6.4.

Table 6.4 Suffixed preposition 'like'

Book	Defective	Plene	Total
Genesis	2	2	4
Exodus	10	1	11
Leviticus	0	2	2
Numbers	1	0	1
Deuteronomy	4	3	7
Torah	17	8	25
Judges	0	3	3
1 Samuel	1	2	3
2 Samuel	1	2	3
1 Kings	0	7	7
2 Kings	3	2	5
Former Prophets	5	16	21
Isaiah	0	4	4
Jeremiah	1	4	5
Ezekiel	1	0	1
Minor Prophets	2	3	5
Latter Prophets	4	11	15
Psalms	0	7	7
Job	5	2	7
Poetry	5	9	14
Lamentations	0	1	1
Nehemiah	1	2	3
Chronicles	1	4	5
Other Writings	2	7	9
Total	33	51	84

•Type 31. Words ending in הֹ- or וֹ (not 'his')

Type 31	Low	Middle	High	Total
Archaic	X	X	757	757
Standard	X	X	739	739
Total	X	X	1496	1496

Example: $z\bar{o}$, 'this,' זוֹ זֹה. Words ending in -$\bar{o}$, excluding the suffix 'his', which has been eliminated on statistical grounds, may be spelled with the *defective* archaic הֹ- or with the standard וֹ-. The archaic הֹ- was never made *plene* הוֹ- in

the MT, although it is found at Qumran, as in the spelling
פרעוה. This type includes prepositions כמו, etc., which when
not suffixed are always spelled with ו (compare Type 30). The
free forms are כמו כמו למו, never *כמה, etc. Their distribution is shown in Table 6.5.

Table 6.5 Free form prepositions 'in,' 'like,' 'to'

Form	Isaiah	Psalms	Job	Other
כמו	3	1	5	0
כמו	6	20	11	20
למו	0	0	4	0

Another set of words in this type consists of the infinitives
absolute of ל"ה roots; see also Type 38. (In studying the spelling of the infinitive absolute, it needs to be remembered that
its use declined after the Exile.) The spelling of ninety-eight
infinitives absolute of this type is shown in Table 6.6.

Table 6.6 Infinitives absolute

Section	Archaic	Standard	Total
Pentateuch	14	4	18
Former Prophets	18	2*	20
Latter Prophets	24	22	46
Poetry	6	2	8
Other Writings	4	2	6

* Note: Both in Samuel, and one still has the archaic form
when repeated in 1 Chronicles 21:24.

As already mentioned, the original writing of the suffix -ō,
'his,' was ה-, superseded almost totally by י-, which occurs
7,710 times. This process was carried through completely in
the Samaritan Pentateuch. In the Masoretic Text some fifty-
five instances of the old spelling survive. Some are found in

fixed spellings -- 'his tent,' אָהֳלֹה (Genesis 9:21; 12:8; 13:3; 35:21 [Mp of L says four instances, but there is a masoretic tradition for five such spellings, the fifth being in Genesis 26:25 -- Ginsburg 1897-1905: IV § 171]); 'all of it,' כֻּלֹּה (× 18: 2 Samuel 2:9, Isaiah 15:3; 16:7; Jeremiah 2:21; 8:6, 10, 10; 15:10; 20:7; 48:31, 38; Ezekiel 11:15; 20:40; 36:10; Hosea 13:2; Nahum 2:1; Habbakuk 1:9, 15; curiously, never in the Pentateuch). Others are genuinely archaic -- סוּתֹה עִירֹה (Genesis 49:11, with two cases of וֹ- in parallel!); בְּעִירֹה (Exodus 22:4); כְּסוּתֹה (Exodus 22:26, compare swt in Kilamuwa [8]); בְּרֵעֹה (Exodus 32:17) and פַרְעֹה (Exodus 32:25), both problematic; נֻסְכֹּה (Leviticus 23:13); וּבְנֻחֹה (Numbers 10:36); קֻבֹּה (Numbers 23:8); לֵחֹה (Deuteronomy 34:7); וּשְׁפֶלָתֹה (Joshua 11:16); שֹׁוכֹה (Judges 9:49); קִצֹה (2 Kings 19:23, with qere, as in Isaiah); נְכֹתֹה (2 Kings 20:13 = Isaiah 39:2); תְּבוּאָתֹה (Jeremiah 2:3; Ezekiel 48:18); בֹּה (ketib in Jeremiah 17:24); הֹדֹה (Jeremiah 22:18); עֶזְרֹה (Ezekiel 12:14); הֲמוֹנֹה (Ezekiel 31:18; 32:31, 32; 39:11); בְּתוֹכֹה (Ezekiel 48:15,21); בְּסֻכֹּה (Psalm 10:9; 27:5); שִׁירֹה (Psalm 42:9); מָעֻזֹּה (Daniel 11:10). Others survived because the ה- was interpreted otherwise, for example as a feminine noun ending. מְנֻחָה (Genesis 49:15) should be מנחה as the masculine טוב shows.

This phenomenon's distribution needs to be viewed in the light of the number of opportunities, book by book. One must ask if there were scribal conventions, assisted perhaps by phonetic factors, that preferred one or the other spelling depending on the pronoun suffix. This might obtain for some books (locally), if not for the whole Bible uniformly.

There are enough specimens from sixth-century books to indicate that the style was still in vogue at that time (it is still in evidence in the Lachish Letters). With the exception of one occurrence in Daniel, the old spelling is not found in any certainly post-exilic works.

The alternative spellings of word-terminal -ō as ה- or וֹ- where the suffix is not 'his' are met in proper nouns: שִׁילֹה in Genesis 49:10; שִׁילוֹ in Judges 21:21, 21; Jeremiah 7:12; שִׁלֹה twenty-one times in the Former Prophets plus Jeremiah 26:6; שִׁלוֹ in Judges 21:19; 1 Samuel 1:24; 3:21; 14:3; Jeremiah 7:14; 26:9; 41:5; שֹׂכֹה or שֹׂוכֹה five times in the Former Prophets; שֹׂוכוֹ three times in Chronicles. Et cetera.

Among the particles, פֹה is generally used (× 57), with פוֹ only in Ezekiel 40-41 (× 24 -- פֹּה thirteen times, eleven in Chapter 40!), and פֹא once (Job 38:11). זֹי occurs eleven times

(unless more are hiding as זֶה); זוּ in Hosea 7:16 and Psalm
132:12; but never זוּא, in spite of זאת. ᵉp̄ō is three ways:
אֵיפֹה (× 10); אֵפוֹא (× 11); אֵפוֹ (× 4, all in Job, which also has the
other two). Compare אֵיכֹה (2 Kings 6:13).

There are other words in which it is an archaic suffix of unknown identity -- 'animal,' חַיְתוֹ (× 8), 'son of,' בְּנוֹ (× 3), and
מַעְיְנוֹ (Psalm 114:8).

The picture of the spelling of word-terminal /ō/ is thus
quite complex, and there are no firm indications of just when
the switch from ה- to וֹ took place; but there is no indication
that the old spelling was used routinely after the sixth century.

Excluded from Type 31 is כֹה (× 577), invariant. Next to
this the most common words with this spelling are שְׁלֹמֹה (×
293) and פַּרְעֹה (× 274), always with the archaic spelling. פרעו
is found in the Genesis Apocryphon. On the other hand, ᵒō, 'or,'
(× 320) is always אוֹ, never אֹה.

It is a question whether any of these variants should come
under the rubric of *ketib/qere*. Levita (Ginsburg 1867b: 179)
declared that any such cases were scribal errors --

וכולם טעותי סופרים כי לא נמצא לעולם מלה

דכתיב בסופה ה''א בחולם וקרי בוי''ו

Gordis (1937: List 4) considers them all to have *qere*, but
Mm 2264 and 2480 do not cover all the facts and L does not
recognize all instances. The following *ketibin* in ה- have been
given *qariᵒan* in וֹ, at least in L:

קָצֹה קצו -- 2 Kings 19:23

נְכֹחֹה נכחו -- 2 Kings 20:13

כֹה כו -- Jeremiah 17:24

הַמוֹנֹה המונו -- Ezekiel 32:32

We have seen (§ 2.3.5) that -ō, 'his,' is thought to follow
Path 1. To judge from cuneiform transcriptions, place names,
which use this spelling, originally ended in -ā. Thus עַכּוֹ was
Akka, but *Akku* from the eighth century onwards. We cannot be

certain of the sound behind the spelling of such words.

•Type 32. The negative particle 'not' לֹא

Type 32	Low	Middle	High	Total
Defective	X	4996	X	4996
Plene	X	188	X	188
Total	X	5184	X	5184

In Deuteronomy 3:11 it is spelled לֹה. (Compare Judges 20:7.) There are also some well-known cases of confusion with לֹו, 'to him,' which might be written לֹא and vice versa; that is, לֹו might be 'not.' At 1 Samuel 2:16 and 20:2 לֹו has qere לֹא. A further complication is lū, spelled לֹו or לֻא (Gordis 1937: List 5). Many of the *plene* spellings of 'not' are due to a secondary convention that prefers the *plene* spelling for הֲלֹוא, 'is it not?' There is also a tendency to use the *plene* when 'not' is preceded by a preposition. A similar effect is not present with וְלֹא. See Table 6.7. (*bĕ lō ʾ* includes בּ, כּ, לֹ, and שׁ forms.)

Table 6.7 Spelling of 'not'

Form	Defective	Plene	Total
lō ʾ	3252	25	3277
wĕ lō ʾ	1583	7	1590
bĕ lō ʾ	38	7	45
hă lō ʾ	124	148	272
Total	4997	187	5184

Levita (Ginsburg 1867b) found a *massora* to the effect that לֹוא occurs thirty-five times. As is so often the case, the identity of the portion of the Bible to which the count applies has apparently been lost, for there are 187, twenty-one in Jeremiah alone. The list derives from the *massora marginalis* of Leviticus 5:1 (Weil 1968 Mm 681). This is incomplete and confused. It lists לֹא in Isaiah 28:15 as *plene* (but it is *defective* in L and P) as well as all three in Jeremiah 5:12 (only one is in L where it has the *massora* לֹה; there are two in P, each bearing לֹה!). At Jeremiah 5:24 and 49:20, L has לֹה מל, even though the text is *defective*. P had ולא in the first hand at Jeremiah 5:24, but it has the *massora*, and ו has been added. In P at Jeremiah 49:20, both are *defective* with no annotation. Mm 681 cites two instances of לוא in the Torah.

The trend to *plene* spelling of *hă lō ʾ* did not prevail fully. Only fifty-four percent of them are *plene*. The *plene* has not taken hold to the same degree in all parts of the Bible, as Table 6.8 shows.

Table 6.8 Spelling of 'is not?'

Book	Defective	Plene	Total
Pentateuch	17	12(Mm 27)	29
Joshua-Judges	14	3	17
Samuel	0	34	34
Kings	25	20	45
Isaiah 1-39	4	5	9
Isaiah 40-66	2	15	17
Jeremiah	2	14	16
Ezekiel	7	9	16
Minor Prophets	1	27	28
Poetry	31	2	33
Ruth-Nehemiah	3	7	10
Chronicles	18	0	18
Total	124	148	272

There is no clear-cut segregation of *plene* spelling in distinct parts of the Bible. The distribution is instructive. Short books with only one or two cases cannot be expected to show any trend. Larger books show three distinct patterns. 1) All, or nearly all, instances of *hă lō ʾ* are spelled *defective* -- Chronicles (all!), Judges (13 out of 14), Poetry (31 out of 33). 2) All, or nearly all, instances of *hӑlō ʾ* are spelled *plene* -- Samuel (all!), Ezra-Nehemiah, Minor Prophets (27 out of 28), Isaiah II, Jeremiah. 3) Mixed practice is found in the Primary History (except Judges, Samuel) and Megillot. These patterns show that spelling praxis for the Bible as a whole is governed neither by rule nor hazard. In some parts one rule prevails, in some parts the opposite rule; in some parts there seems to be no rule. Each part of the Bible has its own scribal history.

The survival of an uneven distribution pattern is all the more surprising when we remember that the trend towards *plene* spelling of *lō ʾ* was in full swing towards the beginning of the common era. The Nash Papyrus has only לוא (Kutscher 1974: 171). It is an interesting sidelight on scribal habits that Segal's description (*Leshonenu* 15: pp. 27ff.) erroneously gives *defective* spelling three times. The *plene* spelling of 'not' in Qumran manuscripts is notorious (Kutscher 1959: 129, 188). This makes it remarkable that the Masoretic Text preserves the earlier style to such a degree. Not that the text was ever completely frozen. One has only to collate any two manuscripts or editions to discover that this morpheme, perhaps more than any other, varied in spelling. A differs from L in this -- both ways! A is *defective* in Judges 8:2, 2 Kings 8:23, 13:12 against the *plene* of L. But A is *plene* in 1 Kings 14:28 against *defective* in L. The Snaith edition is *defective* in Judges 8:2, 2 Kings 8:23, 13:12, Ezekiel 17:10 against the *plene* of L. It looks as if L has drifted a little. Even so, only a handful of the 272 occurrences of *hӑlō ʾ* show variations in the manuscripts from the facts in Table 6.8. Thus the manuscripts are agreed in the striking difference between Samuel and Chronicles. This needs emphasis, because it is the opposite of what one might have expected. Chronicles has resisted the pressure to modernize; Samuel has succumbed completely. It is reasonable to infer from this that Chronicles was written before this spelling came upon the scene.

•Type 33. *Nota accusativi* $^{\jmath}\bar{o}t$, אֵת אוֹת

Type 33	Low	Middle	High	Total
Defective	1031	X	X	1031
Plene	357	X	X	357
Total	1388	X	X	1388

This allomorph is used only with pronoun suffixes. There is an option of אֶתְהֶם or אוֹתָם. אוֹתְכֶם (Joshua 23:15), אוֹתְהֶם (Ezekiel 23:45), and אוֹתְהֶן (Ezekiel 23:47) occur, but this variation was forced on the masoretes by the *plene* spelling. We have no way of knowing how many instances of אֶתְכֶם (× 300), אֶתְהֶם (× 5), and אֶתְהֶן (× 13), all pointed -אֶת, were originally pronounced $^{\jmath}\bar{o}t$- and so could be added to the *defective* spellings of this alloform of the preposition.

The *nota accusativi* is not distributed evenly through the Bible (Andersen and Forbes 1983). There is an increasing use of *plene* spelling, with very few in the Pentateuch (fifty-four out of 656, or eight percent), more in the Former Prophets (112 out of 324, or thirty-six percent), even more in the Latter Prophets (182 out of 353, or fifty-one percent). The sample in the Writings is small due to its sparse use in poetry and a decline in its use with pronoun objects in the work of the Chronicler. Result: nineteen out of sixty-five, or twenty-eight percent. The conservatism of the Pentateuch is impressive.

The question naturally arises: How are the scribal options exercised in the documentary sources of the Pentateuch? Table 6.9 shows the distribution. Table 6.10 shows the estimated cell counts for analysis of Table 6.9 under the model of independence (§ 1.8). Table 6.11 shows the standardized residuals. We find $\chi^2 = 9.59$ for these residuals. At the 99% confidence level with five degrees of freedom, statistical tables give $\chi^2_{99\%} = 15.09$. We therefore reject the hypothesis of nonhomogeneous spelling across the sources. The outlier threshold, $r_{99\%}$ equals 1.12, so only the overuse of *plenes* by D and the underuse of *plenes* by P draw (mild) interest.

Table 6.9 ʾōt in the Pentateuchal sources

Source	את	אות	Total
L	30	1	31
J	64	6	70
E+C	78	9	87
D	65	12	77
H	41	5	46
P	324	21	345
Total	602	54	656

Table 6.10 ʾōt in the sources: estimates

Source	את	אות	Total
L	28.45	2.55	31
J	64.24	5.76	70
E+C	79.84	7.16	87
D	70.66	6.34	77
H	42.21	3.79	46
P	316.60	28.40	345
Total	602.00	54.00	656

Table 6.11 ʾōt in the sources: residuals

Source	את	אות
L	+0.29	-0.97
J	-0.03	+0.10
E+C	-0.21	+0.69
D	-0.67	+2.25
H	-0.19	+0.62
P	+0.42	-1.39

Thus, the priestly sources show no marked tendency to post-exilic practice. If anything, P is more conservative than the others, and quite out of line with the post-exilic compositions. In particular, the heart of P (Exodus and Leviticus) contains 204 specimens of ʾōt, and only seven are spelled *plene*. Compared with other biblical writings, it is hard to believe that this material was composed after the Exile.

Just how archaic the MT Pentateuch is in this detail is shown by the orthography of 4QExod^f, possibly the oldest fragment of the Hebrew Bible (third century BCE). In thirteen places it has /ō/ *plene* where MT is *defective*. The suffixed *nota accusativi* is *plene* six out of seven times, all *defective* in MT. (*Defective* all three times in 11QpaleoLev [Freedman and Mathews 1985: 78].) MT preserves an earlier text type (orthographically speaking), from the Persian period at the latest.

•Type 34. Stem -ō- (first vowel) in prepositions and nouns

Type 34	Low	Middle	High	Total
Defective	678	188	387	1253
Plene	1020	506	1081	2607
Total	1698	694	1468	3860

Examples: *tōk*, 'inside,' תּוֹךְ תֹּךְ; *môt* ← *mawtu* (Path 3), *māwɛt* (absolute); מֹת מוֹת (not always distinguishable from the infinitive [Type 43]). Most common is יוֹם, 'day' (× 1,505), always *plene*, which has been eliminated on statistical grounds. (The stem is *defective* twice in dual יָמִם.)

•Type 35. Stem -ō- in *hipᶜil* of פ"ו roots

Type 35	Low	Middle	High	Total
Defective	260	X	X	260
Plene	1443	X	X	1443
Total	1703	X	X	1703

Hipᶜils and *nipᶜals* of פ"ו roots have ō ← *aw (Path 3) as the first vowel in the stem. Example: *hōlīd*, 'he engendered,' הוֹלִיד הֹלִיד. The *defective* spelling could be due to any of several factors. Not knowing which, we cannot tell where a particular usage comes in the history of spelling. The *plene* spelling can be archaic (diphthong) or modern (phonetic spelling of a long vowel). In between, *defective* spelling could reflect contraction while consonantal spelling still obtained or phonetic spelling of an unstressed long vowel. The former would be archaic dialectal, as in Job, which has the most such forms in proportion to its size (Freedman 1969a). The latter would be intermediate. There is a disproportionately large number in Samuel, Jeremiah, and Chronicles.

•Type 36. Suffix -$\bar{o}$- in *hip^{c}ils*, etc.

Type 36	Low	Middle	High	Total
Defective	32	0	154	186
Plene	14	0	78	92
Total	46	0	232	278

Some irregular roots have developed a special form in perfect verbs in *qal*, *nip^{c}al*, *hip^{c}il*, *pi^{c}el*. Example: *hăqīmōtī*, 'I erected,' הֲקִימֹתִי. See also the discussion under Type 4 above. The historical origins of this vowel are not known.

•Type 37. Suffix -$\bar{o}$ *(t)* of ל"ה infinitives

Type 37	Low	Middle	High	Total
Defective	103	1	97	201
Plene	101	27	845	973
Total	204	28	942	1174

Example: *libnōt*, 'to build,' לִבְנֹת לִבְנוֹת.

The historical origins of this vowel are not known. It could be an analogous formation to the regular verb, as in *lišmōr*, 'to keep' ($\bar{o}$ ← *$\acute{u}$ -- Path 5). But, if it comes from a feminine variant, which exists for many infinitives, especially those from irregular roots, then there is no way that *labanuytu* or *labunyatu*, or the like, could give /$\bar{o}$/ by known regular sound changes (Köhler 1956: 19). The alloroot *bnw* might account for it, if the stem vowel were *a -- *labnawtu* → *libnōt*, following Path 3. The use of -ōt as a general suffix of infinitive construct in Ethiopic points to the same origin, and Aramaic infinitives in -ū likewise come from *uwt*. Bauer and Leander (1922: 411) propose loss of intervocalic semivowel *galawatu* → *galātu* and *banayatu* → *banātu*, following then Path 4. Comparison is invited with ו in various words in old texts. The *ketib* קצוותו (Exodus 37:8; 39:4) can be accepted as an authentic archaic variant feminine plural, the more so as it occurs twice. It points to *qiṣwōtāw*, the ו in the stem being etymological. By analogy Type 37 infinitives could be *bunwai(u)*. The prominence of ו in the Tell Fehkereye inscription, where it might still be consonantal in apparent plurals, suggests that this morphology might have been more widespread than is usually suspected in early Northwest Semitic, including Hebrew. This would make such words comparable with Types 47 and 48 and explain why the distribution of the spellings is more like that in Types 47 and 48 than that in the other infinitives in Type 44.

•Type 38. Stem -ō- in infinitives absolute

Type 38	Low	Middle	High	Total
Defective	X	X	179	179
Plene	X	X	245	245
Total	X	X	424	424

Infinitive absolute is chiefly represented by *qal* of type *šāmōr*, שָׁמֹר שָׁמוֹר. *Qal* infinitives absolute of ל"י roots are in Type 31. This /ō/ ← *ā (Path 4). The vowel is always stressed.

•Type 39. Stem -ō- in *qal* active participles

Type 39	Low	Middle	High	Total
Defective	1954	636	1679	4269
Plene	282	100	658	1040
Total	2236	736	2337	5309

Example: *šōmēr*, 'watching,' שֹׁמֵר שׁמר.

Strictly speaking, since it is in the first position in the stem, the vowel in question does not bear direct stress. It is pretonic when the second vowel is stressed, and in this position 28.2 percent of its occurrences are spelled *plene*. It is further away from the stress when the stem is suffixed, and in this position thirteen percent of its occurrences are spelled *plene*. Inasmuch as *plene* spellings in all positions are rarer in the earlier books, this could preserve evidence of a stage when the standard pronunciation had not yet fully evolved. We cannot assume that the Old South Canaanite sound shift of $*\bar{a} \rightarrow \bar{o}$ took place uniformly over all dialects of early Hebrew. Some nouns with this phonetic shape could be considered to be participial, but the point is moot if there is no evidence of the existence of any other members of the verb system that would evolve from the same root. We could have added *kōhēn*, 'priest,' and its derivatives to this list, even though there are no other *qal* forms. But it occurs 440 times, always *defective*, so it turns out to be invariant. (See Table 5.1.)

•Type 40. Stem -ō- in *qal* imperfect regular verbs

Type 40	Low	Middle	High	Total
Defective	X	X	1356	1356
Plene	X	X	125	125
Total	X	X	1481	1481

Example: *yišmōr*, 'he will watch,' יִשְׁמֹר יִשְׁמוֹר (Path 5). By this history, the vowel exists only under stress. The much lower incidence of *plene* spelling of this vowel reflects the historical fact that the change $*\acute{u} \rightarrow \bar{o}$ occurred quite late. The distribution of the *plene* spelling throughout the Bible confirms this, and the frequent *plene* spelling of this vowel in Qumran texts completes the picture. The spelling is anomalous by biblical standards and in several occurrences has been overridden by a *qere* "correction" (Gordis 1937: Lists 21, 30, 31).

•Type 41. Stem -ō̱- in *qal* imperfect פ״נ roots.

Type 41	Low	Middle	High	Total
Defective	X	X	192	192
Plene	X	X	44	44
Total	X	X	236	236

Example: *yippōl*, 'he will fall,' יִפֹּל יִפּוֹל (Path 5). By this history, the vowel exists only under stress.

•Type 42. Stem -ō̱- in *qal* imperfect verbs of hollow root

Type 42	Low	Middle	High	Total
Defective	3	7	795	805
Plene	4	5	306	315
Total	7	12	1101	1120

Example: *yābō ͻ*, 'he will come,' יָבֹא יָבוֹא (Path 5, in spite of the convention that normalizes the root to בוא).

In contrast to Type 40, the proportionately greater number of *plene* spellings with Types 41 and 42 represents a tendency to triconsonantalism on the purely orthographic level. If, however, a phonetic difference can be inferred, this could reflect a primal ו in the root.

•Type 43. Stem -ō̱- in regular imperative and infinitive

Type 43	Low	Middle	High	Total
Defective	1	14	859	874
Plene	2	13	187	202
Total	3	27	1046	1076

Because of the morphology, this type includes פ״נ roots. Example: *lišmōr*, 'to watch,' לִשְׁמֹר לִשְׁמוֹר (Path 5).

לֵאמֹר (× 945) and לֵאמוֹר (× 3 — Genesis 48:20; Jeremiah 18:5; 33:19) have been excluded from this count as invariant on statistical grounds.

•Type 44. Stem -ō- in imperative and infinitive of hollow root

Type 44	Low	Middle	High	Total
Defective	82	11	182	275
Plene	39	7	218	264
Total	121	18	400	539

Example: *bō ʾ*, 'come!' בֹּא בֹוא (Path 5). On the marked difference between Types 43 and 44, see the note for Type 42.

•Type 45. Stem -ō- in *pōlēl*

Type 45	Low	Middle	High	Total
Defective	206	X	X	206
Plene	241	X	X	241
Total	447	X	X	447

Derivatives of hollow roots with root-consonant duplication. Example: *bōnēn*, 'consider,' בֹּנֵן בֹונֵן. The historical origins of this vowel are not known. Because of its position, it is never stressed.

•Type 46. Stem -ō- (first vowel) in nouns

Type 46	Low	Middle	High	Total
Defective	1095	X	X	1095
Plene	2976	X	X	2976
Total	4071	X	X	4071

Nouns (excepting those in Type 34) which have ō in the first stem position. Example: קֹומָה (× 35) and קָמָה (× 10). Compare Type 7. The difference between nouns (more *defective*) and verbs is notable. In most such nouns this /ō/ probably followed Path 3, hence the preference for *plene* spelling. But some of them could be agent nouns resembling, or even identifiable as, *qal* active participles. Membership in this type is thus somewhat indeterminate.

A frequently occurring word which could have come here is 'Moses,' מֹשֶׁה (× 766), always *defective* and so statistically invariant. Seemingly, so are 'Noah,' נֹחַ (× 46) and 'Joseph,' יוֹסֵף (× 212); there are too few to remove them by the criteria of § 5.6.3.

Compare the inscriptions: *hwšbt* (Hadad 19), *hwšbny* (Panamuwa 19); but *mšb* (Hadad 8), *mšby* (Hadad 15, 20, 25). Compare חרן (Tell-Qasile ostracon) with חורנן (Mesha inscription).

•Type 47. Plural suffix -ō *(t)* of nouns of hollow roots

Type 47	Low	Middle	High	Total
Defective	553	66	100	719
Plene	320	220	924	1464
Total	873	286	1024	2183

Example: *bānōt*, 'daughters,' בָּנֹת בְּנוֹת (Path 4). When suffixed (low stress), 36.7 percent are *plene*, in construct (middle stress) 76.9 percent, absolute (high stress) 90.2 percent. Compare these figures with those for Type 48. See § 1.6.

•Type 48. Plural suffix -ō *(t)* of nouns, regular roots

Type 48	Low	Middle	High	Total
Defective	810	233	425	1468
Plene	438	649	2140	3227
Total	1248	882	2565	4695

In this type חַטָּאת and חַטָּאות are included as a *defective* and *plene* pair. When suffixed (low stress), 35.1 percent are spelled *plene*, in construct (middle stress) 73.6 percent, absolute (high stress) 83.4 percent. See § 1.6.

•Type 49. Suffix -ōn of nouns

Type 49	Low	Middle	High	Total
Defective	1185	60	626	1871
Plene	267	360	1915	2542
Total	1452	420	2541	4413

Example: ᶜeprōn, 'Ephron,' עֶפְרוֹן עֶפְרֹן. This /ō/ probably
•followed Path 4. The most common one is אַהֲרֹן (× 347), always
defective.

We cannot be certain of the count because, while a word
ending in וֹן has to be -ōn, a similar word ending in ן could be
defective spelling of -ōn, or simply -ān. How did the masoretes
know? The defective spelling is pre-exilic. The spelling on the
wine-jar handles from Gibeon is consistently גבען. This spelling
survives in the Bible only in 1 Kings 3:4 but quite often in the
corresponding gentilic.

•Type 50. Stem -ō- (second vowel) in nouns

Type 50	Low	Middle	High	Total
Defective	1784	268	591	2643
Plene	1233	462	2307	4002
Total	3017	730	2898	6645

Example: gādōl, 'big,' גָּדֹל גָּדוֹל. When suffixed (low
stress), 40.9 percent are spelled plene, in construct (middle
stress) 63.3 percent, absolute (high stress) 79.6 percent. This
set, being a residuum, contains various kinds of /ō/'s so far as
the path of evolution is concerned. If we accept comparative
evidence, the existence of gĕdullâ suggests *gadul. If we
accept orthographic evidence, then early spelling with ו could
indicate *gadāl. Similarly gibbōr ← *gibbur or gibbōr ← *gibbār
← *gabbar. This set could have included אֱלֹהִים and its derivatives, about 2,600 tokens, of which only three are spelled plene
(Mm 3226 -- Psalm 18:47; 143:10: 145:1). They have been eliminated, as per Table 5.1.

•Type 51. Stem -ō- in other proper nouns

Type 51	Low	Middle	High	Total
Defective	34	0	471	505
Plene	33	1	392	426
Total	67	1	863	931

This set is mixed as to word shape. Some members prefer
one or the other kind of spelling. Thus 'Jacob' is יַעֲקֹב (× 344)
and יַעֲקוֹב (× 5 — Mm 822: Leviticus 26:42; Jeremiah 30:18;
33:26; 46:27; 51:19), even though the vowel is always stressed.
Historically this word belongs with Type 40.

•Type 52. Stem -ō- in nipᶜals of irregular roots

Type 52	Low	Middle	High	Total
Defective	65	3	1	69
Plene	39	10	91	140
Total	104	13	92	209

Example: nākōn, 'ready,' נָכֹן נָכוֹן. Origins not known.

•Type 53. Stem -ō- (first vowel) residuum

Type 53	Low	Middle	High	Total
Defective	8	2	87	97
Plene	34	11	528	573
Total	42	13	615	670

•Type 54. Stem -ō- in verbs, residuum

Type 54	Low	Middle	High	Total
Defective	1	1	132	134
Plene	3	0	29	32
Total	4	1	161	166

These are mainly qal perfect verbs of the -u- stem class.

•Type 55. Stem -ō- residuum

Type 55	Low	Middle	High	Total
Defective	382	7	430	819
Plene	29	16	206	251
Total	411	23	636	1070

This miscellaneous group includes ʾānōkī, whose /ō/ followed Path 4. This occurs 359 times, always *defective*, just
under our threshold for declaring statistically invariant. Note
עוֹלָם (× 413) and עֹלָם (× 25), עוֹד (× 473) and עֹר (× 17). The
estimate of the number of *defective* ᶜôd in MT varies with the
manuscript. Theoretically, one might consider other cases of
ᶜd vocalized ᶜad or ᶜēd to be ᶜōd, and ᶜwd (ᶜôd) to be really ᶜd
wrongly fixed as ᶜôd by adding the *mater lectionis*. The latter
occurs at Habbakuk 2:3. The parallelism of יָפֵחַ or יָפִיחַ elsewhere shows that ᶜôd ← *ēd must have occurred late.

Altogether Types 30-55 presented the scribe with 50,852
opportunities to make a spelling choice, 51.7 percent of them
being spelled *plene*. Because the words containing /ō/ are so
numerous and the types so varied, we consolidate some results
with respect to the main paths of evolution of that sound when
this is possible with reasonable confidence. Nearly all word-
terminal /ō/'s from Path 1 are spelled with וֹ. Accepting Types
35 and 37 as good representatives of vowels that followed Path
3, about eighty-four percent are spelled *plene*. Accepting Types
38, 39, 47, 48, 49 as good representatives of Path 4, the sum is
more than seventeen thousand opportunities, of which fifty
percent are spelled *plene*. But when stress is taken into
account, 22.5 percent of low-stress vowels (Path 4) are spelled
plene, 57.2 percent of middle stress, 66.2 percent of high
stress. Accepting Types 40-44 as representatives of Path 5,
only 21.3 percent are spelled *plene*. Recall, however, that many
of the words containing Path 5 /ō/ were eliminated as non-
opportunities for spelling choice because *plene* never became
an option for them, so it was only in certain kinds of words and
then only on a small scale that this vowel was ever spelled
plene. The spelling of the various kinds of /ō/ thus preserves
marks of the history of phonetic development along distinct
paths and reflects the history of orthographic development in
the stages outlined in § 3.2.1. The original diphthong (Path 3)

has highest *plene* spelling; original long (Path 4) is average; original short (Path 5) is lowest. The spelling of Path 4 /ō/ also shows the influence of stress on choice of spelling.

6.5.6 Words containing /ū/

Ten types allowing a spelling option categorize this vowel.

•Type 56. Suffix -*ū*- on finite verb

Type 56	Low	Middle	High	Total
Defective	X	X	312	312
Plene	X	X	511	511
Total	X	X	823	823

Verbs ending in -*ū* may be spelled *defective* or *plene* when they have a pronoun object suffix; the vowel is stressed. When unsuffixed, such verbs are not eligible for *defective* spelling, and their terminal vowels have been marked as fixed. Example: *hōrīdūhū*, 'bring him down!' הוֹרִדֻהוּ הוֹרִידוּהוּ.

•Type 57. Suffix -*ūn* on finite verb

Type 57	Low	Middle	High	Total
Defective	X	X	20	20
Plene	X	X	294	294
Total	X	X	314	314

Never *defective* in the Former Prophets, nor in Genesis. Deuteronomy has most of the *defectives* (archaizing?).

•Type 58. Stem -*ū*- in imperfect verb

Type 58	Low	Middle	High	Total
Defective	7	2	225	234
Plene	15	2	676	693
Total	22	4	901	927

Qal imperfect verbs derived from hollow roots may have /ū/ in the stem. Example: *yāqūm*, 'he will arise,' יָקוּם, יָקֻם.

•Type 59. Stem *-ū-* in imperative and infinitive

Type 59	Low	Middle	High	Total
Defective	6	2	35	43
Plene	30	21	424	475
Total	36	23	459	518

Qal imperative and infinitive verbs derived from hollow roots may have /ū/ in the stem. Example: *qūm*, 'arise!' קוּם קֻם. The *defective* spelling is found throughout the Bible, although it is somewhat rare in the Writings.

•Type 60. Stem *-ū-* in *hopᶜals*

Type 60	Low	Middle	High	Total
Defective	17	X	X	17
Plene	310	X	X	310
Total	327	X	X	327

Hopᶜal verb forms derived from פ״י roots may have /ū/ as the first stem vowel. Example: *hūrad*, 'he was brought down,' הֻרַד הוּרַד. Because of its position, this vowel is always unstressed. There is only one *defective* in the Pentateuch (Genesis 33:11).

•Type 61. Stem *-ū-* in *qal* passive participles

Type 61	Low	Middle	High	Total
Defective	212	32	27	271
Plene	340	85	393	818
Total	552	117	420	1089

The /ū/ in the stem of *qal* passive participles of the type *šāmūr*, 'watched,' שָׁמֻר שָׁמוּר may be spelled either way.

•Type 62. Stem -ū- in nouns of hollow roots

Type 62	Low	Middle	High	Total
Defective	40	26	7	73
Plene	466	233	493	1192
Total	506	259	500	1265

Example: ḥūṣ, 'outside,' חֻץ חוּץ.

The preference for *plene* in words of Types 62 and 63 reflects the combined influences of historical spelling, a tendency toward triconsonantalism (itself the result of an intuition if not a grammatical theory of the root), and analogy (when the two preceding factors do not properly apply).

•Type 63. Stem -ū- (first vowel) in other nouns

Type 63	Low	Middle	High	Total
Defective	37	17	36	90
Plene	101	33	253	387
Total	138	50	289	477

Example: tūšiyyā, 'purpose,' תֻּשִׁיָה תּוּשִׁיָה.

In this instance the Pentateuch is not uniform. The word *mūsabbōt* 'surrounded,' illustrates the trend. Archaic: מסבת (Exodus 28:11; 39:6). Middle: מוסבת (Exodus 39:13; Numbers 32:38). Late: מוסבות (Ezekiel 41:24).

•Type 64. Stem -ū- in other nouns

Type 64	Low	Middle	High	Total
Defective	451	62	406	919
Plene	1367	450	1645	3462
Total	1818	512	2051	4381

Example: tĕšūbā, 'return,' תְּשֻׁבָה תְּשׁוּבָה. Individual words tend to be spelled consistently, especially proper nouns. יְהוּדָה was eliminated as invariant as per Table 5.1.

•Type 65. Stem -$\bar{u}$- residuum

Type 65	Low	Middle	High	Total
Defective	17	1	6	24
Plene	110	3	143	256
Total	127	4	149	280

Here are found the particles אוּלַי, מַדּוּעַ, בַּעֲבוּר, זוּלָתִי, etc., and various verbs.

6.6 The mechanics of type assignment

Based on the foregoing characterizations of the types, a program was written which took as input the reduced texts produced by the winnowing processes of Chapter 5. Its output was a list, each line of which corresponded to one opportunity to make a spelling choice. Each line contained all the information needed to study the distribution patterns of biblical spellings. It gave the location of the opportunity in the text (book, chapter, verse, position in verse); its type, as defined by the preceding sixty-five categories; its stress level; the choice made (*plene* or *defective*); and a transcription of the segment itself (see § 1.7). In addition the "sources" of the Pentateuch, as found in Eissfeldt's *Hexateuchsynopsis*, were included in the location.

Chapter 7. Specification of Text Portions

7.1 The need for careful text portioning

Thus far in this book, we have analyzed only simple two-dimensional contingency tables, those having only rows and columns. The data involved were describable in terms of *nominal* categories, categories involving no intrinsic ordering. No cells were forced by the nature of the situations to hold zero counts. The populations analyzed were such that the contingency table cells were well populated. In all cases, without comment, we partitioned the text into traditional, large subsections (Torah, Former Prophets, Latter Prophets, Writings) or in some other relevant way, as in Tables 6.9 through 6.11 where the documentary sources were used.

In Chapter 8, we first examine the effects of proximity on spelling. Next we study the effects of word frequency (viewed locally) on spelling; and finally we analyze the effects of stress on spelling. For the latter two topics, we use a finely-divided text in the interest of more detailed insight. In Chapter 9, we examine the behavior of each vowel type across the text. Since the populations of the types vary enormously (Type 30 has 84 exemplars, while Type 6 has 12,465), some of the analyses will allow but few portions, while others will allow many. Because we control for the effects of stress (§ 9.1) and because some types cannot have certain levels of stress (see Note in § 6.5.1), portion specification is further complicated. In Chapter 10, we analyze the behavior of portions of text across the vowel types. Thus, for most of the analyses of Chapters 8 through 10, we shall want the text divided into more portions than used heretofore. (And, if possible, we prefer that the portionings here defined be useful in future research.)

7.2 The philosophy of portion definition

To divide the text, one selects some reasonable maximum number of portions. The desire to make fine-grained assertions would lead one to divide the text into myriad chunks. But the smaller a piece, the less compelling any statistical assertions made about it will tend to be, since such assertions will be based on limited data. A trade-off between delicacy of analysis and level of confidence in statistical results must be made.

Two sorts of rough rules to help decide an appropriate number of portions are available from contingency table analysis. Both rules prescribe lower limits on cell populations *if one wishes to keep things simple and use chi-square tests*. (Less familiar tests, which we plan to use in future research, allow one to work with more sparse tables [Fienberg 1980: 174].) The numbers of spelling-choice categories, stress categories, and vowel types have been previously decided, leaving the number of portions as the variable we can adjust to meet the cell population prescriptions.

The first rule has three variants. 1) The classical advice was that "the minimal *expected* cell size should exceed 5" if one tested goodness of fit using Pearson's chi-square (Fienberg 1980: 172). 2) Computer simulations have led to the condition that for our sort of analysis, the minimal *expected* cell size should not go below unity (Fienberg, *ibid.*; Sachs 1982: 475). 3) The third variant is that the *expected* cell size should exceed five for eighty percent of the cells, and exceed unity for all (Agresti 1984: 10). This rule, in its various forms, implies that in order to specify the number of categories used (and thereby determine the table layout), one must know the results of trying out relevant models of contingency. One picks a trial set of categories, fits the models of interest, and looks at the cell *estimates*. If they obey the rule, well and good. If they do not, one must redefine the categories (or resort to other tests of goodness of fit which allow for "more sparse" tables).

The second rule stipulates that chi-square may be used to test goodness of fit for our purposes provided the total table population is "four or five times the number of cells" (Fienberg 1980: 173). (In terms of the analogy of § 1.7, the rule states that the average number of visitors in a cubicle should exceed four or five.) This rule is quite general and bears the aroma of "cook-bookery" but has the virtues of being trivial to apply and allowing portion definition prior to model building.

7.3 The mechanics of text portioning

We shall define the largest set of portions allowed by the second rule but, in addition, shall define sets involving fewer portions for use when our data lead to models which badly disobey the first rule.

We have defined the number of types (sixty-five), stress categories (three), and spelling choices (two). Let the number of portions used be p. Then, a full four-dimension contingency table would have $65 \times 3 \times 2 \times p = 390 \times p$ cells. But, as we saw in Chapter 6, twenty-five of our types have only one level of stress, two have only two levels, and the remaining thirty-eight have all three. Taking these facts into account reduces the number of cells which can hold counts in a four-dimensional table to $286 \times p$. If each of these cells is to hold at least five counts, then our total table population should be greater than or equal to $1430 \times p$. Our total sample size is 108,943 opportunities. From these givens, we easily reckon that in analyzing the full data set, we should define seventy-six or fewer portions, since $1430 \times p \leq 108943$ implies $p \leq 76.2$.

The upper limit on how many portions should be defined depends on how extensive are the data being analyzed. Fewer data imply that fewer categories can be reliably handled. Suppose that rather than investigating the interactions of all four basic variables, we study the behavior of each type individually in terms of the portion, stress, and spelling choice of its member vowels. (In terms of our analogy, we study how the visitors are distributed in each tenement without reference to the other tenements.) The limited population of some types creates problems. For example, Type 30 has *very* few members, presenting only 84 opportunities. It involves only one level of stress. In order to obtain statistically significant results, we should analyze using no more than eight portions, since we desire $10 \times p \leq 84$. We shall conflate portions as necessary as we proceed. (Details will be given in § 7.5 below.)

To make comparisons easier, we attempt to make the portions roughly comparable in size. This implies that on average each portion should contain around 1,430 opportunities. Another decision must be made: whether to allow "scissors-and-paste" portions or require that portions involve canonical sequences of text. With one exception, we opt for the canonical sequence for this study. The exception involves placing Jonah just before Ruth, since Jonah shows more affinity to Ruth than to its adjacent Minor Prophets.

7.4 Specification of seventy-six portions

Seventy-six portions were specified as follows: 1) If the number of opportunities in a book was far less than an average portion should contain, we examined adjacent books to see if a merge was in order. If it was, we made it; if not, we left the entire book as a single (small) portion. 2) If the number of opportunities in a book exceeded those an average portion should contain, we determined how many average size portions the book might divide into. If the book had subdivisions of historical interest, we made the divisions accordingly; if there were none, we divided on the basis of content. The specifications of the resulting portions follow as Table 7.1a-c. (Many of our content descriptions were taken from the IB, which supplied the outlines used in the division.)

Table 7.1a The seventy-six portions

P#	BOUNDARIES	OPPS	CONTENTS
1	GE 1-17	1554	Creation → circumcision covenant
2	GE 18-28	1362	Hebron visit → Jacob at Bethel
3	GE 29-38	1419	Jacob at Paddan-aram → Tamar
4	GE 39-50	1928	most of Joseph cycle
5	EX 1-11	1207	Moses' beginnings → plagues
6	EX 12-24	1550	Passover → covenant
7	EX 25-31	1418	P cultic laws
8	EX 32-40	1489	restoration of covenant → end
9	LE 1-16	1881	worship → rite of atonement
10	LE 17-27	1520	Holiness Code plus appendix
11	NU 1-10:10	1682	sojourn at Sinai [P]
12	NU 10:11-22:1	1549	Sinai-Paran → Kadesh-Moab
13	NU 22:2-36	2144	Balaam story → end
14	DE 1-7	1359	God's acts → conquest of Canaan
15	DE 8-16:17	1213	past lessons → yearly pilgrimages
16	DE 16:18-27	1315	officials' duties → Shechem ceremony
17	DE 28-34	1295	blessings and cursings → Moses' death
18	JS 1-12	1818	conquest of western Palestine
19	JS 13-24	1722	division of land → end
20	JD 1-9	1541	Canaan invasion → story of Abimelech
21	JD 10-21	1608	tale of Tola → end
22	1S 1-12	1453	Samuel's birth → his farewell
23	1S 13-20	1366	independence war → Jonathan
24	1S 21-31	1427	Saul & David at war → Gilboa battle
25	2S 1-12	1561	David at Hebron → Nathan's rebuke
26	2S 13-24	1938	David's court problems → end

Table 7.1b The seventy-six portions

P#	BOUNDARIES	OPPS	CONTENTS
27	1K 1-7	1707	David's last days → building of temple
28	1K 8-14	1386	temple dedication → story of Rehoboam
29	1K 15-22	1221	North-South wars → Jehoshaphat
30	2K 1-8	1062	Elisha narratives
31	2K 9-17	1599	Jehu's revolution → fall of North
32	2K 18-25	1289	Assyrian period → end
33	IS 1-12	1231	superscription → thanksgiving
34	IS 13-27	1379	doom of Babylon → last trumpet
35	IS 28-39	1358	lesson for dissolute → end, 1st Isaiah
36	IS 40-55	1833	Second Isaiah
37	IS 56-66	1150	Third Isaiah
38	JE 1-10	1533	superscription → prayer
39	JE 11-23:8	1552	Jeremiah's life → Judah's king
40	JE 23:9-32	1611	prophets → purchase of field
41	JE 33-44	1604	restoration → Jeremiah in Egypt
42	JE 45-52	1543	oracles against nations, appendix
43	EZ 1-13	1650	superscription → against prophets
44	EZ 14-24	1900	idolators → Jerusalem's fall
45	EZ 25-32	1242	oracles against foreign nations
46	EZ 33-39	1200	restoration of Israel
47	EZ 40-48	1588	restored community
48	HO/JL	1269	Hosea and Joel
49	AM/OB/MI	1541	Amos, Obadiah, Micah
50	NA/HB/ZP	877	Nahum, Habakkuk, Zephaniah
51	HG/ZC/ML	1653	Haggai, Zechariah, Malachi

Table 7.1c The seventy-six portions

P#	BOUNDARIES	OPPS	CONTENTS
52	PS 1-41	2169	Book I
53	PS 42-72	1785	Book II
54	PS 73-89	1276	Book III
55	PS 90-106	1042	Book IV
56	PS 107-119	1119	Book Va
57	PS 120-150	1172	Book Vb
58	JB 1-21	1632	prose prolog → 2nd cycle
59	JB 22-42	1678	3rd cycle → prose epilog
60	PR 1-15	1460	title → Solomon's wisdom, I
61	PR 16-31	1489	Solomon's wisdom, II → end
62	JN/RU	674	Jonah & Ruth
63	SS	624	Song of Songs
64	QO	922	Qohelet
65	LA	694	Lamentations
66	ES	1014	Esther
67	DA	965	Daniel less 2:4-7:28
68	ER	1065	Ezra less 4:8-6:18; 7:12-26
69	NE 1-8	1246	Jerusalem → reading of law
70	NE 9-13	1171	marriage reform → end
71	1C 1-9	1629	genealogies
72	1C 10-20	1453	end of Saul → David's victory
73	1C 21-29	1342	census → David's farewell
74	2C 1-9	1379	reign of Solomon
75	2C 10-25	1853	reign of Rehoboam → Amaziah
76	2C 26-36	1793	Uzziah → last kings of Judah

7.5 Reduction to smaller sets of portions

When the data do not allow seventy-six portions, we combine portions to produce sets of thirty, ten, and five. This choice of set sizes was determined by the requirements of the three-dimensional models used in Chapter 9. The reduced sets of portions are shown in Table 7.2a,b.

Table 7.2a Hierarchy of 5/10/30 divisions

5	10	30	BOUNDARIES	OPPS
Pent	A	i	GE 1-28	2916
		ii	GE 29-50	3347
		iii	EX 1-24	2757
		iv	EX 25-40	2907
	B	v	LE	3301
		vi	NU	5375
		vii	DE 1-16:17	2572
		viii	DE 16:18-34	2610
FP	C	ix	JS	3540
		x	JD	3149
		xi	1S	4246
		xii	2S	3499
	D	xiii	1K	4314
		xiv	2K	3950

Table 7.2b Hierarchy of 5/10/30 divisions

5	10	30	BOUNDARIES	OPPS
LP	E	xv	IS 1-39	3968
		xvi	IS 40-66	2983
		xvii	JE 1-32	4696
		xviii	JE 33-52	3147
	F	xix	EZ 1-24	3550
		xx	EZ 25-48	4030
		xxi	HO/AM/OB/MI	2810
		xxii	NA-ML	2530
Poetry	G	xxiii	PS 1-72	3954
		xxiv	PS 73-150	4609
	H	xxv	JB	3310
		xxvi	PR	2949
Other	I	xxvii	JN/RU-DA	4893
		xxviii	ER-NE	3482
	J	xxix	1C	4424
		xxx	2C	5025

Chapter 8. Possible Confounding Factors

8.1 Influences in spelling choice

The preceding discussion has recognized that many causes could have been at work to produce the final state of spelling in the Hebrew Bible. We have distinguished events in which the writer (author or scribe) evidently had no choice -- the statistically invariant spellings of Table 5.1 -- from those in which there was an opportunity for choice. In this chapter we consider three possible influences on spelling choices -- proximity, frequency, and stress.

8.2 The spelling of nearby lexemes

Does a spelling decision, once made, perpetuate itself? If so, how long does its influence last? When a scribe first spells a particular word or kind of word, will he spell it the same way next time around? To study these questions, our master list of spelling opportunities was read to find each successive pair of occurrences of the same lexeme. The gap separating each such pair was measured by means of the number of intervening segments of text -- zero when the repeated items were contiguous, one when one segment separated them, and so on. The mean verse length over the Hebrew Bible is 20.34 segments. We examined all pairs of repeated items with a separation of thirty-nine or fewer intervening segments. That is, we studied the influence of proximity over an average two-verse range of separation. In the *ketib* text, 18,429 pairs lie in this range. (An item may show up twice, matched with a preceding and with a following mate.) Of these, 17,564 pairs have the same spelling (concordant pairs); the remaining 865 have discordant spelling. Table 8.1a,b shows the numbers of concordant and discordant pairs for each of the forty separation distances under study. Across the corpus the mean percent discordant is 4.7%.

Table 8.1a Pair discordance as function of separation

Separation	Concordant	Discordant	Total	% Discordant
0	132	8	140	5.71
1	355	11	366	3.00
2	582	24	606	3.96
3	677	39	716	5.45
4	855	33	888	3.72
5	711	29	740	3.92
6	727	36	763	4.72
7	654	35	689	5.08
8	638	34	672	5.06
9	672	27	699	3.86
10	581	37	618	5.99
11	603	24	627	3.83
12	567	24	591	4.06
13	485	25	510	4.90
14	465	29	494	5.87
15	502	18	520	3.46
16	483	29	512	5.66
17	507	27	534	5.06
18	465	23	488	4.71
19	395	20	415	4.82
20	427	25	452	5.53
21	379	22	401	5.49
22	411	16	427	3.75
23	377	15	392	3.83
24	353	18	371	4.85
25	354	15	369	4.07

Table 8.1b Pair discordance as function of separation

Separation	Concordant	Discordant	Total	% Discordant
26	366	17	383	4.44
27	354	16	370	4.32
28	313	17	330	5.15
29	301	16	317	5.05
30	324	17	341	4.99
31	288	18	306	5.88
32	281	17	298	5.70
33	329	19	348	5.46
34	298	20	318	6.29
35	355	18	373	4.83
36	242	8	250	3.20
37	242	13	255	5.10
38	237	10	247	4.05
39	277	16	293	5.46

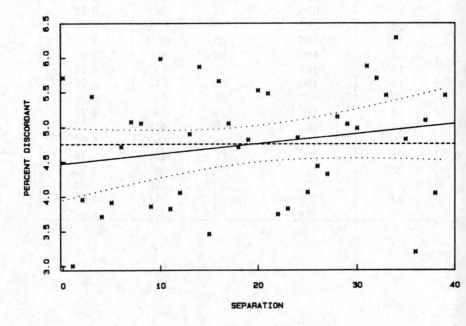

Figure 8.1 Spelling discordance as function of separation

The data of the foregoing table are plotted, on an expanded ordinate, as asterisks in Figure 8.1. When we fit these data with that straight line which best approximates them (regression analysis), the solid line with the slight upward tilt results. The pair of curved dotted lines in the figure bounds a 95% confidence region (as determined via the computational gymnastics specified by Becker and Chambers [1984: 212f.]). The mean for the data, the dashed line in Figure 8.1, lies nicely within the 95% confidence region. So one need not assert that discordance increases with separation. One might more simply assert that the degree of discordance is constant with respect to the space separating the pair items.

When a writer realizes that he is repeating an item, it is reasonable to expect him to remember how he just spelled it, or to examine his recent work and use the same spelling. If the discordant spelling is considered to be an error (or at least an inconsistency) due to failure to remember or to check, we would expect discordant spellings to increase with the distance separating the pairs. The results are contrary to this expectation. This suggests that word-level conditioning or other local rules are controlling. In the last stages of text transmission, of course, there were masoretic notes drawing attention to some of these inconsistencies and guaranteeing their preservation. Without the notes, the text would be more vulnerable to leveling. But the question is why leveling had not occurred long before the rules for copying became so strict.

8.2.1. Andersen (1970a), on the basis of a few examples, suggested that when a word is used twice in close proximity, especially in repetitive poetic parallelism, it is likely to be spelled *plene* first time, to make its identity clear, but *defective* in repetition. Is this generally true?

Table 8.1 indicates that eight of 140 immediately adjacent pairs are discordant. These are:

1) הַקֵּל קוֹל יַעֲקֹב -- Genesis 27:22 (ל חם). The massora draws attention to the unique spelling of this word. וְהַקֹּל occurs in Genesis 45:16.

2) הַבָּנוֹת בְּנֹתַי -- Genesis 31:43

3) אֲבֹתֶיךָ וַאֲבוֹת אֲבֹתֶיךָ -- Exodus 10:6

4) וְעִשָּׂרֹן עִשָּׂרוֹן -- Numbers 28:13 (ה ג מל וב חם). The other defective is in Exodus 29:40. The same repetition occurs four more times; all eight words are *plene*.

5) בֹּארוֹת בֹּארֹת נִשְׁבָּרִים -- Jeremiah 2:13

6) אַל־תַּטִּפוּ יַטִּיפוּן לֹא־יַטִּפוּ -- Micah 2:6 (ל ל ל). We have cited the third member of the same lexeme which follows with a separation of 1. The massora does not flag the uniqueness of each of these three words in terms of spelling as such. They would be unique no matter how spelled.

7) סוֹבֵב סֹבֵב -- Qohelet 1:6

8) אֲבֹתָיו וַאֲבוֹת אֲבֹתָיו -- Daniel 11:24; compare 3) above.

Three of these pairs are *defective-plene*. Three (4, 5, 7) involve simple repetition; two (1, 2) are subject and predicate; two (3, 8) constitute a construct phrase; one (6) involves verbs. By masoretic accentuation, the *plene* form is more stressed than the *defective* for all but 1). See § 8.4.

There are eleven cases when an item is repeated after one intervening segment.

9) בִּשְׁמֹת אֶת־שְׁמוֹת הֶעָרִים -- Numbers 32:38. The first is pause (*zaqep*) yet *defective*; the second is construct, yet *plene*.

10) צִדְקוֹת יהוה צִדְקֹת פִּרְזוֹנוֹ -- Judges 5:11, constructs.

11) יֵקַד יְקֹד בִּיקוֹד אֵשׁ -- Isaiah 10:16 (L, C, A). Disjunctive. Second is construct. 1QIs[a] has יקוד כיקד אש.

12) וּשְׁמֻעָה אֶל־שְׁמוּעָה -- Ezekiel 7:26

13) -- Included in 6) above.

14, 15) אוֹתֹתָם אֹתוֹת -- Psalm 74:4. With secondary accent on the antepenultimate -- ᵓōtōtắm ᵓōtốt. The spelling is consistent: stressed *plene*, unstressed *defective*.

16) לְדֹר וָדוֹר -- Psalm 89:5

17) כְּבֹדָם כָּבוֹד -- Proverbs 25:27

18) עוֹבֵד♦ וְעֹבֵד -- Ruth 4:21-22

19) מַכְאוֹב כְּמַכְאֹבִי -- Lamentations 1:12

For lists of nearby pairs, classified by grammatical categories, see Sperber (1966: 562-74). Unfortunately it is not clear what authorities Sperber is relying on; his examples do not always agree with standard editions. Even BHS cannot be trusted. Thus in Ezekiel 41:16 it has הַחַלֹּנוּת וְהָחַלֹּנוּת as against הַחַלּוֹנוּת וְהָחַלֹּנוּת of sources consulted, including BH3.

8.2.2. With discordant pairs in proximity there is no marked preference for the sequence *defective-plene* (DP -- ×445) over *plene-defective* (PD -- ×415). The scores for the first ten sets of near-by pairs are shown in Table 8.2.

Table 8.2 Spelling in discordant pairs

Separation	PD	DP
0	5	3
1	5	6
2	11	13
3	19	20
4	18	15
5	16	13
6	21	15
7	18	17
8	12	22
9	15	12

The observation made by Andersen (1970a) is illusory. Even when there is no difference in stress level between the pairs there are 355 DP and 336 PD, contrary to Andersen (1970a). Contingency table analysis shows that there is no dependency of the spelling-choice sequence on separation.

8.2.3. Does any other factor, such as stress or word complexity, influence the way the choices in nearby pairs are made? §§ 6.2 and 6.3 discussed stress patterns and word length. There is a connection in that a suffixed word is longer than its unsuffixed counterpart, and its stem is less stressed. There are four possible transitions in the spelling choices between nearby pairs: DD, DP, PD, PP. There are three possible transitions in word complexity/stress between nearby pairs: stress same, when both are suffixed or both are unsuffixed; stress rise (suffixed followed by unsuffixed); stress fall (unsuffixed followed by suffixed). Table 8.3 shows the spelling-choice sequences for nearby pairs with a separation of 0 through 39 in relation to their relative stress.

Table 8.3 Spelling choice and stress sequence

Combination	DD	DP	PD	PP	Total
Stress fall	94	8	62	207	371
Stress same	6968	373	343	10006	17690
Stress rise	98	74	5	191	368
Total	7160	455	410	10404	18429

There is a tendency to change to *defective* spelling with a fall of stress and to change to *plene* spelling with a rise of stress. (Stress fall, stress same, and stress rise are an ordered classification, and hence use of ordinal models is indicated. Such contingency table analyses disclose that no unsaturated models fit the data.)

8.2.4. Do the preferred spelling transitions of nearby pairs change in different portions of the text? A table of the four kinds of transition (DD, DP, PD, PP) in our seventy-six portions was compiled. Contingency table analysis showed that the model of independence did not fit the data. The data are dominated by the preference for identical spellings in successive pairs, and in addition by a general preference for *defective* spellings in the first half of the Bible, for *plene* spellings in the second half. When contingency table analysis was carried out only for changed spelling in a pair (DP, PD), none of the cells attracted suspicion as making a major contribution to the lack of goodness of fit.

8.3 Lexeme frequency and spelling choice

In § 5.6 we eliminated from our general study a number of items whose frequent occurrence and consistent spelling permitted us to declare their spelling statistically invariant. However, a word may be infrequent overall and yet be quite common in some portion of text. Here we elect to study the spelling practices for such locally frequent words, to see if spelling preferences are different when an item occurs frequently from when it occurs rarely. Therefore, frequency assessment for each portion was carried out in terms only of the word population making up that portion. A given word may be high-frequency in one portion and low in all others.

If we defined the frequency threshold in terms of absolute counts, the varying lengths of our portions would affect the outcomes unfavorably. (Short portions would be less likely to have "high-frequency" words than long portions.) A percentage threshold is superior. Hence we specified that if some opportunity-in-a-word accounts for more than one percent of the total opportunities in a portion, that opportunity was labeled high-frequency throughout the portion. The one percent cutoff is arbitrary but gives a set of "high-frequency" opportunities that is intuitively satisfying yet defined objectively.

8.3.1. In order to determine the frequency rating for each opportunity, the computer first made a list containing the number of times each word occurred, ranking the words from most frequent to least. It then threw away all items which made up less than one percent of the total number of opportunities in the portion. The resulting list of high-frequency opportunities was then used to apply a frequency rating to each opportunity.

The grand list containing any word that accounts for at least one percent of the opportunities of at least one portion contains 210 entries. The average portion has almost ten distinct high-frequency lexemes (range: 4 through 18). The high-frequency items tend to be function words, fragments of set phrases, or major themes of the given portions.

8.3.2. Study of the spelling of vowel types as in Chapter 6 is advantageous because word contextuality effects can be "averaged out" by forming classes composed of many similar vowels. But there is a place, too, for study of specific words or collections of very similar words (lexemes). Such study rests on fewer abstractions than does the study of types, but the price paid for concreteness is greater sensitivity to context effects. Use of lexemes, rather than single word forms, somewhat reduces context sensitivity by allowing one to consider normal, suffixed, and pausal forms together. (Study of these differently stressed items can be revealing; see § 8.4 below.) We have previously summarized the spelling distributions for a few selected words. (See Tables 1.1, 1.2, 6.2, 6.3, 6.4, 6.7, 6.8, and 6.9.) The data so tabulated were displayed either to motivate our discussions via simple examples or to characterize spelling-opportunity types made up of one or a few forms. We shall here study the spelling practice for lexemes which are *locally frequent*, that is, which appear with high frequency in at least one portion of text. (A lexeme whose overall frequency is high is termed *globally* frequent.)

We shall address three questions:

1) How are frequent opportunities spelled within the portions where they manifest high frequency?

2) How do locally frequent opportunities differ in their spelling behavior from globally frequent ones?

3) How does the spelling of a locally frequent lexeme compare between portions where the lexeme is of high frequency and those where it is of low frequency?

Of the 9,057 lexemes which contain opportunities, only 161 are ever of high frequency. Four of the locally frequent *lexemes* appear in all portions of the Hebrew Bible: פְּנֵי, לֹא, -ךְ, and יָבֹא. Seven appear in but a single portion: אֶסְתֵּר (fifty-five occurrences in Esther), גִּדְעוֹן (thirty-nine in Judges 1:1-9:57), יְהוֹאָשׁ (seventeen in 2 Kings 9:1-17:41), יִתְרוֹן (ten in Qohelet), מָנוֹחַ (eighteen in Judges 10:1-21:25), רוּת (twelve in Ruth), and שִׁמְשׁוֹן (thirty-eight in Judges 10:1-21:25). Over a hundred items are of high frequency in but one portion; none is of high frequency in all portions. (לֹא is of high frequency in seventy-five of the seventy-six portions. The absent portion is the genealogical material of 1 Chronicles 1-9, wherein the negative appears only five times.)

8.3.3. By ordering the list of *all* opportunity-bearing lexemes from most frequent to least and then associating with each locally frequent item its global rank, the list can be ordered from most to least *globally* frequent. When this is done, only the fifteenth most globally frequent lexeme (יוֹשְׁבִים) is missing from the roster of the top twenty-five locally frequent lexemes. In other words, all but one of the twenty-five globally most frequent lexemes appear in the list of locally frequent lexemes. (יוֹשְׁבִים accounts for less than one percent of the opportunities in each of the seventy-six portions.) By comparing the spelling practices for the globally most frequent lexemes with that of globally less frequent lexemes, we can assess whether globally frequent lexemes behave in special ways.

8.3.4. The first thirty-seven items from our list of 210 include the top twenty-five globally frequent lexemes. For the high-frequency portions (those portions in which a given item appears with high frequency), either the *defective* count or the *plene* count is zero for 172 of the 210 items (82%). That is, four times out of five, the items appear with only one spelling in portions where they are locally frequent. The departures from total dominance for the remaining thirty-eight items can be classified into four convenient categories defined by whether the item is globally or only locally frequent and by whether the deviation is large or small. In high-frequency contexts, there are 1,032 deviant spellings. The first thirty-seven items (having global ranks one through twenty-five) account for 840 of the deviations (eighty-one percent of them).

Sense can be made of this behavior once we note that which spelling is dominant is often the result of happenstance. Consider the Type 47 final vowel in אָבוֹת (*fathers*). The *defective* spelling is dominant, outnumbering the *plene* spelling by 68 to 46 in its high-frequency portions, 11, 31, 71, and 76. (It is thus locally frequent in parts of Numbers, 2 Kings, and Chronicles.) The distribution of spellings in these four high-frequency portions is shown in Table 8.4.

"Threshold" gives the count a word must equal in order to be considered of high frequency in the given portion. ("Threshold" is just over one percent of a portion's number of opportunities.) A shift of five *defectives* to *plenes* in Portion 31 would cause that portion no longer to be of high frequency, causing its opportunities to move into the low-frequency bracket. A further shift of any four *defectives* to *plenes* in any of the three remaining portions would then leave forty-four *defectives* and forty-six *plenes* so that the *plene* spelling would be dominant, and there would be forty-four *defective* deviants where there were forty-six *plene* deviants before the switching of the spelling of the nine items. Thus we see that the dominant high-frequency portion spelling is not to be considered normative *per se*. If one spelling totally dominates the other for an item, we should consider that the item is either very localized in the text or, if it is widely frequent, that the item's spelling is fixed. (The six human names listed above seem to be invariants and are very localized, while the plural common noun אֱלֹהִים [*gods*] is invariant in all portions.)

Table 8.4 Distribution of 'fathers' in its high-frequency portions

Portion	Defective	Plene	Threshold
11	32	1	17
31	20	4	16
71	2	21	17
76	14	20	18

If few deviants occur, we should investigate the context in search of some rule-governed behavior, copyist's error, quoted material, or redaction. If there are many deviants, we should examine the separate behaviors in the high-frequency portions looking for portion-wise homogeneity of spelling of the sort seen in all but the last portion in Table 8.4. Examination of the thirty-eight cases of deviation in terms of the foregoing is instructive. We proceed from most globally frequent to least. The spelling tallies include only high-frequency portions.

לֹא (*not*): Global Rank: 2. *Defective*: 4,991. *Plene*: 188. High-frequency portions: seventy-five in all (71 is missing). This lexeme is the sole member of Type 32. The possibility of its deviant *plene* forms being controlled by local rules has been discussed previously. (See Tables 6.7 and 6.8 with accompanying discussion.)

אֵת (*nota accusativi*): Global Rank: 5. *Defective*: 787. *Plene*: 246. High-frequency portions: twenty-seven in all (none in the Minor Prophets, Poetry, Other Writings). This lexeme is the sole member of Type 33. See the discussion above in Chapter 6, under Type 33.

דָּוִיד (*David*): Global Rank: 7. *Defective*: 719. *Plene*: 239. High-frequency portions: thirteen in all (1 Samuel 13 - 1 Kings 14; Psalms, Books I, II, and Vb; 1 Chronicles 10 - 2 Chronicles 25). This lexeme is the major contributor to Type 9, accounting for seventy-two percent of its *defective* forms and sixteen percent of its *plene* forms. As Table 1.1 shows, each spelling is restricted to specific high-frequency portions. In fact, only three, one, and no forms are deviant in the Former Prophets, Psalms, and Chronicles, considered separately.

יָבֹא (*qal active imperfect of 'come'*): Global Rank: 9. *Defective*: 263. *Plene*: 59. High-frequency portions: thirteen in all (3, 6, 21, 22, 24, 25, 26, 28, 30, 31, 32, 66 and 72). This lexeme contributes more than eighty percent of the opportunities in Type 42. It is a very extensive lexeme, including singular and plural forms of all persons. When the opportunities from *all* of the portions are analyzed, using the four traditional sections of the Bible, evidence of conservative, rule-governed spelling emerges. Among the most common forms, *plene* spelling seems preferred only for the תָבוֹא forms, which are *defective* a total of fifty-one times and are *plene* a total of ninety-five times. The יָבֹאוּ forms are *defective* a total of 242 times and are *plene* a total of eight times. (The breakdown by section is quite uniform. Torah has 56 *defective* and 0 *plene*; Former Prophets has

103 and 3; Latter Prophets has 37 and 2; Poetry has 11 and 1; Other Writings has 35 and 2.) The early practice of avóiding *plenes* in adjacent syllables may have persisted for this very common form. The יָבֹא forms also tend to be *defective*. Clearly, nonhomogeneous spelling for Type 42 may result from the subject matter under discussion. For example, in Ruth, six of the ten opportunities are *plene*, and all are תָּבֹוא forms.

אָבֹות (*fathers*): Global Rank: 11. *Defective*: 68. *Plene*: 46. High-frequency portions: 11, 31, 71, and 76 (Numbers 1-10; 2 Kings 9-17; 1 Chronicles 1-9, 26-36). This lexeme contributes half of the *defectives* and one-fifth of the *plenes* to Type 47. Its spelling in the four high-frequency portions was given in Table 8.4 above. Table 8.5 shows the five words involved in this item. By subdividing the lexeme, our table cells have smaller entries, but one is able cautiously to make inferences not evident from the combined data. The unsuffixed form appears to be basically *plene*. *My fathers* is too rare to suggest a pattern. *His fathers* appears to have remained stably *defective*, perhaps because of the יו ending. Both forms of *their fathers* appear to have changed from *defective*-dominated to *plene*-dominated.

Table 8.5 Spelling of forms of 'fathers'

Form		Torah	FP	LP	Poetry	Other	Total
אָבֹות	D	2	0	0	0	0	2
	P	12	7	9	1	48	77
אֲבֹתַי	D	5	2	0	0	2	9
	P	0	2	1	1	3	7
אֲבֹתָיו	D	9	40	0	1	23	73
	P	0	3	0	1	1	5
אֲבֹתָם	D	43	3	0	0	1	47
	P	2	19	18	7	14	60
אֲבֹתֵיהֶם	D	58	15	14	2	35	124
	P	4	12	38	7	26	87

עַל (*upon*): Global Rank: 17. *Defective*: 1. *Plene*: 58. High-frequency portions: 12, 39, and 46 (Numbers 10-22; Jeremiah 11-23; Ezekiel 33-39). This lexeme contributes only ten percent of the *defectives* but sixty percent of the *plenes* present in Type 13. All fifteen deviants (the one in high-frequency portion 12 at Numbers 4:27 and the rest in Genesis through Numbers) are in the Torah, distributed as shown in Table 6.3. All involve second and third person plural suffixes.

עוֹלָם (*eternity*): Global Rank: 21. *Defective*: 5. *Plene*: 117. High-frequency portions: 37, 54-57 (Third Isaiah and Psalms 73-150). This lexeme contributes negligibly to the *defectives* and twenty percent to the *plenes* of Type 55. The five deviant forms in the high-frequency portions occur at Isaiah 57:11; Psalm 75:10, 92:9, 136:3, and 145:13.

אֶל (*unto*): Global Rank: 24. *Defective*: 15. *Plene*: 121. High-frequency portions: 5, 40, and 41 (Exodus 1-11 and Jeremiah 23-44). This lexeme contributes ninety percent of the *defectives* and thirty-three percent of the *plenes* of Type 13. See Table 6.2 and its associated discussion for the basic facts.

At this point, we have discussed each of the deviant spellings of the first twenty-five globally ranked lexemes. Twenty-eight deviants remain in high-frequency portions for lexemes of lower global rank. Twenty-three of them each involve ten or fewer deviations totaling to eighty-one instances. We shall conclude this survey by taking up the five items showing sizable departures from uniform spelling in high-frequency portions.

נְבִיאִם (*prophets*): Global Rank: 40. *Defective*: 20. *Plene*: 30. High-frequency portions: 29 and 40 (1 Kings 15-22 and Jeremiah 23-32). This lexeme has endings of Types 6, 14, or 25; the significant deviation is for the middle vowel, Type 9. This lexeme is another where examination of its component words is instructive, since some forms are much more stable than others.

Table 8.6 shows the spellings of the normal, construct, and suffixed forms for the Hebrew Bible.

Table 8.6 Spelling of 'prophets'

Form		Torah	FP	LP	Poetry	Other	Total
Normal	D	0	6	23	0	4	33
	P	1	28	31	0	6	66
Construct	D	0	0	1	0	0	1
	P	0	12	7	0	0	19
Suffixed	D	0	0	0	0	1	1
	P	0	4	12	1	11	28

The construct and suffixed forms appear invariant. Twenty-one
of the *defectives* for the normal form in the Latter Prophets
come from Jeremiah.

מִשְׁפָּחוֹת (*families*): Global Rank: 80. *Defective*: 106. *Plene*: 14.
High-frequency portions: 11, 13, and 19 (Numbers 1-10, 22-36;
Joshua 13-24). The final vowel is of Type 48. The deviant forms
are scattered among the dominant forms with no apparent factors conditioning their use.

אַבְשָׁלוֹם (*Absalom*): Global Rank: 163. *Defective*: 16. *Plene*: 82.
High-frequency portion: 26 (2 Samuel 13-24). The final vowel is
of Type 51. *All* of the deviant forms for this name occur in the
single high-frequency portion. No conditioning factors are obvious.

מִגְרָשִׁים (*pastures*): Global Rank: 166. *Defective*: 49. *Plene*: 52.
High-frequency portions: 19 and 71 (Joshua 13-24 and 1 Chronicles 1-9). The final vowel is of Type 14 or 25. Here one portion
uses one form and the other uses the other. Portion 19 uses
the lexeme fifty-eight times. The ָ -suffixed form is *defective*
forty-nine times and *plene* once. Portion 71 uses the lexeme

forty-three times with all forty-one ָ-suffixed forms *plene*.

פֹּה (*here*): Global Rank: 211. *Defective* (strictly "archaic"): 11. *Plene* (strictly "standard"): 24. High-frequency portion: 47 (Ezekiel 40-48). The vowel is of Type 31 (with one instance like Type 32). By our hypothesis, the deviant spellings are the eleven *defectives*. But in all other portions of the Bible the segment appears forty-seven additional times, always spelled *defective*. All twenty-four of the *plene* forms occur in Ezekiel 40:11-41:26, always in the word מִפֹּה. In chapters 40-41, Ezekiel also has the word מִפֹּה eleven times. This form never occurs elsewhere in the Hebrew Bible.

One might go on to expound the deviant spellings found in low-frequency portions, but little new insight would be gained. Few major lexemes would be added to the stock just characterized. The full list of low-frequency deviants contains eighty-seven items, amounting to a total of 1,475 deviants. It is worth noting that for 202 of the items (all but eight), which spelling dominates is the same in low-frequency contexts as in high. Also, in all but a dozen instances, the percentage of deviants for a given item is higher in the low-frequency portions than in the high.

8.4 Stress

In § 6.2 provision was made for classifying all opportunity vowels in terms of their relative stress. Masoretic accentuation permits recognition of three grades of stress; and, in accordance with the views generally held by Hebraists, we call these "low," "middle," and "high." This suggests ordering. Vowels are supposed to be longer under stress, so the question arises whether increased length under greater stress (or simply stress itself) enhances the chances that the vowel in question will be spelled *plene*. Any such effect might change over time; it might be handled differently by different scribal schools, and so the resulting spelling choices might vary from portion to portion. They might vary also with vowel type, and, for any given vowel type, the manifold influences are likely to be relative.

Just how the stress categories should be ordered, if indeed they should be, is not clear. From the statistical point of view the study of possible dependence of spelling on stress is complicated by the disproportionate way in which vowels of some types occur under the two or three grades of stress possible for them. Middle stress mainly applies to construct nouns; proclitic verbs are rare. So some types have hardly any specimens under middle stress. When the table of vowels of any given type is dominated by those with one stress, the table can often be collapsed on the grounds that no significant inhomogeneity due to stress is observed. (When the counts are very disproportionate, the result would be much the same if the very small samples of the rare stress state were simply ignored.)

8.4.1. Evidence has already been presented, and more is given in Chapter 9, to confirm the general impression that the use of *matres lectionis* increased with the passage of time. When the usual canonical order is accepted as a roughly chronological arrangement, there is a general trend towards more use of *matres lectionis* in the later parts of the Bible. This leads to a further and more nuanced question whether the differential effects of stress on the probability of choosing a *plene* spelling for any given vowel are constant throughout the corpus, or whether they change from portion to portion.

8.4.2. Figure 8.2 shows the percentages of opportunities which are low, middle, and high stress plotted across the Hebrew Bible divided into thirty portions (Chapter 7). The distribution among the three grades of stress is fairly constant. There are always relatively fewer middle-stress vowels, and more high- than low-stress vowels, except in Ezekiel 1-24, where they are equal. The fluctuations from portion to portion reflect varying use of suffixes with nouns and verbs. Whether this is due to content, genre, or individual style is not yet known. The highest percentage of low-stress vowels occurs in Ezekiel 1-24 and in Leviticus. The highest percentage of middle-stress vowels occurs in Exodus 25-40, presumably because of a greater use of construct noun phrases.

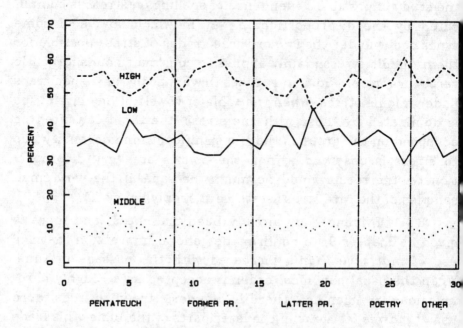

Figure 8.2 Percent of opportunities versus portion

8.4.3. Such fluctuations would interfere with any general trends in spelling preference due to stress as such, but they are nothing compared to the behavior of individual vowel types across the Bible. Because the frequency with which a vowel of any given type occurs varies from portion to portion, Figures 8.3 and 8.4 present plots of the percentages of the spelling choices for the three grades of stress for Types 47 and 48 across the Bible as thirty portions. (These types were considered in combination in § 1.6.) First impressions are that the spelling of these vowel types is erratic, but some patterns can be discerned.

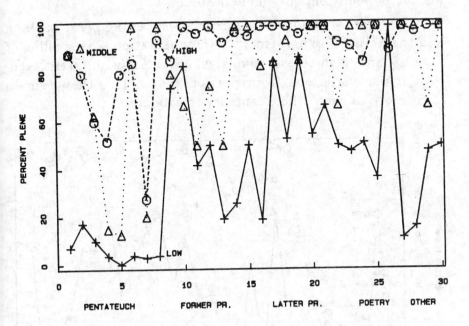

Figure 8.3 Percent plene across portion for Type 47

The percentage of *plene* spellings of high-stress Type 47 vowels is generally high, except in Exodus and the first half of Deuteronomy. The percentage of *plene* spellings of low-stress Type 47 vowels is very low (below 20%) in the Pentateuch, fairly low (around 20%) in Kings, Deutero-Isaiah, Megilloth and Ezra-Nehemiah. In some portions it is quite high (Proverbs!). The spelling of middle-stress Type 47 vowels fluctuates, *plene* being low in Exodus 25-40, Leviticus, and the first half of Deuteronomy; elsewhere it is generally high, with variations.

For Type 48 (Figure 8.4) all vowels prefer *defective* spelling in the Pentateuch, with a deviation for high and middle stress in Genesis 29-50. High and middle stress prefer *plene* spelling in the rest of the Bible (middle somewhat less than high in 2 Kings and Ezra-Nehemiah). The spelling of low-stress Type 48 vowels fluctuates wildly outside the Pentateuch.

For Types 47 and 48 low-stress vowels evoke *plene* spelling less than others, in agreement with expectation. The spelling of middle- and high-stress vowels is not clearly differentiated. With minor variations from portion to portion, they remain fairly close to each other, contrary to expectation.

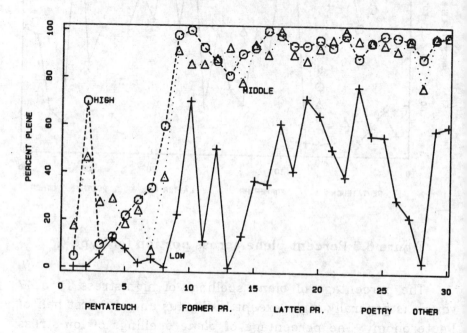

Figure 8.4 Percent plene across portion for Type 48

Comparison of Figure 8.3 with 8.4 also supports the hunch that spelling choices might be dependent in some measure (at least in some portions) on word length. Words with Type 47 vowels are shorter than those with Type 48 vowels. Note also the differences between Types 40 and 42, and Types 43 and 44 (tables in Chapter 6). The spelling of low-stress vowels shows similar trends in Figures 8.3 and 8.4, but in the Pentateuch high- and middle-stress vowels of Type 47 go in for *plene* spellings more than those of Type 48. (In comparing the spelling of middle-stress vowels of Types 47 and 48 with the aid of Figures 8.3 and 8.4, it needs to be remembered that the lower incidence of middle-stress Type 47 vowels partly accounts for the wider variance in the percentage of *plene* spellings in Figure 8.3.)

8.4.4. The result of studying all spelling choices across the five sections of the Bible is shown in Figure 8.5. The picture for "all stresses" is a general trend towards more *plene* spellings as we move through the Bible. This is also true of high stress; but within the Writings, the Poetry shows the highest preference for *plene* spelling of low-stress vowels, but a remarkably low preference for *plene* spelling of middle-stress vowels, which are almost on a par with the spelling of high-stress vowels.

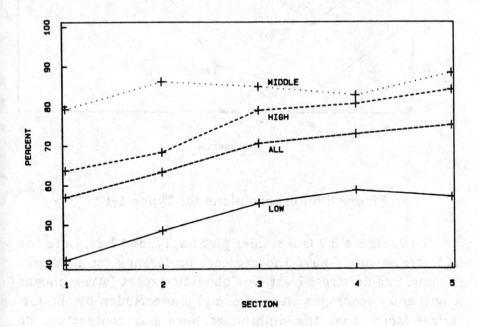

Figure 8.5 Percent plene for all opportunities

8.4.5. Figure 8.6 is a similar plot of the spelling of Types 1-12. The relatively large number of *defective* spellings in the Former Prophets (Section 2) reflects the local concentration of 'David' with consonantal spelling. Middle stress shows a consistently greater preference for *plene* spelling, so if stress has anything to do with spelling choice, the term "middle" is a misnomer.

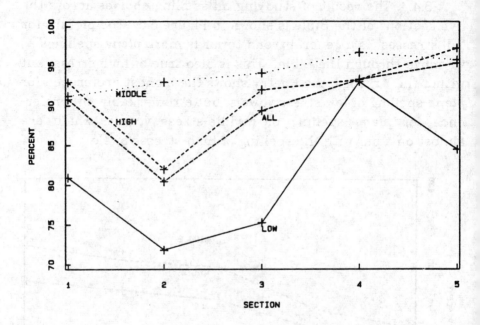

Figure 8.6 Percent plene for Types 1-12

8.4.6. Figure 8.7 is a similar plot for Types 13-24. Here the high-stress vowels have the greatest preference for *defective* spelling, middle-stress least. The phonetic aspect (stress means length and encourages *plene* spelling) is overridden by the historical factor that the diphthongs were not contracted, no matter what the stress, during the biblical period. The masoretic vocalization of these vowels represents an artificial and unhistorical normalization to a standard which emerged only at the end of, or even after, the biblical period.

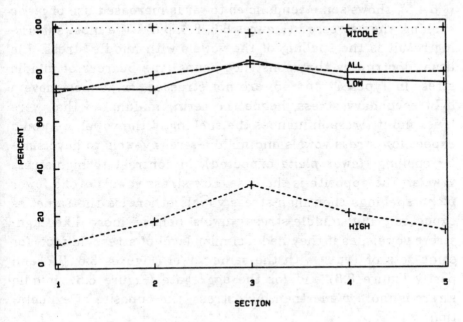

Figure 8.7 Percent plene for Types 13-24

8.4.7. Figure 8.8 does the same thing for Types 30-55. Here the trends are more consistent. Each stress level follows a similar path. The peculiar behavior of middle-stress vowels in the Poetry (Section 4), already remarked in Figure 8.5, is seen to be due to this vowel. The expected ordering low-middle-high is found only in the Writings.

8.4.8. Figure 8.9 is for Types 56-65. Here the spelling of high-stress vowels is the most erratic. In the Former Prophets, they are more *defective* than any others, and the Latter Prophets is the only section with the ordering low-middle-high.

8.4.9. From this discussion we see that, while stress does influence spelling choice, it varies from vowel to vowel. The primally long vowels (Figures 8.6 and 8.9) and the primal diphthong (Figure 8.7) show very little systematic response of spelling to stress. The vowel /ō/, whose history is very complex (§ 6.4.5), shows some tendencies towards increased use of *plene* spelling when stressed (Figures 8.3, 8.4, 8.8). The most surprising result is the spelling of the vowels with middle stress. The usual doctrine is that construct nouns (the bearers of middle stress in Types 47 and 48) are not stressed, or at most have a light secondary stress; hence the term "middle." If that were true, and if stress influences the spelling of the vowel, we would expect low-stress vowels and middle-stress vowels to have similar spelling (fewer *plene* expected), in contrast to high-stress vowels. The opposite is the case. Low-stress vowels evoke fewer *plene* spellings than high-stress vowels otherwise the same, as expected. But middle-stress vowels behave more like high-stress vowels, as if they had a similar level of stress. In fact, for some sets of Types with the same vowel (Figures 8.6, 8.7, and partly Figure 8.8) and for the aggregate (Figure 8.5), middle stress is more *plene* than high stress, the opposite of expectation.

Clearly, stress is a complex matter requiring full study in its own right. For the purposes of our present work, we neither attempt to explain the effects of stress fully nor do we ignore stress. It suffices to control for stress in subsequent analyses by investigating partial associations rather than marginal associations when necessary. We shall take these matters up in Chapter 9.

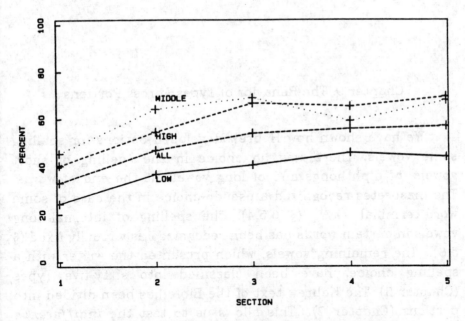

Figure 8.8 Percent plene for Types 30-55

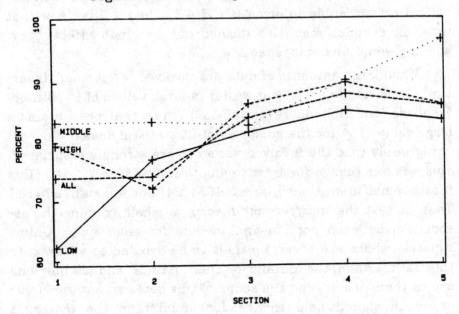

Figure 8.9 Percent plene for Types 56-65

Chapter 9. The Behavior of Types Across Portions

We have shown how Hebrew developed options for spelling some vowels. There was no choice in the spelling of short vowels, of diphthongs and of long vowels at the end of words. The masoretes recognized a pseudo-choice in the case of some word-terminal /ā/'s (§ 6.5.4). The spelling of internal long vowels in certain words has been recognized as virtually fixed (§ 5.6). The remaining vowels, which presented the writer with a spelling choice, have been classified into sixty-five Types (Chapter 6). The Hebrew text of the Bible has been divided into portions (Chapter 7). This allows us to test the *indifference theory* of text transmission which posits that our texts lack historical orthographic information (§ 4.2). In § 4.9, we saw that were all encoder statistics washed out by chain effects, text spelling would be homogeneous.

When large amounts of data are involved, even small departures from homogeneity can result in large values of χ^2 (Bishop, Fienberg, and Holland 1975: 329-332). Thus, that one obtains a large value of χ^2 for the goodness-of-fit statistic does *not* necessarily imply that the involved variables are strongly associated. This was our reason for introducing Cramér's v in § 1.11. (This measure has limitations [Agresti 1984: 24] but will suffice here.) Thus, to test the *indifference theory*, we shall examine the association between portion and spelling for each type. Unfortunately, there are several pitfalls to be avoided as we execute this task. While the details of their nature and of how one avoids them are beyond the scope of this book, an outline of our approach should help the reader understand the materials presented in § 9.2 below.

9.1 Assessing the *indifference theory*

In carrying out the contingency table analyses for each vowel type, we addressed the following five questions:

1) How are the effects of stress to be handled?

2) Which observations (if any) are suspicious?

3) Which of the suspicious observations are outliers?

4) Is Cramér's v for the type made spuriously large by a few dominant outliers?

5) How do the portion-choice and portion-verse parity associations compare?

We next expound the organization of the material in § 9.2 by explaining how that material documents the answers to these five questions.

9.1.1. We get at the effects of stress (or lack thereof) by performing three-dimensional contingency table analyses for each type which allows more than one level of stress. For each multiple-stress type in § 9.2, the first box following the type number gives the results of the three-dimensional analysis. The top item tells the *number* of the model which best fits the data for the type. (Thus, for Type 2, we read that 3-D Model #7 best fits the data.) What does this mean?

While two-dimensional analysis for non-ordered categories allows only one model of interest, the model of independence (§ 1.8), inclusion of a third dimension allows a total of eight interesting models (Fienberg 1980: 27). (For reasons discussed in § 8.4, we have elected to treat stress as non-ordered.) The analogy of § 1.7 is a ready vehicle for specifying the eight interesting models (plus a ninth having zero degrees of freedom). The nine models involve:

1) All three variables totally independent.

2) Position (portion) and story (stress) associated, independent of cubicle choice (spelling choice).

3) Position and cubicle choice associated, independent of story.

4) Story and cubicle choice associated, independent of position.

5) Position and choice independent, given story.

6) Story and choice independent, given position.

7) Position and story independent, given choice.

8) The interaction of each pair of variables independent of the third.

9) The interactions of pairs dependent on the remaining variable (saturation).

Viewed causally, some of these models seem puzzling. It is best to interpret them in terms of contingency analysis of sub-tables. Thus, for example, model #5 simply implies that the two-dimensional model of independence applies separately to each story of the tenement. (Only Type 14 obeys this model.)

The usefulness of determining which of these models best fits each multiple-stress type results from a theorem we shall not attempt to explain (Agresti 1984: 36-38). The theorem's implication is easy to state: If Models #5 or #8 or #9 best fit the data, then the relation of portion and choice should be studied by analyzing the two-dimensional tables at each level of stress. For the other models, stress may be ignored by "collapsing" the table on stress; that is, by analyzing the two-dimensional table which results when we sum over the stress dimension. (In terms of our analogy, one sends each upper-story occupant to the ground story cubicle directly under the one he first inhabits.) In the first situation, we are forced to analyze what the literature refers to as *partial* tables. In the second case, we may analyze *marginal* tables. So much for the top item in the 3-D box.

The bottom row in the 3-D box gives the first five items next described. All eight items next described are given both in boxes dealing with marginal (collapsed) tables ("Stress LMH") and in boxes characterizing partial tables ("Stress L," say).

1) the number of portions used in the analysis (p) as dictated by the population rule(s) of § 7.2.

2) the mean cell population (λ).

3) the number of degrees of freedom of the best model ($d.f.$).

4) a Pearson chi-square-like measure of the model fit for the spelling choice data (G_s^2).

5) the 99% confidence chi-square threshold introduced in § 1.10 ($\chi_{99\%}^2$).

6) a Pearson chi-square-like measure of the model fit for the verse parity-portion data (G_v^2).

7) Cramér's v_s for portion-spelling.

8) Cramér's v_v for portion-parity.

There is much subtlety buried in these items. The reckoning of item 3, the degrees of freedom, requires special care (Bishop, Fienberg, and Holland 1975: 114-6). Items 4 and 6 are called *log likelihood-ratio test statistics.* · They are similar to Pearson's chi-square statistic, but are better suited for the sort of model selection being described here (Fienberg 1980: 56-60).

The upshot of the three-dimensional analyses is that for twenty-two of the vowel types, analysis of partial tables is preferable to analysis of marginal tables. Many of these preferences for analysis of partial tables may be artifacts resulting from the large goodness-of-fit statistics generated by our large datasets (Gokhale and Kullback 1978: 124).

9.1.2. To discover suspicious cells, the informal method of § 1.11 was used. In order to evaluate the threshold of suspicion ($r_{99\%}$), the involved two-dimensional tables had first to be fitted via the model of independence. The results of these fittings are given by the boxes headed "Independence Model for Stress ..." in § 9.2. The row entry items are as above.

The homogeneity or inhomogeneity of the (sub)type under consideration was determined by examining whether χ^2 was less than or greater than $\chi_{99\%}^2$. In some cases the homogeneity of the data could be due to the small size of the sample, e.g., Type 10, middle stress. In other cases, a high-frequency type exhibited the same behavior evenly across all portions.

9.1.3. Prospecting for suspicious cells turned up three thousand candidates, indicative of a situation of considerable inhomogeneity. True outliers were detected by the "leave-one-out" strategy described by Bishop, Fienberg, and Holland (1975: 140). The details need not detain us. Only the five most suspicious cells for each table were tested by the strategy. We were especially interested in those portions of the Bible which make a major contribution to the inhomogeneous spelling of any given vowel type (§ 9.3). In the boxes headed "Outlier Portions," we list the outliers in decreasing order of contribution to inhomogeneity (G_1^2). In characterizing each outlier, we report its deviation in terms of overuse (+D) or underuse (-D) of *defective* spelling, and likewise for *plene*, whichever is appropriate. The counts of *defective* and *plene* spellings for deviant portions are also given.

9.1.4. The next step was to examine the outlier portions to determine the cause(s) of the behavior. In most cases, the behavior was produced by a multiplicity of forms. But, as noted below where appropriate, in some cases a single word or few words led to the behavior.

9.1.5. The extent of association between portion and choice for (collapsed) types is summarized by Figure 9.1. (To assess association for partial tables, examine the v_s entries in § 9.2.) The upper solid line shows Cramér's v_s for the types, ranked for ease of study from least association to most. The dotted bar at each rank shows the 95% confidence interval for that rank. The number at the upper limit of the bar identifies the type; the vowel shown at the lower limit shows what kind of vowel the type is. The lower solid line shows the association between portion and verse parity for each type. Note that in almost all cases, portion and spelling show considerably more association than portion and verse parity. The upper curve discloses some quite high degrees of association, leading us to assert that the

indifference model of text transmission is *not* tenable. Orthographic information has survived passage through the transmission chain.

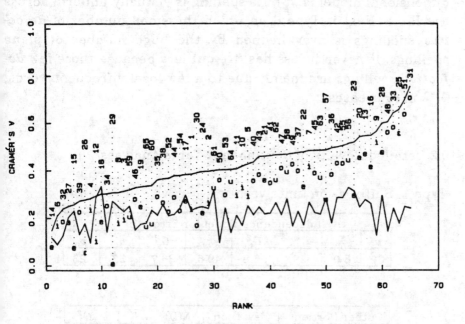

Figure 9.1 Ranked v_s with 95% C.I. plus v_v

The types on the righthand side of the figure show the
highest association of spelling choice with portion. The extreme
is Type 31, and the outliers given below show that this is the
result of concentration of special vocabulary items with invariant spelling (proper nouns in the first two outliers). Type 51,
with the next highest association, is similar ('Jacob' and 'Absalom'). The next, Type 25, results from the different but consistent spelling of the same word, locally frequent in Joshua and
Chronicles (§ 8.3.4). The fourth highest association of portion
and spelling is shown by Type 33, *nota accusativi*, discussed in
detail in Chapter 6. Next is Type 48, which started our

discussion (§ 1.6). See also Figure 8.4. At the other end of the plot, the least association between portion and choice of spelling is shown by Type 14 (it is the only one whose three-dimensional model is #5). Its spelling is virtually uniform across the Bible. Next is Type 6, in which the small number of *defective* spellings is overwhelmed by the huge number of *plene* spellings. It nevertheless has five outliers because those few *defective* spellings are mainly due to a few locally frequent words, גּוֹיִם in four cases.

9.2 Detailed Results of Contingency Table Analyses

•Type 1. Suffix -ī- on finite verb

Independence Model for Stress H							
p	λ	$d.f.$	G_s^2	$\chi_{99\%}^2$	G_{η}^2	v_s	v_{η}
30	8.0	29	56.2	49.6	26.7	.38	.23

Outlier Portions	Deviation	N(D)	N(P)	G_1^2
Ex 25-40	+D -P	4	4	10.8
1 Samuel	+D -P	6	14	9.8
Ez 1-24	-D	0	42	6.7

•Type 2. Stem -ī- in *qal* of hollow root

Stress LMH 3-D Model #7				
p	λ	$d.f.$	G^2	$\chi_{99\%}^2$
10	10.0	25	40.8	44.3

Independence Model for Stress LMH							
p	λ	$d.f.$	G_s^2	$\chi_{99\%}^2$	G_{η}^2	v_s	v_{η}
30	10.0	29	75.1	49.6	37.0	.40	.24

Outlier Portion	Deviation	N(D)	N(P)	G_1^2
1 Samuel	+D -P	7	10	20.0

•Type 3. Stem $-\bar{\iota}$- in perfect of לה root

Stress LMH 3-D Model #1				
p	λ	$d.f.$	G^2	$\chi^2_{99\%}$
30	7.1	140	163.5	181.8

Independence Model for Stress LMH							
p	λ	$d.f.$	G_s^2	$\chi^2_{99\%}$	G_ν^2	v_s	v_ν
76	8.4	75	88.5	106.3	70.2	.31	.23

Outlier Portion	Deviation	N(D)	N(P)	G_1^2
Je 45-52	+D -P	17	8	11.6

Type 3 is homogeneous when gauged by G_s^2 but is inhomogeneous when gauged by Pearson's χ_s^2, which equals 125.4.

•Type 4. Stem $-\bar{\iota}$- in $hip^c il$ forms

Stress LMH 3-D Model #8				
p	λ	$d.f.$	G^2	$\chi^2_{99\%}$
76	12.4	99	120.7	134.6

Independence Model for Stress L							
p	λ	$d.f.$	G_s^2	$\chi^2_{99\%}$	G_ν^2	v_s	v_ν
76	7.8	75	214.9	106.4	80.4	.40	.25

Outlier Portions	Deviation	N(D)	N(P)	G_i^2
Je 33-44	+D -P	14	0	14.8
1 Sa 1-12	+D -P	13	0	12.9
1 Ki 15-22	+D -P	12	0	7.8
Je 11-23:8	+D -P	14	0	6.7

Stress M: Sample too small for analysis ($p \leq 4$).

Independence Model for Stress H							
p	λ	$d.f.$	G_s^2	$\chi_{99\%}^2$	G_ν^2	υ_s	υ_ν
76	29.1	75	312.5	106.4	53.5	.26	.11

Outlier Portions	Deviation	N(D)	N(P)	G_i^2
2 Sa 1-12	+D -P	20	40	26.4
1 Ki 1-7	+D -P	11	24	13.2
De 1-7	+D -P	11	26	11.7
1 Sa 13-20	+D -P	15	48	11.3
Ez 25-32	+D -P	9	21	10.1

•Type 5. Stem -ז- in forms from פ״י roots

Independence Model for Stress L							
p	λ	$d.f.$	G_s^2	$\chi_{99\%}^2$	G_ν^2	υ_s	υ_ν
30	6.0	29	60.6	49.6	23.9	.43	.25

Outlier Portions	Deviation	N(D)	N(P)	G_i^2
Ex 25-40	+D -P	4	1	12.1
1 Samuel	+D -P	8	10	11.9
Ps 1-72	-D	0	29	8.2

•Type 6. Suffix $-\bar{\iota}\,(m)$ of plural nouns

Independence Model for Stress H							
p	λ	$d.f.$	G_s^2	χ_{99z}^2	G_v^2	v_s	v_v
76	82.0	75	557.6	106.4	98.3	.21	.09

Outlier Portions	Deviation	N(D)	N(P)	G_i^2
Ez 33-39	+D -P	30	102	53.8
Nu 22:2-36	+D -P	34	232	28.7
Ez 25-32	+D -P	26	146	28.3
Is 56-66	+D -P	16	101	14.8
Hg-Zc-Ml	+D -P	23	194	13.4

•Type 7. Stem $-\bar{\iota}-$ (first vowel) in other nouns

Independence Model for Stress L							
p	λ	$d.f.$	G_s^2	χ_{99z}^2	G_v^2	v_s	v_v
76	6.9	74	274.8	105.2	80.7	.49	.27

Outlier Portions	Deviation	N(D)	N(P)	G_i^2
1 Sa 21-31	+D -P	14	1	25.3
1 Ch 1-9	-D +P	3	47	21.8
Je 33-44	+D -P	8	0	18.1
1 Sa 13-20	+D -P	24	13	16.8
Is 40-55	+D -P	12	3	14.5

•Type 8. Stem $-\bar{\iota}-$ in nouns with hollow roots

Stress LMH 3-D Model #9				
p	λ	$d.f.$	G^2	χ_{99z}^2
10	10.9	0	0	0

Independence Model for Stress L							
p	λ	$d.f.$	G_s^2	$\chi_{99\%}^2$	G_ν^2	v_s	v_ν
10	14.2	9	20.2	21.67	9.1	.28	.18

Outlier Portion	Deviation	N(D)	N(P)	G_1^2
Ezekiel-MP	+D	7	32	11.3

Low stress Type 8 is homogeneous by G_s^2 and (barely) inhomogeneous by χ_s^2, which equals 21.8.

Independence Model for Stress M							
p	λ	$d.f.$	G_s^2	$\chi_{99\%}^2$	G_ν^2	v_s	v_ν
5	7.2	4	6.8	13.3	3.3	.34	.21

Outlier Portion	Deviation	N(D)	N(P)	G_1^2
Ps-Jb-Pr	+D	2	12	6.7

Middle stress Type 8 is homogeneous by both measures of fit. This is no surprise, as there are only two *defective* forms.

Independence Model for Stress H							
p	λ	$d.f.$	G_s^2	$\chi_{99\%}^2$	G_ν^2	v_s	v_ν
10	15.0	9	31.7	21.7	31.5	.36	.31

Outlier Portion	Deviation	N(D)	N(P)	G_1^2
Le-Nu-De	+D -P	8	27	19.8

•Type 9. Stem -$\bar{\imath}$- (second vowel) in nouns

Stress LMH 3-D Model #9				
p	λ	$d.f.$	G^2	$\chi^2_{99\%}$
76	13.6	0	0	0

Independence Model for Stress L							
p	λ	$d.f.$	G^2_s	$\chi^2_{99\%}$	G^2_v	v_s	v_v
76	11.3	65	211.6	106.4	71.3	.35	.20

Outlier Portions	Deviation	N(D)	N(P)	G^2_1
Je 23:9-32	+D -P	20	15	36.3
Je 33-44	+D -P	8	8	11.8
2 Ch 26-36	+D -P	6	7	7.8
Je 45-52	+D -P	9	16	7.6
2 Sa 13-24	+D -P	7	11	6.8

Independence Model for Stress M							
p	λ	$d.f.$	G^2_s	$\chi^2_{99\%}$	G^2_v	v_s	v_v
30	9.5	29	62.8	49.6	60.5	.36	.32

Outlier Portions	Deviation	N(D)	N(P)	G^2_1
Je 1-32	+D -P	10	20	20.8
2 Samuel	+D -P	5	13	8.0

Independence Model for Stress H							
p	λ	$d.f.$	G^2_s	$\chi^2_{99\%}$	G^2_v	v_s	v_v
76	25.9	75	1892.3	106.4	110.0	.69	.17

Outlier Portions	Deviation	N(D)	N(P)	G_1^2
2 Sa 1-12	+D -P	195	54	385.8
1 Sa 21-31	+D -P	174	62	309.5
1 Sa 13-20	+D -P	122	27	252.3
2 Sa 13-24	+D -P	95	73	97.9

All these outliers are dominated by the *defective* spelling of
דָּוִד. See § 1.2.

•Type 10. Stem -ī- in other proper nouns

Stress LMH 3-D Model #9				
p	λ	$d.f.$	G^2	$\chi_{99\%}^2$
10	9.2	0	0	0

Independence Model for Stress L							
p	λ	$d.f.$	G_s^2	$\chi_{99\%}^2$	G_ν^2	ν_s	ν_ν
5	9.1	3	5.4	11.3	8.2	.24	.28

Low stress Type 10 is homogeneous.

Middle stress Type 10 sample is too small for analysis ($p \le .2$).

Independence Model for Stress H							
p	λ	$d.f.$	G_s^2	$\chi_{99\%}^2$	G_ν^2	ν_s	ν_ν
30	7.7	25	110.1	44.3	25.0	.47	.21

Outlier Portions	Deviation	N(D)	N(P)	G_1^2
Judges	+D -P	46	15	55.1
Is 1-39	-D +P	0	16	12.3
Ezra-Nehemiah	-D +P	5	28	12.0
2 Ki 9-25	-D +P	1	21	9.1

These outliers are dominated by the prominence of certain

tribes or persons in the stories -- Benjamin in Judges, Jehoiakim in 2 Kings.

•Type 11. Suffix $-\bar{\imath}(t)$ of feminine nouns

Stress LMH 3-D Model #6				
p	λ	$d.f.$	G^2	$\chi^2_{99\%}$
10	10.4	11	15.3	24.7

Independence Model for Stress LMH							
p	λ	$d.f.$	G^2_s	$\chi^2_{99\%}$	G^2_v	v_s	v_v
30	10.4	29	89.8	49.6	29.8	.41	.21

Outlier Portions	Deviation	N(D)	N(P)	G^2_τ
Numbers	+D -P	11	24	23.5
Leviticus	+D -P	13	46	19.3

•Type 12. Residuum of $-\bar{\imath}-$ opportunities

Stress LMH 3-D Model #1				
p	λ	$d.f.$	G^2	$\chi^2_{99\%}$
5	4.0	22	30.0	40.3

Independence Model for Stress LMH							
p	λ	$d.f.$	G^2_s	$\chi^2_{99\%}$	G^2_v	v_s	v_v
10	6.1	9	10.8	21.7	10.9	.29	.29

This residuum presents a small sample which is completely homogeneous and yields no points of interest.

•Type 13. Stem-terminal -$\bar{e}$- in prepositions

			Independence Model for Stress L				
p	λ	$d.f.$	G_s^2	$\chi^2_{99\%}$	G_ν^2	υ_s	υ_ν
76	6.6	74	303.8	105.2	85.2	.55	.28

Outlier Portions	Deviation	N(D)	N(P)	G_1^2
Ex 1-11	+D -P	17	11	31.7
Ge 39-50	+D -P	20	18	30.6
Ex 12-24	+D -P	12	8	21.7
Le 17-27	+D -P	10	6	19.1
Ex 32-40	+D -P	5	2	13.3

•Type 14. Stem-terminal -$\bar{e}$- in nouns

		Stress LM 3-D Model #5		
p	λ	$d.f.$	G^2	$\chi^2_{99\%}$
76	24.0	150	139.3	193.2

			Independence Model for Stress L				
p	λ	$d.f.$	G_s^2	$\chi^2_{99\%}$	G_ν^2	υ_s	υ_ν
76	15.0	75	106.6	106.4	119.8	.30	.22

Outlier Portion	Deviation	N(D)	N(P)	G_1^2
Ge 1-17	+D -P	6	9	29.2

			Independence Model for Stress M				
p	λ	$d.f.$	G_s^2	$\chi^2_{99\%}$	G_ν^2	υ_s	υ_ν
76	33.1	75	32.7	106.4	114.0	.13	.15

Middle stress Type 14 is homogeneous; six *defective* out of 5,028.

•Type 15. Stem-initial -$\bar{e}$- in verbs

Independence Model for Stress L							
p	λ	$d.f.$	G_s^2	$\chi_{99\%}^2$	G_ν^2	ν_s	ν_ν
10	5.9	9	8.8	21.7	6.6	.26	.23

Type 15 is homogeneous.

•Type 16. Stem -$\bar{e}$- in verbs from ל״י roots

Stress LMH 3-D Model #3				
p	λ	$d.f.$	G^2	$\chi_{99\%}^2$
5	6.6	18	21.6	34.8

Independence Model for Stress LMH							
p	λ	$d.f.$	G_s^2	$\chi_{99\%}^2$	G_ν^2	ν_s	ν_ν
10	9.9	9	60.8	21.7	14.7	.55	.26

Outlier Portions	Deviation	N(D)	N(P)	G_1^2
Jn/Ru-Ne	+D -P	22	2	41.3
Ezekiel-MP	-D +P	9	44	9.6

The first outlier is dominated by הַרְבֵּה.

•Type 17. Stem -$\bar{e}$- in verbs from other roots

Stress LMH 3-D Model #1				
p	λ	$d.f.$	G^2	$\chi_{99\%}^2$
30	5.1	147	113.8	189.8

Independence Model for Stress LMH							
p	λ	$d.f.$	G_s^2	$\chi_{99\%}^2$	G_ν^2	ν_s	ν_ν
76	6.1	74	107.3	105.2	85.9	.38	.30

Outlier Portion	Deviation	N(D)	N(P)	G_1^2
Je 33-44	-D +P	11	5	12.8

•Type 18. Stem -$\bar{e}$- in nouns from hollow roots

Stress LMH 3-D Model #2				
p	λ	$d.f.$	G^2	$\chi_{99\%}^2$
10	13.3	29	31.5	49.6

Independence Model for Stress LMH							
p	λ	$d.f.$	G_s^2	$\chi_{99\%}^2$	G_ν^2	ν_s	ν_ν
76	5.3	75	56.1	106.4	99.1	.30	.33

Type 18 is homogeneous by both measures of fit.

•Type 19. Stem -$\bar{e}$- (first vowel) in other nouns

Stress LMH 3-D Model #8				
p	λ	$d.f.$	G^2	$\chi_{99\%}^2$
10	11.8	18	26.4	34.8

Independence Model for Stress L							
p	λ	$d.f.$	G_s^2	$\chi_{99\%}^2$	G_ν^2	ν_s	ν_ν
30	7.8	29	55.6	49.6	22.1	.35	.21

Outlier Portion	Deviation	N(D)	N(P)	G_1^2
Ps 1-72	-D +P	11	10	19.3

Independence Model for Stress M							
p	λ	$d.f.$	G_s^2	$\chi_{99\%}^2$	G_v^2	v_s	v_v
5	7.5	4	.85	13.3	1.3	.11	.13

Middle stress Type 19 is homogeneous.

Independence Model for Stress H							
p	λ	$d.f.$	G_s^2	$\chi_{99\%}^2$	G_v^2	v_s	v_v
10	8.2	9	23.6	21.7	9.7	.37	.24

•Type 20. Stem $-\bar{e}-$ (second vowel) in nouns

Stress LMH 3-D Model #9				
p	λ	$d.f.$	G^2	$\chi_{99\%}^2$
10	6.8	0	0	0

Independence Model for Stress L							
p	λ	$d.f.$	G_s^2	$\chi_{99\%}^2$	G_v^2	v_s	v_v
10	11.5	9	8.7	21.7	6.8	.19	.17

Low stress Type 20 is homogeneous.

Independence Model for Stress M							
p	λ	$d.f.$	G_s^2	$\chi_{99\%}^2$	G_v^2	v_s	v_v
10	8.3	8	108.8	20.1	10.0	.79	.24

Outlier Portions	Deviation	N(D)	N(P)	G_1^2
Is-Je	+D -P	21	7	41.2
Ezekiel-MP	+D -P	14	1	23.5
Psalms	+D -P	4	1	7.2

High stress Type 20 sample is too small for analysis ($p \le 1.2$).

•Type 21. Stem -$\bar{e}$- (first vowel) in proper nouns

Independence Model for Stress L							
p	λ	$d.f.$	G_s^2	$\chi_{99\%}^2$	G_ν^2	v_s	v_ν
30	6.5	26	91.4	45.6	19.8	.46	.22

Outlier Portions	Deviation	N(D)	N(P)	G_1^2
2 Kings	+D -P	51	12	26.5
1 Chronicles	-D +P	16	38	13.2
Ezra-Nehemiah	+D -P	28	9	9.4

•Type 22. Stem -$\bar{e}$- (second vowel) in proper nouns

Stress L H 3-D Model #9				
p	λ	$d.f.$	G^2	$\chi_{99\%}^2$
10	9.0	0	0	0

Independence Model for Stress L							
p	λ	$d.f.$	G_s^2	$\chi_{99\%}^2$	G_ν^2	v_s	v_ν
5	6.8	3	8.4	11.3	8.2	.32	.34

Low stress Type 22 is homogeneous.

Independence Model for Stress H							
p	λ	$d.f.$	G_s^2	$\chi_{99\%}^2$	G_ν^2	v_s	v_ν
10	14.6	8	52.6	20.1	2.6	.50	.09

Outlier Portions	Deviation	N(D)	N(P)	G_1^2
Joshua-2 Samuel	-D +P	23	12	39.7
Genesis-Exodus	-P	160	0	24.9

•Type 23. Stem -$\bar{e}$- (first vowel) residuum

Independence Model for Stress L							
p	λ	$d.f.$	G_s^2	$\chi_{99\%}^2$	G_ν^2	ν_s	ν_ν
10	5.9	9	26.6	21.7	12.4	.52	.31

Outlier Portion	Deviation	N(D)	N(P)	G_1^2
Job-Proverbs	+D -P	6	4	14.4

•Type 24. Stem -$\bar{e}$- residuum

Stress LMH 3-D Model #2				
p	λ	$d.f.$	G^2	$\chi_{99\%}^2$
5	3.8	11	16.4	24.7

Independence Model for Stress LMH							
p	λ	$d.f.$	G_s^2	$\chi_{99\%}^2$	G_ν^2	ν_s	ν_ν
10	5.7	9	20.7	21.7	7.3	.52	.31

Type 24 is homogeneous when judged by G_s^2 but inhomogeneous when judged by χ_s^2, which equals 31.8. No outliers.

•Type 25. Stem-terminal /$\bar{\varepsilon}$/ in nouns

Independence Model for Stress H							
p	λ	$d.f.$	G_s^2	$\chi_{99\%}^2$	G_ν^2	ν_s	ν_ν
76	16.2	75	356.7	106.4	80.1	.66	.18

Outlier Portions	Deviation	N(D)	N(P)	G_1^2
Js 13-24	+D -P	49	22	290.7
De 28-34	-D	0	107	7.0

•Type 26. Stem /$\bar{\varepsilon}$/ in verbs

Independence Model for Stress H							
p	λ	$d.f.$	G_s^2	$\chi_{99\%}^2$	G_ν^2	v_s	v_ν
10	7.3	9	11.0	21.7	4.8	.28	.18

Type 26 is homogeneous; no outliers.

•Type 27. Suffix -$t\bar{a}$ of perfect verbs

Stress LMH 3-D Model #6				
p	λ	$d.f.$	G^2	$\chi_{99\%}^2$
30	10.7	25	35.4	44.3

Independence Model for Stress LMH							
p	λ	$d.f.$	G_s^2	$\chi_{99\%}^2$	G_ν^2	v_s	v_ν
76	12.7	75	133.6	106.4	86.4	.25	.20

Outlier Portion	Deviation	N(D)	N(P)	G_1^2
Ps 1-41	-D +P	11	5	8.2

•Type 28. Suffix -$n\bar{a}$ of feminine plural verbs

Independence Model for Stress L							
p	λ	$d.f.$	G_s^2	$\chi_{99\%}^2$	G_ν^2	v_s	v_ν
30	5.7	29	102.5	49.6	34.5	.60	.30

Outlier Portions	Deviation	N(D)	N(P)	G_1^2
Ex 25-40	+D -P	5	0	21.8
Ge 1-28	+D -P	5	3	11.9
Ge 29-50	+D -P	8	12	11.1
Ex 1-24	+D -P	6	7	9.9
De 16:18-34	+D -P	2	0	8.6

•Type 29. Suffix -$\bar{a}$ of intensive imperatives

Independence Model for Stress H							
p	λ	$d.f.$	G_s^2	$\chi_{99\%}^2$	G_v^2	v_s	v_v
30	5.3	29	13.4	49.6	27.7	.31	.27

Type 29 is homogeneous when judged by χ_s^2, which equals 12.9.
No outliers.

•Type 30. The preposition כְּמוֹ

Independence Model for Stress H							
p	λ	$d.f.$	G_s^2	$\chi_{99\%}^2$	G_v^2	v_s	v_v
5	8.4	4	13.0	13.3	5.1	.39	.24

Type 30 is homogeneous.

Outlier Portion	Deviation	N(D)	N(P)	G_1^2
Pentateuch	+D -P	17	8	12.3

•Type 31. Words ending in ה- or וֹ (not 'his')

Independence Model for Stress H							
p	λ	$d.f.$	G_s^2	$\chi_{99\%}^2$	G_v^2	v_s	v_v
76	9.8	75	1059.5	106.4	95.4	.76	.24

Outlier Portions	Deviation	N(D)	N(P)	G_1^2
1 Ki 1-7	+D -P	95	1	125.9
Ge 39-50	+D -P	92	2	114.4
Le 1-16	-D +P	4	92	107.7

The *"defective"* spelling is strictly speaking archaic. The word
שְׁלֹמֹה occurs frequently in the first outlier, פַּרְעֹה in the second,
אוֹ in the third. The spelling אֹה never occurs.

•Type 32. The negative particle 'not' לֹא

Independence Model for Stress L							
p	λ	$d.f.$	G_s^2	$\chi_{99\%}^2$	G_ν^2	v_s	v_ν
76	34.1	75	291.8	106.4	82.9	.24	.13

Outlier Portions	Deviation	N(D)	N(P)	G_1^2
Je 1-10	-D +P	125	21	29.7
2 Sa 1-12	-D +P	39	8	13.3
Hg-Zc-Ml	-D +P	65	10	12.5
2 Ki 1-8	-D +P	42	8	12.4
1 Sa 21-31	+P	59	9	11.2

•Type 33. *Nota accusativi* ʾ$\bar{o}t$, אֵת אוֹת

Independence Model for Stress L							
p	λ	$d.f.$	G_s^2	$\chi_{99\%}^2$	G_ν^2	v_s	v_ν
76	9.1	68	601.2	98.0	88.7	.64	.24

Outlier Portions	Deviation	N(D)	N(P)	G_1^2
Jd 10-21	-D +P	2	35	83.2
Ez 14-24	-D +P	14	40	57.9
Jd 1-9	-D +P	2	19	40.3
Js 1-12	-D +P	14	23	22.4

• Type 34. Stem -ō- (first vowel) in prepositions and nouns

Stress LMH 3-D Model #9				
p	λ	$d.f.$	G^2	$\chi^2_{99\%}$
76	8.5	0	0	0

Independence Model for Stress L							
p	λ	$d.f.$	G^2_s	$\chi^2_{99\%}$	G^2_ν	v_s	v_ν
76	11.2	75	395.0	106.4	69.0	.46	.20

Outlier Portions	Deviation	N(D)	N(P)	G^2_1
Ge 29-38	+D -P	44	2	68.0
Ex 1-11	+D -P	25	1	39.0
Ez 1-13	-D +P	3	33	22.3

Independence Model for Stress M							
p	λ	$d.f.$	G^2_s	$\chi^2_{99\%}$	G^2_ν	v_s	v_ν
30	11.6	29	85.7	49.6	35.0	.33	.22

Outlier Portions	Deviation	N(D)	N(P)	G^2_1
Proverbs	+D -P	10	4	12.2
De 1-16:17	-D +P	0	16	10.3
Ez 25-48	+D -P	10	12	9.8
Je 33-52	-D +P	2	29	9.0

Independence Model for Stress H							
p	λ	$d.f.$	G^2_s	$\chi^2_{99\%}$	G^2_ν	v_s	v_ν
76	9.7	75	301.2	106.4	79.8	.43	.23

Outlier Portions	Deviation	N(D)	N(P)	G_1^2
Ge 1-17	+D -P	44	44	23.9
1 Ch 21-29	+D -P	12	2	22.0
2 Ch 10-25	+D -P	18	9	19.6
Ps 90-106	+D -P	17	12	13.7
2 Ch 26-36	+D -P	11	6	11.1

•Type 35. Stem -$\bar{o}$- in *hip^{c}il* of ‎י''פ roots

Independence Model for Stress L							
p	λ	$d.f.$	G_s^2	$\chi_{99\%}^2$	G_ν^2	v_s	v_ν
76	11.2	75	226.1	106.4	80.9	.36	.21

Outlier Portions	Deviation	N(D)	N(P)	G_1^2
2 Sa 1-12	+D -P	14	13	20.0
Ps 1-41	-D +P	0	53	17.9
Jb 22-42	+D -P	16	21	17.0
2 Sa 13-24	+D -P	13	14	16.5
Je 45-52	+D -P	7	6	10.5

•Type 36. Suffix -$\bar{o}$- in *hip^{c}ils*, etc.

Stress LMH 3-D Model #6				
p	λ	$d.f.$	G^2	$\chi_{99\%}^2$
5	9.3	5	5.8	15.1

Independence Model for Stress LMH							
p	λ	$d.f.$	G_s^2	$\chi_{99\%}^2$	G_ν^2	v_s	v_ν
10	13.9	9	78.0	21.7	9.0	.50	.18

Outlier Portions	Deviation	N(D)	N(P)	G_1^2
Genesis-Exodus	+D -P	33	0	28.7
1-2 Chronicles	-D +P	4	19	26.3
Le-Nu-De	+D -P	4	31	8.7

• Type 37. Suffix $-\bar{o}\,(t)$ of לה'' infinitives

Stress LMH 3-D Model #8				
p	λ	$d.f.$	G^2	$\chi^2_{99\%}$
30	6.5	44	64.7	68.7

Independence Model for Stress L							
p	λ	$d.f.$	G^2_s	$\chi^2_{99\%}$	G^2_v	v_s	v_v
10	10.2	9	70.7	21.7	16.7	.55	.27

Outlier Portions	Deviation	N(D)	N(P)	G^2_1
Le-Nu-De	+D -P	30	2	33.3
Ezekiel-MP	-D +P	4	25	20.0
Psalms	-D +P	1	10	9.2

Middle stress Type 37 sample is too small to analyze ($p \le 2.8$).

Independence Model for Stress H							
p	λ	$d.f.$	G^2_s	$\chi^2_{99\%}$	G^2_v	v_s	v_v
76	6.2	75	204.4	106.4	68.9	.50	.26

Outlier Portions	Deviation	N(D)	N(P)	G^2_1
Ex 12-24	+D -P	10	4	30.5
Ex 32-40	+D -P	12	11	26.2
Ge 18-28	+D -P	6	7	11.1
Le 1-16	+D -P	5	5	10.1
Ex 25-31	+D -P	4	5	7.0

•Type 38. Stem -ō- in infinitives absolute

Independence Model for Stress H							
p	λ	$d.f.$	G_s^2	$\chi_{99\%}^2$	G_v^2	v_s	v_v
30	7.1	29	63.7	49.6	31.3	.37	.26

Outlier Portions	Deviation	N(D)	N(P)	G_1^2
Joshua	-D +P	0	9	10.0
1 Samuel	+D -P	15	6	7.7
Je 33-52	+D -P	15	6	7.7

•Type 39. Stem -ō- in *qal* active participles

Stress LMH 3-D Model #9				
p	λ	$d.f.$	G^2	$\chi_{99\%}^2$
76	11.6	0	0	0

Independence Model for Stress L							
p	λ	$d.f.$	G_s^2	$\chi_{99\%}^2$	G_v^2	v_s	v_v
76	14.7	75	245.6	106.4	92.4	.32	.20

Outlier Portions	Deviation	N(D)	N(P)	G_1^2
Pr 16-31	-D +P	16	12	16.1
Ps 73-89	-D +P	12	10	14.6
Ps 42-72	-D +P	21	12	12.4
Ne 1-8	-D +P	40	16	10.4
Jonah/Ruth	-D +P	6	5	7.2

Independence Model for Stress M							
p	λ	$d.f.$	G_s^2	$\chi_{99\%}^2$	G_v^2	v_s	v_v
30	12.3	29	79.4	49.6	38.2	.32	.22

Outlier Portions	Deviation	N(D)	N(P)	G_1^2
2 Chronicles	-D +P	29	17	17.2
Judges	-D +P	19	12	12.8
2 Kings	-P	30	0	9.0

Independence Model for Stress H							
p	λ	$d.f.$	G_s^2	$\chi^2_{99\%}$	G_v^2	v_s	v_v
.76	15.4	75	332.8	106.4	72.1	.36	.17

Outlier Portions	Deviation	N(D)	N(P)	G_1^2
Lamentations	-D +P	4	15	21.3
2 Ch 26-36	-D +P	2	11	18.2
Nu 22:2-36	+D -P	47	3	16.3
Qohelet	-D +P	25	29	15.9
2 Ch 1-9	-D +P	6	13	13.4

•Type 40. Stem -ō- in *qal* imperfect regular verbs

Independence Model for Stress H							
p	λ	$d.f.$	G_s^2	$\chi^2_{99\%}$	G_v^2	v_s	v_v
76	9.7	74	258.9	105.2	72.0	.44	.21

Outlier Portions	Deviation	N(D)	N(P)	G_1^2
Jb 1-21	-D +P	35	20	35.2
Hosea-Joel	-D +P	12	12	29.1
Is 40-55	-D +P	19	7	7.9
Is 56-66	-D +P	10	5	7.5

•Type 41. Stem -ō- in *qal* imperfect יׄ״פ roots.

Independence Model for Stress H							
p	λ	$d.f.$	G_s^2	$\chi^2_{99\%}$	G_v^2	v_s	v_v
10	11.8	9	61.5	21.7	11.7	.46	.22

Outlier Portions	Deviation	N(D)	N(P)	G_1^2
Joshua-2 Samuel	+D -P	49	0	23.0
Job-Proverbs	-D +P	14	11	9.8
Is-Je	-D +P	12	10	9.3
Genesis-Exodus	-P	19	0	8.2

•Type 42. Stem -$\bar{o}$- in *qal* imperfect verbs of hollow root

Stress LMH 3-D Model #3				
p	λ	$d.f.$	G^2	$\chi^2_{99\%}$
30	6.2	116	74.7	154.4

Independence Model for Stress LMH							
p	λ	$d.f.$	G_s^2	$\chi^2_{99\%}$	G_v^2	v_s	v_v
76	7.4	75	302.1	106.4	100.9	.50	.29

Outlier Portions	Deviation	N(D)	N(P)	G_1^2
Esther	-D +P	2	12	20.6
Ez 33-39	-D +P	0	8	20.4
Ne 1-8	-D +P	1	9	17.2
Ez 40-48	-D +P	2	8	11.7
Je 1-10	-D +P	6	11	10.0

•Type 43. Stem -$\bar{o}$- in regular imperative and infinitive

Stress LMH 3-D Model #3				
p	λ	$d.f.$	G^2	$\chi^2_{99\%}$
30	6.0	106	83.9	143.8

Independence Model for Stress LMH							
p	λ	$d.f.$	G_s^2	$\chi^2_{99\%}$	G_v^2	v_s	v_v
76	7.1	75	242.0	106.4	71.0	.46	.25

Outlier Portions	Deviation	N(D)	N(P)	G_i^2
Qohelet	-D +P	21	27	35.4
2 Ch 26-36	-D +P	10	11	12.2
2 Ch 10-25	-D +P	9	10	11.2
2 Ch 1-9	-D +P	4	6	8.4

•Type 44. Stem -ō- in imperative and infinitive of hollow root

Stress LMH 3-D Model #9				
p	λ	$d.f.$	G^2	$\chi_{99\%}^2$
10	9.0	0	0	0

Independence Model for Stress L							
p	λ	$d.f.$	G_s^2	$\chi_{99\%}^2$	G_ν^2	v_s	v_ν
10	6.1	9	38.2	21.7	14.1	.52	.32

Outlier Portions	Deviation	N(D)	N(P)	G_i^2
Genesis-Exodus	+D -P	23	1	13.9
Joshua-2 Samuel	-D +P	14	16	7.8
Psalms	-D +P	0	3	7.0

Middle stress Type 44 sample is too small for analysis ($p \leq 1.8$).

Independence Model for Stress H							
p	λ	$d.f.$	G_s^2	$\chi_{99\%}^2$	G_ν^2	v_s	v_ν
30	6.7	29	74.0	49.6	31.4	.41	.27

Outlier Portions	Deviation	N(D)	N(P)	G_i^2
Ex 1-24	+D -P	8	0	12.8
2 Chronicles	-D +P	3	16	7.9
1 Kings	+D -P	11	3	6.6

•Type 45. Stem -ō- in $p\bar{o}l\bar{e}l$

Independence Model for Stress L							
p	λ	$d.f.$	G_s^2	$\chi_{99\%}^2$	G_v^2	v_s	v_v
30	7.5	29	115.3	49.6	25.5	.49	.22

Outlier Portions	Deviation	N(D)	N(P)	G_1^2
Ezra-Nehemiah	+D -P	27	5	21.7
Ps 73-150	-D +P	8	40	20.6
Ps 1-72	-D +P	11	39	14.0

•Type 46. Stem -ō- (first vowel) in nouns

Independence Model for Stress L							
p	λ	$d.f.$	G_s^2	$\chi_{99\%}^2$	G_v^2	v_s	v_v
76	26.8	75	473.0	106.4	94.5	.33	.15

Outlier Portions	Deviation	N(D)	N(P)	G_1^2
Ge 39-50	-D +P	4	150	69.2
1 Ki 15-22	+D -P	34	5	63.3
Le 1-16	+D -P	67	89	19.4

•Type 47. Plural suffix -ō (t) of nouns of hollow roots

Stress LMH 3-D Model #9				
p	λ	$d.f.$	G^2	$\chi_{99\%}^2$
30	12.1	0	0	0

Independence Model for Stress L							
p	λ	$d.f.$	G_s^2	$\chi_{99\%}^2$	G_v^2	v_s	v_v
76	5.7	73	441.6	104.0	94.5	.65	.30

Outlier Portions	Deviation	N(D)	N(P)	G_i^2
Ez 14-24	-D +P	2	40	69.2
Nu 1-10:10	+D -P	39	1	29.2
Je 1-10	-D +P	1	16	25.9
Js 13-24	-D +P	6	20	18.1

Independence Model for Stress M							
p	λ	$d.f.$	G_s^2	$\chi_{99\%}^2$	G_v^2	v_s	v_v
10	14.3	9	49.9	21.7	10.1	.38	.19

Outlier Portions	Deviation	N(D)	N(P)	G_i^2
Genesis-Exodus	+D -P	29	36	20.0
Jonah/Ruth-Ne	-D +P	0	22	12.1
Ezekiel-MP	-D +P	3	38	8.2

The need to use only ten portions puts Genesis and Exodus together and obscures the difference between them. The excess of *defective* spellings is contributed mainly by Exodus ($\times$ 26), most of the deficiency in *plene* ($\times$ 9).

Independence Model for Stress H							
p	λ	$d.f.$	G_s^2	$\chi_{99\%}^2$	G_v^2	v_s	v_v
76	6.7	73	239.6	104.0	108.1	.53	.31

Outlier Portions	Deviation	N(D)	N(P)	G_i^2
De 1-7	+D -P	9	2	32.6
Ex 32-40	+D -P	10	9	22.9
De 8-16:17	+D -P	7	4	19.4
Ex 1-11	+D -P	6	5	14.1
Ex 12-24	+D -P	8	16	10.3

•Type 48. Plural suffix $-\bar{o}\,(t)$ of nouns, regular roots

Stress LMH 3-D Model #9				
p	λ	$d.f.$	G^2	$\chi^2_{99\%}$
76	10.3	0	0	0

Independence Model for Stress L							
p	λ	$d.f.$	G^2_s	$\chi^2_{99\%}$	G^2_v	v_s	v_v
76	8.2	75	527.0	106.4	94.1	.59	.26

Outlier Portions	Deviation	N(D)	N(P)	G^2_1
Nu 1-10:10	+D -P	60	1	45.3
Nu 22:2-36	+D -P	39	0	34.4
Ps 1-41	-D +P	6	26	29.5
Ez 14-24	-D +P	16	38	29.1
Ez 1-13	-D +P	9	24	19.9

Independence Model for Stress M							
p	λ	$d.f.$	G^2_s	$\chi^2_{99\%}$	G^2_v	v_s	v_v
76	5.8	75	509.0	106.4	74.3	.73	.27

Outlier Portions	Deviation	N(D)	N(P)	G^2_1
Nu 22:2-36	+D -P	32	7	55.7
Nu 1-10:10	+D -P	21	2	44.9
Ex 32-40	+D -P	23	6	36.8
Ge 1-17	+D -P	14	4	21.2

Independence Model for Stress H							
p	λ	$d.f.$	G^2_s	$\chi^2_{99\%}$	G^2_v	v_s	v_v
76	16.9	75	1095.5	106.4	102.4	.71	.20

Outlier Portions	Deviation	N(D)	N(P)	G_1^2
Ex 32-40	+D -P	52	6	155.9
Ex 25-31	+D -P	45	8	123.6
Le 1-16	+D -P	28	6	72.6
Ex 12-24	+D -P	21	1	68.6
Nu 1-10:10	+D -P	22	5	55.9

The spelling of Type 48 is strongly inhomogeneous, and the large counts permit the use of seventy-six portions for all three stress levels.

•Type 49. Suffix -$\bar{o}n$ of nouns

Stress LMH 3-D Model #9				
p	λ	$d.f.$	G^2	$\chi^2_{99\%}$
76	9.7	0	0	0

Independence Model for Stress L							
p	λ	$d.f.$	G_s^2	$\chi^2_{99\%}$	G_v^2	v_s	v_v
76	9.6	75	332.1	106.4	104.6	.47	.26

Outlier Portions	Deviation	N(D)	N(P)	G_1^2
Pr 16-31	-D +P	4	12	24.7
Jb 22-42	-D +P	4	9	16.3
2 Ch 10-25	-D +P	1	5	12.6
Ps 120-150	-D +P	8	10	12.5
Pr 1-15	-D +P	12	12	12.0

Independence Model for Stress M							
p	λ	$d.f.$	G_s^2	$\chi^2_{99\%}$	G_v^2	v_s	v_v
30	7.0	29	116.5	49.6	26.1	.58	.24

Outlier Portion	Deviation	N(D)	N(P)	G_1^2
Ez 1-24	+D -P	13	5	33.2

Independence Model for Stress H							
p	λ	$d.f.$	G_s^2	$\chi^2_{99\%}$	G_v^2	v_s	v_v
76	16.7	75	972.2	106.4	99.4	.62	.20

Outlier Portions	Deviation	N(D)	N(P)	G_1^2
Le 1-16	+D -P	71	7	161.8
Ex 25-31	+D -P	52	8	106.2
Nu 10:11-22:1	+D -P	59	27	76.8
Nu 1-10:10	+D -P	55	25	71.6
Ex 32-40	+D -P	34	7	63.0

•Type 50. Stem $-\bar{o}-$ (second vowel) in nouns

Stress LMH 3-D Model #9				
p	λ	$d.f.$	G^2	$\chi^2_{99\%}$
76	14.6	0	0	0

Independence Model for Stress L							
p	λ	$d.f.$	G_s^2	$\chi^2_{99\%}$	G_v^2	v_s	v_v
76	19.8	75	945.7	106.4	68.9	.53	.15

Outlier Portions	Deviation	N(D)	N(P)	G_1^2
Js 1-12	-D +P	25	141	145.7
2 Ch 10-25	-D +P	31	92	60.8
1 Ki 8-14	+D -P	164	31	55.3
1 Ki 1-7	+D -P	83	6	53.0

Independence Model for Stress M							
p	λ	$d.f.$	G_s^2	$\chi_{99\%}^2$	G_ν^2	v_s	v_ν
30	12.2	29	160.1	49.6	25.6	.45	.18

Outlier Portions	Deviation	N(D)	N(P)	G_1^2
Numbers	+D -P	39	18	25.7
Is 40-66	-D +P	0	17	21.3
Ezra-Nehemiah	+D -P	23	7	20.8

Independence Model for Stress H							
p	λ	$d.f.$	G_s^2	$\chi_{99\%}^2$	G_ν^2	v_s	v_ν
76	19.1	75	525.5	106.4	82.1	.43	.17

Outlier Portions	Deviation	N(D)	N(P)	G_1^2
Ex 1-11	+D -P	39	11	78.2
Le 1-16	+D -P	50	34	63.5
Nu 22:2-36	+D -P	27	27	23.9
Ez 14-24	+D -P	21	17	22.7

•Type 51. Stem -$\bar{o}$- in other proper nouns

Stress LMH 3-D Model #3				
p	λ	$d.f.$	G^2	$\chi_{99\%}^2$
30	5.2	104	127.4	140.5

Independence Model for Stress LMH							
p	λ	$d.f.$	G_s^2	$\chi_{99\%}^2$	G_ν^2	v_s	v_ν
76	6.1	62	554.0	90.8	65.3	.70	.25

Outlier Portions	Deviation	N(D)	N(P)	G_1^2
Ge 29-38	+D -P	110	3	123.2
2 Sa 13-24	-D +P	82	16	66.4

The first outlier is dominated by יַעֲקֹב, the second by אַבְשָׁלוֹם.

•Type 52. Stem -ō- in *nip^c als* of irregular roots

Stress LMH 3-D Model #7				
p	λ	$d.f.$	G^2	$\chi_{99\%}^2$
5	7.0	16	24.3	32.0

Independence Model for Stress LMH							
p	λ	$d.f.$	G_s^2	$\chi_{99\%}^2$	G_v^2	v_s	v_v
10	10.5	9	29.9	21.7	9.7	.37	.21

Outlier Portions	Deviation	N(D)	N(P)	G_1^2
Job-Proverbs	-D +P	4	31	10.3
Ezekiel-MP	+D -P	16	13	7.1

•Type 53. Stem -ō- (first vowel) residuum

Stress LMH 3-D Model #9				
p	λ	$d.f.$	G^2	$\chi_{99\%}^2$
10	11.2	0	0	0

Low stress Type 53 sample is too small for analysis ($p \leq 4.2$). Middle stress Type 53 sample is too small for analysis ($p \leq 1.3$).

Independence Model for Stress H							
p	λ	$d.f.$	G_s^2	$\chi_{99\%}^2$	G_v^2	v_s	v_v
30	10.3	29	105.3	49.6	39.7	.43	.25

Outlier Portions	Deviation	N(D)	N(P)	G_1^2
Ezra-Nehemiah	+D -P	15	5	39.8
Je 33-52	+D -P	12	21	10.9
Ez 25-48	-D +P	0	33	10.4

•Type 54. Stem -ō- in verbs -- residuum

Stress LMH 3-D Model #3				
p	λ	$d.f.$	G^2	$\chi_{99\%}^2$
5	5.5	16	17.5	32.0

Independence Model for Stress LMH							
p	λ	$d.f.$	G_s^2	$\chi_{99\%}^2$	G_v^2	v_s	v_v
10	8.3	9	28.9	21.7	10.1	.38	.24

Outlier Portion	Deviation	N(D)	N(P)	G_1^2
Genesis-Exodus	-P	21	0	9.7

•Type 55. Stem -ō- residuum

Stress LMH 3-D Model #9				
p	λ	$d.f.$	G^2	$\chi_{99\%}^2$
30	5.9	0	0	0

Independence Model for Stress L							
p	λ	$d.f.$	G_s^2	$\chi_{99\%}^2$	G_v^2	v_s	v_v
30	6.9	28	59.9	48.3	30.4	.46	.26

Outlier Portions	Deviation	N(D)	N(P)	G_1^2
Nehemiah	-D +P	2	4	14.4
Proverbs	-D +P	4	3	7.2

Middle stress Type 55 sample is too small for analysis ($p \leq 2.3$).

Independence Model for Stress H							
p	λ	$d.f.$	G_s^2	$\chi^2_{99\%}$	G_ν^2	v_s	v_ν
30	10.6	29	150.3	49.6	71.7	.47	.33

Outlier Portions	Deviation	N(D)	N(P)	G_1^2
Ps 1-72	-D +P	13	46	57.6
Ge 1-28	+D -P	36	2	17.8
Ps 73-150	-D +P	27	31	12.1
Proverbs	-D +P	4	10	9.2

•Type 56. Suffix -$\bar{u}$- on finite verb

Independence Model for Stress H							
p	λ	$d.f.$	G_s^2	$\chi^2_{99\%}$	G_ν^2	v_s	v_ν
76	5.4	73	251.7	104.0	98.9	.52	.33

Outlier Portions	Deviation	N(D)	N(P)	G_1^2
Ps 1-41	+D -P	29	14	17.7
2 Ch 10-25	-D +P	1	25	16.2
Ps 120-150	-D +P	2	27	15.4
Le 17-27	+D -P	7	0	13.7
Ex 1-11	+D -P	8	1	10.3

•Type 57. Suffix -$\bar{u}n$ on finite verb

Independence Model for Stress H							
p	λ	$d.f.$	G_s^2	$\chi^2_{99\%}$	G_ν^2	v_s	v_ν
30	5.2	25	45.7	44.3	29.1	.49	.28

Outlier Portion	Deviation	N(D)	N(P)	G_1^2
Proverbs	+D -P	5	2	20.7

•Type 58. Stem $-\bar{u}-$ in imperfect verb

Stress LMH 3-D Model #3				
p	λ	$d.f.$	G^2	$\chi^2_{99\%}$
30	5.2	114	77.4	152.0

Independence Model for Stress LMH							
p	λ	$d.f.$	G^2_s	$\chi^2_{99\%}$	G^2_ν	υ_s	υ_ν
76	6.1	73	227.7	104.0	77.9	.47	.28

Outlier Portions	Deviation	N(D)	N(P)	G^2_1
Js 1-12	+D -P	13	4	20.0
Nu 10:11-22:1	+D -P	14	6	18.1
Ps 42-72	-D +P	0	26	15.4
2 Ch 26-36	+D -P	6	3	6.9

•Type 59. Stem $-\bar{u}-$ in imperative and infinitive

Stress LMH 3-D Model #1				
p	λ	$d.f.$	G^2	$\chi^2_{99\%}$
10	8.6	47	67.1	72.4

Independence Model for Stress LMH							
p	λ	$d.f.$	G^2_s	$\chi^2_{99\%}$	G^2_ν	υ_s	υ_ν
30	8.6	28	55.0	48.3	33.6	.32	.25

Outlier Portion	Deviation	N(D)	N(P)	G^2_1
Je 33-52	+D -P	9	20	13.4

•Type 60. Stem $-\bar{u}-$ in $hop^c als$

Independence Model for Stress L							
p	λ	$d.f.$	G_s^2	$\chi_{99\%}^2$	G_v^2	v_s	v_v
30	5.5	28	34.2	48.3	18.5	.34	.23

Type 60 is homogeneous. No outliers.

•Type 61. Stem $-\bar{u}-$ in qal passive participles

Stress LMH 3-D Model #9				
p	λ	$d.f.$	G^2	$\chi_{99\%}^2$
30	6.1	0	0	0

Independence Model for Stress L							
p	λ	$d.f.$	G_s^2	$\chi_{99\%}^2$	G_v^2	v_s	v_v
30	9.2	29	117.3	49.6	29.6	.44	.22

Outlier Portions	Deviation	N(D)	N(P)	G_1^2
Numbers	+D -P	70	32	47.3
1 Chronicles	-D +P	0	11	10.8
Ps 73-150	-D +P	1	15	9.2
Ex 25-40	+D -P	16	4	7.4

Independence Model for Stress M							
p	λ	$d.f.$	G_s^2	$\chi_{99\%}^2$	G_v^2	v_s	v_v
10	5.9	9	26.0	21.7	11.3	.47	.30

Outlier Portion	Deviation	N(D)	N(P)	G_1^2
Ezekiel-MP	+D -P	11	4	16.2

Independence Model for Stress H							
p	λ	$d.f.$	G_s^2	$\chi_{99\%}^2$	G_ν^2	υ_s	υ_ν
30	7.0	29	46.3	49.6	32.6	.34	.27

High stress Type 61 is homogeneous.

Outlier Portion	Deviation	N(D)	N(P)	G_1^2
1 Sa 21-31	+D -P	6	16	10.2

•Type 62. Stem $-\bar{u}$- in nouns of hollow roots

Stress LMH 3-D Model #8				
p	λ	$d.f.$	G^2	$\chi_{99\%}^2$
30	7.0	36	57.8	58.6

Independence Model for Stress L							
p	λ	$d.f.$	G_s^2	$\chi_{99\%}^2$	G_ν^2	υ_s	υ_ν
30	8.4	29	89.8	49.6	38.2	.52	.26

Outlier Portions	Deviation	N(D)	N(P)	G_1^2
Ex 25-40	+D -P	9	6	28.3
De 1-16:17	+D -P	6	2	22.6

Independence Model for Stress M							
p	λ	$d.f.$	G_s^2	$\chi_{99\%}^2$	G_ν^2	υ_s	υ_ν
10	13.0	9	34.8	21.7	10.6	.31	.20

Independence Model for Stress H							
p	λ	$d.f.$	G_s^2	$\chi_{99\%}^2$	G_ν^2	υ_s	υ_ν
30	8.3	29	20.1	49.6	36.2	.23	.26

High stress Type 62 is homogeneous.

•Type 63. Stem $-\bar{u}-$ (first vowel) in other nouns

Stress LMH 3-D Model #9				
p	λ	$d.f.$	G^2	$\chi^2_{99\%}$
10	8.0	0	0	0

Independence Model for Stress L							
p	λ	$d.f.$	G^2_s	$\chi^2_{99\%}$	G^2_ν	v_s	v_ν
10	6.9	9	32.2	21.7	2.8	.49	.14

Outlier Portions	Deviation	N(D)	N(P)	G^2_1
Genesis-Exodus	+D -P.	15	6	22.2
Jonah/Ruth-Ne	-D +P	2	29	10.4

Independence Model for Stress M							
p	λ	$d.f.$	G^2_s	$\chi^2_{99\%}$	G^2_ν	v_s	v_ν
5	5.0	4	20.1	13.3	3.1	.56	.25

Outlier Portions	Deviation	N(D)	N(P)	G^2_1
Ps-Jb-Pr	-D +P	0	12	11.9
Is-Je-Ez-MP	+D -P	11	4	8.8

All twelve cases in the poetic books are מוּסָר.

Independence Model for Stress H							
p	λ	$d.f.$	G^2_s	$\chi^2_{99\%}$	G^2_ν	v_s	v_ν
10	14.5	9	12.5	21.7	6.5	.21	.15

High stress Type 63 is homogeneous. No outliers.

•Type 64. Stem -$\bar{u}$- in other nouns

Stress LMH 3-D Model #9				
p	λ	$d.f.$	G^2	$\chi^2_{99\%}$
76	9.6	0	0	0

Independence Model for Stress L							
p	λ	$d.f.$	G_s^2	$\chi^2_{99\%}$	G_ν^2	v_s	v_ν
76	12.0	75	260.9	106.4	87.6	.36	.22

Outlier Portions	Deviation	N(D)	N(P)	G_1^2
Esther	-D +P	0	65	37.9
Ex 25-31	+D -P	26	13	31.1
Ex 32-40	+D -P	23	20	16.6
1 Ch 21-29	+D -P	15	10	14.1
Nu 1-10:10	+D -P	16	13	12.4

Independence Model for Stress M							
p	λ	$d.f.$	G_s^2	$\chi^2_{99\%}$	G_ν^2	v_s	v_ν
30	8.5	29	77.9	49.6	34.3	.39	.25

Outlier Portions	Deviation	N(D)	N(P)	G_1^2
Ez 25-48	-D	1	54	8.8
2 Samuel	+D -P	4	3	8.3
Nahum-Malachi	+D -P	4	4	7.0

Independence Model for Stress H							
p	λ	$d.f.$	G_s^2	$\chi^2_{99\%}$	G_ν^2	v_s	v_ν
76	13.5	75	710.2	106.4	84.5	.61	.19

Outlier Portions	Deviation	N(D)	N(P)	G_1^2
Js 1-12	+D -P	130	15	367.9
Ex 25-31	+D -P	12	3	25.4
De 28-34	+D -P	13	8	18.0
Hg-Zc-Ml	+D -P	12	8	15.7

•Type 65. Stem -$\bar{u}$- residuum

Stress LMH 3-D Model #3				
p	λ	$d.f.$	G^2	$\chi_{99\%}^2$
5	9.3	16	30.0	32.0

Independence Model for Stress LMH							
p	λ	$d.f.$	G_s^2	$\chi_{99\%}^2$	G_ν^2	υ_s	υ_ν
10	14.0	9	29.0	21.7	9.1	.34	.18

Outlier Portion	Deviation	N(D)	N(P)	G_1^2
Ezekiel-MP	+D -P	8	14	15.0

9.3 Discussion

To satisfy the requirements of contingency table analysis the Hebrew Bible was divided into portions in four ways (§§ 7.4 and 7.5). The outliers are thus of four different sizes. The list of outliers reported in § 9.2 is not exhaustive. Of the thousands of outlier cells, only the most suspicious are given, and never more than five for any one situation. In spite of these limitations, valid impressions may be gained, especially when consistent patterns can be discerned.

The finest distinctions and closest comparisons can be made when the division into seventy-six portions is used. The division into thirty portions is also useful, since many of these portions are identical with individual books.

9.3.1. Pentateuch. When seventy-six portions are used, fifty-five conspicuous outliers are reported in § 9.2. Exodus has more than any other book (× 21), and all of these are +D-P; that is, each is an outlier in both excess of *defective* spelling and lower-than-expected *plene* spelling. Leviticus and Numbers together contribute twenty more +D-P outliers. In fact, fifty-two of the fifty-five are +D-P. When thirty portions are used, the Pentateuch accounts for seventeen of the outliers reported in § 9.2. Of these, sixteen are +D-P. The exception is Deuteronomy 1:1-16:17 for middle stress Type 34 (-D+P -- none *defective*). When ten portions are used, the Pentateuch yields ten outliers in § 9.2. Of these, seven are +D-P and three are -P. The one outlier consisting of the complete Pentateuch is also +D-P. Of the eighty-three outliers in § 9.2, seventy-six are +D-P and three are -P, while three are -D+P and one is -D. The one instance of -D is due to Type 25, which is problematic (see § 5.5.5). The three -D+P outliers from the Pentateuch in § 9.2 are: Genesis 39-50, low stress Type 46 due to local concentration of יוֹסֵף; Leviticus 1-16 Type 31 due to אִו (invariant) concentrated there; and Deuteronomy 1:1-16:17 middle stress Type 34 which has no *defective* spellings. So with four exceptions, two of which result from concentration of one fixed-spelling vocabulary item due to subject matter, and one of which is dubious, seventy-nine out of eighty-three Pentateuch outliers are deviant with an excess of *defective* spellings and low use of *plene* spellings. In general terms, Pentateuchal spelling is consistently more conservative than the rest of the Bible, especially in the vowel types present in the seventy-six +D and seventy-nine -P outliers. Exodus, Leviticus, Numbers are more conservative than Genesis, Deuteronomy. The rest of the Bible contributes seventy-nine more +D-P outliers to § 9.2, only three more than the Pentateuchal contribution.

9.3.2. Former Prophets. Using seventy-six portions, thirty-two outliers are supplied by the Former Prophets to § 9.2. Of these, twenty-two are +D-P, ten are -D+P. Of the former, only three are from Joshua-Judges. Of the latter, five come from Joshua-Judges. Clearly Samuel-Kings is closer to the Pentateuch in its conservative spelling than Joshua-Judges. Using thirty portions, the Former Prophets contribute nine outliers in § 9.2. Of these, seven (six from Samuel-Kings) are +D-P, and two are -D+P (both from Joshua-Judges). Same pattern. Using ten portions, the Former Prophets supply six outliers to § 9.2. Of these, three are +D-P, one is -P, two are -D+P. Using five portions, the Former Prophets supply no outliers to § 9.2. Of the forty-seven Former-Prophets outliers reported in § 9.2, thirty-two are +D-P, one is -P. Of these thirty-three outliers with conservative spelling preferences, twenty-eight come from Samuel-Kings; of the fourteen with less conservative spellings, ten are in Joshua-Judges.

9.3.3. Latter Prophets. Using seventy-six portions, thirty-two outliers are contributed by the Latter Prophets to § 9.2. Of these, seventeen are +D-P (eight from Jeremiah), fifteen are -D+P (seven from Ezekiel). Using thirty portions, the Latter Prophets contribute twelve outliers to § 9.2. Of these, six (four from Jeremiah) are +D-P, four are -D+P (one from Jeremiah), and two are -D. Using ten portions, the Latter Prophets give ten outliers to § 9.2. Of these, one is +D, five are +D-P, four are -D+P. Using five portions, the Latter Prophets as a whole yield one outlier to § 9.2. It is middle stress Type 63 (+D-P); the sample is small. For the fifty-five Latter-Prophets outliers in § 9.2, the picture is more mixed. Of the thirty outliers with conservative spelling, fourteen come from Jeremiah; of the twenty-five with less conservative spellings, only six are in Jeremiah. Jeremiah is generally more conservative than the other Latter Prophets.

9.3.4. Poetry (Psalms, Job, Proverbs). Using seventy-six portions, fifteen outliers are contributed by the Poetry to § 9.2. Of these, three are +D-P, twelve are -D+P. Using thirty portions, the Poetry contributes twelve outliers reported in § 9.2. Of these, two are +D-P, one is -D, nine are -D+P. Using ten

portions, the Poetry yields six outliers to § 9.2. Of these, two
are +D-P, four are -D+P. Using five portions, the Poetry yields
two outliers to § 9.2. One is middle stress Type 8 (+D) (the two
defective spellings of this type occur here); the other is middle
stress Type 63 (-D+P) (all due to the twelve occurrences of
מוּסָר). Of the thirty-five Poetry outliers in § 9.2, only eight are
due to an excess of conservative spelling.

9.3.5. Other Writings. Using seventy-six portions, twenty-
three outliers are contributed by the Other Writings to § 9.2. Of
these, six are +D-P (all from Chronicles), seventeen are -D+P.
Using thirty portions, the Other Writings contribute ten outliers
in § 9.2. Of these, four are +D-P (all from Ezra-Nehemiah), six
are -D+P. Using ten portions, the Other Writings yield four
outliers to § 9.2. Of these, one is +D-P, three are -D+P. Using
five portions, the Other Writings yield no outliers to § 9.2. Of
the thirty-seven Other-Writings outliers in § 9.2, only eleven are
due to an excess of conservative spelling. Chronicles is more
conservative than the rest of the Other Writings.

9.3.6. Summary. The steady trend away from conservative
spelling through the canon in its usual order is summarized in
Table 9.1.

Table 9.1 Outliers in type-portion-spelling cells

Section	+D	+D-P	-P	SbTot	-D	-D+P	+P	SbTot	Tot
Pent.	-	76	3	79	1	3	-	4	83
Fm.Pr.	-	32	1	33	-	13	1	14	47
Lt.Pr.	1	29	-	30	2	23	-	25	55
Poetry	1	7	-	8	1	26	-	27	35
Writ.	-	11	-	11	-	26	-	26	37
Total	2	155	4	161	4	91	1	96	257

Chapter 10. The Behavior of Portions Across Types

In Chapter 9, we examined the behavior of types across portions, showing that the spelling choices for most types are associated with portion. Given that association, interest naturally arises as to the relations among the portions. In terms of the analogy of § 1.7, we are interested to study the similarities of patterns of cubicle occupancy for the various hall positions. Earlier chapters have communicated various possible groupings of portions; now we wish to get at these groupings systematically. The research questions may be posed as relating to finding an optimal ordering of the portions in time or to describing the similarities among the portions.

10.1 Ordering the portions

One very attractive way of organizing the portions would be to array them along a time-line, showing the date of production of each. In other words, we would treat the portion category as ordinal. But rather than assigning an order score to each, as is the standard practice for ordinal contingency table analysis (Fienberg 1980: 61-68), we would let the unknown dates be parameters of the model to be determined in the course of fitting the model. The mathematics for doing this exist in the form of *log-multiplicative* models (Agresti 1984: 138-146). We have not taken this route for three reasons:

1) Log-multiplicative models are new, and their behavior is not yet well understood. At times they produce strange results, such as requiring that variables' natural ordering be violated (Clogg 1982: 253).

2) Proper use of log-multiplicative models would require that the effects of stress be well understood. However, the influence of stress on orthographic choice remains unclear (§ 8.4).

3) Spelling updating (§ 4.8) may have distorted the apparent relations among texts, making their arraying along a time-line difficult and/or misleading.

Given these considerations, it seems wiser to examine the affinities among portions than to attempt to array them along a time-line.

10.2 Preparing the data

We wish to study spelling choices independent of type incidence. One way of doing this involves fitting our data with a variant of three-dimensional log-linear model #5 of § 9.1.1. We gauge the distance between portions by computing χ^2 between the data and the model which assumes choice and portion are independent, given type. (This involves fitting 2×2×93-tables for each pair of portions, since there are two portions being considered at a time, there are two possible spelling choices, and there are ninety-three [sub-]types involved when partial and marginal sub-tables are arranged for.)

We have carried out the analysis just outlined. We shall not present the results here, since very similar results are obtained when we go about things in a much more straightforward way. The simpler approach is as follows. Suppose we "standardize the marginals" for our choice data by replacing the counts of *defective* and *plene* spellings by the related percentages. Thus, a pair of cells which reports ten *defective* spellings and forty *plene* spellings is adjusted to hold twenty (percent) and eighty (percent), respectively. Such a stratagem removes the information relating to type incidence from the data. But there is a price paid: whether a pair of cells holds counts of zero and one thousand or zero and one, the percentages will be zero and one hundred. This is unacceptable, as it ignores the issue of sample size. Table 10.1 shows the percentage of cell pairs that are rejected from consideration if we require that their total counts exceed the four threshold values shown.

Table 10.1 Percent of rejected cell pairs

Number of Portions	Threshold Value			
	0	10	20	30
5	2.6%	9.7%	15.7%	20.0%
10	4.0%	16.6%	28.0%	36.0%
30	8.1%	37.8%	54.5%	66.0%
76	17.1%	61.5%	78.9%	87.0%

If we set the threshold too low, tiny counts may distort our results. If we set the threshold too high, relevant information will not be reflected in our results. In the interest of preserving as much relevant information as possible, for most of the analyses reported below we require that a pair involve at least ten choices and analyze in terms of thirty portions. Fully one-third of the pairs are excluded from contributing information. Note that since we have standardized the marginals (by making the choice cell pairs sum to one hundred), only one of the choice options needs to be carried along in the remaining analysis. We elect to work in terms of percent *defective*.

A final data preparation task remains to be considered: attribute standardization (Romesburg 1984: 78). Consider the behavior of Type 47 at high stress as shown by the octagon-surrounded data-points of Figure 8.3. The mean percent *plene* score for the Former Prophets through the end of the text hovers quite close to one hundred percent. Yet in the

Pentateuch, the scores are considerably lower. The question to be addressed is: Do we analyze in terms of absolute percentages or in terms of departures from the mean? In most cases, ours being one of them, the better practice is to standardize the attributes (Romesburg 1984: 91). This renders the data dimensionless (not necessary for us since the data already are percentages) and causes each (sub-)type to contribute equally to the final results (so that no one [sub-]type dominates the results). For our analyses, we standardize by subtracting the average percent *defective* count (averaged across the portions) from each cell's (percent) count and then dividing the result by the (sample) standard deviation (again computed across the portions). As a result, when we sum cell entries across an attribute, the result is zero; when we sum the squares of the cell entries, the result is unity. See Romesburg (1984: 78f.) for full details.

Performing the two sorts of standardization discussed above yields three two-dimensional tables of positive and negative numbers. There are five or ten or thirty rows, corresponding to the sets of portions used. There are ninety-three columns, corresponding to the (sub-)types involved in an analysis properly controlled for stress. That is, each portion is characterized in terms of ninety-three attributes.

10.3 Displaying the data

How do we recognize affinities among the portions based on the choices made in spelling the types? It is a commonplace of statistics that graphical displays of data can suggest affinities. Great ingenuity has been expended in creating ways of displaying multi-dimensional data. Figure 10.1 illustrates one such approach, Chernoff faces (Becker and Chambers 1984: 312). It's as though all Mr. Vowel's relatives have gathered at the urban complex of § 1.7, and our task is to group them by examining their faces. Each of the fifteen facial features

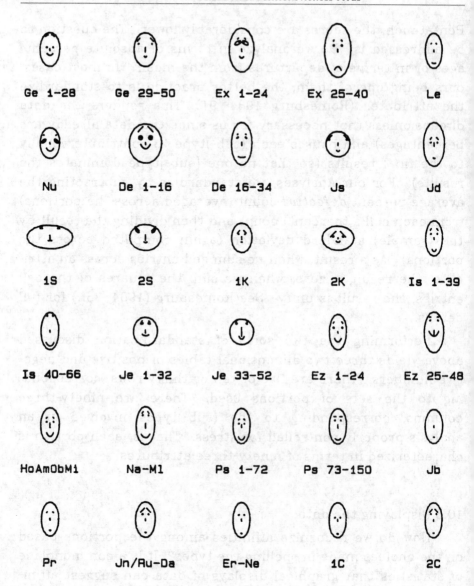

Figure 10.1 Chernoff faces for marginal Types 1-15

corresponds to a type, collapsed on stress. The correspondences are given in Table 10.2.

Table 10.2 Facial features and types

Facial feature	Type	Facial feature	Type	Facial feature	Type
Area of face	1	Mouth width	6	Eye width	11
Shape of face	2	Eye location	7	Pupil location	12
Nose length	3	Eye spacing	8	Brow location	13
Mouth location	4	Eye angle	9	Brow angle	14
Curve of smile	5	Eye shape	10	Brow width	15

Valid insights flow from examination of the faces. Why has 1 Samuel such a wide face? Because, as we found in Chapter 9, he is a strong Type 2 outlier. Why is Exodus 25-40 not smiling? His Type 5 behavior differs strongly from that of his relatives. This fact can be verified by consulting the list of Type 5 outliers in Chapter 9, where Exodus 25-40 is the lead item. And so on.

10.4 Quantitating similarity

All this is still not enough. Outliers pop out of such a display, but attempted inclusion of ninety-three attributes would lead to impossible elaboration. Furthermore, even for the limited display of Figure 10.1, deciding where portions fit in the family tree is not easy. A way of measuring the *distance* between portions, a metric, is needed. For our purposes, the Euclidean metric, the usual means of quantitating the distance between points, will do. Its generalization to ninety-three-dimensional space is straightforward: to measure the distance between two portions, one simply takes the square-root of the sum of the squares of the differences between the corresponding attribute values (the Pythagorean theorem). Table 10.3 shows the distances between the five portions of Table 7.2a,b.

Table 10.3 Distances between pairs of portions

	Pent	FP	LP	Poetry	Other
Pent	0.00				
FP	14.00	0.00			
LP	15.25	12.55	0.00		
Poetry	16.36	14.62	10.39	0.00	
Other	16.02	13.04	11.30	11.15	0.00

(The distances are based on ninety-three [sub-]types with the threshold of Table 10.1 set at ten.) One can read off the distances between portions precisely as one reads the usual mileage chart on a map. Thus, the two closest portions are the Latter Prophets and the Poetry, which are separated by 10.39 units. (The distances should be viewed as relative, their absolute size having no readily interpretable meaning.) The two portions furthest apart are the Pentateuch and the Poetry, which are separated by 16.36 units. These distances are helpful summary numbers, but a good bit of study is required to gain from them a picture of the affinities among the portions. This is profoundly the case, when we move from the five-portion situation (where only ten distances are involved) to the thirty-portion situation (where 435 distances must be mastered).

10.5 Discovering affinities

This leads to *hierarchical clustering*, a useful way of discovering affinities among objects. The basic ideas involve only simple arithmetic and are well described by Romesburg (1984: 9). We shall here explain only the method of clustering we have used, the "complete linkage" or "furthest neighbor" algorithm. This algorithm considers each of the objects it is supplied to be a cluster. (Five portions yield five initial clusters.) Its first step is to combine the two closest objects to form a new cluster. For the case whose distances are shown in Table 10.3, LP and Poetry are combined. The distance between this new cluster and each remaining (single-object) cluster is defined *for this approach* to be the distance between a (single-object) cluster and the member of the (two-object) cluster furthest away from it. Thus, after the first stage of clustering, the revised distance table, known as the *resemblance matrix*, is as shown in Table 10.4.

Table 10.4 First-stage resemblance matrix

	Pent	FP	LP/Poetry	Other
Pent	0.00			
FP	14.00	0.00		
LP/Poetry	16.36	14.62	0.00	
Other	16.02	13.04	11.30	0.00

Next, the two closest clusters are combined. According to Table 10.4, these are Other and LP/Poetry. The distances are revised, yielding Table 10.5.

Table 10.5 Second-stage resemblance matrix

	Pent	FP	LP/Poetry/Other
Pent	0.00		
FP	14.00	0.00	
LP/Poetry/Other	16.36	14.62	0.00

At this stage, the Former Prophets and Pentateuch are closest, so they are clustered, yielding the matrix of Table 10.6.

Table 10.6 Third-stage resemblance matrix

	Pent/FP	LP/Poetry/Other
Pent/FP	0.00	
LP/Poetry	16.36	0.00

As the final stage, the Primary History and the rest are clustered. The ordering of the agglomerations reflects the affinities of the objects being clustered. Thus, we may assert that the Latter Prophets, Poetry, and Other Writings form a natural cluster. The Pentateuch and Former Prophets, while less similar to each other than are the other three portions, nonetheless cluster naturally to form a Primary-History cluster.

In the form of a *tree* or *dendrogram*, Figure 10.2 summarizes the clustering results just obtained. (The threshold used was ten.) The various clusters merge at the distances indicated on the scale at the top of the figure. Thus, we read off of the dendrogram that LP and Poetry are separated by about 10.3 units, while the final two clusters are separated by about 16.4 units. That the Primary History and rest of the Hebrew Bible form two quite dissimilar units when studied from the perspective of orthography is the strongest result in this chapter. The clusters are insensitive to all manner of variant forms of the data supplied.

As we increase the number of portions used in clustering, the robustness of the results deteriorates steadily due to sample-size effects. In the gallery of clusters which follows, therefore, one should make less and less of details as we move from five to ten to thirty portions. Sensitivity to threshold choice can be assessed by comparing the results when different thresholds are used. Table 10.7 lists the clusterings presented in Figures 10.2 through 10.10.

Table 10.7 Gallery of dendrograms

Figure	Portions	Thresh	Description
10.2	5	10	All types
10.3	10	10	All types
10.4	10	20	All types
10.5	30	10	All types
10.6	30	20	All types
10.7	30	10	All types less outliers
10.8	30	20	All types less outliers
10.9	30	10	All types: verse parity
10.10	30	20	All types: verse parity

In examining the dendrograms, the reader should notice that clusters can be repositioned from one figure to the next and appear to involve greater structural differences than are the case. For example, in Figures 10.5 and 10.6, the Samuel/Kings/Jeremiah 33-52 cluster migrates from the bottom to the middle of the dendrogram. Note also the relative stability of the Pentateuchal clusters as compared with the rest. Figures 10.7 and 10.8 result when the data leading to Figures 10.5 and 10.6 are reduced by removing the following proper-noun-dominated (sub-)types: Type 9 (High stress), 31, 46, 49 (High stress), 50 (Low stress), and 51. These six (sub-)types may show strong contextuality effects because of the *dramatis personae* they contain.

The clusterings take place in a sequence that does not necessarily reflect the *kind* of similarity between any two portions linked. Figures 10.3 and 10.4 are similar in some details, different in others. They cluster the portions of the Primary History in the same way. In each, Chronicles is the last portion to be clustered with its five mates. But those five portions cluster differently in each case. In Figure 10.4, the Latter Prophets cluster together, as do all the Writings. In 10.3, Psalms clusters with the Latter Prophets. We suspect that, just as the two portions of the Pentateuch are the first to cluster in Figures 10.3 and 10.4 because of shared conservative spellings, as against all the rest (as we have seen many times) so Ezekiel-Minor Prophets and Psalms cluster next in Figure 10.3 because they contain the highest use of modern spellings. The positions on the dendrograms do not necessarily correspond to ranking in terms of oldness or newness of spelling.

In the dendrograms for thirty portions (Figures 10.5-10.8), canonically   adjacent   portions   often   cluster   together. 1 and 2 Samuel, 1 and 2 Kings, 1 and 2 Chronicles cluster in the first three figures, and Ruth/Jonah-Nehemiah cluster in all four. Joshua and Judges cluster in Figures 10.5 and 10.7. (Compare the two portions of Deuteronomy.) The portions of Ezekiel cluster in Figures 10.6-10.8 and are close in 10.5. Portions of Psalms cluster in Figure 10.5 and are close in 10.6-10.8. Portions of other big books (Genesis, Exodus, Isaiah, and Jeremiah) do not cluster immediately, or even early, with each other. These details suggest that some single books (or kindred books) came down as wholes through the transmission channel(s) and might have had a similar compositional history as well. But the exceptions suggest that the differences still found within some large books might represent the survival of differences which were within them from the beginning due to their assemblage from sources which differed in orthography. (See § 4.11.)

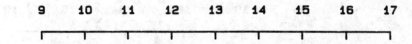

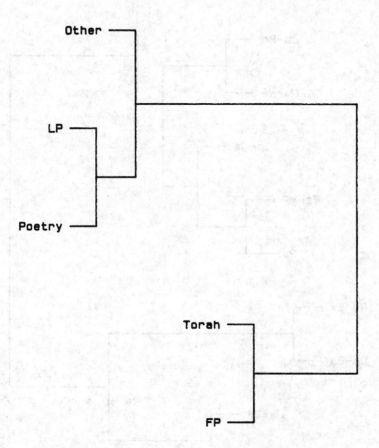

Figure 10.2 Spelling: five portions, all types

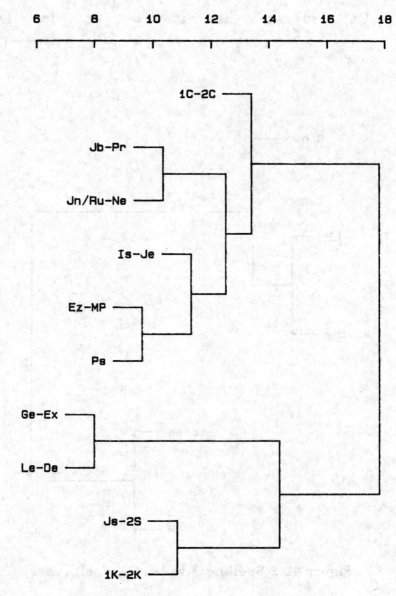

Figure 10.3 Spelling: ten portions (Threshold = 10)

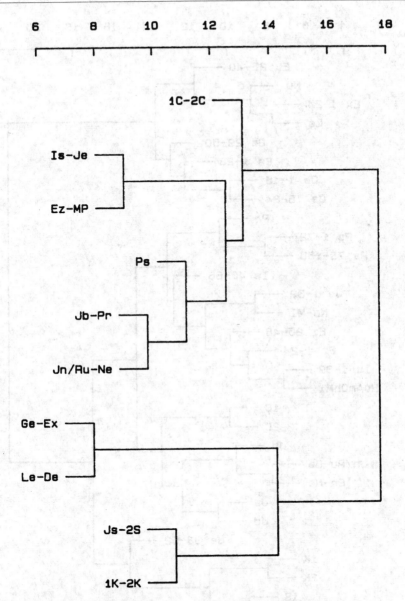

Figure 10.4 Spelling: ten portions (Threshold = 20)

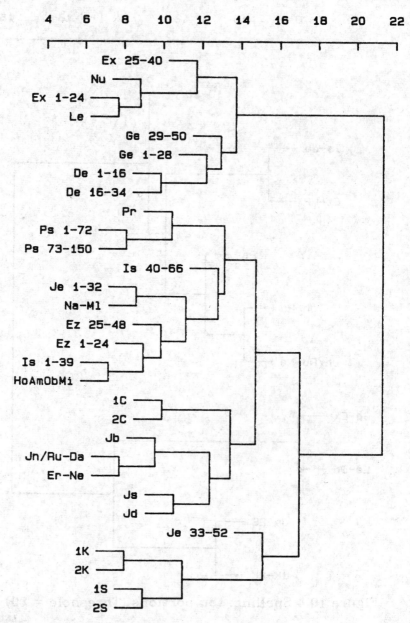

Figure 10.5 Spelling: thirty portions (Threshold = 10)

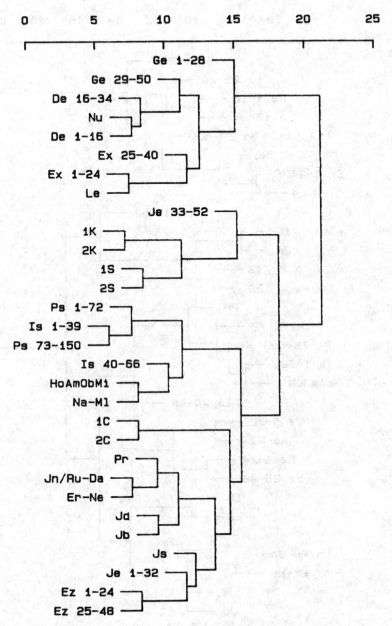

Figure 10.6 Spelling: thirty portions (Threshold = 20)

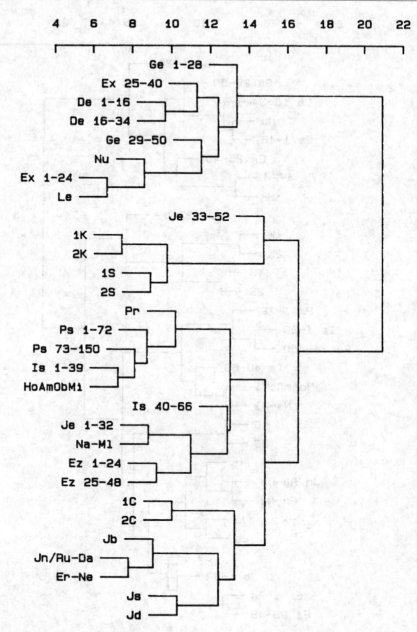

Figure 10.7 Spelling: without outliers (Threshold = 10)

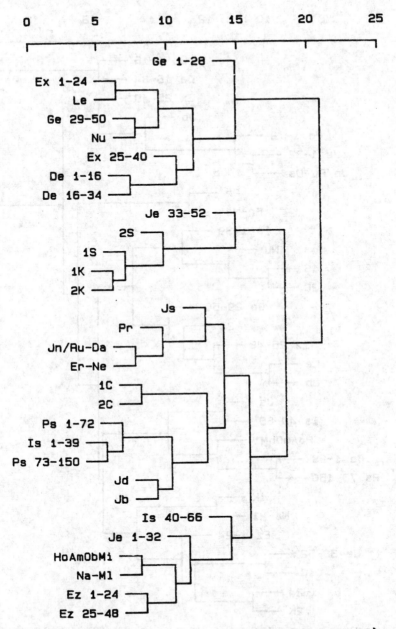

Figure 10.8 Spelling: without outliers (Threshold = 20)

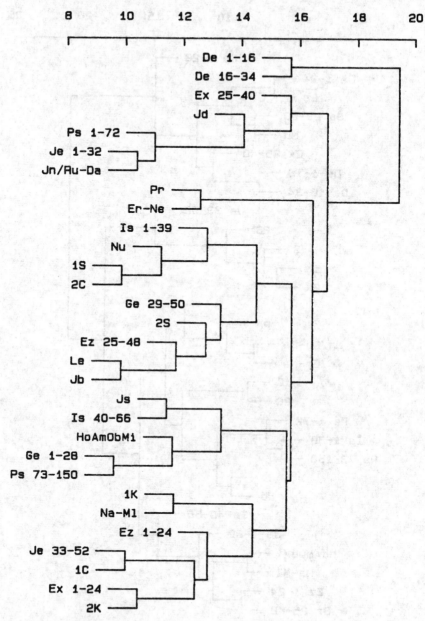

Figure 10.9 Verse-parity clusters (Threshold = 10)

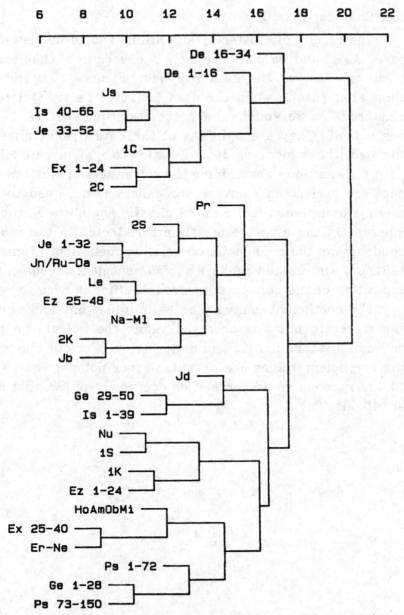

Figure 10.10 Verse-parity clusters (Threshold = 20)

10.6 Checking results

The results of clustering algorithms should be viewed with care. As should be clear from their description, they produce clusters whatever the data supplied. Figures 10.9 and 10.10 show what results when the data for verse parity (§ 1.12) are clustered. As we would expect, the resulting clusters are curious indeed. They are figments of the data's randomness and the algorithm's plodding determination to agglomerate all in its path. In addition to examining the robustness of clusters as the data are varied, an exercise our gallery is designed to allow, there is a mathematical method of assessing how well the facts inherent in the distance matrix are reflected in the resulting dendrogram: the cophenetic correlation coefficient (Romesburg 1984: 24). Interested readers should consult Romesburg for an exposition of the concepts involved. Suffice it here to remark that the coefficient can vary between minus one and plus one. The closer to one the observed value, the better the match between distance matrix and dendrogram. For our clusterings, the coefficient values are acceptable but not perfect. (Figure 10.2 has a cophenetic correlation coefficient of .82; that of Figure 10.5 is .75.)

Chapter 11. Summary and Conclusions

11.1 The use of *matres lectionis*

In the first section of this chapter we shall review briefly the extent to which the vowel letters came into use in the spelling of vowels in biblical Hebrew texts.

11.1.1 The use of י as *mater lectionis*

1) For /ī/ (§ 6.5.1): (i) With two or three exceptions (§ 3.4.1), short /i/ is never spelled *plene*. (ii) With four exceptions, all rectified by *qere* (1 Kings 8:48; Ezekiel 16:59; Psalm 140:13; Job 42:2), word terminal /ī/ is always *plene*. (iii) Word-medial /ī/ may be spelled either way. Leaving out the two residue types (10 and 12), which gather in cases in which the length of /i/ is hard to determine, there are over 30,000 indubitable long /ī/'s of which about seven percent are spelled *defective*. This gives a measure of the high degree to which the spelling of this vowel has been standardized. This standardization has been carried through more completely in the later books.

2) For /ē/ (§ 6.5.2): It is not possible to summarize the spelling of /ē/ with exactitude, because the history of many of the specimens is not known. The indications are: (i) Nearly always ē ← *ay is *plene* (historical spelling). Of the few exceptions, those under Type 13 (אֵל and עֵל) may be illusory, since the archaic *defective* spelling may reflect the primal form which has not taken on the pseudo-plural stem. Nouns with ē ← *ay in the stem are rarely *defective*. We cannot be sure of the exact number because we do not always know the root. Nouns with ē ← *ay in the suffixed or construct plural stem (Type 14) are *defective* only when the stem ends in י -- and there are only six cases in construct (§ 5.5.4).

Since פ״י roots sometimes have a biconsonantal by-form (Andersen 1970b), and, in reverse, the root טב has an allo-root יטב, the forms of Types 15 and 19, illustrated by מֵטַב מֵיטַב מֵטָב, could be derivatives from different roots rather than different spellings of the same word. We have no way of knowing, however.

(ii) Nearly always $\bar{e}$ ← $\acute{\iota}$ is *defective*. This means that י never established itself as the phonetic spelling -- true *mater lectionis* -- for long /$\bar{e}$/ as such in biblical texts. (The story is quite different later on [Weinberg 1975].) It suggests furthermore that the change $\bar{e}$ ← $\acute{\iota}$ did not take place until quite late, not in time to intrude into proto-masoretic texts. This is evident in the fact that segolates represented by סֵפֶר are never *plene*. Even at Qumran *plene* spelling of $\bar{e}$ ← $\acute{\iota}$ is rare: מית for *mēt* in 1QIs^a (Kutscher 1959: 113), but $^c\bar{e}d$ is still עד.

A special case is the $\overset{+}{\iota}$ in the stem of *hip$^c\hat{\iota}l$* forms, with development into /$\bar{\iota}$/ by analogy (Bauer and Leander 1922: § 46), into /$\bar{e}$/ by the usual phonetic change, into /a/ by Philippi's Law. We suspect that *defective* spelling is a genuine archaism (it could reflect the primal short vowel). The masoretic vocalization reflects a standardized and perhaps theoretical morpho-phonemic pattern, so we do not know if the *defective* spelling of /$\bar{\iota}$/ (Type 4) should be /$\bar{e}$/, which is usually *defective* as in Type 17, or whether the *plene* spelling of /$\bar{e}$/ (Type 17) should be /$\bar{\iota}$/, which is usually *plene* (Type 4).

3) The spelling of /$\bar{\varepsilon}$/: The spelling -יִ - retains its diphthong character and is spelled *defective* in only about one percent of its occurrences, many of them dubious (§ 5.5.5.2).

It emerges from all this that י became *mater lectionis* in the strict sense only in the case of /$\bar{\iota}$/. The *plene* spelling of /$\bar{e}$/ and /$\bar{\varepsilon}$/ remained almost entirely historical.

4) The use of י in words like בָּנָיו, 'his sons,' is a peculiar and late development, purely graphic in function (§ 11.3.10).

11.1.2 The use of ה as *mater lectionis*

The consonant ה never became a full-fledged *mater lectionis* in the sense of being an optional auxiliary for spelling /ā/ as such. It is never used to represent word-medial /ā/; every certain word-terminal /ā/ is spelled *plene* with ה. The uniformity of the masoretic text in this matter is astounding. The only exceptions arise from the ligaturing of a few compound proper nouns (Weil 1981: 676). The only discernible trend is a slight tendency to use א as *mater lectionis* for /ā/, even within a word occasionally (§ 3.3.1.2).

The apparent *defective* spelling of word-terminal /ā/ probably represents an alternative pronunciation, lost in masoretic standardization. The preference of the consonantal text for the apparently *defective* spelling of word-terminal /ā/ in the case of a very few morphological classes (Types 27, 28, 29) is a genuine archaism.

As a consequence we are unable to use the variations in the use of word-terminal ה as an index of the evolution of the spelling of a constant vowel /ā/ as such.

11.1.3 The use of ו as *mater lectionis*

This letter came to be used for every word-terminal /ū/, with the proviso that the scribes might have missed a few or found too many. Similarly for the majority of word-terminal /ō/'s, with the alternative ה- surviving as a not uncommon archaism. ה-, 'his,' survived this normalization in fifty-five cases. It is found in Ezekiel, once in Daniel, but not in any other post-exilic books. Scribes continued to leave it when copying old texts, even if they did not use it in writing new ones.

Within words ו is used optionally for /ū/ and /ō/. The *plene* spelling of /ū/ has taken hold more extensively (about 80 percent) than the *plene* spelling of /ō/ (46.5 percent -- Table 6.1). This is clearly due to the fact that long /ū/ is primal in Hebrew whereas long /ō/ is entirely secondary. There are sixty

cases (§ 3.4.2) in which the masoretes interpreted ן as
anomalous spelling of short /u/ (from their point of view).
These should probably be taken as mixed forms which can be
read as /ū/ or /u/. The same is true of the thirty-six cases
where the consonantal text has ן and the vowel is *qameṣ*
(§ 3.4.3).

Unlike ׳, which rarely spells /ē/ ← *í plene*, ן spells all
kinds of /ō/, but to differing degrees depending on the type of
vowel, the type of word, and the age of the text. Bearing in mind
that the history of all long /ō/ vowels is not known with uniform
certainty, from the spelling behavior of /ō/ in words of Types
30-55 above (§ 6.5.5), the following picture emerges. 1) The suffix 'his,' ō is spelled with ן in 99.3 percent of its occurrences.
2) Long /ō/ from Path 3 (primal diphthong), as attested by
Types 34, 35, 36 (more than ten thousand cases), is spelled
plene about eighty-four percent of the time. 3) Long /ō/ ← *ā
is *plene* about fifty percent of the time. Types 38, 39, 47, 48, 49
supply the clearest cases. 4) Long /ō/ ← *ú has taken up *plene*
spelling the least. In § 5.6 over 4,800 such vowels, all *defective*,
were eliminated as statistically invariant. Their inclusion would
have lowered the percentage of *plene* spellings of this kind of
/ō/ substantially. In Types 40-44 and 54 (verbs), the vowel is
twenty-one percent *plene*. Specimens in Types 50-53, and 55
could not be segregated because their history is uncertain. The
historical differences between the main kinds of long /ō/ are
still manifest in the different degrees to which *plene* spelling is
used.

11.2 Spelling in the various portions of the Bible

The spelling in the *textus receptus* still reflects a stage in
the transmission of the text that is later than pre-exilic times
but not as late as Greek times. It falls in the Exilic and Persian
Periods, 600-300 BCE. It has moved beyond pre-exilic practice,
which had developed the use of *matres lectionis* only partially;

but it has not moved as far as the more luxuriant use of the *matres lectionis* found in early rabbinic times. That long but all-important period in the history of the Hebrew Bible is, unfortunately, quite lacking in manuscript evidence and deficient in Hebrew inscriptions. Evidence becomes available only from the Third Century BCE onwards with the earliest Qumran manuscripts (Freedman and Mathews 1985). Hence we are unable to monitor the development before that time using external controls. The reconstruction of the history of the text by internal analysis of its spelling can yield only broad and tentative results. See § 4.11.

11.2.1. The Primary History as a whole is more conservative in its spelling than the rest of the Bible, which thus falls into two parts of almost equal size. Recognizing that this is a single continuous work that, according to the notices at the end of the book of Kings, could have been completed by about 560 BCE, one can attribute the generally conservative spelling found throughout this gigantic work to its early recognition as canon. The Pentateuch is the most conservative of all (§ 9.3.1). In spite of differences among the five books which could be partly due to the fact that each existed and was transmitted as a separate scroll, and hence probably was copied by different scribes at the same time, the Pentateuch is more uniform in orthographic character than any other part of the Bible. Recall how its portions clustered together in the Figures in Chapter 10. There are three possible explanations for this.

1) The Torah was canonized first and canonized early. The usual critical theories do not place this event earlier than the time of Ezra. If it was a matter of recognizing an old and already fixed text, that would permit an earlier canonization. But if it was a matter of publishing an edition, including post-exilic priestly works (document P), then we have to explain why that work does not display more evidence of the influence of post-exilic spelling; more particularly, why it is so different in its spelling from the contemporary work Ezra-Nehemiah.

2) The Torah which found its way into the present masoretic corpus had a different transmission history (in Persian times) from the rest of the Bible. It represents a local text-type which has not undergone as much modernization in its spelling as other parts of the Bible. Cross (1966, 1985) recognizes that the Pentateuch does not have the developed orthography of other parts of the Bible, but does not go into details (1966: 90; see also pages 93-94). The text is "pristine" (p. 86), a term he does not define.

3) "The Jewish sages took tremendous pains clarifying the orthographic text of the Torah, but did not exercise the same care with respect to the text of the prophets and hagiographa" (Breuer 1976: XXXII).

All these factors combined do not fully explain why the Pentateuch is so very different from the rest. More important, they do not explain why the book of Kings is, by most criteria, almost as conservative as the Torah. Compare 4QSam[b].

11.2.2. So far as spelling is concerned, the most conservative book in the Pentateuch is Exodus, followed by Leviticus, Numbers, Genesis, Deuteronomy. That is, Exodus and Leviticus have by far the most old-fashioned spelling in the entire Bible; and they are dominated by priestly material. There is a lot of P in Numbers too, and about one quarter of Genesis is P. So, the more P, the older the spelling. This means either that old spellings were still in use in priestly circles well after the Exile, or -- more likely -- that the P document is actually a pre-exilic composition, and that the whole of the Pentateuch was complete by the time of the onset of the Exile. The outliers in the Pentateuch given in Chapter 9 deserve close study in this connection.

11.2.3. The Former Prophets, while generally more conservative than the Latter Prophets and Writings (although not as conservative as the Pentateuch), are far from homogeneous. The two parts of Samuel are quite similar, as are the two parts of Kings. In other words, these are single books each of whose parts shared the same transmission history. But the transmission history of the two books was quite different, to judge from the spelling. Joshua and Judges are different again, although they have a lot in common against the rest of the Former Prophets; and they have more modern spellings than Samuel or Kings.

In many matters Kings is almost as conservative as the Pentateuch. See the dendrograms in Chapter 10. Samuel is a mixture. It combines some quite conservative features, such as the spelling of 'David,' with advanced ones, such as the spelling of הָלוֹא.

11.2.4. The Latter Prophets consists of four books which are, in the main, not as conservative as the Primary History but more conservative than the Writings. But within the Latter Prophets there are considerable differences. Jeremiah is the most conservative, and some of its differences from Ezekiel are quite striking, considering that they are near contemporaries. One is tempted to see in Jeremiah the last expression of the spelling practices of Palestine at the beginning of the sixth century BCE, while Ezekiel already exhibits the new style that would come increasingly to the fore in the exiled community in Babylon and would continue to do so in post-exilic times. At the same time it preserves some quite archaic features, such as the spelling ה-, 'his,' which makes it less likely that it was composed after the Exile. See also § 11.3.10. Isaiah's text has more modern spellings than either of the other two Major Prophets, and chapters 40-66 are even more modern than chapters 1-39.

The Minor Prophets are different again, but remarkably homogeneous in their spelling. The Book of the Twelve was evidently edited and transmitted as a single scroll. It need not have been completed until the end of the sixth century, but we cannot tell whether the differences it displays when compared with the three Major Prophets are due to rapid changes in spelling practice at the end of the sixth century or to changes to this book during its subsequent transmission. The Minor Prophets stand out in one particular. They have a high incidence of *plene* spelling of long /ō/ ← *ū* and this is found in all parts of the collection, including books from eighth-century prophets.

11.2.5. Within the Writings, the two parts of the book of Chronicles are similar, as befits a single scroll. In contrast to Ezra-Nehemiah, Chronicles is remarkably conservative in its orthography, with some notable exceptions, such as the spelling of 'David.' This is not what we would have expected, given the usual views about its provenance. In passages that are parallel to Samuel and Kings, it often displays systematic updating of the spelling of selected words; but in other matters it is as conservative as Kings, and more so than Samuel.

11.2.6. The poetic books are mixed. Their orthography is advanced, but not as far as the prose works in the Writings (excepting Chronicles, which is a special case). The poetic works follow a similar tradition, but share with the Minor Prophets an increased number of *plene* spellings of /ō/ ← *ū*, especially in verb forms.

The Megillot are rather mixed, and, being smaller, it is harder to make inferences about their individual character. Qohelet, Song of Songs, and Esther are in some details the most generous users of *matres lectionis*.

11.2.7. In the long chain of transmission, who knows how many times these texts have been copied? And every time a new copy was made was a moment of peril for the text. It required only a careless scribe, or a conscientious but misguided one, to bring about substantial changes. Samuel evidently suffered such a calamity, as we have known for a long time through study of the LXX, and as has now been confirmed by 4QSam[b]. And, if that new copy replaced the old as a standard, the better details of the original could be lost forever (see Chapter 4). Fortunately other forces worked against such lasting injuries. First, the very nature of the craft and mentality of the scribe. His job was to copy, and to copy exactly. That ideal was inculcated in the apprentices in the scribal academies from the earliest times. If a scribe set himself to correct or improve, he fancied himself a textual scholar. Doubtless the scribes continually fell into this temptation, but more likely in piecemeal fashion than systematically. More probably they made unconscious "corrections," just as they made unconscious mistakes (the two can hardly be distinguished in the readings, for the distinction depends on what the scribe thought he was doing, not what he did). But a real error is more harmless than a pseudo-correction, for it sticks out and is likely to be corrected in "proofing," or in the making of the next copy. Whereas a change that looks all right will be perpetuated.

A second constraint arises from the communal character of scribal work. Spelling is a community convention, and the community of scribes and the community of manuscripts diminish the statistical consequences of slips by an individual scribe and blemishes in an individual manuscript.

Spelling variations would seem to be the most harmless of all the alterations a scribe could make. Easy on the conscience too. That being so, we repeat, it is astonishing that the spelling in the Bible is as varied as it is, and that the variations turn up consistently in different parts of the corpus. Most remarkable is the fact that the differences leave a clear trail. We can infer, with all due caution, that the more archaic the spelling, the earlier the completion and publication (canonization, if you like) of the work, and the greater the veneration that shielded it from drastic changes from that time onward. While this confirms in a general way the common belief that the Law, the Prophets, and the Writings constitute a three-part canon, established in that order, the evidence of spelling suggests that the Primary History was the proto-canon, with the three Major Prophets as accompanying documents, already in exilic times. After that, it is harder to trace the accession of the remaining works. The fixed order of the books in the Primary History in all listings contrasts with the chaos in the sequence of the other books, Latter Prophets as well as Writings. This is another indication of later promulgation, lesser prestige, and greater vulnerability to change. But a greater and simpler cause of the main differences between the two parts of the Hebrew Bible is the likely circumstance that the Primary History was finished in the sixth century BCE and still reflects exilic spelling praxis; whereas the other books were edited or written after the Exile and contain more indications of the spelling that set the norms for sacred scripture. The earlier books were never brought up completely to those norms, and no part of the Bible ever departed significantly from them. (See § 11.4.)

11.3 The history of spelling in the Hebrew Bible

11.3.1. The spelling rules exhibited by the Hebrew Bible are those of old Northwest Semitic alphabetic writing as developed from the beginning of the Iron Age and especially during the first half of the First Millennium BCE. These rules are applied more generously in biblical texts than in pre-exilic inscriptions, but, for the most part, they are the same rules.

There are two conspicuous exceptions to this statement, and they are very important. There are two kinds of pre-exilic spelling which have been replaced almost completely in the Bible by two new rules. In pre-exilic inscriptions word-terminal $\hat{o}$ is spelled ה-. No proven exceptions. In biblical texts the standard spelling of word-terminal $\hat{o}$ is ו-. Many archaic spellings of this vowel survived the modernization process, in both the suffix 'his' and other words, notably proper nouns (Type 31).

The second innovation was probably connected with the first one (see § 11.3.10). It is the use of י as an almost universal marker of masculine plural noun stems, whether it represented a long vowel /ī/ (Type 6), the diphthong /ɛy/ (Type 25), the contracted diphthong /ê/ (Type 14), the diphthong /āy/, or no

sound at all, as in *bānāw*, 'his sons,' which was spelled originally בנו but in late standard usage בניו.

11.3.2. There is no trace in the Hebrew Bible of texts using
purely consonantal (Phoenician) spelling. If any ancient Israelite texts ever existed in such a form, all trace of them has been
washed out in transmission. Or nearly all. It is legitimate to
suspect that some orthographic features of texts that have
been shown to be very ancient on other grounds could be ac-
counted for as survivals of archaic spellings, but it is difficult to
prove that this is ever the case. Any such sources from the earliest stages of Israelite literacy that were incorporated into the
sacred scriptures must have been almost completely adjusted
to the later prevailing usages.

11.3.3. The spellings used in the masoretic texts of the
Hebrew Bible exhibit a higher level of utilization of the *matres
lectionis* than the inscriptions of pre-exilic times.

11.3.4. The spellings used in the masoretic texts of the
Hebrew Bible do not exhibit the level of utilization of *matres
lectionis* found in Hebrew texts from around the turn of the
era, outside those biblical texts which can be recognized as
proto-masoretic. It cannot be assumed that Qumran practice
was in the main stream so far as the use of *matres lectionis* is
concerned; but Qumran spelling displays, albeit in an extreme
form, the trend to more *plene* spellings. The contrast with biblical usage is startling.

11.3.5. In view of §§ 11.3.3 and 11.3.4, it can be inferred
that the tradition of spelling in masoretic texts comes from the
period during which the Hebrew Bible was taking final shape,
that is, between 600 and 300 BCE. Since, however, its spelling is
noticeably more advanced than that of the latest pre-exilic inscriptions (early decades of the sixth century) and noticeably
more conservative than the earliest manuscripts (second century BCE), this interval may be narrowed to 550-350 BCE or
more particularly to the Persian period.

It is precisely during this period that tradition and scholarship locate the most intensive literary activities that produced the Hebrew Bible in its present form. Criticism suggests that the sixth century was the first vital period when ancient records were salvaged and edited, the time when their canonical prestige was established or reaffirmed. It is highly likely that the Primary History was the major result of this literary activity. How much of the remainder of the Bible already existed in written form alongside this opus is more disputable.

Tradition associates Ezra with another phase of intense work on the texts, and it speaks of his achievements in terms of finality. The value of this tradition is variously estimated. While later legend has undoubtedly adorned the tale, many scholars find Ezra's reputation generally credible. Others (Rivkin 1969) find very little that survives stringent historical testing. Houtman (1981) reviews the wide range of available critical opinions. Adopting a middle position, we do not need to know how much Ezra himself had to do with it (or even his date!); but we can at least acknowledge that the making of most of the Hebrew Bible into its definitive form took place over a period of one or two centuries at the most, a time which includes the developments associated with Ezra.

Is it possible within this period to locate more precisely the kinds of work done on the text? Is it possible to trace more accurately the development of spelling practice during this period? And, if so, is it possible to associate those developments with the literary and codicological history of the corpus?

11.3.6. Unfortunately the history of Hebrew writing and spelling is not well attested in inscriptional evidence for the period under investigation. That is, the spelling now exhibited by the Hebrew Bible represents a transition from early Hebrew to rabbinic Hebrew, and there are no non-biblical texts of any scope from the ancient world which exhibit the same profile of spelling habits. The texts we have are clearly in the main stream of trends and developments which may be traced steadily, but not continuously, throughout the entire First Millennium BCE and which, presumably, went on through the poorly attested Babylonian and Persian periods. We may safely infer that the tradition displayed by the surviving texts represents the practices of Jewish scribes during that period of final formation and early transmission. After that period (and already during that period, for all we know), the transmission of the texts led to diversification and divergence, yielding textual recensions or text types, possibly on a regional basis. But the text itself had now been fixed, and even the spelling had stabilized almost completely.

To sum up. Redaction, editing, and normalization went on during the sixth and fifth centuries. After that, and certainly by the third century BCE, we have a canon that was scarcely open to alteration. And any changes in the text from then on were purely scribal.

11.3.7. Two new spelling rules, mentioned briefly in § 11.3.1, were introduced during the period of collecting and editing. No new spelling rules were introduced during the period of scribal transmission. To give some extreme examples: the Bible contains no trace of the use of double *matres lectionis* for single vowels as found in Qumran manuscripts. The inroads into biblical texts of such post-biblical practices are negligible.

Because of its etymological status, the combination of א with a bona fide *mater lectionis* does not constitute an exception to this rule. Other apparent exceptions can be explained otherwise. Thus קצוותו (Exodus 37:8; 39:4) preserves an archaic detail in which the first ו is a primal root consonant.

11.3.8. There is one obvious occasion which contained the factors which best explain the distinctive, enduring, and remarkably consistent spelling usage which is still found in the Hebrew Bible. That occasion was the change-over to the Aramaic 'square' character. The rabbis called the old writing

'Hebrew,' the new 'Assyrian' (Naveh 1982: 112-124). We do not know whether this movement had begun during the Exile, but there is every reason to believe that it was complete by the end of the fifth century. The abundant Aramaic secular documents from the fifth century attest the prevailing practice, even in Jewish circles. Not that the paleo-Hebrew script died out all at once. Apart from its perpetuation in the Samaritan community, it continued to be used, if only for the divine name, right down into early rabbinic times. Manuscripts in this script from Qumran attest late use (Freedman and Mathews 1985). Origen still knew of manuscripts in which the tetragrammaton was written in paleo-Hebrew. Such manuscripts have now come to light among the Dead Sea Scrolls, and even copies of books which were entirely written in the old script.

11.3.9. The Talmud (*B. Sanhedrin* 21b-22a; *Megilla* 71a-b; compare *T. Sanhedrin* 5:7) connects Ezra with a second publication of the Torah and with the authorized use of the Assyrian writing. This tradition probably remembers the final detachment of the five books of Moses from the Primary History of which up until that time it had constituted an integral part. With enhanced authority, the Torah from then on was less vulnerable to scribal changes than any other parts of the Hebrew Bible. We can accordingly conclude that its spelling represents the official spelling of the fifth century. Tradition also credits Ezra with the conservation of the traditional pronunciation. In due time legend interpreted this as the provision of the vowel points. The grain of truth in this is probably a memory that Ezra produced an edition, standardized in spelling as well as in letter shapes, and that after him no changes were to be permitted. The task of the scribes was now to copy the text with scrupulous fidelity. They may not always have succeeded. But that was their ideal.

This is admittedly speculative, but it is a reasonable hypothesis. Biblical spelling is Ezra's spelling. It owes its establishment to his introduction of "Assyrian" characters. He seized the opportunity to make a complete revision of all sacred texts in accordance with standardized rules. The remarkable uniformity and consistency of the spellings in our present Hebrew Bible, notwithstanding all the deviations which we have brought to light in the preceding discussion, are best explained as the imprint of a single mind. Considering the enormous size of the Hebrew canon, this was a monumental achievement. It is understandable that tradition links a panel of experts (the men of הכנסת הגדולה) with Ezra in this task. Again we do not have to accept this at face value; it is doubtless anachronistic. But it probably preserves a memory of the transfer of the custody of the sacred writings to a chain of scholars. It is a recognition that after Ezra the Bible was transmitted by scribes.

11.3.10. The impact of the Aramaic square character on Hebrew writing and spelling, which we have connected with Ezra's role as "a ready scribe" (Ezra 7:6), did not mean the wholesale imitation of Aramaic spelling rules. As we have seen, the old rules for the use of ו, י, and ה as *matres lectionis* were essentially the same for all Northwest Semitic languages except Phoenician during the early first millennium BCE. By the fifth century their use was general for all long word-terminal vowels and optional for long word-medial vowels except /ā/. The standardization of the spelling in the sacred texts which we can associate with their promulgation in early post-exilic times was also a conservation within the Hebrew spelling tradition. The old rules remained in force; their use was simply carried through more completely. At the same time two new rules were introduced, either then or soon after.

The first new rule was the writing of word-terminal -ô with ו instead of ה. This was not Aramaic usage and so was not part of the package when square character was taken over. It has no proven precedent in pre-exilic usage. It must have been thought out deliberately. It was carried through with amazing thoroughness, at least in the case of the suffix 'his.' The latter occurs 7,765 times, only 55 of which are spelled with ה in the *ketib* text. The innovation probably represented an attempt to resolve the ambiguity in the use of ה for more than one word-terminal vowel (as well as sometimes for a word-terminal consonant, the latter usually a pronoun suffix). The prime use of ה as a *mater lectionis* was for word-terminal long /ā/. Its attestation is early in both Aramaic and Hebrew, and evidently every word-terminal long /ā/ was so represented. On the other hand ו was well established as the historical and possibly phonetic *plene* spelling of long /ō/ within words. The Hebrew use of ה for word-terminal ŏ (Path 1 in § 6.4.5) was thus anomalous. Hebrew spelled the same sound, /ō/, with two different *matres lectionis*, ו and ה, and used the same *mater lectionis*, ה, to spell at least two different word-terminal vowels, /ā/ and /ō/. This confusion did not arise in Aramaic. The solution for Hebrew was obvious: use ו for word-terminal /ō/, abandoning the pre-exilic spelling of the suffix 'his,' departing at the same time from the matching graphic practice of Aramaic. Incidentally, the fact that א was not brought in as an appropriate *mater lectionis* for writing word-terminal long /ā/ (this happened only later, and on a limited scale) shows that this letter still represented a real consonant, even in the Aramaic article, and was not yet perceived as one of the *matres lectionis*.

The use of ו rather than ה to write word-terminal long /ō/, however, created another ambiguity in Hebrew. For ו at the end of a word was already well established as the writing of long /ū/ and as well could still represent a real consonant. The former ambiguity would not cause as much confusion in Hebrew as in Aramaic, because of the complementary distribution of these word-endings among distinct word classes in Hebrew. In Hebrew it is rare for a noun to end in /ū/; that suffix is characteristic of plural verbs. In Aramaic, however, it is found on nouns as well. In Hebrew it is rare for a verb to end with /ō/, except when, as with nouns, it is the suffix 'his' or 'him.' Hence the pronunciation of word-terminal ו in Hebrew is usually settled by the morphological identity of the word as a whole, assisted by context when the form (the root) is not unique. At least for a verb, it must be either plural $-\bar{u}$ or the suffix 'him.' With nouns, however, one difficulty remained, and this can be seen as the underlying reason for the introduction of the second new spelling rule into post-exilic Hebrew. In the old orthography it was not possible to distinguish 'his son' from 'her son,' both spelled בנה, unless aided by context. The new convention wrote בנו and בנה respectively. But this created a new problem. In the old orthography בנו was the regular spelling of $b\bar{a}n\bar{a}w$, 'his sons,' but now this could be read as $b\bar{a}n\hat{o}$. Other forms of plural nouns had the *plene* spelling of the long vowel in $b\bar{a}n\bar{i}m$ or of the stem-terminal diphthongs in the suffixed forms, such as בניהם, 'their sons.' The remedy again was obvious. Spell all plural nouns (masculine or of masculine type) with ' whether it was pronounced or not. Hence the artificial בניו, $b\bar{a}n\bar{a}w$, 'his sons,' in which the ' is purely graphic.

The adjustment of the spelling of all plural nouns, most of them masculine, with the suffix 'his' to this new convention with $-(y)w$ was not carried through completely. Some books preserve quite a few words in the earlier style without '. This residue of unnormalized spellings yielded a crop of *ketib/qere* variants. Once the vowel points had been supplied, this device for resolving the ambiguity of the consonantal text was no longer needed. The manuscripts show extensive differences in their presentation of this kind of *ketib/qere* pair. Comparison of Ginsburg's list (1897-1905: II 55-74) with Gordis' (1937: Lists 3a, 3b, 3c) shows that over 180 examples can be found. More than half of these are due to Samuel and Ezekiel. The indeterminacy of the lists could be due either to a delayed provision of the device or to its partial abandonment once the writing of the vowel points rendered it unnecessary.

In any case, whatever the later history of this device, it is noteworthy that the old spelling of word-terminal $-\bar{a}w$, 'his,' on plural nouns is the only one attested in pre-exilic inscriptions: אנשו, 'his men' (Lachish 3:18); אלו, 'to him,' (Yavneh-Yam 13).

It is still present in texts, such as Ezekiel, produced in exilic times, and the few examples later than Ezekiel (Daniel 11:10; Ezra 3:3; 4:7) are dubious. The spelling of word-terminal -ō with ה has a similar distribution. This suggests that the early conventions remained in use, if not in vogue, until the fifth century. The switch from ה to ו and from ו to וי seems to have been made in the period of establishing texts from the sixth century to the end of the fifth, or else very early in the period of their ensuing transmission.

The history of the spelling of words like 'his sons' is thus the reverse of what was previously believed. It was argued that the *plene* masoretic spelling בניו represented a triphthong *banayw* in which the י is etymological and that the diphthong *ay* contracted to *ā* (Bauer and Leander 1922: §§ 251, 26c; GKC § 91i), so that the *defective* spelling is the later, phonetic, development. But in this case the *defective* spelling is the archaic one, even though this still leaves the irregular development of the stem ending to be explained.

11.4 Conclusion

The spelling rules and procedures which prevail in the masoretic texts combine the conservation of old rules with the adoption of two new ones, along with a certain drift towards phonetic spelling of long vowels with *matres lectionis*. Uniformity was never achieved. The formative period may be located in the period of two hundred years or more during which the Hebrew Bible was receiving its final shape. The application of rules would be self-conscious on the part of scribes, the drift to *plene* spellings more adventitious. If the latter dominated, we would expect the results to be more randomized than they turn out to be; if the former dominated, we would expect the results to be more uniform than they are. A similar mix would result if different portions of the Bible or different types of vowels had been subjected to normalizing policies to differing degrees.

Possibly all these factors were at work.

The resultant usage may be called "biblical spelling." It would be anachronistic to call it "masoretic," even though masoretic spelling remains biblical in the sense we have given that word. (Some scholars use the term "proto-masoretic.") The masoretes received and preserved a consonantal text that had been fixed long before their time, essentially fixed, even in its spelling, during the Persian period. Insofar as biblical spelling is uniform, it may be associated with the completion and fixation of the canonical text. Deviations from its norms are few and slight, but they are very revealing.

Viewed in this way, the spellings of all vowels in the Hebrew Bible which present a scribe with a spelling choice may be classified under three headings: 1) standard, when the majority of vowels of that type are spelled in the same way, whether *defective* or *plene*; 2) archaic, when a vowel of a type whose standard spelling is *plene* is spelled *defective*; 3) recent, when a vowel of a type whose standard spelling is *defective* is spelled *plene*. The specific details of these three patterns have been summarized in Chapters 9 and 10. This classification scheme is valid only for vowels whose ancient spelling is *defective* and whose standard spelling became *plene*, notably long /ī/ and /ū/, and /ō/ ← /ā/, and for vowels whose ancient spelling was *defective* and whose standard spelling remained *defective*, notably primally short /i/ → /ē/ and primally short /u/ → /ō/. Long vowels derived from primal diphthongs were spelled historically *plene*, and this became the standard spelling once the etymological consonant was interpreted phonetically as a *mater lectionis*. The *defective* spelling of such a vowel is equivocal. It could be archaic, a survival of consonantal spelling of words containing such a vowel from the (Phoenician) usage of a dialect in which the diphthong had monophthongized. It could be archaizing, if the choice of *defective* spelling, known to be an option for long vowels, was preferred in order to imitate the usage of ancient texts. Such usage would be logographic if a word such as 'house' were spelled בת in imitation of venerable Phoenician spelling, even if the dialect in question still said *bayt*. It could be phonetic, since long /ē/ as such was normally spelled *defective*.

Some spellings represent the survival of archaic usage. These are more evident in the older portions of the canon, notably in the Primary History and especially in the Torah. They possibly represent a resistance to normalization in texts already settled and hallowed before the work of standardization could be carried through completely.

Other deviations from the norms represent drift towards later usage, due mainly to scribal variations (but always within the limits of recognized biblical options) in copying manuscripts. The latter process never ceased. Its consequences can be observed all over the corpus, but they are more evident in those portions of the canon which were composed or compiled or edited during the time when the production of the entire Hebrew Bible was nearing finality.

Epilog

So far as we know, this is the first study of its kind. It is new in having examined the spelling of every vowel of the Hebrew Bible with the aid of the computer. It is new also in the use of various kinds of statistical analyses to measure the homogeneity (or inhomogeneity) of the spelling practices in the various portions of the Bible. The study is exploratory, preliminary, provisional.

Over the years, many hours of discussion have preceded methodological decisions. Looking back, we realize that some of these decisions could now be improved in the light of subsequent experience. The decision to use the Masoretic Text as found in L has left us uneasy. A check needs to be made by doing the study all over again for another manuscript of high quality. We can also be faulted for accepting the vocalization of the Masoretic Text at face value (§ 3.2.1.), especially since we criticize other scholars for using the same vocalization with ancient inscriptions (§ 2.3.1.).

Some arbitrary decisions were made in selecting and classifying data. Thus, § 5.6 reports a mixture of historical and statistical criteria for declaring certain vowels not opportunities for spelling choices. The ninety-five percent confidence limit and the one percent threshold are stringent enough (§ 5.6.3), but applying these criteria to lexemes rather than, say, to individual words or to word types is arbitrary in another way.

The history of all vowels is not known with the same certainty; hence some of the types defined in Chapter 6 are not cleanly defined. Types 7, 19, 20, 34, 46, 50, and 51 have mixed membership, as do the residual types. In view of the fact that prominent participants tend to have their names spelled invariantly and tend to be locally frequent (but not often frequent enough to be eliminated under the criteria of § 5.6.3), it would have been better to have separated the proper nouns from Types 31, 46, 49, and 50.

In deciding the maximal number of portions to divide the text into (§ 7.2), we followed conservative practice for contingency table analysis utilizing the chi-square distribution. At the cost of rendering our methods much less accessible, we could have allowed more portions had we used other distributions. This would have allowed the orthographic peculiarities of individual books to be studied closer up.

In studying the effects of proximity on the spelling of repeated lexemes (§ 8.2), we limited our range of interest to approximately two verses (forty segments). Of course, the results suggest that no longer-range effects exist. In our analysis of the effects of word frequency (§ 8.3), we picked one percent incidence as the threshold above which a word is said to be of high frequency in a portion, again an arbitrary point.

The inclusion of stress as a variable in our analysis led to puzzling results. It is hoped that more refined methods might allow the history of Hebrew spelling to suggest the history of stress (§ 8.4). Likewise for the history of diphthongs.

We reported clustering results using only a Euclidean metric and only for the furthest-neighbor algorithm. Other metrics and clustering methods should be tried. And other methods of detecting affinities should be used as cross-checks. (In fact, we applied classical multi-dimensional scaling to our data, with results quite similar to those set forth in Chapter 10.)

Of theoretical interest is the impasse reached at the end of Chapter 4. Is there any way of analyzing the orthographic inhomogeneity of the established text so as to separate the effects of scribal transmission from the features of the original (or updated) text? A comprehensive study of the orthography of all ancient non-biblical Hebrew texts might yield a measure of the rate of increase in the use of *matres lectionis*. A similar study of all early Aramaic texts might also be useful. Assuming that the Primary History was completed by 550 BCE, assuming that its orthography was then similar to that of the latest pre-exilic Hebrew inscriptions, and assuming further that the spelling of the Torah was (more or less) fixed by 450 BCE and that the most modernized spelling found in any book represents the virtual close-out of updating by, say, 250 BCE, it might be possible to calculate the rate of increase in the use of *matres lectionis* over those centuries.

Within the Bible itself, a systematic measurement of orthographic distances between two recensions of the same text (portions of the Primary History repeated in Isaiah, Jeremiah, Psalms, Chronicles) might give another estimate of the rate of spelling changes.

It would be unwise to look to Qumran for a control on the stage reached by Hebrew at the turn of the era. The lavish use of *matres lectionis* is eccentric and not in the mainstream of transmission. A better idea of early rabbinic spelling of non-biblical texts might be gained by systematic study of the orthography of the Kaufmann Manuscript of the Mishnah.

Clearly, much work remains to be done.

Bibliography

Abou-Assaf, A.
   1981 "Die Statue des HDYS^cY, Konig von Guzana," *MDOG*
         113: 3-22.

Abou-Assaf, A., Bordreuil, P., and Millard, A. R.
   1982 *La Statue de Tell Fekhereye et son inscription bi-
         lingue assyro-araméenne*. Paris: Editions Recherche
         sur les civilizations.

Agresti, A.
   1984 *Analysis of Ordinal Categorical Data*. New York: John
         Wiley & Sons.

Aharoni, Y.
   1970 "Three Hebrew Ostraca from Arad," *BASOR* 197: 16-42.
   1975 *Arad Inscriptions (Heb.)*. Jerusalem: Bialik Institute
         and Israel Exploration Society.
   1981 *Arad Inscriptions (Eng.)*. Jerusalem: Israel Explora-
         tion Society.

Albrektson, B.
   1978 "Reflections on the Emergence of a Standard Text of
         the Hebrew Bible," *VTS* 29: 49-65.

Albright, W. F.
   1943 "The Gezer Calendar," *BASOR* 92: 16-26.

Althann, R.

1982 "Consonantal *ym*: Ending or Noun in Isa 3, 13; Jer 17, 16; 1 Sam 6, 19," *Biblica* 63: 560-65.

Andersen, F. I.

1966 "Moabite Syntax," *Orientalia* 35: 81-120.

1970a "Orthography in Repetitive Parallelism," *JBL* 89: 343-4.

1970b "Biconsonantal Byforms in Biblical Hebrew," *ZAW* 82: 270-274.

Andersen, F. I., and Forbes, A. D.

1976a *A Linguistic Concordance of Ruth and Jonah: Hebrew Vocabulary and Idiom. The Computer Bible Volume IX.* Wooster, Ohio: Biblical Research Associates.

1976b *Eight Minor Prophets: A Linguistic Concordance. The Computer Bible Volume X.* Wooster, Ohio: Biblical Research Associates.

1978a *Jeremiah: A Linguistic Concordance. I Grammatical Vocabulary and Proper Nouns. The Computer Bible Volume XIV.* Wooster, Ohio: Biblical Research Associates.

1978b *Jeremiah: A Linguistic Concordance. II Nouns and Verbs. The Computer Bible Volume XIVA.* Wooster, Ohio: Biblical Research Associates.

1983 "'Prose Particle' Counts of the Hebrew Bible," pp. 165-183 in *The Word of the Lord Shall Go Forth. Essays in Honor of David Noel Freedman in Celebration of His Sixtieth Birthday*, eds. C. Meyers and M. O'Connor. Philadelphia: ASOR.

1985a "Orthography and Text Transmission," *TEXT* 2: (in the press).

1985b "The Vocabulary of the Pentateuch," *Proceedings of the International Conference on Computer-Assisted Study of Ancient Languages*, ed. H. V. D. Parunak. Ann Arbor: University of Michigan.

Andersen, F. I., and Freedman, D. N.
1980 *Anchor Bible 24: Hosea*. Garden City: Doubleday.

Anderson, G. W.
1979 *Tradition and Interpretation*. Oxford: Clarendon.

Aspesi, F.
1977 "Sistema fonematico 'complessivo' e sistemi fonematici 'morfologici': un'interpretazione di alcuni fatti semitici," *AION* 37/4: 393-401.

Audet, J. P.
1950 "A Hebrew-Aramaic List of Books of the Old Testament in Greek Transcription," *JTS* 1: 135-154.

Auld, A. G.
1979 "Joshua: the Hebrew and Greek Texts," *SVT* 30: 1-14.

Avigad, N.
1953 "The Epitaph of a Royal Steward from Silwan Village," *IEJ* 3: 137-52.
1976 "Bullae and Seals from a Post-Exilic Judean Archive," *Qedem 4*. Jerusalem: Hebrew University.

Bachrach, J. b. M.
1854 ספר היהם לכתב אשורי ותולדות הנכדות והתעסם Warsaw (*non vidi*).

Baillet, M.
1979 "Trois inscriptions samaritaines au musée de l'Ecole Biblique de Jerusalem," *RB* 86: 583-593.

Bange, L. A.
1971 *A Study in the Use of Vowel-Letters in Alphabetic Consonantal Writing.* Munich: UNI-DRUCK.

Bardowicz, L.
1894a *Studien zur Geschichte des Orthographie des Althebräischen.* Frankfort am Main: Kauffmann.
1894b "Das allmähliche Überhandnehmen der matres lectionis im Bibel-texte," *Monatsschrift für Geschichte und Wissenschaft des Judenthums* 38: 117-21; 157-67.

Barnes, W. E.
1900 "Ancient Corrections in the Text of the Old Testament (Tikkun Sopherim)," *JTS* 1: 387-414.

Barr, J.
1967a "St. Jerome and the Sounds of Hebrew," *JSS* 12: 1-36.
1967b "Vocalization and the Analysis of Hebrew among the Ancient Translators," *Hebräische Wortforschung: Festschrift zum 80. Geburtstag von Walter Baumgartner. SVT* 16: 1-11.
1968 *Comparative Philology and the Text of the Old Testament.* Oxford: Clarendon.
1978 "Some Notes on $b\hat{e}n$ 'between' in Classical Hebrew," *JSS* 23: 1-22.
1981 "A New Look at KETHIBH-QERE," *OTS* 21: 17-37.

Barth, J.
1906 "Formangleichung bei begrifflichen Korrespondenzen," pp. 787-796 in *Orientalische Studien . . . Th. Noeldeke*, ed. C. Bezold. Giessen: Alfred Töpelmann.

Barthelemy, D.
1976 "History of Hebrew Text," pp. 878-84 in *The Interpreter's Dictionary of the Bible Supplement*, ed. Keith Crim. Nashville: Abingdon.

Bauer, H., and Leander, P.

1922 *Historische Grammatik der hebräischen Sprache.* Hildesheim: Georg Olms [Photomechanical reprint 1965].

Becker, R. A., and Chambers, J. M.

1984 *S: An Interactive Environment for Data Analysis and Graphics.* Belmont, CA: Wadsworth.

Bishop, Y., Fienberg, S., and Holland, P.

1975 *Discrete Multivariate Analysis: Theory and Practice.* Cambridge: The MIT Press.

Blake, F. R.

1940 "The Development of Symbols for Vowels in the Alphabets Derived from the Phoenician," *JAOS* 60: 391-413.

Blau, J.

1968 "Some Difficulties in the Reconstruction of 'Proto-Hebrew' and 'Proto-Canaanite'," pp. 29-43 in *In Memoriam Paul Kahle* [*BZAW 103*], eds. M. Black and G. Fohrer. Berlin: de Gruyter.

1976 *A Grammar of Biblical Hebrew: Porta linguarum orientalium N. S. 12.* Wiesbaden: Harrassowitz.

Blau, J. and Loewenstamm, S. E.

1970 "Zur Frage der Scriptio Plena im Ugaritischen und Verwandtes," *Ugaritische Forschungen* 2: 19-33.

Bonk, H.

1891 "Über die Verwendbarigkeit der doppelformigen mit *yohô* und *yo* anlautenden Namen im Alten Testament für die historische Quellenkritik," *ZAW* 11: 125-156.

Bravmann, M. M.

1977 *Studies in Semitic Philology.* Leiden: Brill.

Breuer, M.
 1976 *The Aleppo Codex and the Accepted Text of the Bible*.
 Jerusalem: Mosad Harav Kook.

Brock, S. P.
 1972 Review of Goodwin 1969, *JSS* 17: 260.

Chavel, C. B., tr.
 1971 *Commentary on the Torah*. New York: Shilo.

Clogg, C.
 1984 "Some Models for the Analysis of Association in Multi-
 way Cross-Classifications Having Ordered Categories,"
 pp. 224-60 in *The Analysis of Cross-Classified Data
 Having Ordered Categories*, L. A. Goodman. Cambridge: Harvard University Press.

Cramér, H.
 1946 *Mathematical Methods of Statistics*. Princeton: The
 Princeton University Press.

Cross, F. M.
 1953 "A New Qumran Biblical Fragment Related to the Original Hebrew Underlying the Septuagint," *BASOR* 132:
 15-26.
 1961 "The Development of the Jewish Scripts," pp. 133-202
 in *The Bible and the Ancient Near East. Essays in
 Honor of William Foxwell Albright*, ed. G. E. Wright.
 Garden City: Doubleday.
 1966 "The Contribution of the Qumran Discoveries to the
 Study of the Biblical Text," *Israel Exploration Journal*
 16: 81-95.
 1973 *Canaanite Myth and Hebrew Epic*. Cambridge: Harvard University Press.
 1975 "The Evolution of a Theory of Local Texts," pp. 293-525

in *Qumran and the History of the Biblical Text*, eds. F. M. Cross and S. Talmon. Cambridge: Harvard University Press.

1985 "New Directions in Dead Sea Scroll Research. Part I: The Text behind the Text of the Hebrew Bible," *Bible Review* 1 (Summer): 12-25.

Cross, F. M., and Freedman, D. N.
1952 *Early Hebrew Orthography: A Study of the Epigraphic Evidence. AOS 36.* New Haven: American Oriental Society.
1972 "Some Observations on Early Hebrew," *Biblica* 53: 413-420.

Cross, F. M., and Talmon, S.
1975 *Qumran and the History of the Biblical Text.* Cambridge: Harvard University Press.

Dahood, M.
1982 "The Hapax ḥārak in Proverbs 12,27," *Biblica* 63: 60-62.

Degen, R.
1969 *Altaramaische Grammatik der Inschriften des 10.-8. Jh. v. Chr.* Wiesbaden: Harrassowitz.

Delitzsch, F.
1920 *Die Lese- und Schreibfehler im Alten Testament nebst den dem Schrifttexte einverliebten Randnöten klassifiziert: ein Hilfsbuch für Lexicon und Grammatik, Exegese und Lekture.* Berlin: de Gruyter.

Dhorme, E.
1967 *A Commentary on the Book of Job*, H. Knight, tr. Nashville: Nelson [1984 reprint].

Diakonoff, I. M.

1976 "Ancient Writing and Ancient Written Language: Pitfalls and Peculiarities in the Study of Sumerian," pp. 99-121 in *Sumeriological Studies in Honor of Thorkild Jacobsen. AS 20.* Chicago: University of Chicago.

Dion, P.-E.

1974 *La langue de Ya'udi. Description et classement de l'ancien parler de Zencirli dans le cadre des langues sémitiques du nord-ouest.* Waterloo: Corporation for the Publication of Academic Studies in Religion in Canada.

Donner, H., and Rollig, W.

1962-4 *Kanaanäische und aramäische Inschriften; mit einem Beitrag von O. Rössler.* Wiesbaden: Harrassowitz.

Feller, W.

1968 *An Introduction to Probability Theory and Its Applications (Third Edition)* N.Y.: John Wiley & Sons.

Fienberg, S.

1980 *The Analysis of Cross-Classified Categorical Data* (Second Edition). Cambridge: The MIT Press.

Fitzmyer, J. A.

1967 *The Aramaic Inscriptions of Sefire. Biblica et Orientalia 19.* Rome: PBI.

1979 *A Wandering Aramean: Collected Aramaic Essays. SBL MS 25.* Missoula, Montana: Scholars Press.

Freedman, D. N.

1955 "*Pšty* in Hosea 2:7," *JBL* 74: 275.

1962 "The Massoretic Text and the Qumran Scrolls: A Study

in Orthography," *Textus* 2: 87-102.

1963 "The Law and the Prophets," *SVT* 9: 250-265.

1969a "Orthographic Peculiarities in the Book of Job," *Eretz-Israel* 9: 35-44.

1969b "The Orthography of the Arad Ostraca," *IEJ* 19: 52-56.

1983a "The Earliest Bible," *Michigan Quarterly Review* 22 No. 3: 167-175.

1983b "The Spelling of the Name 'David' in the Hebrew Bible," *Hebrew Annual Review* 7: 89-104.

Freedman, D. N., and Andersen, F. I.

1985 "The Orthography of the Aramaic Portion of the Tell Fekhereye Bilingual," *Fensham Festschrift* [Forthcoming].

Freedman, D. N., and Mathews, K. A.

1985 *The Paleo-Hebrew Leviticus Scroll (11QpaleoLev)*. Winona Lake: Eisenbrauns [for ASOR].

Freedman, D. N., and Ritterspach, A.

1985 "The Use of Aleph as a Vowel Letter in the Genesis Apocryphon," *Revue de Qumran* 22: 293-520.

Frensdorff, S.

1876 *Die Massora Magna*. New York: KTAV [1968 reprint].

Garbini, G.

1969 "Studi Aramaici 1-2," *AION, NS* 19: 1-15.

1977a "Sulla datazione dell'iscrizione di Aḥiram," *AION* 37/1: 81-89.

1977b "I dialetti del fenicio," *AION* 37/3: 283-294.

1977c "Analisi di iscrizione fenicie," *AION* 37/4: 403-416.

1978a "Penseri su Ebla (ovvero: Le uova di Babilonia)," *AION* 38/1: 41-52.

1978b "Su un'iscrizione ebraica da Khirbet el-Kom," *AION* 38/2: 195-204.

1978c "Sull'alfabetario di ᶜIzbet arṭah," *Or. Ant.* XVII/4: 289-295.

1979 "Storia e problemi dell'epigrafia semitica," *Supplement n. 19 agli AION* 39/2: 1-100.

1981 "Gli incantesimi fenici di Arslam Tas," *Or. Ant.* XX/4: 277-294.

Gasov-Ginsberg, A.
1959 "ᶜAR--strana MO'ABA," *Palestinskii sbornik* 4(67): 12-16.

Gelb, I. J.
1969 *Sequential Reconstruction of Proto-Akkadian. Assyriological Studies 18.* Chicago: University of Chicago Press.

Gibson, J. C. L.
1971 *Textbook of Syrian Semitic Inscriptions. Vol. I. Hebrew and Moabite Inscriptions.* Oxford: Clarendon.

Gill, J.
1767 *A Dissertation Concerning the Antiquity of the Hebrew Language Letters, Vowel-Points and Accents.* London: Keith, et. al.

Ginsberg, H. L.
1942 "Aramaic Studies Today," *JAOS* 62: 229-238.

Ginsburg, C. D.
1867a *Jacob ben Chajim ibn Adonijah's Introduction to the Rabbinic Bible.* Reprinted with Prolegomenon by N. H. Snaith. New York: KTAV [1968 reprint].
1867b *The Massoreth Ha-Massoreth of Elia Levita.* New

York: KTAV [1968 reprint].

1897 *Introduction to the Massoretico-critical Edition of the Hebrew Bible*. Reprinted with Prolegomenon by H. M. Orlinsky. New York: KTAV [1966 reprint].

1897-1905 *The MASSORAH Compiled from Manuscripts*. Reprinted with Prolegomenon by A. Dotan. New York: KTAV [1975 reprint].

Girdlestone, R. B.

1892 *The Foundations of the Bible: Studies in Old Testament Criticism*. London: Eyre and Spottiswoode.

GKC

1910 *Gesenius' Hebrew Grammar*. 2nd edition, ed. A. E. Cowley. Oxford: Clarendon Press.

Gokhale, D. V., and Kullback, S.

1978 *The Information in Contingency Tables*. New York and Basel: Marcel Dekker, Inc.

Goodwin, D. W.

1969 *Text-Restoration Methods in Contemporary U. S. A. Biblical Scholarship*. Napoli: Istituto Orientale Di Napoli.

Gordis, R.

1937 *The Biblical Text in the Making: A Study of the Kethib-Qere*. Reprinted with Prolegomenon by R. Gordis. New York: KTAV.

1971a "The Origin of the Masoretic Text in the Light of the Rabbinic Literature and the Qumran Scrolls," *Prolegomenon to the reprint of Gordis 1937*. New York: KTAV.

1971b *Poets, Prophets and Sages: Essays in Biblical Interpretation*. Bloomington: University of Indiana Press.

1976   *The Word and the Book: Studies in Biblical Language and Literature.* New York: KTAV.

1978   *The Book of Job.* New York: KTAV.

Gordon, R. P.
1978   "Aleph apologeticum," *JQR* 69/2: 112-16.

Goshen-Gottstein, M.
1960   "The Authenticity of the Aleppo Codex," *Textus* 1: 17-58.

1967   "Hebrew Bible Manuscripts: Their History and Their Place in the HUBP Edition," *Biblica* 48: 243-90.

Grabbe, L. L.
1977   *Comparative Philology and the Text of Job: A Study in Methodology. SBL Dissertation Series 34.* Missoula, Montana: Scholars Press.

Greenberg, M.
1965   *Introduction to Hebrew.* Englewood Cliffs: Prentice-Hall.

Hamming, R. W.
1980   *Coding and Information Theory.* Englewood Cliffs: Prentice-Hall.

Harary, F., Lipstein, B., and Styan, G.
1970   "A Matrix Approach to Nonstationary Chains," *Operations Research* 18: 1168-1181.

Harris, Z. S.
1939   *The Development of the Canaanite Dialects: an Investigation in Linguistic History.* New Haven: American Oriental Society.

Höfner, M.
  1943. *Altsudarabische Grammatik.* Leipzig: Harrassowitz.

Houtman, C.
  1981 "Ezra and the Law," *OTS* 21: 91-115.

Huffmon, H. B.
  1965 *Amorite Personal Names in the Mari Texts: A Structural and Lexical Study.* Baltimore: Johns Hopkins Press.

Isaacson, D. L. and Madsen, R. W.
  1976 *Markov Chains Theory and Applications.* New York: John Wiley & Sons.

Israel, F.
  1979 "The Language of the Ammonites," *Orientalia Lovaniensia Periodica* 10: 143-59.

Jamme, A.
  1962 *Sabaean Inscriptions from Maḥram Bilqîs (Mârib).* Baltimore: Johns Hopkins University Press.

Jellicoe, S.
  1974 *Studies in the Septuagint: Origins, Recensions and Interpretations. Library of Biblical Studies,* ed. H. M. Orlinsky. New York: KTAV.

Kahle, P.
  1945 "Problems of the Septuagint," *SP* 1/1: 328-338.
  1956 "The Masoretic Text of the Bible and the Pronunciation of Hebrew," *JJS* 7: pp. 493-513 in Leiman 1974.
  1959 *The Cairo Geniza.* Oxford: Blackwell.

Kaufman, S. A.
  1982 "Reflections on the Assyrian-Aramaic Bilingual from
       Tell Fakhariyeh," *Maarav* 3 No. 2: 137-175.

Koehler, L.
  1950-1 "Bemerkungen zur Schreibung und Aussprache der
         Tiberischen Masora," *HUCA* 23, 1: 137-55.
  1956 "Problems in the Study of the Language of the Old Tes-
       tament," *JJS* 1: 3-24.

Kutscher, E. Y.
  1959 .הלשון והרקע הלשוני של מגילת ישעיהו השלמה ממגילות ים המלח
       Jerusalem: Hebrew University.
  1974 *The Language and Linguistic Background of the
       Isaiah Scroll (1QIsa^a)*. Leiden: Brill.
  1982 *A History of the Hebrew Language*, ed. R. Kutscher.
       Jerusalem/Leiden: Magnes Press/Brill.

Lambdin, T. O.
  1971 "The Junctural Origin of the West Semitic Definite Arti-
       cle," pp. 315-33 in *Near Eastern Studies in Honor of
       William Foxwell Albright*, ed. H. Goedicke. Baltimore:
       John Hopkins University Press.

Leiman, S. Z.
  1974 *The Canon and Massorah of the Hebrew Bible: An
       Introductory Reader. Library of Biblical Studies*, ed.
       H. M. Orlinsky. New York: KTAV.
  1976 *The Canonization of Hebrew Scripture: The Talmudic
       and Midrashic Evidence*. Hamden: Archon Books, for
       the Connecticut Academy of Arts and Sciences.

Lemaire, A.
  1977a *Inscriptions Hébraïques. Tome I Les Ostraca*. Paris:
       Les éditions du Cerf.

1977b "L'épigraphie paléo-hébraïque et la Bible," *SVT* 29 165-76.

Liebetrau, A. M.
1983 *Measures of Association*. Beverly Hills: Sage Publications.

Loewenstamm, S. E.
1980 *Comparative Studies in Biblical and Oriental Literatures*. Kevelaer/Neukirchen-Vluyn: Butzon and Bercker/Neukirchener.

Lowth, R.
1787 *Lectures on the Sacred Poetry of the Hebrews*. N.Y.: Garland Publishing [1971 reprint].
1868 *Isaiah: A New Translation. 17th ed.* London: Tegg.

Martin, M.
1958 *The Scribal Character of the Dead Sea Scrolls*. Louvain: Publications Universitaires.

Morag, S.
1962 *The Vocalization Systems of Arabic, Hebrew and Aramaic. Janua Linguarum XIII*. The Hague: Mouton.
1974 "On the Historical Validity of the Vocalization of the Hebrew Bible," *JAOS* 94: 307-15.

Murtonen, A.
1953 "The Fixation in Writing of Various Parts of the Pentateuch," *VT* 3: 46-53.
1975 "On the Interpretation of the Matres Lectionis in Biblical Hebrew," *Abr-Nahrain* 16: 66-121.

Naveh, J.

1973 "Some Semitic Epigraphical Considerations on the Antiquity of the Greek Alphabet," *AJA* 77: 1-8.

1982 *Early History of the Alphabet. An introduction to West Semitic epigraphy and palaeography.* Jerusalem: Magnes Press.

O'Connor, M.

1983 "Writing Systems, Native Speaker Analyses, and the Earliest Stages of Northwest Semitic Orthography," pp. 439-65 in *The Word of the Lord Shall go Forth. Essays in Honor of David Noel Freedman in Celebration of His Sixtieth Birthday*, eds. C. Meyers and M. O'Connor. Philadelphia: ASOR.

Orlinsky, H. M.

1940-1 "The Import of the Kethib-Kere and the Masoretic Note on לְכָה, Judges 19.13," *JQR* 31: 59ff.

1941 "On the Present State of Proto-Septuagint Studies," *JAOS* 61: 81-91.

1947 "Current Progress and Problems in Septuagint Research," pp. 145-161 in *The Study of the Bible Today and Tomorrow*, ed. H. R. Willoughby. Chicago: University of Chicago Press.

1966 "The Masoretic Text: a Critical Evaluation," *Prolegomenon to the reprint of Ginsburg 1897, pp. I-XLV.* New York: KTAV.

1974 *1972 and 1973 Proceeding IOMS.MS1.* New York: KTAV.

Owen, J.

1659 "Of the Integrity and Purity of the Hebrew and Greek Text of the Scripture," pp. 345-421 in Vol. 16 of *The Works of John Owen (1850-1853 edition).* London: Banner of Truth [1968 reprint].

Palva, H.
1977 "The Descriptive Imperative of Narrative Style in Spoken Arabic," *FO* 18: 5-26.

Pardee, D.
1978 "Letters from Tel Arad," *UF* 10: 289-336.

Pardee, D, Sperling, S. D., Whitehead, J. D., and Dion, P.-E.
1982 *Handbook of Ancient Hebrew Letters. SBL Sources for Biblical Studies 15.* Chico: Scholars Press.

Parunak, H. V. D.
1978 "The Orthography of the Arad Ostraca," *BASOR* 230: 25-32.

Parzen, E.
1962 *Stochastic Processes.* San Francisco: Holden-Day.

Petracek, K.
1979 "Die semitische Laryngaltheorie und die Sprache von Ibla," *AION* 39/3: 385-394.

Plackett, R. L.
1981 *The Analysis of Categorical Data.* London and High Wycombe: Charles Griffin.

Puech, E.
1980 "ABECEDAIRE et list alphabétique de noms hébreux du debut du IIe s. A. D.," *RB* 87: 118-126.

Rahlfs, A.
1916 "Zur Setzung der Lesemütter im Alten Testament," *Nachrichten von der Königlichen Gesellschaft der Wissenschaften zur Göttingen.* Philologisch-historische Klasse: 315-347.

Rainey, A. F.
    1972   "The Word םי in Ugaritic and in Hebrew," *Lesonenu* 36: 186-89.

Reider, J.
    1930   "The Present State of Textual Criticism of the Old Testament," *HUCA* 7: 285-315.

Rendsburg, G. A.
    1980   "Laqtil Infinitives Yipᶜil or Hipᶜil?" *Orientalia* 51/2: 231ff.
    1982   "A New Look at Pentateuchal HW ᵓ," *Biblica* 63: 351-69.

Revell, E. J.
    1970   "Studies in the Palestinian Vocalization of Hebrew," pp. 51-100 in Wevers and Redford (1970).

Rivkin, E.
    1969   "Prolegomenon" to the KTAV reprint of *Judaism and Christianity*. New York: KTAV, pp. VII-LXX.

Roberts, B. J.
    1949a   *The Old Testament Text and Versions: the Hebrew Text in Transmission and the History of the Ancient Versions*. Cardiff: University of Wales Press.
    1949b   "The Divergences in the Pre-Tiberian Massoretic Text," *JJS* 1: 147-155.
    1964   "The Hebrew Bible since 1937," *JTS* 15: 253-264.
    1979   "The Textual Transmission of the Old Testament (including modern critical editions of the Hebrew Bible)," pp. 1-52 in Anderson (1979).

Romesburg, H. C.
    1984   *Cluster Analysis for Researchers*. Belmont, CA: Wadsworth.

Sachs, L.
    1982 *Applied Statistics: A Handbook of Techniques*. New
          York: Springer-Verlag.

Sarfatti, G. B.
    1982 "Hebrew Inscriptions of the First Temple Period,"
          Maraav 3: 55-83.

Scholem, G.
    1959 "Fresh Information about R. Joseph Askenazi, the
          Taana from Safed," *Tarbiz* 28: 75.

Schwarz, W.
    1955 "Discussion on the Origin of the Septuagint," *Princi-
          ples and Problems of Biblical Translation*. Cam-
          bridge: Cambridge University Press [1970 reprint].

Sedelow, W. A. and S. Y.
    1983 *Computers in Language Research: Trends in Linguis-
          tics. Studies and Monographs 19*. The Hague: Mouton.

Segal, M. H.
    1953 "The Promulgation of the Authoritative Text of the
          Hebrew Bible," *JBL* 72: 35-47.

Segert, S.
    1961 "Semitische Marginalien III. Zur Phonetik und Morpho-
          logie des Nordwestsemitischen," *ArOr* 29: 106-118.
    1978 "Vowel Letters in Early Aramaic," *JNES* 37: 111-114.

Siegel, J. P.
    1974a "The Severus Scroll and 1QIs[a]," *IOMS.MS* 1: 159-65.
    1974b "An Orthographic Convention of 1QIs[a] and the Origin
          of Two Masoretic Anomalies," pp. 99-110 in Orlinsky
          1974.

Sperber, A.

1939 "Hebrew Based Upon Biblical Passages in Parallel Transmission," *HUCA* 14: 153-249.

1942-3 "Problems of the Masora," *HUCA* 17: 293-394.

1943 *Hebrew Grammar: A New Approach*. New York: Jewish Theological Seminary.

1959 *Grammar of Masoretic Hebrew*. Copenhagen: Gad.

1966 *A Historical Grammar of Biblical Hebrew*. Leiden: Brill.

Stefaniak, L. W.

1969 "Old Hebrew Inscriptions from Tel Arad," *FO* 11: 265-277.

Suen, C. Y.

1979 "n-Gram Statistics for Natural Language Understanding and Text Processing," *IEEE Trans. on Pattern Recognition and Machine Intelligence*, *1*(2), 164-172.

Sundberg, A. C.

1968 "The 'Old Testament': A Christian Canon," *CBQ* 30: 143-155.

Talmon, S.

1962 "The Three Scrolls of the Law that were found in the Temple Court," *Textus* 2: 14-27.

Torczyner, H., Harding, L., Lewis, A., and Starkey, J. L.

1938 *Lachish 1: The Lachish Letters*. London, New York, Toronto: Oxford University Press.

Viganò, L.

1977 "Quelques exemples du singular feminin en -ôt en Ezekiel," *SBF* 7: 239-245.

Weil, G. E.
    1968 "Prolegomenon" to the reprint of Frensdorff's *Die Mas-*
          sorah Magna (1876). New York: KTAV.
    1971 *Massorah Gedolah iuxta codicem Leningradensem B*
          19a. Vol. I Catalogi. Rome: PBI.
    1981 "Les décomptes de versets, mots et lettres du Penta-
          teuque selon le manuscrit B 19a de Leningrad," pp.
          651-703 in *Mélanges Dominique Barthelemy. Etudes*
          Bibliques offertes a l'occasion de son 60e anniver-
          saire: Orbis Biblicus et Orientalis 38, eds. P. Casetti,
          O. Keel and A. Schenker. Fribourg/Göttingen: Edi-
          tions Universitaires/Vandenhöck und Ruprecht.

Weinberg, W.
    1975 "The History of Hebrew *Plene* Spelling: From Antiquity
          to Haskalah," *HUCA* 46: 457-487. Reprinted in *The*
          History of Hebrew Plene *Spelling*. (Cincinnati: HUC
          Press, 1985): 1-31.

Weingreen, J.
    1982 *Introduction to the Critical Study of the Text of the*
          Hebrew Bible. Oxford: Clarendon Press.

Wernberg-Møller, P.
    1958 "Studies in the Defective Spellings in the Isaiah Scroll
          of St. Mark Monastery," *JSS* 3: 244-264.

Wevers, J. W., and Redford, D. B., eds.
    1970 *Essays on the Ancient Semitic World*. Toronto:
          University of Toronto Press.

Würthwein, E.
    1979 *The Text of the Old Testament*. An Introduction of the
          Biblia Hebraica. E. F. Rhodes, tr. Grand Rapids: Eerd-
          mans.

Yeivin, I.
1980 *Introduction to the Tiberian Masorah. JBLMasS 5.* Missoula, Montana: Scholars Press.

Zadok, R.
1977 "On Five Biblical Names," *ZAW* 89: 266-268.

Zeitlin, S.
1966 "Were there Three Torah-Scrolls in the Azarah?" *JQR* 56: 269-272.

Zevit, Z.
1977 "The Linguistic and Textual Arguments in Favor of a Hebrew 3m.s. Suffix -Y," *UF* 9: 315-28.
1980 *Matres Lectionis in Ancient Hebrew Epigraphs. ASOR Monograph Series 2.* Cambridge: ASOR.

Citation Index

Genesis

1:21	137
2:7	167
2:19	167
2:25	96
4:4	137
5:29	137
6:7	164
6:16	142
6:18	26
9:11	26
9:17	26
9:21	184
10:4	168
10:5	136
10:8	33
10:20	136
10:31	136
10:32	136
12:3	148
12:8	184
13:3	184
14	92
14:6	176
16:5	146
17:6	174
17:7	26
17:19	26
18:18	136
20:6	86
22:12	96
22:18	136
22:22	129
23:6	83
23:11	84
25:23	136
25:24	88
26:3	26
26:4	136
26:25	184
27:3	133
27:22	218
27:29	93
30:11	86
30:34	143
31:43	218
33:11	202
34:23	137
35:21	184
36:21	69
36:24	175
36:25	69
36:30	69
37:24	175
38:18	145
38:25	145
38:27	88
41:27	175
43:26	90
43:28	93
44:13	93
44:29	88
45:16	218
47:17	137
47:30	143
48:4	164
48:20	195
49:6	173
49:10	69, 168, 184
49:11	184
49:15	184
49:22	92

Exodus

2:9	164
2:10	164
2:16	142
2:25	172
3:5	146
3:18	168
6:4	26
10:6	218
13:5	71
13:9	71
13:11	71
13:16	71, 74

14:10	167
14:13	86
16:12	96
20:18	167
20:20	167
22:4	184
22:26	184
23:15	164
25:31	136, 151, 173
28:11	203
29:40	218
31:6	164
31:11	164
31:18	10
32:8	164
32:17	184
32:25	184
33:13	144
34:18	164
36:19	175
37:8	193, 321
39:4	193, 321
39:6	203
39:13	203

Leviticus
4:25	73
4:30	73
4:34	73
5:1	186
11:43	87
15:10	75
21:5	92
23:13	184
23:17	90
23:42	74
23:43	74
26:42	199
26:9	26, 27

Numbers
7:1	75
10:36	184
11:4	88
11:11	87
11:15	135
11:17	88
11:20	82
11:25	88
13:9	84
14:20	143
15:20	70, 137
15:21	70
15:24	86
17:17	137
17:25	96
21:15	48
21:20	70
21:28	48
23:8	184
23:22	89
23:28	70
24:8	89
24:24	168
28:13	218
29:33	137
30:8	144
31:9	137
32:26	137
32:38	203, 218
33:49	70
34:4	91

Deuteronomy
1:11	137, 138
2:9	48
2:18	48
2:29	48
3:11	83, 186
3:19	137
3:24	145
4:13	10
4:35	174
5:24	135
5:27(24)	135
6:8	71, 74
6:9	71, 74
7:5	138
9:11	10
9:12	164
9:15	10
11:12	88
11:18	74
11:20	71

12:21	164
13:12	167
15:18	145
17:13	167
19:20	167
19:21	145
21:7	91, 146
21:21	167
23:15	141, 143
23:17	90
24:8	164
24:10	88
25:9-10	146
25:12	145
28	78
28:1	136
28:57	87
29:4	146
32:7	46
32:10	70
32:13	99
32:47	175
33:17	89
33:21	174
33:27	134
34:6	86
34:7	184

Joshua

1:8	144
3:17	175
4:3	175
4:14	167
5:15	146
6:7	94
7:21	135
8:11	86
9:7	94, 99
9:11	150, 177
10:24	84
11:16	184
12:3	70
12:20	90
13:20	70
15:4	91
15:55	96
18:12	91

18:14	91
18:19	91
21	145
23:15	189
24:3	135
24:8	135

Judges

4:19	87, 91
4:21	83
5:11	218
7:16	175
8:1	91
8:2	188
9:4	175
9:41	89
9:49	184
11:3	175
11:31	164
11:35	164
13:8	96
13:17	144, 147
13:18	89
15:14	87
18:21	96
18:29	96
19:9	145
20:7	186
21:19	69, 184
21:20	93
21:21	69, 184

1 Samuel

1:17	88
1:24	69, 184
1:28	164
2:16	186
2:24	75
2:35	26, 27
3:21	184
4:7	167
4:15	92
7:7	167
7:9	93
8:2	138
9:26	134
10:6	87

10:10	93
10:13	87
13:19	93
14:3	184
14:30	84
14:33	89
15:13	26, 27
15:16	94
17:4	176
17:11	167
17:17	84
17:23	176
17:35	95
17:46	164
19:17	164
20:2	186
21:3	164
22:15	99
23:19	70
23:24	70
24:19	135
25:8	86
25:31	99
25:33	164
26:1	70
26:3	70
28:8	99
28:24	86

2 Samuel
1:16	146
2:9	184
2:35	27
3:7	69
3:8	164
5:2	86
6:20	175
7:12	26, 27
7:21	96
7:23	96
10:17	83
10:19	167
11:1	83
11:24	84, 144
12:1	83
12:4	83
12:18	167

14:19	88
14:31	144
18:9	132
18:12	84
19:7	84
19:14	86
20:5	90
20:9	85
20:15	175
22:33	96
22:40	85
23:20	90

1 Kings
1:37	134
2:5	146
2:26	141
3:4	198
3:12	146
3:14	4, 5
6:12	26
7:23	133
7:36	5, 10
8:9	10
8:26	144, 147
8:29	144
8:40	167
8:48	163, 309
9:5	26
9:9	93
11:4	4, 5
11:36	4, 5
11:39	89
12:3	94
12:7	93
12:12	86
12:21	94
14:28	188
16:9	83
16:26	62
18:36	144, 147
21:21	86
21:23	175
21:29	86
22:13	144, 147
22:49	91

2 Kings

2:21	94
2:22	88
4:3	175
6:13	185
7:10	68
7:11	68
8:23	188
9:33	94
9:37	134
10:4	167
11:4	82
11:9	82
11:10	82
11:15	82
13:6	87
13:12	188
14:13	94
16:7	89
16:10	96
16:15	94
17:31	136
19:23	184, 185
19:25	88
20:13	184, 185
20:15	164
20:18	93
22:5	93
23:36	96
24:10	92

Isaiah

1:29	176
1:30	143
3:8	176
3:24	79
5:5	96
9:3	45
10:13	89, 174
10:16	218
10:33	94
15:1	48
15:3	184
15:5	145
16:7	184
16:8	96
18:4	99
18:7	169
20:2	146
22:5	169
23:1	168
23:3	70
23:12	168
26:1	175
26:20	99
27:5	96
28:12	84
28:15	186
28:16	96
28:27	96
29:3	26
29:8	175
30:5	84
30:6	138
32:11	78
33:4	79
33:7	79, 103
33:20	84
34:7	89
37:17	144, 145
37:19	93
37:26	88
39:2	184
39:7	93
40:4	142
40:31	111, 136
41:22	88
41:23	135
41:25	89
42:16	164
42:24	95
43:8	95
43:19	70
43:20	70
44:14	99
44:17	99
45:13	164
48:8	146
48:18	84
51:4	96
53:4	136
53:5	138
54:10	142
55:4	96

58:14	99	27:20	99
59:2	172	29:10	26
61:8	99	29:23	164
63:1	133	30:16	84, 89
63:15	145	30:18	199
63:19	84	31:34	96
		31:39	133
Jeremiah		32:35	87
1:5	99	33:8	99
2:3	184	33:9	136
2:10	168	33:14	26
2:13	218	33:19	195
2:15	91	33:26	199
2:18	70	38:11	111, 136
2:21	184	38:22	146
2:24	62	39:16	86
5:10	48	40:16	134
5:12	187	41:5	69, 184
5:24	187	42:16	134
6:17	26	44:7	138
6:21	41, 61	44:8	111, 136
7:12	69, 184	44:9	138
7:14	69, 184	46:27	199
8:6	184	48:6	142
8:10	184	48:31	184
9:17	87, 142	48:38	184
10:11	52, 149	48:41	92
11:16	96	49:17	145
15:10	164, 184	49:20	138, 187
15:16	144, 147	50:6	92
17:8	135	50:20	141
17:24	184, 185	51:9	94
18:5	195	51:19	199
18:10	133	51:29	92
18:21	142	51:56	92
18:23	135		
19:8	145	Ezekiel	
19:15	86	1:14	84
20:7	184	4:12	142
22:6	91	7:11	138
22:18	184	7:21	93
23:3	138	7:26	218
23:4	26	9:8	84
23:5	26	10:12	138
26:6	69, 111, 136, 184	11:15	184
26:9	69, 87, 184	12:14	184
27:1	91	13:19	142

14:4	83		36:10	184
16:34	96		36:13-15	136
16:57	83		37:6	174
16:59	163, 309		37:19	164
16:60	26, 27		37:22	92
16:62	26, 27, 28		39:2	164
17:10	188		39:11	184
20:18	96		39:26	87
20:40	184		40:48	176
21:21	88		41:8	87
21:28	99		41:15	83, 133
23:16	135		41:16	219
23:41	96		41:24	203
23:43	92, 135		42:5	86, 90
23:45	189		43:17	138
23:47	189		43:27	84
23:49	141		44:3	99
24:2	99		44:30	70
24:11	175		45:3	134
24:23	138		46:9	94
24:25	96		47:8	84
25:6	83		47:16	89
25:9	70		48:15	184
26:2	92		48:18	184
27:6	168		48:21	184
27:15	99			
27:19	97		Hosea	
28:14	135		2:5	164
28:16	87		2:7	56
28:24	84		2:17	45
28:26	84		3:5	5
29:3	164		4:6	83
30:23	163		7:6	138
31:5	83		7:16	185
31:11	164		8:12	99
31:15	174		9:15	90
31:18	184		10:14	84, 89, 97
32:25	145		13:2	184
32:31	184			
32:32	184, 185		Joel	
33:25	138		2:6	84
34:14	138		4:19	84
34:23	4, 26			
34:29	26		Amos	
35:11	142		4:3	143
35:12	92		4:4-5	93
36:5	83		7:8	99

8:2	99		14:3	45
9:4	145		14:4	175
Obadiah			Psalms	
1:20	175		2:12	185
			6:4	135
Jonah			10:9	184
1:14	84		10:15	100
			11:1	86
Micah			12:7	144
1:3	99		16:10	143
1:8	151		18:35	92
1:15	86		18:40	85
2:6	218		18:47	198
2:12	142		20:4	145
3:2	133		21:2	142
5:4	137		22:22	89
6:3	174		27:5	184
7:17	167		29:6	89
			31:5	97
Nahum			36:7	144
1:3	100		37:39	97
1:12	164		42:9	184
2:1	100, 184		42:10	90
2:8	138		43:2	97
2:11	84		45:10	95, 96
			45:14	97
Habakkuk			49:6	97
1:9	184		50:13	90
1:15	184		51:4	135
2:2	10		52:9	97
2:3	200		55:16	70
			58:8	87
Zephaniah			68:8	70
2:9	111		68:14	92
			68:29	97
Haggai			73:2	91
1:8	134		74:4	218
1:12	88		74:6	135
1:14	88		77:13	146
2:2	88		78:40	70
			78:60	69
Zechariah			78:63	97
1:16	133		81:2	97
5:9	87		89:5	219
11:5	89		89:11	94
12:3	136		89:29	100

90:4	45		Job	
90:8	138, 180		1:10	135
90:15	46		1:21	87
92:11	89		3:8	46
95:8	45		5:7	97
99:6	89		5:12	97
101:5	100		6:14	87
102:5	97		6:19	177
105:18	62		6:19-20	93
105:28	62		8:8	88
106:14	70		9:9	177
107:4	70		14:3	144, 145
114:8	185		15:5	97
119	143		15:31	88
119:9	143		16:16	91
119:11	144		17:5	142
119:16	143		18:3	87
119:17	143, 144		22:1	177
119:25	143		22:6	97
119:28	143		22:28	132
119:37	144		31:7	89
119:41	144		32-35	84
119:42	143		32:11	85
119:65	143		32:18	87
119:74	144		33:21	90
119:81	144		38:11	184
119:98	145		39:9	89
119:101	143		39:10	89
119:102	174		41:17	87
119:105	143		42:2	163, 309
119:107	143		42:5	145
119:147	144, 147		42:12	170
119:148	144			
119:160	143		Proverbs	
119:161	144, 147		1:10	85
119:169	144		5:18	145
127:2	83		6:21	145
132:12	185		10:4	83
134:2	138		11:25	83
139:20	86, 87		12:11	175
140:13	163, 309		16:27	62
143:10	198		16:30	83
144:13	91		22:8	100
145:1	198		22:11	100
145:6	97		22:14	100
145:8	100		25:27	219
			27:10	133

28:15	79	1:4	97
28:19	175	2:9	145
29:18	138	6:3	97
30:17	95	9:27	93
30:18	134		
31:16	134	Daniel	
31:18	133	1:4	89
		1:15	141
Ruth		2:4-7:28	149
1:8	135	2:5	98
1:14	87, 142	3:10	98
1:20	83	3:29	92
2:3	143	5:6	98
2:9	87	5:21	98
2:20	138	7:10	98
3:15	86	8:8	143
4:4	134	9:5	145
4:7	97	9:12	62
4:7-8	146	9:16	145
4:21-22	219	9:18	135
		11:10	184, 326
Song of Songs		11:19	97
4:4	4	11:24	218
4:9	164	11:30	132, 168
		11:44	83
Qohelet			
1:6	218	Ezra	
1:10	138	2:64	84
3:14	167	2:69	91
4:8	62	3:3	93, 326
4:14	86	4:7	326
7:22	135	4:8-6:18	149
10:8	97	6:21	111, 136
11:9	145	7:6	323
		7:12-26	149
Lamentations		8:18	90
1:7	144	8:25	100
1:12	219	10:12	144, 147
2:7	45		
2:8	175	Nehemiah	
2:22	45	2:7	90
3:12	83	2:17	90
4:17	91	2:20	90
5:1	135	3:5	87
5:21	134	3:13	86
		3:14	86
Esther		3:15	94

5:7	84, 89
5:13	175
6:8	89
6:16	167
7:65	97
7:66	84
7:71	84
9:6	135
9:32	138
10:1	136
10:38	70
11:15	97
12:38	84, 90
13:10	92
13:16	84
13:23	100

1 Chronicles

1:7	168
1:10	33
1:38	70
1:41	70
1:42	70
2:48	69
2:49	83
3:5	97
4:30	95
5:26	83, 89
7:15	142
7:34	100
11:22	90
11:31	95
12:1	95
12:21	95
12:39	88
13:5	70
17:2	27
17:11	26, 27
17:19	97
18:10	100
20:8	97
21:24	183
26:7	84
27:18	84

2 Chronicles

| 2:7 | 97 |

5:10	10
7:18	26, 27, 28
9:10	97
9:11	97
9:21	97
13:7	175
31:7	95
32:13	111, 136
32:17	111, 136
34:22	100
36:14	100

Scholar Index

Abayye 72
Abravanel 133
Agresti, A. 19, 206, 240, 242, 288
Aharoni, Y. 36, 166
Albright, W. F. v, vi, viii, ix, xi, 63
Althann, R. 45
Andersen, F. I. 33, 38, 52, 139, 144, 167, 189, 217, 219, 220, 310
Baillet, M. 176
Bange, L. A. 38, 63, 64, 65, 85, 92
Barr, J. 76, 102
Barth, J. 46, 126
Barthelemy, D. 73
Bauer, H. 2, 36, 41, 160, 193, 310, 326
Becker, R. A. 217, 291
Bishop, Y. 16, 23, 240, 243, 244
Blake, F. R. 53
Blau, J. 45, 63, 127, 160
Bonk, H. 6
Bravmann, M. M. 46
Breuer, M. 78, 99, 314
Brock, S. P. 44
Cassuto, U. vi
Chambers, J. M. 217, 291
Chavel, C. B. 72
Clogg, C. 288
Cowley, A. 68, 93, 95, 111, 112, 114, 326
Cramer, H. 23
Cross, F. M. viii, ix, 33, 54, 59, 61, 63, 64, 65, 115, 314
Dahood, M. v-xi, xiii, xv, 31, 63
Delitzsch, F. 77
Dhorme, E. 93
Diakonoff, I. M. 102

Dion, P.-E. 55, 58
Eissfeldt, O. 204
Feller, W. 110
Fienberg, S. 16, 18, 23, 206, 207, 240, 241, 243, 244, 288
Forbes, A. D. 189
Freedman, D. N. ix, xiii, xv, 5, 6, 33, 38, 49, 52, 54, 56, 60, 61, 63, 64, 65, 139, 140, 141, 144, 177, 191, 192, 313, 322
Frensdorff, S. 27, 99, 135, 175
Gasov-Ginsberg, A. 48
Garbini, G. 37
Gelb, I. J. 58
Gesenius, W. 68, 93, 95, 111, 112, 114, 326
Gibson, J. 36
Gill, J. 76
Ginsberg, H. L. vi, 58, 126
Ginsburg, C. D. 4, 27, 29, 71, 72, 74, 77, 78, 80, 82, 84, 88, 90, 95, 99, 100, 133, 135, 137, 143, 149, 152, 175, 176, 184, 185, 325
Girdlestone, R. B. xiii
Gokhale, D. V. 243
Goodwin, D. W. 63
Gordis, R. 28, 29, 62, 73, 76, 82, 86, 91, 149, 185, 186, 194, 325
Gordon, R. vi, 85
Goshen-Gottstein, M. 73, 78
Grabbe, L. L. 76
Greenberg, M. 2
Hahn, H. 100
Hamming, R. W. 105, 107
Harary, F. 123
Harris, Z. S. 37, 41, 42, 49, 53, 63
Höfner, M. 44, 45

Holland, P. 16, 23, 240, 243, 244
Houtman, C. 320
Ibn Adoniyahu 74
Ibn Ezra 2, 72, 77, 79
Isaacson, D. L. 107, 123, 124
Jamme, A. 45
Josephus 71
Kahle, P. 2, 3, 32, 36
Kautzsch, E. 68, 93, 95, 111, 112, 114, 326
Kennicott 80
Koehler, L. 84, 192
Kullback, S. 243
Kutscher, E. 5, 46, 89, 90, 91, 96, 140, 160, 180, 188, 310
Lambdin, T. O. 82, 185
Leander, P. 2, 36, 41, 160, 193, 310, 326
Leiman, S. Z. 60
Levita 27, 133, 137, 149, 185, 186
Liebetrau, A. 23
Lipstein, B. 123
Loewenstamm, S. 63
Lowth, R. 76
Madsen, R. W. 107, 123, 124
Maimonides, M. 80
Mandelkern, S. 14
Martin, M. 70, 90
Mathews, K. A. 49, 191, 313, 322
Morag, S. 32, 76
Murtonen, A. 2, 3, 14, 70
Nachmanides 72
Naveh, J. 31, 322
O'Connor, M. 31, 63, 65
Orlinsky, H. M. 62, 135, 181
Owen, J. 76
Pardee, D. 56
Parunak, H. V. D. 58, 166
Parzen, E. 124
R. Abulafua 79
R. J. Ashkenazi 80
R. Hillel 73
R. Ishmael 71, 74

R. Isaac 72
R. Joseph 72
R. Meir Nehmad 80
R. Nehemiah 134
R. Ramban 72
R. Shammai 73
R. Simeon 74
R. Tam 74
Rahlfs, A. 70
Rainey, A. F. 45
Rashi 75
Rendsburg, G. 135
Rivkin, E. 320
Romesburg, H. 290, 291, 308
de Rossi, J. 80
Sachs, L. 8, 206
Sarfatti, G. B. 31, 45, 56, 58, 59, 63, 67, 166
Scholem, G. 80
Segal, M. H. 188
Segert, S. 37
Snaith, N. 28, 100, 188
Sperber, A. 46, 75, 79, 82, 133, 134, 219
Stade, B. 6
Styan, G. 123
Suen, C. Y. 108, 109
Talmon, S. 134
Torczyner, H. 45
Viganò, L. 46
Weil, G. E. 92, 186, 311
Weinberg, W. xii, 37, 310
Wernberg-Møller, P. 90, 176
Würthwein, E. 2, 3
Yeivin, I. 32
Zadok, R. 59
Zeitlin, S. 134
Zevit, Z. 59, 61, 63, 64, 65, 81, 166

Subject Index

/ā/, spelling of, 179-181
A, 5, 26, 28, 78, 79, 80, 82, 86, 87, 95, 99, 100, 188, 218
Akkadian, 45
alef
  mater lectionis, 49, 81-91, 132
  omitted, 85
  redundant, 84, 88
alphabet
  Aramaean, 31, 34
  Canaanite, 31
  Hebrew, 1
  Northwest Semitic, 53
  Phoenician, 31, 32, 52
  Ugaritic, 31
alphabetic writing, 31-33
  Northwest Semitic, 318
Amarna, 45
analogy, tenement, 25, 241, 242
  introduction of, 15-16
analysis of types, discussion of, 284-287
anti-repetition spelling rule, 111
anti-successive-syllables spelling rule, 111
Arad, 133, 168, 170
Arad ostraca, 36, 45, 48, 56, 166
  assessment of spelling of, 56
Aramaean, 31, 34
Aramaic, 37, 40, 43, 47, 50, 51, 53, 54, 55, 59, 81, 82, 92, 98, 193, 324
  square characters, 321, 323
association
  introduction of, 22-23
  portion and choice, 244
  section and vowel pair, 113
  verse-parity, 24
assumption, type preservation, 116

assumptions needed for separability, 125
attributes, standardization of, 290-291
autograph writer, spelling choices of, 101
Babylonian MS240, 144, 168
Barth-Ginsberg dissimilation, 126
BH3, 219
BHS, 27, 29, 95, 143, 219
books, post-exilic, 94, 184, 190, 311
British Museum G86, 80
C, 5, 26, 27, 87, 99, 146, 218
Canaanite, 31, 53, 64
chain
  convergence, 123
  effect examples, 118-123
  equations, 124
  memory loss, 123
  nonstationary, 123
  strong, 120-121
  weak, 121-123, 122
channel
  definition of, 106
  description of, 115-118
  effects on text, 110
  effects, options for dealing with, 125
  equations, 117
  probabilities, 116
characteristics of source-encoder, 109-115
checking clustering results, 308
Chernoff faces, 292
  introduction of, 291
chi-square
  distribution, 20
  statistic for large datasets, 240
  statistic, definition of, 19

threshold, definition of, 20
choice of
  ketib text, 28-29
  manuscript studied, 25-30
  spelling, 101-102
classification of vowels, 155-156
clustering
  complete linkage, 294-297
  furthest-neighbor, 294
  hierarchical, 294-297
  results, checking, 308
  sequence, 298
complete linkage clustering, 294-297
components of our problem, 30
conclusions, 326-328
confidence intervals
  definition of, 8
  for 'David', 9
  for "invariants", 151
  for -$\bar{o}t$, 11-14
  for 'three', 10
confidence level, definition of, 21
confidence region for proximity data, 217
confounding factors, possible, 214
contingency table
  collapsed, 244
  definition of collapsed, 242
  definition of marginal, 242
  definition of partial, 242
  marginal, 243, 289
  partial, 243, 289
contingency table analysis
  and double-vowel incidence, 113-114
  and portions, 205
  applicability of, 123
  for stress change, 220
  for types, 246-284
  log-multiplicative, 288
  ordinal, 288
  procedures, 16
  results, discussion of, 284-287

three-dimensional, 241
verse-parity, 24-25
cophenetic correlation coefficient, introduction of, 308
copyists'
  attitudes, 99
  mistakes, 14
  mistakes, views on seriousness of, 72-73
  spelling decisions, 102
Cramér's v, 243, 244
  as measure of association, 23, 240
  definition of, 23
  for channel input, 119
  for double-vowel analysis, 113
  for weak channel output, 123
critiques of Cross and Freedman analysis, 63-65
Cross and Freedman analysis, 54, 63
data
  displaying the, 291-293
  preparing the, 289-291
'David', spelling of, 4
decoder, definition of, 106
defective spelling, definition of, 1
definitions
  channel, 106
  chi-square statistic, 19
  chi-square threshold, 20
  confidence interval, 8
  confidence level, 21
  contingency table, collapsed, 242
  contingency table, marginal, 242
  contingency table, partial, 242
  Cramér's v, 23
  decoder, 106
  defective spelling, 1
  degrees of freedom, 21
  diacritics, 66
  encoder, 106
  equilibrium, 120

degrees of freedom
  definition of, 21
  in double-vowel analysis, 113
  in -ōt analysis, 21-22
  reckoning of, 243
dendrogram, introduction of, 296
dendrograms, 299-307
  interpretation of, 298
diacritics, definition of, 66
diphthong
  aw, spelling of, 44-48
  ay, spelling of, 48-49
  contraction of word-terminal, 42
  monophthongization of ancient, 44-49
  spelling of primal, 49-51
  word-medial, 51
diphthongization, secondary, 38
displaying the data, 291-293
distance, 294, 295
  in higher dimensional space, 293
document
  D, 165
  E, 165
  J, 165
  P, 14, 165, 190, 191, 313, 314
documentary source, 189
documents, model of independence for, 189
double-vowel incidence analysis, 111-114
  /ē/, spelling of, 170-178
  /ḗ/, spelling of, 178-179
effect of
  lexeme frequency, 221-230
  proximity, 214-221
  sample size, 7
  stress, 230-239
  word length, 158
el-Kadr javelin, 85
encoder
  definition of, 106

statistics, effects of Markov chain on, 118-121
epigraphic material. *See also* inscriptions
Amarna, 45
Arad, 133, 168, 170
Arad ostraca, 36, 45, 48, 56, 166
el-Kadr javelin, 85
Gezer Calendar, 33, 34, 51, 52, 56
Gibeon wine-jar handles, 198
Hadad, 44, 55, 59, 60, 197
Kilamuwa, 85, 184
Lachish Letters, 45, 169, 170, 184, 325
Mesha, 65, 85, 197
Murabbaᶜat phylactery, 70, 71
Panamuwa, 44, 55, 59, 60, 197
Samaria ostraca, 48, 59
Siloam Tunnel Inscription, 38, 41, 45, 46, 55, 61, 85, 169
Silwan Epitaph, 60
Tell Fekhereye, 33, 34, 43, 52, 55, 59, 60, 133
Tell-Qasile Ostracon, 55, 197
Yavneh-Yam, 61, 325
equilibrium, 121
  definition of, 120
error-free theory, 121-123
  introduction of, 103
Ethiopic, 47, 193
Ezra, 320, 322, 323
'fathers', spelling of, 227
frequency effect, 221-230
furthest-neighbor clustering, 294
Genesis Apocryphon, 185
Gezer Calendar, 33, 34, 51, 52, 56
  assessment of spelling of, 56-57
Gibeon wine-jar handles, 198
goodness of fit
  assessing, 20-22

measuring, 19-20

Hadad, 44, 55, 59, 60, 197

hapax legomena, 75, 129

he

as *mater lectionis*, 38-44, 91-92, 132-135, 311

syncope of intervocalic, 41

hierarchical clustering, 294-297

'his', spelling of, 39-43

historical spelling, 35

argument, 36

history of spelling in the Hebrew Bible, 318-326

homogeneity of strong chain output, 121

homogeneous

portions, input of, 119

text, hypothetical, 7

/ī/, spelling of, 163-170

ignorance model, introduction of, 17

indifference theory

assessing the, 241-246

introduction of, 103

untenable, 244-245

information theory and textual transmission, 105-107

inhomogeneity of weak chain output, 121

inscriptions. *See also* epigraphic material

Aramaic, 50

pointing of, 36

pre-exilic, 39, 40, 42, 45, 56, 61, 67, 81, 160, 166, 168, 318, 319

usefulness of information from, 31

introduction of

association, 22-23

Chernoff faces, 291

cophenetic correlation coefficient, 308

dendrogram, 296

error-free theory, 103

ignorance model, 17

indifference theory, 103

mixed theory, 103

model of independence, 17-18

resemblance matrix, 295

tenement analogy, 15-16

verse parity, 23-25

'is not?', spelling of, 187

ketib text, 9, 11, 111, 112

choice of, 28-29

ketib/qere

text, 111, 112, 149, 154

variants, 28-29, 73, 93, 134, 143, 144, 147, 180, 185, 325

Kilamuwa, 85, 184

L, 5, 10, 26, 27, 28, 29, 62, 70, 78, 79, 83, 84, 86, 87, 89, 92, 95, 96, 99, 100, 103, 105, 124, 132, 135, 137, 138, 142, 145, 146, 151, 154, 173, 175, 184, 185, 186, 187, 188, 218, 329

Lachish Letters, 45, 169, 170, 184, 325

languages

Akkadian, 45

Aramaic, 37, 40, 43, 47, 50, 51, 53, 54, 55, 59, 81, 82, 92, 98, 193, 324

Canaanite, 53, 64

Ethiopic, 47, 193

Moabite, 34, 35, 37, 51

Old South Arabic, 44

Old South Canaanite, 160, 194

Phoenician, 37, 50, 57, 63, 319, 323, 327, 328

Ugaritic, 37, 41, 43, 59, 63, 64

Ya'udi, 55, 58

lexeme

definition of globally frequent, 223

definition of locally frequent, 221

fixed, 153-154

frequency effect, 221-230

frequency threshold, definition of, 221

lexeme frequency threshold, 221
lexemes, globally frequent, 223
lexemes, locally frequent, 221
Markov chain, 117
mater lectionis, 1
opportunity for spelling choice, 104
outlier, 22-23
Pearson's chi-square, 19
plene spelling, 1
portions, five/ten/thirty, 212-213
portions, seventy-six, 209-211
residual outlier threshold, 22
residuals, standardized, 19
sampling zero, 163
sink, 106
source, 106
spelling choice opportunity, 104
standardized residuals, 19
structural zero, 163
Type 1, 163-165
Type 2, 165
Type 3, 165-166
Type 4, 166
Type 5, 167
Type 6, 167-168
Type 7, 168-169
Type 8, 169
Type 9, 169
Type 10, 169
Type 11, 170
Type 12, 170
Type 13, 170-172
Type 14, 173
Type 15, 173
Type 16, 174
Type 17, 174-175
Type 18, 175-176
Type 19, 176
Type 20, 177
Type 21, 177
Type 22, 177
Type 23, 178
Type 24, 178
Type 25, 178
Type 26, 179
Type 27, 179-180
Type 28, 180-181
Type 29, 181
Type 30, 181-182
Type 31, 182-186
Type 32, 186-188
Type 33, 189-191
Type 34, 191
Type 35, 191-192
Type 36, 192
Type 37, 192-193
Type 38, 193
Type 39, 193-194
Type 40, 194
Type 41, 195
Type 42, 195
Type 43, 195
Type 44, 196
Type 45, 196
Type 46, 196-197
Type 47, 197
Type 48, 197
Type 49, 198
Type 50, 198
Type 51, 199
Type 52, 199
Type 53, 199
Type 54, 199
Type 55, 200-201
Type 56, 201
Type 57, 201
Type 58, 201-202
Type 59, 202
Type 60, 202
Type 61, 202
Type 62, 203
Type 63, 203
Type 64, 203
Type 65, 204
updater, 115
vowel types, 162

'like', spelling of, 182

log-likelihood ratio statistic, 243

long /ō/ paths, 159-161

long vowels, plene spelling of, 81-94

LXX, 70, 137, 144, 145, 172, 176, 200, 316

manuscripts
1QIs^a, 5, 26, 128, 132, 133, 140, 146, 176, 218, 310
1QIs^b, 132, 133
4Q161, 5
4Q174, 5
4Q177, 5
4QExod^f, 191
4QSam^b, 314, 316
11QpaleoLev, 191
A, 5, 26, 28, 78, 79, 80, 82, 86, 87, 95, 99, 100, 188, 218
Babylonian MS240, 144, 168
British Museum G86, 80
C, 5, 26, 27, 87, 99, 146, 218
Genesis Apocryphon, 185
L, 5, 10, 26, 27, 28, 29, 62, 70, 78, 79, 83, 84, 86, 87, 89, 92, 95, 96, 99, 100, 103, 105, 124, 132, 135, 137, 138, 142, 145, 146, 151, 154, 173, 175, 184, 185, 186, 187, 188, 218, 329
LXX, 70, 137, 144, 145, 172, 176, 200, 316
Nash Papyrus, 188
P, 26, 27, 70, 79, 84, 89, 95, 99, 136, 137, 144, 146, 164, 186, 187
Rabbinic Bible, 28
Samaritan Pentateuch, 14, 46, 70, 134, 147, 176, 183
Snaith, 28, 100, 188
studied, choice of, 25-30
Tittle Bible, 80

marginal associations, 238

marginals, standardization of, 289-290

Markov chain. See chain

definition of, 117

effects of, 118-121

Markov channel. See channel

Markov model of source-encoder, 110

Markov process, 107-109
backward, 110

Markov property, 109

Markovian order of source-encoder, 111

masoretic vocalization, 76

Massora, 4, 27, 70, 134, 143, 164
Mm 18, 96
Mm 27, 187
Mm 605, 144
Mm 681, 186, 187
Mm 816, 27
Mm 822, 199
Mm 898, 88
Mm 907, 84
Mm 1145, 144
Mm 1267, 146
Mm 2264, 185
Mm 2480, 185
Mm 2489, 69
Mm 2841, 27
Mm 3226, 198
Mm 3440, 100

mater lectionis
ambiguity-resolving use of, 2
arguments based on, 73-75
definition of, 1
fortuitous use of, 2
mystical use of, 2
rule-governed use of, 2
space-saving nonuse of, 2
use and nonuse of, 2-3

matres lectionis
biblical development of, 67-70
development of, 66-81
evolution of, 52, 54
further pre-exilic developments of, 55-60
in MT, 66
letters used as, 32

long vowels, summary of, 94
masoretic development of, 76-79
masoretic period, 76
modern development of, 81
origin of, 53
post-exilic developments of, 60-62
post-exilic use of, 51
post-masoretic development of, 79-81
pre-masoretic development of, 70-71
Qumran, 70
rabbinic development of, 71-76
used for word-internal long vowels, 57-60
mean-cell population rule, 207
measure of association. *See* Cramér's v
mechanics of
type assignment, 204
vowel marking, 149-154
Mesha, 65, 85, 197
metric in higher dimensional space, 293
Midrash on לוּחַ, 10
minimal expected cell-size rule, 206
Mishnah, 68, 331
mixed theory, 103
Moabite, 34, 35, 37, 51
model
contingency, three-dimensional, 241-242
of independence for documents, 189
of independence, introduction of, 17-18
log-multiplicative, 288
of probabilistic text generation, 108
of source-encoder, Markov, 110
monophthongization of ancient diphthong, 44-49

Mr. Vowel, 15, 291
multidimensional scaling, 330
Murabbaᶜat phylactery, 70, 71
Nash Papyrus, 188
non-opportunities
elimination of, 130-131
statistical, 329
nonuse of
defective option, 132-149
plene option, 131-132
Northwest Semitic, 53
alphabetic writing, 318
writing, stages of, 32-33
'not', spelling of, 186
/ō/, spelling of, 10, 162, 181-201
Old South Arabic, 44
Old South Canaanite, 160, 194
opportunity for spelling choice, definition of, 104
options for dealing with channel effects, 125
ordinal contingency table analysis for stress change, 220
-ōt
in documents, spelling of, 189
spelling of, 11-14
outlier
definition of, 22-23
detection via data displays, 293
patterns for type analysis, 284-287
outliers
Former Prophets, 285
Latter Prophets, 286
leave-one-out strategy for discovering, 244
Other Writings, 287
Pentateuchal, 285
Poetry, 286
P, 26, 27, 70, 79, 84, 89, 95, 99, 136, 137, 144, 146, 164, 186, 187

Panamuwa, 44, 55, 59, 60, 197
partial associations, 238
Pearson's chi-square, definition of, 19
period, pre-exilic, 36, 198
Philippi's law, 166, 310
Phoenician, 31, 32, 37, 50, 52, 57, 63, 319, 323, 327, 328
plene spelling
  definition of, 1
  of long vowels, 81-94
  of short /i/, 95
  of short /o/, 98-100
  of short /u/, 95
  of short vowels, 95-100
portion hierarchy, 212
portioning
  need for careful text, 205
  philosophy of, 206-207
portions
  and contingency table analysis, 205
  definition of five/ten/thirty, 212-213
  definition of seventy-six, 209-211
  distance between, 289
  ordering the, 288-289
possible confounding factors, 214
possible improvement, 329-331
  clustering method, 330
  encoder-channel impasse, 330
  lexemes out, 329
  mixed types, 329
  other metrics, 330
  proper nouns, 330
  proximity range, 330
  sparse tables, 330
  stress effects, 330
  text choice, 329
post-exilic
  books, 94, 184, 190, 311
  developments of *matres lectionis*, 60-62
  practice for 'David', 5

use of *matres lectionis*, 51
pre-exilic
  inscriptions, 39, 40, 42, 45, 56, 61, 67, 81, 160, 166, 168, 318, 319
  practice for 'David', 5
  spelling, 63
preparing the data, 289-291
primal diphthongs, spelling of, 49-51
Primary History, 100, 114, 161, 166, 188, 296, 313, 315, 317, 318, 322, 328, 331
  publication date of, 60
  spelling practice in, 61
probabilistic
  spelling rule, 109
  text generation model, 108
probability
  coin flipping, 20
  conditional, 108
  simple, 108
  spelling choice, 7-9
problem, components of our, 30
'prophets', spelling of, 229
proximal pairs, spelling of, 215
proximity
  and stress, 220
  effect, 214-221
quantitating similarity, 293-294
Qumran, 5, 70, 81, 89, 90, 91, 98, 128, 129, 132, 133, 140, 150, 176, 180, 183, 188, 194, 310, 313, 319, 321, 322, 331
1QIs^a, 5, 26, 128, 132, 133, 140, 146, 176, 218, 310
1QIs^b, 132, 133
4Q161, 5
4Q174, 5
4Q177, 5
4QExod^l, 191
4QSam^b, 314, 316
11QpaleoLev, 191
Rabbinic Bible, 28
regression analysis for proximity, 217

rejected cell pairs, 290
relative frequencies, interpreting, 6-9
resemblance matrix, 295-296
residual outlier threshold
definition of, 22
double-vowel, 113
residuals
definition of standardized, 19
for documents, 189
for double-vowel analysis, 113
rule
anti-repetition spelling, 111
anti-successive-syllables
spelling, 111
mean-cell population, 207
minimal expected cell-size,
206
probabilistic spelling, 109
spelling, 35-36, 62, 318, 321
text portioning, 206
word-terminal spelling, 111
word-terminal vowel spelling,
2
rules
GKC's spelling, 110
scribal spelling, 72, 73
summary of GKC spelling, 114
winnowing, 150-151
Samaria ostraca, 48, 59
Samaritan Pentateuch, 14, 46,
70, 134, 147, 176, 183
sample size, effect of, 7, 20
sampling zero, definition of,
163
scribal rules, 72, 73
separability, assumptions
needed for, 125
Septuagint. See LXX
short
/i/, plene spelling of, 95
/o/, plene spelling of, 98-100
/u/, plene spelling of, 95
vowels, plene spelling of, 95-
100
vowels, spelling of, 129

significance level. One minus
confidence level, which see
Siloam Tunnel Inscription, 38,
41, 45, 46, 55, 61, 85, 169
Silwan Epitaph, 60
similarity
discovering, 294-297
quantitating, 293-294
sink, definition of, 106
sledding, heavy, 115-125
Snaith edition, 28, 100, 188
source, definition of, 106
source-encoder
and channel separability,
124-125
characteristics, 109-115
spelling
aesthetic, 104
argument, historical, 36
change mechanisms, 102-103
choice, 101-102, 104
choice opportunity, definition of, 104
choice probability, 7-9
conditions fixing, 126-128
conventional, 51
critiques of Cross and Freedman analysis of, 63-65
Cross and Freedman analysis
of, 54, 63
definition of plene, 1
effects of proximity on, 205
effects of stress on, 205
error-free theory of, 103
fixed (proper nouns), 130
historical, 35, 52-5
hypothesis, 101-102
in Former Prophets, 314-315
in Hebrew Bible, history of,
318-326
in Major Prophets, 315
in Minor Prophets, 315-316
in the Bible, 312-318
in the Writings, 316
in Torah, 313-314

spelling (*continued*)
  indifference theory of, 103
  mixed theory of, 103
  needed, study of, 78
  of /ā/, 179-181
  of 'David', 4
  of diphthong *aw*, 44-48
  of diphthong *ay*, 48-49
  of /ē/, 170-178
  of /ɛ̄/, 178-179
  of 'fathers', 227
  of 'his', 39-43
  of /ī/, 163-170
  of 'is not?', 187
  of 'like', 182
  of long vowels, *plene*, 81-94
  of 'not', 186
  of /ō/, 10, 162, 181-201
  of -ōt, 11-14
  of -ōt in documents, 189
  of primal diphthongs, 49-51
  of 'prophets', 229
  of proximal pairs, 215
  of short /i/, *plene*, 95
  of short /o/, *plene*, 98-100
  of short /u/, *plene*, 95
  of short vowels, 129
  of short vowels, *plene*, 95-100
  of theophoric names, 41
  of 'three', 9-10
  of /ū/, 10, 201-204
  of 'unto', 171
  of 'upon', 172
  of vowel classes, 129, 130
  of word classes, 129
  of word-terminal /ā/ in MT, 57
  of words, 129
  options, 104
  phonetic, 37
  practice in Primary History versus rest, 61
  practice, Hebrew, 1-4
  pre-exilic, 63
  ridiculous, study of, 77-78
  rule, 35-36, 62, 321
  rule, probabilistic, 109
  rules, 318
  rules, GKC's, 110
  rules, summary of GKC, 114
  scribal, 101
  statistically invariant, 133, 151-153
  study of Hebrew, 63-65
stage of development
  biblical, 67-70
  masoretic vocalization, 76-79
  modern, 81
  post-masoretic, 79-81
  pre-masoretic, 70-71
  rabbinic, 71-76
stages of development, 66-81
  Northwest Semitic writing, 32-33
standardization of
  attributes, 290-291
  marginals, 289-290
standardized residuals, definition of, 19
stress
  and proximity, 220
  category ordering, 231
  controlling for, 238
  effects, 230-239
  grades of, 157
  levels across MT, 232
  patterns, 156-158
structural zero, 25
  definition of, 163
Talmud, 72, 73, 74, 75, 81, 322
  Babylonian, 134
  Jerusalem, 134
telephone example, 107
Tell Fekhereye, 33, 34, 43, 52, 55, 59, 60, 133
Tell-Qasile Ostracon, 55, 197
tenement analogy, 25, 241, 242
  introduction of, 15-16
text
  Aramaic, 149
  hypothetical homogeneous, 7
  portion hierarchy, 213
  portioning mechanics, 207-208

portioning philosophy, 206
portioning rule, 206
transmission channel, description of, 115-118
transmission system, information theoretic nature of, 106
transmission and information theory, 105-107
transmission, theories of, 102-104
textus receptus, 79, 80, 81, 86, 87, 145, 312
theophoric names, spelling of, 41
theories of textual transmission, 102-104
'three', spelling of, 9-10
Tittle Bible, 80
transmission channel equations, 117
type
  assignment, mechanics of, 204
  preservation assumption, 116
Type 1, 58
  analysis of, 246
  definition of, 163-165
Type 2, 166, 241, 293
  analysis of, 246
  definition of, 165
Type 3, 163
  analysis of, 247
  definition of, 165-166
Type 4, 139, 174, 192, 310
  analysis of, 247
  definition of, 166
Type 5, 78, 173, 293
  analysis of, 248
  definition of, 167
Type 6, 136, 205, 228, 246, 318
  analysis of, 249
  definition of, 167-168
Type 7, 196, 329
  analysis of, 249
  definition of, 168-169
Type 8, 250

analysis of, 249
definition of, 169
Type 9, 226, 228, 297
  analysis of, 251
  definition of, 169
Type 10, 243, 309
  analysis of, 252
  definition of, 169
Type 11
  analysis of, 253
  definition of, 170
Type 12, 309
  analysis of, 253
  definition of, 170
Type 13, 228, 309
  analysis of, 254
  definition of, 170-172
Type 14, 136, 228, 229, 242, 246, 309, 318
  analysis of, 254
  definition of, 173
Type 15, 167, 310
  analysis of, 255
  definition of, 173
Type 16
  analysis of, 255
  definition of, 174
Type 17, 139, 310
  analysis of, 255
  definition of, 174-175
Type 18
  analysis of, 256
  definition of, 175-176
Type 19, 175, 257, 310, 329
  analysis of, 256
  definition of, 176
Type 20, 329
  analysis of, 257
  definition of, 177
Type 21
  analysis of, 258
  definition of, 177
Type 22
  analysis of, 258
  definition of, 177
Type 23
  analysis of, 259

definition of, 178
Type 24
  analysis of, 259
  definition of, 178
Type 25, 141, 147, 228, 229, 245, 285, 318
  analysis of, 259
  definition of, 178
Type 26, 141, 147
  analysis of, 260
  definition of, 179
Type 27, 133, 135, 150, 311
  analysis of, 260
  definition of, 179-180
Type 28, 133, 150, 311
  analysis of, 260
  definition of, 180-181
Type 29, 133, 150, 311
  analysis of, 261
  definition of, 181
Type 30, 183, 205, 208
  analysis of, 261
  definition of, 181-182
Type 31, 61, 160, 185, 193, 230, 245, 285, 297, 318, 330
  analysis of, 261
  definition of, 182-186
Type 32, 226, 230
  analysis of, 262
  definition of, 186-188
Type 33, 72, 226, 245
  analysis of, 262
  definition of, 189-191
Type 34, 196, 285, 312, 329
  analysis of, 263
  definition of, 191
Type 35, 69, 200, 312
  analysis of, 264
  definition of, 191-192
Type 36, 312
  analysis of, 264
  definition of, 192
Type 37, 193, 200
  analysis of, 265
  definition of, 192-193
Type 38, 183, 200, 312
  analysis of, 266

definition of, 193
Type 39, 78, 141, 160, 200, 312
  analysis of, 266
  definition of, 193-194
Type 40, 195, 199, 234
  analysis of, 267
  definition of, 194
Type 41
  analysis of, 267
  definition of, 195
Type 42, 196, 226, 227, 234
  analysis of, 268
  definition of, 195
Type 43, 191, 196, 234
  analysis of, 268
  definition of, 195
Type 44, 193, 234
  analysis of, 269
  definition of, 196
Type 45
  analysis of, 270
  definition of, 196
Type 46, 285, 297, 329, 330
  analysis of, 270
  definition of, 196-197
Type 47, 141, 193, 200, 224, 227, 232, 233, 234, 235, 238, 312
  analysis of, 270
  definition of, 197
  stress levels across MT, 233
Type 48, 141, 193, 200, 229, 232, 233, 234, 235, 238, 245, 312
  analysis of, 272
  definition of, 197
  stress levels across MT, 234
Type 49, 200, 297, 312, 330
  analysis of, 273
  definition of, 198
Type 50, 297, 329, 330
  analysis of, 274
  definition of, 198
Type 51, 229, 245, 297, 329
  analysis of, 275
  definition of, 199

Type 52
  analysis of, 276
  definition of, 199
Type 53
  analysis of, 276
  definition of, 199
Type 54, 312
  analysis of, 277
  definition of, 199
Type 55, 228, 278, 312
  analysis of, 277
  definition of, 200-201
Type 56, 58
  analysis of, 278
  definition of, 201
Type 57
  analysis of, 278
  definition of, 201
Type 58
  analysis of, 279
  definition of, 201-202
Type 59
  analysis of, 279
  definition of, 202
Type 60
  analysis of, 280
  definition of, 202
Type 61, 281
  analysis of, 280
  definition of, 202
Type 62, 203, 282
  analysis of, 281
  definition of, 203
Type 63, 203
  analysis of, 282
  definition of, 203
Type 64
  analysis of, 283
  definition of, 203
Type 65
  analysis of, 284
  definition of, 204

Types
  1-12, 236
  1-15, 292, 293
  13-24, 236, 237
  30-55, 200, 237, 239, 312
  40-44, 200, 312
  50-53, 312
  56-65, 237, 239
/ū/, spelling of, 10, 201-204
Ugaritic, 31, 37, 41, 43, 59, 63, 64
'unto', spelling of, 171
updater
  definition of, 115
  effects of, 289
  problems produced by, 115-116
'upon', spelling of, 172
variants, *ketib/qere*, 28-29, 73, 80-81, 93, 134, 143, 144, 147, 180, 185, 325
verse parity, 241, 243, 244
  for checking, use of, 308
  introduction of, 23-25
vowel
  classes, spelling of, 129, 130
  classification, 155-156
  classification features, 15, 104-105
  history, 158-162
  marking mechanics, 149-154
  points, 32
  points, authority of, 76
  types, definition of, 162
vowels, summary of *matres lectionis* for long, 94
waw as *mater lectionis*, 37-8, 92, 148-149, 311-312
winnowing rules, 150-151
word classes, spelling of, 129
writing vowels, 33-55
Ya'udi, 55, 58
Yavneh-Yam, 61, 325
yod as *mater lectionis*, 37, 92, 135-148, 309-310